The lyrical doc and evocation of place

KT-130-672

Catherine Russell

Experimental Ethnography

Duke University Press Durham and London

1999

© 1999 Duke University Press
All rights reserved   Printed in the United States
of America on acid-free paper ∞
Designed by C.H. Westmoreland
Typeset in Minion with Frutiger display by Tseng
Information Systems, Inc.

Library of Congress Cataloging-in-Publication Data
appear on the last printed page of this book.

Images on title page: *(Top)* Still from *Unsere
Afrikareise* (Peter Kubelka, 1966).
(Bottom) Still from *Les Maîtres fous*
(Jean Rouch, 1954).

For Marco

Contents

Acknowledgments

As the inspiration for this book originates in the work of filmmakers, my first debt of gratitude goes to those whose films I have written about, and also to many film- and videomakers who do not appear here. My goals may be critical and theoretical in this project, but they are vitally dependent on the textual experiments of several generations of filmmakers, and my hope is that this book is of use in expanding the critical discourse that supports alternative film practices.

In the preparation of this book, Ivone Margulies was absolutely instrumental. I cannot thank her enough for her meticulous and detailed reading of the manuscript, for posing challenging questions, and for insisting on a rigor that was vital in shaping an often unwieldy beast. A number of additional people helped me at various stages of the writing, including David James, Cheryl Simon, Bill Nichols, and Bill Wees. Most of the material was first developed in the context of M.F.A. seminars at Concordia University from 1993 to 1997, and I would like to thank all the students who took part in those classes for their patient support of my attempts to teach experimental ethnography while I was figuring out what it was. Many of their insights have no doubt found their way into this book. Invaluable research assistance was provided by Hong Nguyen, Angela Fong, John Spezzacatena, and Jean Bruce. Thanks also to Paul Litherland, who assisted me in the production and selection of film stills.

Many individuals and institutions helped in the collection of stills: Danielle Carter, Blaine Allen, Craig Baldwin, Jonas Mekas, Su Friedrich, Leslie Thornton, Women Make Movies, the Library of Congress, Yamagita International Film Festival, Canadian Filmmakers Distribution Center, Museum of Modern Art, Interama, Martin and Osa Johnson Safari Museum, Walker Art Center, and the Andy Warhol Foundation.

Versions of some of this material have been previously published in a variety of places, including "Twilight in the Image Bank," in *David Rimmer: Films and Tapes, 1967–1993* (Toronto: Art Gallery of Ontario, 1993); "Playing Primitive: *In the Land of the Headhunters* and/or *War Canoes*," *Visual Anthropology* 8 (1996); "Culture as Fiction: The Ethnographic Impulse in the Films of Peggy Ahwesh, Su Friedrich, and Leslie Thornton," in *New American Cinema*, ed. Jon Lewis (Durham: Duke University Press, 1998); "Subjectivity Lost and Found: Bill Viola's *I Do Not Know What It Is I Am Like*," in *Documenting the Documentary*, ed. Barry Grant and Jeannette Sloniowski (Detroit: Wayne State University Press, 1998) and "Dystopian Ethnography: Peter Kubelka's *Unsere Afrikareise* Revisited," in *Canadian Journal of Film Studies* 7:1 (1998). Portions have also been presented at Visible Evidence, Society for Cinema Studies conferences, and Film Studies Association of Canada conferences over the past few years. I would like to thank all the editors and panel chairs who supported this project, as these opportunities were invaluable for developing the various parts of the book.

This project was funded by several research grants, including Concordia University's faculty grants, the Social Sciences and Humanities Research Council of Canada, and the Fonds pour la Formation de Chercheurs et l'Aide à la Recherche. My work on early cinema in Quebec was done in the context of a research team headed by André Gaudreault. The work of writing this book took place in Montreal, Tokyo, and Georgian Bay, and I would like to thank Choeur Maha, the Japan Foundation, and Marco Leyton for providing the different kinds of home that made the effort possible.

Preface

Experimental film and ethnographic film have long been considered separate, autonomous practices on the margins of mainstream cinema. Each has been endowed with its own set of critical categories, its own historical lineage, and its own concerns drawn largely from the domains of modernism and anthropology respectively. However, within the contemporary critical context of postmodernism and postcolonialism, both ethnography and experimental film have begun to fill new cultural roles. The last ten or fifteen years have seen a great deal of film- and videomaking that challenges the neat compartmentalization of these modes of film practice. In light of these developments, a history of experimental ethnography emerges as a re-visioning of films that have fallen through the disciplinary gaps of film history.

The term "experimental ethnography" has begun to circulate in postcolonial anthropological theory as a way of referring to discourse that circumvents the empiricism and objectivity conventionally linked to ethnography. Examples of its literary manifestations abound, and an enormous amount of critical work has been produced on experimental forms of written ethnography.[1] Immediately apparent in the work of James Clifford, George Marcus, Stephen Tyler, Michael Taussig, and others is that once the terms "experimental" and "ethnography" are brought together, both terms undergo a transformation. In any medium, experimental ethnography refers to a rethinking of both aesthetics *and* cultural representation.

Experimental ethnography is intended not as a new category of film practice but as a methodological incursion of aesthetics on cultural representation, a collision of social theory and formal experimentation. In the dissolution of disciplinary boundaries, ethnography is a means of renewing the avant-gardism of "experimental" film, of mobilizing its play with language and form for historical ends. "Ethnography" likewise becomes an expansive term in which "culture" is represented from many different, fragmented, and mediated perspectives. For different reasons, both experimental and ethnographic film practices have been declared dead in postmodern and postcolonial culture, and yet in their ghostly convergence, they survive as a site of radical praxis at the end of the twentieth century.

The effect of bringing experimental and ethnographic film together is one of mutual illumination. On the experimental side, ethnography provides a critical framework for shifting the focus from formal concerns to a recognition of avant-garde filmmakers' cultural investment and positioning. On the ethnographic side, the textual innovations that have been developed by experimental filmmakers indicate the ways that "the critique of authenticity" has been played out in the cinema. Experimental film can be seen as a kind of laboratory in which the politics of representation and the conventions of observational cinema are brought under scrutiny. Therefore the method of this book is dialectical, moving in two directions. Textual analyses of thirty-five different films and videos will focus on an ethnographic cinema freed from its social science origins, and colonial and postcolonial forms of looking and documenting will be identified within the history of experimental film.

From the interpenetration of the avant-garde and ethnographic cinemas emerges a subversive form of ethnography in which cultural critique is combined with experiments in textual form. If ethnography can be understood as an experimentation with cultural difference and cross-cultural experience, a subversive ethnography is a mode of practice that challenges the various structures of racism, sexism, and imperialism that are inscribed implicitly and explicitly in so many forms of cultural representation. Taking both ethnography and the avant-garde in their broadest possible senses, their points of contact describe the parameters of a cultural practice that may not be "new," but is newly visible.

The critical method of this book proceeds by way of historical juxtaposition and generic disjunction. A selective, interpretive gaze back at historical texts, reviewing them on video, is not only a process of revision but also a dialectical method of montage. I want to place different films and videos against one another, not as instances of a historical teleology, but as historical interruptions. Because experimental ethnography is a textual practice that is in many cases legible only retrospectively, an exhaustive history of it is not possible. It is not a form, but a critical method produced in and through film and video. Experimental ethnography is not simply a new tendency in contemporary film, but also a means of re-visioning the long history of the intersection of the avant-garde and anthropology. The filmmakers with whom this book is concerned are all perceived as "others," regardless of their ethnic identity. Their various cultural orientations are deeply embedded in their work, and much of my analysis is devoted to unraveling the subjective spaces produced by the contradictions *and* intentions of these texts. One of the key effects of bringing ethnography and the avant-garde together is a conjunction of cultural critique and aesthetic appreciation. In other words, not all the filmmakers or their works will emerge unscathed.

The book is divided into five parts. In the first, introductory part, a theoretical framework will be sketched in chapter 1, followed by analyses of two exemplary experimental ethnographic films in chapter 2. My perspective on postmodern ethnography will be developed in the first chapter by way of brief histories of experimental and ethnographic cinemas, along with its potential as a critical practice. One of the key thinkers in this theorization of experimental ethnography is Walter Benjamin. Benjamin realized the political potential of the new media of the twentieth century, and his aesthetics have generally been recognized as a theorization of "an historical avant-garde," one committed to social transformation. This involves the immersion of art in everyday life, and the lack of autonomy of the artwork, a position Benjamin shared with many of the surrealists and dadaists of his time. In chapter 2, the terms of a surrealist ethnographic project will be introduced by way of two films that document the horror of colonial culture in extraordinarily experimental ways: Luis Buñuel's *Las Hurdes* (1932) and Tracey Moffatt's *Night Cries* (1990). The radical ambiguity of surrealism is a crucial point of reference for documentary forms that resist the closures of realist representation, and these two films are good examples of texts that evade the "correctness" of a realist mandate.

The second part of the book, "Documentary before Documentary," contains three chapters, each exploring a different aspect of nonfiction film in the silent period. Chapter 3 is about the role of the body in the cinema of attractions, including the protocinematic photography of Eadweard Muybridge. The visibility of the body, the sensations of the body, and the commodification of the body were all transformed in the new techniques of representation, transportation, and industrialization that proliferated in the early twentieth century. Cinema played a crucial role in this process, particularly as it intersected with science, tourism, and ethnology. The affinities between the avant-garde and "primitive cinema," expressed in *From the Pole to the Equator* (Yervant Giankian and Angela Ricci Lucchi, 1987) and by structural filmmaker David Rimmer (*Seashore*, 1971), will be explored as a modernist form of ethnography. Notions of travel and utopian social formations are introduced in chapter 4 in analyses of early actualities shot in Quebec in 1903, Georges Méliès's *Voyage dans la lune* (1903), and the quotation of the Méliès film in a 1982 ethnographic film by Brazilian filmmaker Paula Gaitan (*Uaka*). Chapter 5 is about Edward Curtis's film *In the Land of the Headhunters*, its deployment of Hollywood melodrama in 1914, and its "restoration" in 1973. Rethinking early cinema as an archival cinema casts the myth of primitivism as a model for an alternative form of documentary practice that preceded the documentary mode institutionalized by Flaherty in 1922. These films may have been made at the height of colonial culture, and yet they display a textual openness that lends itself much more readily to postcolonial misreadings and appropriations than later documentary forms tend to allow.

Part 3 consists of two chapters about the gaze as a disciplinary structure. In chapter 6, ethnography will be mapped onto the shared terrain of pornography and zoology. The disciplinary techniques of containment and voyeurism are techniques of mastery that can be, and have been, dismantled by texts that deploy an "undisciplined" gaze, as exemplified by five very different films: *Microcultural Incidents at Ten Zoos* (Ray Birdwhistell, 1969), *Unsere Afrikareise* (Peter Kubelka, 1966), *Simba* (Martin and Osa Johnson, 1928), and *Hide and Seek* (Su Friedrich, 1996). Chapter 7 is about structural film as a representation of the gaze that creates a realism quite unlike the objectivity of documentary realism, or the diegetic realism of narrative film. Chantal Akerman, Andy Warhol, David Rimmer, Joyce Wieland, James Benning, and Bill Viola are filmmakers who have brought a formal minimalism to bear on "documentary" material. Their gaze is a fixed stare that produces certain panopticonic effects, but their "undisciplined" aestheticism creates a visceral tension between viewer and viewed, clearing a visual space for intercultural experience and representation.

The fourth part, entitled "Other Realities," contains two chapters on particular intersections of avant-garde and ethnographic practices that challenge the epistemological foundations of visual knowledge and cultural history. Chapter 8 addresses the modernist fascination with possession rituals. Analyses of *Trance and Dance in Bali* (Margaret Mead and Gregory Bateson, 1952), *Divine Horsemen* (Maya Deren, 1947–1985), *Les Maîtres fous* (Jean Rouch, 1954), and *I Do Not Know What It Is I Am Like* (Bill Viola, 1986) indicate how trance films demarcate the limits of visual knowledge and produce the subjectivity of the Other as a discourse of excess. Found-footage filmmaking will in turn be discussed, in chapter 9, as a discourse of the body in representation. Through analyses of *A Movie* (Bruce Conner, 1958), *Atomic Café* (The Archives Project, 1982), *Tribulation 99* (Craig Baldwin, 1991), and *Handsworth Songs* (Black Audio Film Collective, 1985), I will argue that archival film practices articulate an historiography of radical memory. The "other reality" of these films is the ethnographic sphere of the image bank in which the body is the indexical sign of historical memory in a culture of amnesia.

The concluding chapter on "autoethnography" addresses the confluence of personal cinema and cultural representation in several examples of diary filmmaking: *Reminiscences of a Journey to Lithuania* (Jonas Mekas, 1972), videos by Sadie Benning and George Kuchar, Kidlat Tahimik's *Why Is Yellow the Middle of the Rainbow?* (1993), and Chris Marker's *Sans Soleil* (1982). In the interstices of travel and autobiography, these filmmakers develop the theme of personal and cultural memory as a function of the film and video mediums. They also explore the limits of self-representation in different cultural contexts, and the contradictions implicit in the autoethnographic mode. Diary filmmaking and the use of autobiographical material are extremely effective and widely used means of "politicizing the personal," and in many ways, the micropolitics of everyday life have become the terrain across which subjectivity is inscribed. And yet autobiography in film and video is rarely a source of truth and authenticity, but a dispersal of representation, subjectivity, experience, and cultural history. I want to suggest that the gaps between these layers and temporalities are foregrounded in diary filmmaking, and that their failure to cohere in an originary source named "the author" functions as a form of radical ethnography.

Benjamin's own theoretical method was one of montage, bringing together diverse quotations, aphorisms, and objects of study. He also advocated a radical sense of historical discontinuity through an embrace of new technologies of representation. The subtitle of this book refers to his landmark essay of 1935, "The Work of Art in the Age of Mechanical Reproduction," in which he argued that film was more than another art form, but had greatly changed the political and social role of art in culture.[2] At the end of the twentieth century, it is video, along with an intimation of other forms of electronic imaging in a rapidly changing technological environment, that has brought about another shift, of equal magnitude, in visual culture. One of the themes of this book is a revision of ethnographic historiography from a paradigm of lost and "vanishing" cultures to one of cultural transformation. The relation between film and video serves as an analogy for ethnographic historiography and, at the same time, as a methodological intervention into film history.

The age of video refers to a time when the cinema is enjoying a kind of rebirth. Video brings to film new and valuable means of dissemination, enabling us to see and explore film history, to preserve and restore it, and also to intervene through processes of fragmentation, recombination, and colorization. Experimental and independent practitioners may be drawn to video for its economics and flexibility, often exploring its own principles of medium specificity, but they equally often draw on the techniques and lessons of the cinema. It cannot be true that video is replacing cinema, when digital technologies are enabling us to see so much more cinema. I would prefer to argue that video is an extension of cinema, often functioning as an allegory of cinema's vanishing aura. Film and video are in many respects interdependent, intermingled media, in terms of production practices, spectatorship, and aesthetics.[3]

By way of video, film has emerged from the rarefied space of the theater and penetrated the home, the office, and the ethnographic field itself. Video is a medium that extends far beyond the art world to a wide range of cultural practices, from broadcast television to surveillance, medical, and domestic uses. Video not only has changed the cultural role of film but has become a cultural tool that has had an impact on many aspects of everyday life in many parts of the world. It is better described as a "media practice" than a "technical device" because video is always part of culture, embedded in a network of social relations.[4] Although a number of videos will be discussed (works by Bill Viola, George Kuchar, and Sadie Benning), this book is not about video but about the ways that video enables us to see film differently, and the implications of this perspective to the cultural roles of the avant-garde and ethnography.

Ethnography in its most expansive sense refers not to the representation of other cultures but to the discourse of culture in representation. Any and all films could thus be described as ethnographic insofar as they can be read as cultural texts. One direction that this book might have taken is the one leading from Italian neorealism to the many examples of dramatic narratives set in a culturally specific milieu, using professional and nonprofessional actors. Films such as Shirley Clarke's *The Cool World* (1964) and *The Connection* (1961), Nick Gomez's *Laws of Gravity* (1992), Peggy Ahwesh and Margie Strosser's video *Strange Weather* (1993), and dozens of other texts made in many different countries might be described as experimental ethnographies. Iranian directors Kiarostami and Makhmalbar are extraordinarily playful with the theatrical and narrative conventions of the neorealist heritage. Especially in cross-cultural viewing situations, many films take on ethnographic aspects, as "ethnography" becomes less of a scientific practice and more like a critical method, a means of "reading" culture and not transparently representing it. Although this project is restricted to "nonnarrative film," a term that denotes the field of documentary and the avant-garde, it should be borne in mind that the neorealist tendency has taken on a number of postmodern guises as filmmakers interrupt the illusionistic humanism of the neorealist project.

A history of antidocumentary, poetic documentary, and subjective documentary that would include the films of Joris Ivens, Humphrey Jennings, and Johan van der Keuken and the various *cinéma direct, cinéma vérité* and free cinema movements of the 1950s and 1960s would address many of the issues in this book.[5] My focus on the avant-garde takes a slightly different path through film history, guided by Benjamin's call for an awakening from the dream of history, which has been in film history largely a dream of humanism. Experimental ethnography involves, above all, dismantling the universalist impulse of realist aesthetics into a clash of voices, cultures, bodies, and languages. "The human condition" needs to be rethought as one of ongoing cultural encounter, translation, and transition, and it is the avant-garde, I believe, more so than "documentary," that provides the tools for this operation.

A growing sense of something new is developing as film and video practices evolve into an "intercultural" exploration of social representation.[6] Within the various discussions of ethnographic revisionism, spearheaded by theorists such as James Clifford, Bill Nichols, and Trinh Minh-ha, there is a surprising poverty of attention to formal aspects of contemporary film and video. Certainly the emergence of new voices, new technologies, and new social formations (including diasporic, gay, feminist, and postcolonial) are key to the new film and video forms that are in circulation. From this contemporary situation, a history of experimental ethnography is emerging in retrospect, and it is the project of this book to illuminate that history. It is not meant to be in any way exhaustive or complete. It is intended as a cartography of experimental ethnography, a mapping, in which history is represented as a fantastic, flexible, and inauthentic text.

Once ethnography is understood as a discursive structure, its affinities with filmic ontologies of memorialization, redemption, and loss become a rich source of allegorical possibility. If the cinema itself has taken on some of the aura of a "vanishing culture" as it gradually evolves into the multiple forms of digital and electronic media, experimental ethnography refers to a mode of representation that understands itself as a practice that is historical, that takes place in a moment, or across several moments in time. As a practice grounded in colonial culture, ethnographic film has exploited cinematic realism as a form of preservation, but that realism is now in decay. As archaic textual forms become legible as discourses of imperialism, as the gaze of power is dethroned, new histories can emerge. Reworking memory and tradition as fantastic forms of cultural desire — rather than sites of authenticity — ontologies of loss can become allegories of desire.

I

INTRODUCTION TO EXPERIMENTAL

ETHNOGRAPHY

Still from *Simba, The King of Beasts*
(Martin and Osa Johnson, 1928).

1 Another Look

I am kino-eye, I am a mechanical eye.

I, a machine, show you the world as only I can see it.

—DZIGA VERTOV, "We: Variant of a Manifesto"

In the last fifteen years, experimental film has diversified into a range of different media, styles, and practices, many of which impinge on both documentary and fiction. Parallel to an increasing interdisciplinary interest in visual culture, experimental filmmaking is flourishing within a postcolonial, postmodern context. More and more artists and theorists are turning to film and video as a means of addressing social questions, from gay and lesbian identities, to diasporic politics, cultural and family memory, and histories of oppression, resistance, and criminal justice systems. These "issues" are all questions of representation and cannot be separated from the way that they enter and circulate in the media. To consider this vast spectrum of filmmaking as "ethnographic" is to recognize the expanding horizon of visual anthropology. To consider it as "experimental" is to recognize its challenge to conventional forms of representation and the search for new languages and forms appropriate to a more pluralist social formation.

A new critical vocabulary is desperately needed, appropriate to filmmaking that is simultaneously "aesthetic" and "ethnographic," work in which formal experimentation is brought to bear on social representation. Theorists and critics preoccupied with form, with modernism/postmodernism debates, with mainstream media, and with various political agendas have failed to keep up with this innovative work. And yet, as interest in experimental film has faltered in film studies, it has ironically been rediscovered by anthropologists and ethnographic theorists. George Marcus, for example, has embraced cinematic montage as an invaluable technique to "disrupt and reconceive the way social and cultural process as action is represented in ethnography." Marcus argues that cinema is the medium most suited to the "increasing de-territorialized nature of cultural process" because it is able to articulate the complex relations of time and space that characterize postmodern, postcolonial culture.[1] I want to suggest that ethnographic theory might provide the critical tools appropriate to recent developments in experimental film and video practice—and even to the historical convergence of ethnographic and experimental cinemas.

Trinh T. Minh-ha has been one of the most prominent of recent filmmakers to deploy a radical film practice within a specifically ethnographic milieu. Her written critique of the conventions of ethnographic objectivity has been a catalyst in the rethinking and renovation of documentary practice.[2] Trinh's most cogent critique of ethnographic film is the way it implies a division of the world into those "out there" (the subjects of ethnography) and those "in here" (in the theater, looking at them). She argues that the assumptions of documentary truth and veracity perpetuate a Cartesian duality between mind and matter in which the Other is objectified and the filmmaker and his or her audience are the subjects of perception.[3] A more fluid conception of reality is required to transcend this paradigm, one in which meaning is not "closed" but escapes and evades representation. It is the otherness of reality itself that she argues must be reconceptualized, although she offers little advice on how this might be put into (film) practice. My objective in this book is to demonstrate how filmmakers have in fact experimented with the "otherness" of reality, and how that paradigm of objective realism is also a temporal historical one, with great implications to forms of cultural memory.

In her own films, Trinh is preoccupied with rural Third World cultures (in *Reassemblage* [1982], *Naked Spaces* [1985], and *Shoot for the Contents* [1991]), and to a large extent, her filmmaking remains locked within the ethnographic model that James Clifford has described as "the salvage paradigm":[4] "In a salvage/pastoral setup most non-Western peoples are marginal to the advancing world system. Authenticity in culture or art exists just prior to the present."[5] In his key article "On Ethnographic Allegory," Clifford explains, "the most problematic, and politically charged aspect of this 'pastoral' evocation is its relentless placement of others in a present-becoming-past."[6] The ethnographic pastoral embraces the myth of primitivism but is also characteristic of the very structure of ethnographic representation. "Every description or interpretation that conceives itself as 'bringing culture into writing,' moving from oral-discursive experience . . . to a written version of that experience . . . is enacting the structure of salvage. To the extent that the ethnographic process is seen as inscription, the representation will continue to enact a potent, and questionable, allegorical structure."[7]

Johannes Fabian has argued that anthropology constructs Otherness by "using" time. The salvage paradigm is a "denial of coevalness" that is part and parcel of the forms of ethnographic representation: "Time is involved in any possible relationship between anthropological discourse and its referents."[8] This is especially true of film, which feeds on photographic properties of preservation, fixing its referents in the prior time of shooting. In the cinema, the pastoral allegory becomes exaggerated by the role of technology in the act of representation, further splitting "the modern" from "the premodern." → Past decade ...

Ethnographic allegory also refers to the process by which individuals are abstracted into general social patterns; individual subjects become representative of cultural practices and even "human" principles. Although ethnography will always be allegorical, Clifford argues that "the assumption that something essential is lost when a culture becomes 'ethnographic'" can be avoided through a "recognition of allegory" in ethnographic practice itself. In other words, ethnographic practices of salvage can be transformed by means of a structure of doubled representation in which singularities persist within the techniques of textual meaning production. Indeed, such a structure is necessary for a transformation of ethnographic practices. aware of what making?

Clifford insists that resistance to the salvage paradigm lies not in abandoning its allegorical structure "but by opening ourselves to different histories."[9] By this I take him to mean two different things, both of which I intend to take up as forms of experimental ethnography. "Different histories" refers first of all to the voices and histories of the colonized, and to new forms of subjectivity articulated through texts that might be described as autoethnographies and indigenous ethnographies. Secondly, and not unrelated to these different histories, the salvage paradigm is also the expression of a teleological historiography. The primitive Other comes to represent the childhood of civilization only within a modernist historiography of progress. The recognition of this allegory is born of a different historiography, one that understands history as a series of disparate moments that have no "necessary" relation, progressive or otherwise. Such a perspective is associated with postmodernism and can lead to a dystopian view of historical repetition, stasis, and banality (the Baudrillardian position). Another perspective on postmodern historiography is provided by Walter Benjamin, who suggests that allegory itself is a means of articulating utopian desires for historical transformation within a nonteleological critique of modernist progress. It is this theory that seems particularly appropriate to experimental ethnography in film and video.

Allegory is not a formula or a prescriptive method but a structure of representation that, in Craig Owens's words, has the "capacity to rescue from oblivion that which threatens to disappear."[10] But allegory does so by means of fragmentation, appropriation, and intertextuality, resisting both symbolic and narrative relations as well as teleological forms. Developing Benjamin's theory, Owens describes the domain of allegory as "the arbitrary, the conventional, the unmotivated."[11] Allegory embraces the salvage paradigm as a temporal inscription that renders representation a form of writing, in which meaning is produced as a supplement that is added to a text, not derived from it hermeneutically. The allegorical photographic image marks a historical break with its referent, which belongs to that other time of the profilmic (the pre-filmic; the time of shooting), and the relation between the two moments is dialectical.

The recognition and exploration of ethnographic allegory implies a foregrounding of "the time machine" of anthropological representation, a discursive production of the Other that may construct an Edenic, pastoral, authentic site of otherness, but only as a fantasy. The textual construction of otherness can be positioned as a form of cultural memory that is not grounded in empirical facticity, but is dynamic and dialectical, producing an ethnography that is oriented toward a history of the future. One of the themes of this book will be the fate of the primitive in postmodernity, which, I will argue, is the inversion of the salvage paradigm into a science fiction narrative. The task of postcolonial ethnography is not only to include the Other within modernity but to revise the terms of realist representation. If we seem to be launched into a postmodernity that threatens to obliterate historical memory, ethnography offers an alternative theory of radical memory. In its revisionist form, ethnography offers techniques for looking forward and backward at the same time.

Technologies, like cultures, are constantly evolving into new forms, generating a host of cultural effects in the process. Although I would insist that the relation between film and video is one of hybridity, it can also be construed as an instance of ethnographic allegory. Electronic digital media at the end of the twentieth century have begun to alter many of our most precious assumptions about visual representation, as the image is no longer linked ontologically or indexically to something "out there" in the real world. Unlike the cinematic image, preserved on celluloid, the video image is made anew at every transmission; and digital image processing has opened up the possibility of infinite manipulation. In the light of the TV monitor, the cinema is reinvented as a site of disappearance, loss, and memory.

The replacement of film by video remains incomplete, as do the transformations of postcolonial societies. My intention is neither to declare film "dead" nor to salvage it as a lost medium. By drawing a tacit parallel between the cinema and "traditional" societies, I wish to foreground a relation between the aesthetics of "pure form," media specificity, and cinematic ontology on the one hand, and the status of cultural essences and purities in ethnography on the other. Both are "auratic" in Walter Benjamin's sense of the term. "The work of cinema" refers to the struggle of film to survive in postmodernity, but also to film's altered role. As a tool of cultural production, film's autonomy as a "work of art" is precisely what is vanishing. In 1935 Walter Benjamin argued that "mechanical reproduction," specifically the arts of film and photography, had altered the status and role of art as a social and cultural form. Video and digital media constitute yet another turn in that process, rendering film itself as a kind of historical horizon. For Benjamin, the vanishing of the aura is commensurate with the production of historical memory as a form of representation that is inherently allegorical.

Benjamin never directly addressed the question of ethnographic representation, but his merging of theory and practice was always a merging of viewer and viewed. In his theory of experience, subjective and objective poles of perception were potentially united. The *flâneur* is thus the field-worker and the first *vérité* observer; he is part of the crowd, but not part of the crowd. Benjamin's particular understanding of the collusion of ethnography and the avant-garde can be traced to his conception of experience, or "aura," as a lost quality of modernity. Benjamin's invention of aura on the verge of its extinction replicates the logic of the salvage paradigm and the invention of the primitive as the sign of cultural loss. Aura becomes visible only as it disappears. Auratic experience cannot be "salvaged" or resurrected in modernity, but it can be represented in allegorical form. Benjamin thus offers a way out of a typical conundrum of postmodern and postcolonial thought — how to theorize cultural memory without mystifying it as an originary site.

The loss of aura in mechanical reproduction is the sign of a new function of art, as it is released from its ritualistic basis in "the cult of beauty," and the "criterion of authenticity ceases to be applicable to artistic production."[12] And yet equally important for Benjamin is the utopian aspect of a "second-degree" realism: "The sight of immediate reality has become an orchid in the land of technology."[13] In the vanishing of aura, authenticity, and contemplative aesthetics, a new form of experience emerges that is immediate, fragmentary, and bound to the physicality of the viewing experience. Referentiality is conceived as a temporal process in which the past is always receding, the present is momentary, and the future is a kind of mirror image of the past, a projection of auratic experience, otherwise known as desire.

When Benjamin declares that film offers, "precisely because of the thoroughgoing permeation of reality with mechanical equipment, an aspect of reality which is free of all equipment,"[14] he is suggesting that as a technology, film invents the fantasy of a nontechnologized reality. This seems to me the image of analog visual media (film and photography) that is created by digital imaging: a "pastoral allegory" of transparent representation. Benjamin follows this provocative statement with "and that is what one is entitled to ask from a work of art," referring to the assemblage of an image of reality from the fragments produced by the mechanics of cinematic *découpage*. It is precisely the doubling of technologized reality with its auratic fantasy that Benjamin reads as the historical dialectics of modernism. The myth of primitivism is likewise produced in colonial culture as an effect of technology seeking its other in the wholeness of cultures "free of all equipment."

Ethnographic truth, like the vanishing aura of Benjamin's modernism, is a realism that is conditional on the fragmented and transient present. Benjamin does make reference in "The Work of Art" to the techniques that would subsequently be identified with ethnographic film. He suggests that film will enable an analysis of behavior because "it can be isolated more easily." Margaret Mead and Gregory Bateson began to apply film to fieldwork in Bali only a few years later for precisely this purpose, as I will discuss in chapter 8. Benjamin, however, also foresaw "the mutual penetration of art and science" implicit in such a practice and proclaimed it "one of the revolutionary functions of film." He goes on to explain that it is "evidently a different nature [that] opens itself to the camera than opens to the naked eye—if only because an unconsciously penetrated space is substituted for a space consciously explored by man."[15] The camera introduces "unconscious optics" into the field of vision, rendering the image a "second nature," a reality that has been penetrated by a technology of desire. Benjamin's poetics are grounded in a materialist dialectic in which the body, the *physis,* is given a new dynamic of experience, a dynamic that includes the body's mortality. "For the film, what matters primarily is that the actor represent himself to the public before the camera, rather than represent someone else. . . . For the first time—and this is the effect of the film—man has to operate with his whole living person, yet forgoing its aura."[16] Thus allegorical representation in the cinema begins with performance as a process of doubling in which the body functions as the principal site of a loss of aura. Benjamin effectively demonstrates why cinema and ethnography are drawn together, and how they are two sides of a similar modernist preoccupation with loss.

Against the modernist myth of progress, Benjamin developed a radical theory of memory. In his major, unfinished study of the Paris Arcades, he suggests that the past persists in the present in the form of a dream, often commodified as a wish image. This conception of the past is precisely the allegory of the ethnographic pastoral, and it also captures the lingering traces of the modern in postmodernity, and the aura of cinematic pleasure in video culture. Anne Friedberg has drawn out some of the implications of Benjamin's theorization of modernity to the cinema: "The imaginary *flànerie* of cinema spectatorship offers a spatially mobilized visuality but also, importantly, a temporal mobility." The shopper in the Paris Arcades of the nineteenth century, like the tourist and the VCR time shifter, enacts a virtual gaze in and of history. Benjamin recognized that film and photography brought about a great change in "the subjective role of memory and history."[17] Mechanical reproduction broke history down into discrete fragmentary moments, generating a discontinuity that Benjamin saw as having revolutionary dialectical possibilities.

Transience is a discourse of mortality and decay, but for Benjamin it signifies the fundamental impermanence of history and its dialectical potential. "Allegories are, in the realm of thoughts, what ruins are in the realm of things."[18] If the ruin contains the trace of original form, it is a model of representation that is in constant flux, bearing a shifting relation to a prior site of authenticity. In 1935 the cinema marked a great change in the status of the original authenticity of the artwork. If the cinema is on the leading edge of "the ragged break" between the modern and the postmodern, video constitutes an extension of that process. Video may realize the allegorical potential of cinema more completely, being a medium that always "ruins" a photographic image by converting it to an electronic signal. The transient movements of immigration, exile, and displacement are likewise very much part of the shifting paradigms of modernity and postmodernity. Spatial and temporal forms of transience come together in cinematic practices of cross-cultural representation that enable us to release the Other from the ahistoricism of premodernity.

Ethnographic Film: The Danger of Becoming Art

Ethnographic film is an inherently contradictory mode of film practice. Like experimental film, it has a canon of exemplary works, and a body of literature celebrating them and justifying their methods.[19] Ethnography is the branch of anthropology concerned with the documentation of culture, and in whatever medium — film, photography, writing, music, or sound — it implies a regime of veracity. Ethnographic film theory and criticism is an ongoing discussion of issues of objectivity, subjectivity, realism, narrative structure, and ethical questions of representation. The links to social science imply a commitment to objectivity, and the role of film is principally to provide empirical evidence. And yet there is little agreement as to the "rules" of ethnographic film; nor is there a set of conventions on which all ethnographic filmmakers might agree.[20] The ideal ethnographic film is one in which social observation is presented as a form of cultural knowledge, but given the colonial context of the development of anthropology and its ethnographic branch, this "knowledge" is bound to the hierarchies of race, ethnicity, and mastery implicit in colonial culture. The history of ethnographic film is thus a history of the production of Otherness.

It may be true that "ethnography" is antithetical to the ideals of a postcolonial culture in which imperial forms of domination might be completely overcome. The implied hierarchy within the act of representation cannot be sustained in a global culture in which the Other is neither mute nor "vanishing," but I would like to think that the term "other" can be transformed, expanded, and modified. Otherness is still very much with us as new hierarchies and forms of difference are constantly being produced in postcolonial culture. New hybrid, intercultural identities are being enacted and constructed in audiovisual representation more than ever before. Ethnography in its experimental form serves as an ideal language for this ongoing process of cultural struggle and encounter. Experimental ethnography involves a reconceptualization of the historical nature of Otherness, including not only how the Other was (and is) constructed in colonial discourse but also how cultural difference and "authenticity" are related in the postcolonial present and future.

Indigenous ethnography, along with a recognition of alternative film practices produced in non-Western cultures and by minority filmmakers, is clearly one way of inverting the salvage paradigm. Among the most important developments in experimental film culture is the 1980s work of the Black Film co-ops in Britain: Sankofa and Black Audio, along with films by Australian Aboriginal filmmaker Tracey Moffat and the late gay African American Marlon Riggs. Their use of experimental film forms is closely bound to the cultural politics of racism and post-colonialism. These filmmakers have, however, been plagued by debates about the "positive images" demanded by their respective communities. Their embrace of experimental form does not sit easily with the "authenticity" of their racial and ethnic identities.[21]

Within the arena of ethnographic film, "handing the camera over" to a native filmmaker often simply perpetuates the realist aesthetics that experimental film form has dislodged. The "authentic identity" of the film- or videomaker is not, in other words, a sufficient revision of ethnographic practice because differences exist within cultures and communities just as surely as they do between cultural identities. Rachel Moore goes so far as to call indigenous ethnography a "savage impiricism [sic]."[22] Faye Ginsberg has described the impact of indigenous ethnography on visual anthropology as a "parallax effect." Indeed, it is not the "correctness" of indigenous ethnography so much as the opening of multiple perspectives that has shifted the emphases of visual anthropology.[23]

Since the 1970s, ethnographic film might be said to be in a state of crisis, not because no one is making films (the advent of video and the opening of broadcast possibilities have increased production exponentially), but because the status of "visible evidence" has faltered radically. As David MacDougall explains: "The early strident calls for ethnographic film to become more scientific (or else redefine itself as 'art') have been tempered by the realization that many previously unquestioned assumptions about scientific truth are now widely questioned. It is more generally accepted that the positivist notion of a single ethnographic reality, only waiting for anthropology to describe it, was always an artificial construct."[24]

As a subcategory of documentary film, ethnography has a major stake in cinematic realism. As a scientific instrument of representation, ethnographic film assumes that the camera records a truthful reality, "out there"—a reality distinct from that of the viewer and filmmaker. Yet to achieve this realism, the filmmaker must observe a number of cardinal rules, chief among them the admonition to ethnographic subjects not to look at the camera. But then reflexivity itself becomes the signature of realism, and that look back, along with various other techniques, becomes another level of truth. As Trinh says, "What is presented as evidence remains evidence, whether the observing eye qualifies itself as being subjective or objective."[25] In postmodern culture, when reflexive techniques have become recognizable as "style," the evidentiary character of visual culture necessarily shifts. Documentary filmmaking has become increasingly "subjective," and the great divide between subject and object, mind and matter, is potentially breaking down. In this context, ethnography is liberated from its bond with the real, and from its assumptions about truth and meaning. Even more so than the avant-garde, ethnography is dead and awaits rebirth.

Despite this sense of recent crisis, ethnographic film has a rich history of experimentation. Before World War II, ethnographic filmmakers were travelers, adventurers, and scientific missionaries intent on documenting the last traces of vanishing cultures. Film promised the possibility of an archive of cultural documents, a practice that preserved the "authentic" as always already lost to a world where cinema itself signified the inevitable spread of industrialization. Fatimah Tobing Rony has described the techniques deployed in this cinema as having three overlapping phases: the positivist mode of scientific research, the taxidermic mode canonized in *Nanook of the North* (1922), and commercial exploitation films. Her description of the picturesque aesthetic sums up the conflicting desires at work in salvage ethnography:

In the "picturesque" cataloguing of peoples in Melanesia, the Americas and so on, anthropology provided the justification for what was in many cases genocide: a central premise of much of anthropology was that the native was already vanishing, and the anthropologist could do nothing but record and reconstruct, racing against the evolutionary clock. Often accompanying this premise, however, was "abstracted" guilt, as a nostalgia for lost origins, and as a fear — contemplation of death in the abstract leading to one's own fear of death.[26]

Ethnographic practice was clearly bound up with a range of other modernist aesthetics, theories, and practices. Its uneven alignment with the avant-garde may not have been apparent at the time, but at the end of the twentieth century, the contradictions and ironies of this cinema have become legible. Cinema was an important instrument in the colonialist production of an ethnographic body, but at the same time, early ethnographers were experimenting with techniques and strategies of representation. My reading of "Documentary before Documentary" goes against the grain of projects such as Curtis's, Muybridge's and Méliès's; it is a misreading designed to produce histories other than the "progressive" ones of evolutionary anthropology and narrative cinema.

The turning point in most accounts of ethnographic film was the advent of *cinéma vérité*, lightweight sixteen-millimeter equipment, and the humanist ideas of Jean Rouch in the 1950s. His conception of "shared anthropology" and "participatory ethnography," exemplified in films such as *Chronique d'une été* (1960) and *Jaguar* (1967), opened up the field to new methods and new audiences. Rouch's innovations were closely linked to developments in fiction filmmaking, specifically Italian neorealism and the French New Wave. In fact, most of the developments in ethnographic film are closely linked to stylistic changes in film culture in its broadest sense. Within the somewhat fragmented and diverse canon of ethnographic film, there is a rich history of experimentation with film language. From Flaherty to Trinh Minh-ha, filmmakers have struggled to find a means of representing "culture" that is in some way appropriate to the intercultural experience.

In many respects, ethnographic film is a marginal film practice, sharing with experimental cinema a limited audience, limited funds, and a certain flexibility in terms of length, format, and style. However, it has by no means shaken the scientific yoke. Many ethnographic films are still made and distributed within the scope of anthropological knowledge, subsuming "culture" within a regime of academic authority,[27] and are often intended to be seen accompanied by a package of "study materials" designed to complete the knowledge conveyed by the film. We also need to remember that despite the incredible innovations and shifts in the very ideas of cultural knowledge and observation, one can still see the most conventional of ethnographic films broadcast daily on television. The conventions of explanatory voice-over narration and rural, impoverished people of color with exotic customs have become reified as a generic commodity in Western culture. Any exploration of experimental ethnography must therefore take place within a fragmented culture in which the postcolonial revision of anthropological knowledge remains a breakthrough only *in potentia*.

As MacDougall implies, ethnographic film is in constant danger of becoming art. But what happens when we claim it as an art? What kind of art is it? It has always been an aesthetic practice, drawing from a wide range of formal devices to structure its treatment of culture. These include everything from the beautiful Arctic landscapes of *Nanook of the North*, to the analytic editing of Timothy Asch's *The Ax Fight* (1975), to the psychological narrativity of *Dead Birds* (Robert Gardner, 1963), to the long takes of *To Live with Herds* (David and Judith MacDougall, 1971) and *Forest of Bliss* (Robert Gardner, 1986). Ethnography may even be considered an experimental practice in which aesthetics and cultural theory are combined in a constantly evolving formal combination. There may be little consensus on what ethnographic film should or could become, except that it is a practice of representation, a production of textual form from the material history of lived experience. Experimental ethnography has a long history and a very open future, which may be better mapped if it is revisited within the context of the avant-garde.

Experimental Film: The Canon and Its Discontents

Experimental film has been plagued by debates over canonization. As an avant-garde, it has been beleaguered by a peculiar institutional drag since the 1960s that has hampered the recognition of innovation and kept academic criticism way behind the developments of praxis. In a seminal article published in *Screen* in 1978, Constance Penley and Janet

Bergstrom reviewed several new books on avant-garde cinema. They pointed out how tightly the critical theory was linked to the promotion of "great works." In the American context, this meant a fairly narrow phenomenological approach, in which film was apprehended as an "analogue of consciousness": "Cinema replays unconscious wishes, the structures of which are shared by phenomenology: the illusion of perceptual mastery with the effect of the creation of a transcendental subject." Within this theoretical paradigm, the films of Stan Brakhage, Michael Snow, Hollis Frampton, and others became high points in cinematic modernism. Penley and Bergstrom point out that this criticism is unable to account for the work of filmmakers who "investigate and analyze the question of who speaks." They in turn advocate a set of films that confirm their commitment to discourse theory: work by Straub and Huillet, Marguerite Duras, Chantal Akerman, and Jean-Luc Godard. These "great works" conformed more closely to Penley and Bergstrom's feminist concerns.[28]

The authors echo an earlier essay by Peter Wollen on the "two avant-gardes," in which he describes a shift from an idealist cinema grounded in an ontology of the medium, to a materialist cinema related to Brecht's politics of representation.[29] Implicit in these accounts is a split between European and American filmmaking, corresponding to a parallel split between politicized and strictly aesthetic practices. Armed with the critical tools of semiotics and psychoanalysis, the *Screen* critics replaced one canon with another, without rethinking the role of "the good text" or the avant-garde artist in critical practice.

By the 1980s, the division had shifted to a split between generations. The "new generation," brought up on TV, is supposedly inclined toward postmodern forms, video, feminism, and cultural politics. The so-called older generation, many of whom are still working, are concerned with personal expression, film language, and abstraction.[30] In 1989 an International Film Congress held in Toronto threw this generational divide into relief. A group of American filmmakers boycotted the event, protesting the way that the congress continued to promote the "Institutional Canon of Masterworks of the Avant-Garde." Their statement-manifesto included the observation that "it is time to shift focus from the History of Film to the position of film within the construction of history."[31] In a long-standing avant-garde tradition, they proclaimed the death of the avant-garde. As Paul Mann has pointed out, the pertinent question is never whether the avant-garde is really dead, but how that death can be used. "The avant-garde's death is . . . one of its fundamental purposes." [32]

Implicit in this debate is a conception of the avant-garde as a category rather than a method or practice. The blurring of "experimental film" with "the avant-garde" has not helped to loosen the canonical framework that has evolved. Part of the problem is the formalist orientation of most of the major theoretical texts on experimental film. Marxist and feminist critiques of this tendency provide a starting point for an alternative critical framework for avant-garde filmmaking, as they contest the presumed autonomy of the aesthetic realm. I would like to propose an ethnographic critical method for the avant-garde that might circumvent some of these debates by rethinking some of the canonical works and, at the same time, opening up the category by cutting a swath through it. As new filmmakers deploy experimental techniques for new effects and purposes, the idea of experimental film needs to be rethought.

One of the real barriers between the "old" and the "new" film avant-gardes is the concept of "the social." In the modernist aesthetics that governed the canonization of the avant-garde, "the social" constituted an impurity, a crude interruption of the examination of medium specificity and personal expression. And yet the social is never completely banished; even the withdrawal from "the social" is a social practice. Within the work on film language and filmic principles and axioms, the desire to see is never entirely eradicated. Whether we describe this desire as scopophilia or as epistophilia, as observational cinema or as "the subject in (visual) language," the desire to see is socially configured. It is an engagement, whether it be passive or active, whether it be a poetics or a scientific study. Because structural filmmakers worked so hard to strip film down to its bare essentials, they have in many ways excavated the "elements" with which ethnographers need to know how to work. Going back to these films, in the light of ethnography, searching out the traces of "the social" is to break through the barrier between the avant-gardes, and to link aesthetic innovation to social observation.

The opposition of generations forces a duality that is not borne out by close examination of experimental practices. The canon may be loaded down with masters, masterpieces, and techniques of mastery, but like colonialism, the canon needs to be thoroughly deconstructed before being dismissed because the lessons it has to offer are invaluable. The flicker films of Paul Sharits and Peter Kubelka only indicate the larger denigration of "content" that informed the canonical avant-garde. But images there were, and often these were images of people, either anonymous people (the escalator passengers in Standish Lawder's 1969 film *Necrology*) or friends (the amateur performers in Jack Smith and George Kuchar's films). In many ways, an ethnographic element provided an invaluable support system for the play with film language.

The most prominent examples of this ethnographic undercurrent are perhaps Andy Warhol and Jonas Mekas. Two very different film-makers, they were both interested in developing film languages that could convey something about the microcultures in which they lived and worked, two overlapping pockets of the New York art world of the 1960s. For Warhol, this meant using cinema as a machine through which his actor friends were transformed into cultural commodities; for Mekas, it meant using cinema as a romantic form of expression in which his filmmaker friends were the poets of a new world. These filmmakers were concerned not with "documentary" but with new means of repre-senting culture, in which people and art could be fused in new forms of cultural production that lay resolutely outside the film industry and all that it represented.[33] Warhol begins to give himself over to the profilmic and to disappear, himself, into the machine that is the cinema. And yet the people in his films, the denizens of his factory, become a little like the ethnographer's "own" villagers, whom he or she has come to know well enough to film. Mekas called his film journal "Film Culture," indi-cating the relationship between cinema and a specific social formation that the films were documenting.

The ethnographic aspect of experimental film extends beyond the various representations of cultures and communities. An important part of the project of this book is to return to the canonical avant-garde and reevaluate its significance for experimental ethnography. The phenomenological aspect of the "transcendental gaze," once described as a "metaphor of vision,"[34] needs to be rethought as a technology of seeing. Filmmakers such as Michael Snow, Joyce Wieland, and Peter Kubelka employed a minimalist cinematic method that constituted an exploration of the apparatus of vision that is the cinema. Taken out of its art historical context, structural film is in many ways a replication of panopticism, deploying a rigidity and mechanization that lays bare the powers and desires of a certain mode of visual culture. In the 1970s and 1980s, filmmakers such as Chantal Akerman and James Benning adopted some of the strategies of structural film to better "frame" and expose these social aspects of the form.

The affinity of the avant-garde with early cinema constitutes a version of the myth of primitivism as a minimalist film form. Dubbed "Primitive Cinema" by Noel Burch, filmmaking before 1907 (before Griffith) represents a historical otherness akin to the otherness that anthropologists are attracted to in "underdeveloped" cultures. Experimental filmmakers embraced early cinema as an alternative to the narrative realism that came to dominate the institutionalization of cinema. The romantic aestheticization of this cinematic Eden ironically reproduces colonial culture in a modernist film form, enabling a perspective on the primitive as a modernist construction. Primitivism is not a site of authenticity but a reduction of film language to its basic elements as a technology of modernity. Looking at early cinema through the lens of the avant-garde offers a kind of visual historiography in which several layers of mediation render "the primitive" allegorical.

As an archival cinema, the avant-garde provides a model of historiography that is of great relevance to ethnographic practices. Collage films and the incorporation of "found" material into original footage have been prevalent since the 1950s. If one of the conventions of ethnographic film is the experiential encounter of the filmmaker and the filmed, found footage thoroughly mediates that encounter. Already filmed, already screened, decontextualized and recontextualized, found footage bears the trace of a complex social constellation of production, consumption, and disposal. In chapter 9, I will argue that found-footage filmmaking produces an ethnographic discourse of radical memory. The preoccupation with apocalypse in found-footage filmmaking combines a critique of technological "progress" with a critique of cultural representation, suggesting how ethnographic discourse is produced as a counterhistory of mass media. It therefore invokes a historical paradigm that has a remarkable resemblance to salvage ethnography. That early (primitive) cinema frequently appears in collage films only adds to the force of the parallel process of rescue, redemption, and loss.

Experimental filmmakers are drawn not only to the marginalia of media culture but also to marginal cultures. Affinities between artists and cultural minorities are often born of a romantic opposition to mainstream bourgeois culture, and for many filmmakers, the foray into ethnography is grounded in an identification with the cultural other. Anthropology as a site of alterity has given rise to an Orientalist literary and artistic trope that can be highly problematic. In the attempt to transcend colonial relations, modernist orientalism can also produce a subjectivity that is split and fragmented. Thus the critique of an ethno-avant-garde is a necessary step in the process of decentering the colonial construction of subjectivity. My analyses of films by Peter Kubelka and Chris Marker and Bill Viola's videos will argue that these film- and videomakers remain implicated in paradigms of modernism and colonialism, even as they seek ways of revising the production of otherness in representation.

Postmodern Ethnography

The utopian project of experimental ethnography is to overcome the binary oppositions of us and them, self and other, along with the tension between the profilmic and the textual operations of aesthetic form. These are the binaries of modern culture, and they are not easily overcome. More than a few of the films discussed here will point to failures of representation. Teasing apart the discursive layers of audiovisual culture is often a means of exposing the limits of epistemological forms. Much of this book will be preoccupied with examples of modernist culture, revisited from a postcolonial, postmodern perspective. Postmodern ethnography itself may or may not actually exist. In any case, it is not my aim to define it or to establish its characteristics. Stephen Tyler has described postmodern ethnography as a "document of the occult," a textual evocation rather than representation, "to provoke an aesthetic integration that will have a therapeutic effect."[35] If ethnography is to become poetry, poetry can likewise become an ethnographic practice, but Tyler's position must be augmented with a politicization of the real for experimental ethnography to be an avant-garde practice.

Photography, as Benjamin quickly realized, never really had a firm grasp on the real, and the subsequent history of film, video, and new digital technologies has further collapsed the claims on authenticity made by "visible evidence." Many commentators trace the popular and political dissolution of the truth-value of visual culture to the Rodney King trials (1992–1993), in which the self-evident "proof" captured by a home video camera was interpreted very differently by different "sides."[36] That the debate was also fundamentally about American racism and civil rights brought the hitherto "merely academic" questions about visible evidence into the center ring of political discourse.

With the extensive mixing of visual media, furthermore, notions of aesthetic purity and medium specificity have been superseded by the significance of image manipulation. Digital technologies that create "virtual spaces" composed of disparate images relegate the real far outside the domain of representation; they also politicize "the real" as a new form of historical materialism.

Postmodernism denotes, among other things, a perspective from which a number of "modernisms" can be distinguished, not all of which have vanished. The lingering dualities of now and then, center and periphery, us and them, he and she, persist within postmodern cultural forms, as does the utopian aspiration of radical praxis. If overcoming those dualities in global culture entails leaving behind oppositional critical practice, we need perhaps to retain a sense of the modern within the postmodern. This is where I find Benjamin's model of critical practice so useful. In so many ways, he foresaw the developments of postmodernism, describing them from within the context of modernism. He draws our attention to the fundamental imbrication of form and content in politicized cultural praxis and offers the tools of allegorization needed to renew an ethnographic avant-garde.

From a postmodern perspective, modernism is not simply an aesthetic but corresponds to the network of cultural activities and practices within which this aesthetic flourished — specifically, the emergence of bourgeois capitalism and its colonialist mandate. Ethnographic and experimental film practices originated within a culture that understood itself as being "modern" in its most progressive sense, and they shared a common fantasy of the alterity of the primitive. In the multiple modernisms of the twentieth century, primitivism needs to be read as an allegorical discourse that combines utopian imagination with cultural difference.

Science fiction, like ethnography, takes on new meanings and social roles in postmodern culture, mapping the transformations of the human subject as it becomes increasingly fused with technology. Donna Haraway reminds us that a truly transformative practice can and must take place within the spheres of representation and technology,[37] and as the age of film blurs into the age of video, it becomes increasingly difficult to deny that representation is a technology. Experimental ethnography brings science, in the form of mechanical and electronic forms of reproduction, together with fiction, in the form of image culture, for "a different kind of journey."[38] The mandate of the avant-garde might thus be refigured as a discourse of science fiction that remains grounded in experience and memory. As Stephen Tyler describes postmodern ethnography, it is a new kind of realism, one that evokes "a possible world of reality already known to us in fantasy."[39] In the late 1920s, Dziga Vertov had already begun to imagine a prototypical cyborg consciousness, theorizing the film camera as a technological extension of human vision dedicated to utopian forms of ethnographic representation.[40]

Many of the developments in feminist film theory provide a foundation for postcolonial theory, which may be described as a second phase of the politics of representation in film studies. Analysis of "the gaze" originated within the politics of sexual difference, and the theoretical understanding of film as a coded language of representation has been instrumental to theorizing postcolonial cinema. The limitations of apparatus theory, too, with its narrow conception of spectatorship, are significant to ethnographic film theory. Critical strategies of revisioning, rereading, and misreading, viewing "against the grain" of dominant culture, were all developed within feminist film theory and practice. These strategies are fundamental to my practice of looking again at films that were produced under quite different auspices for very different ideal viewers.

Feminism, postmodernism, and experimental ethnography are linked by an imbrication of theory in textual form. From an anthropological perspective, Stephen Webster argues that "experimental ethnographic form has taken shape in ethnographic accounts that reproduce in textual form the hermeneutic or reflexive theory of fieldwork or of social change. . . . In one way or another, postmodernist ethnographic forms . . . seek to integrate with, rather than represent, the social practices that are their object. This integral relationship with practice is, at the same time, their form and their theory."[41] From *Riddles of the Sphinx* (Laura Mulvey and Peter Wollen, 1977) to *The Man Who Envied Woman* (Yvonne Rainer, 1985) and *Adynata* (Leslie Thornton, 1983), the integration of theory with praxis has been a fundamental means by which women filmmakers have managed to interrogate the very forms of representation with which they work. Avant-garde film has always had a strained but significant relationship with theory, but it has been feminism that has dominated the conception of "the social."[42]

Experimental ethnography is very much about prying apart identity and authenticity so as to evade doctrines of political correctness alongside realist aesthetics. Autobiography can, however, be an important form of experimental ethnography and points to another intersection of feminism and ethnographic representation. The interest in "everyday life," the representation of detail, and the routines of daily life are also crucial ways in which feminist concerns have combined with ethnographic forms in the renewal of an alternative film culture. Chantal Akerman, a filmmaker who bridged the two so-called avant-gardes of the 1970s, has brought dramatic narrative and ethnography in extraordinarily close alignment in an aesthetic described by Ivone Margulies as "the politics of the singular." [43] The question of representativeness, of types and stereotypes, of people "standing in" for abstract categories of culture, is central to the dynamics of experimental ethnography and its recovery and reinvention of subjectivity within cultural representation.

The cumulative effect of these various intersections of feminism and ethnography is a critical methodology that will be taken up at various points in the pages that follow. Analyzing discourses of gender in texts produced within colonial culture is often a means of opening them up and identifying some of their strategies of representation. It is primarily through gender studies that the two-sided process of cultural critique and textual analysis has developed; my conception of experimental ethnography is part of that project.

Criticism of experimental film may be implicitly tied to the promotion of "great works," but in successive generations of critics, the meaning of each term, "great" and "work," tends to change. Discussion of ethnographic film is often limited to content. One of the things that experimental film brings to ethnography is what Nichols describes as the ability to *see film* as cultural representation—as opposed to *seeing through* film.[44] It is a difference between discourse analysis and content analysis, and it requires a selection of texts that are exemplary of particular configurations of culture and representation. We need to shift the emphasis from "great works" to "exemplary texts," in keeping with the new role of art as it merges with culture, and discuss texts as historical productions with historically shifting significance.

The affinities between revisionist anthropology and contemporary art practices revolve around their mutual negotiation of textuality—a recognition of the discursive construction of the real—and a "longing for referentiality." Hal Foster has described the emergence of "the artist as ethnographer" along with what he sees as the dangers associated with this practice. If the shared terrain of fieldwork, interdisciplinarity, reflexivity, and contextualization is organized around an ideal of reconciling theory and practice, Foster is concerned that this ideal practice "might be projected onto the field of the other, which is then asked to reflect it as if it were not only authentically indigenous but innovatively political." [45] In the primitivist fantasy produced by anthropology and psychoanalysis, the Other is apprehended as a site of authenticity that, he feels, is being resurrected in the recent turn to ethnography. And on the other side, he questions the renewed authority of the anthropologist as textual reader. Foster's critique is ultimately directed to a critical practice that he associates with a waning of aesthetic value in light of identity politics.

Although Foster is concerned with the plastic arts, his reservations about the artist as ethnographer are extremely relevant to the question of experimental ethnography in film and video. Benjamin's essay "The Author as Producer" is a model of critical method that privileges a conjunction of form and content as the means of producing socially engaged, politicized art. Foster is afraid that the artist as ethnographer has lost sight of the solidarity with the Other — the proletariat — that Benjamin advocated on the level of technique. The potential trap is not one of "speaking for the Other" but one of relocating the space of politics outside the sphere of aesthetics to an "elsewhere" that is loosely named the social or the cultural. For this reason, we must understand film and video as social and cultural practices, even (especially) in the context of formal and aesthetic analysis. If we can understand film and video as means by which "culture" is translated into technologies of representation, we can potentially see, in Rey Chow's words, "how a culture is 'originally' put together, in all its cruelty." [46]

For Benjamin, the term "technique" referred to the position of an artwork within the relations of production; technique refers to neither form nor content, but the means by which a work engages with social relations. In this sense, film is a technology, producing a relation between a fantastic (filmed) body and a physical (viewing) body. As cinematic representation becomes itself threatened by new technologies, the "elsewhere" of the social can less and less be assumed. Especially in the age of video, aesthetic value is deeply implicated in technique as a cultural phenomenon and in social relations of production. Following from Benjamin's dialectical critical method, experimental ethnography seeks to combine textual analysis with representation, to be able to represent culture (ethnography) from within culture (experimental film).

A study such as this also risks the danger of what Caren Kaplan calls a "theoretical tourism" producing "sites of escape or decolonization for the colonizer" while the Third World "functions simply as a metaphorical margin for European oppositional strategies, an imaginary space, rather than a location of theoretical production itself."[47] Kaplan's critique applies to many of the experimental films and filmmakers who empathize with the marginality of native peoples, and my attempt to sketch the terms and effects of this alignment is not intended to reproduce it. No doubt a critical authority is assumed by my readings, and a certain degree of "projection" is assumed, but it is in the interests of destabilizing representation and, along with it, the authenticity of the Other as referent.

As a forging of critical method, this book seeks to develop other ways of looking at both experimental and ethnographic films. The question of "distance" is raised by ethnography and the avant-garde in many overlapping ways. Critical distance and geographical distance were important criteria for modernist aesthetics and anthropological representation. Postmodernity entails a collapse of these distances: as the Other is one's neighbor, one's family becomes an ethnographic field; in the eclipse of referentiality, the distance between signified and signifier closes down, and a new realism of identity politics emerges. In many respects, the coevalness that anthropology has denied may finally be on the horizon, but its attainment is at the expense of historical thought. Allegory is a means of reinscribing "distance" as a discursive practice that enables the critic to use history as a critical tool; science fiction is the narrativization of that distance in an imaginary form.

Once otherness is perceived as a discursive construction and a fantasy that is reified in colonial culture, it is not simply thereby deconstructed and dismissed. Otherness remains a structural component of desire, both historical and psychological, the linchpin of the historical subject. If for Benjamin the Other was the proletariat, in postmodern culture it is, as Foster argues, the cultural other. But for many filmmakers, this cultural other is "within" — within themselves, their families, their communities and their nations. Once we know each other to be each the Other's other, a much more fluid Deleuzean subjectivity takes hold, but it does not come about by banishing the Other as a concept. Thus, if we want to trace the transformation of "personal expression" in the avant-garde to a more culturally based theory of identity, criticism needs to turn to ethnography as a discourse of othering. And if this discourse is conceived in terms of desire and fantasy, it ceases to be limited by the realism that Foster objects to in the primitivist fantasy.

Experimental ethnography is thus an allegorical discourse, one that apprehends otherness as fundamentally uncanny. It marks the point of a vanishing and transitory subjectivity that is at once similar and different, remembered and imagined. Through the analyses of films that explore cultural marginalia on multiple levels, a critical distance will be assembled, rather than assumed, from the conjunction of cultural critique and formal analysis. Keeping these two methodologies in constant contact is an attempt at a dialectical form of film criticism. The uncanniness of the Other in representation is the knowledge of its unknowability, the knowledge that to see is not, after all, to know. From that unknowability unfolds a resistance in and of representation.

The failure of realism to present evidence of the real is the radical possibility of experimental ethnography. Criticism that aims to fracture the edifice of realism apprehends all texts allegorically, as traces of a reality that is beyond the text, in history. "The real" conceived as history differs from "the real" of referentiality in that it includes the spectator and the filmmaker in its scope. Beyond the limits of representation exist other realities of experience, desire, memory, and fantasy. These realities are historical and produce real effects, especially in the institutions and practices of colonial culture. The decolonization of ethnographic film is therefore commensurate with the experimental critique of realist film languages—both narrative and documentary—and the development of new forms of audiovisual representation.

2 Surrealist Ethnography

To state the contrast schematically, anthropological humanism begins
with the different and renders it — through naming, classifying, describing,
interpreting — comprehensible. It familiarizes. An ethnographic surrealist
practice, by contrast, attacks the familiar, provoking the irruption of
otherness — the unexpected.

— JAMES CLIFFORD, *The Predicament of Culture*

The mutual influence and interpenetration of ethnography and the
avant-garde requires a wholesale realignment of the familiar opposition of art and social science. In the twentieth century, ethnography,
James Clifford argues, has been an inherently modernist preoccupation, meaning not only that it shares a great deal with the arts, but
that it begins "with a reality deeply in question."[1] The humanist recognition and appreciation of other peoples, other aesthetics, other social
practices, and other forms of everyday life has produced a cultural
relativism that is often masked by the critique of colonialism. Clifford
describes ethnography as more than an "empirical research technique,"
but a "more general cultural disposition" that shares a great deal with
twentieth-century art and writing (121). He focuses particularly on the
shared ground of surrealism and ethnography, two faces of a fascination with the familiar and the strange, the exotic and the banal.

The conjunction of ethnography and surrealism can be traced to
the journal *Documents,* edited by Georges Bataille, of which seven-
teen issues were published from 1929 to 1930. Its contributors included
anthropologists, surrealists, former surrealists, and future anthropologists. One of the journal's main objectives was the promotion of an
anti-aesthetic mode of representation, which meant, in part, an attrac-

tion to the grotesque and the "dirty," but equally to the collection and description of objects and practices that resisted the marketplace logic of use and exchange value. Stripped of "beauty" and "good taste," the journal challenged bourgeois humanist norms of art *and* museology. As Dennis Hollier explains, "The official ideological contract was an aesthetic of the irretrievable." The collusion of ethnologists and artists was not without friction, but *Documents* was in all respects grounded in "an aggressive realism." The status of the document was the nemesis of poetic metaphor: "Photography takes the place of the dream."[2] Objets trouvés, like the related Duchampian readymade, were the aesthetic predecessors of found footage, appropriated and recontextualized. But the dream is never completely banished, nor is the dream-work, when the accumulation of cultural detritus is reassembled into a phantasmagoria. "Heterogeneous and foreign, [the document] has an impact, it shocks (it has shock-value) as a trauma would" (21).

Documents included written texts, some as short as a paragraph, photographs, and so-called dictionary definitions. Its technique of juxtaposition, creating ironic effects of cultural collision, brought together the "high" and the "low," the familiar (European) and the strange (mainly African). It included film reviews—of *Hallelujah* ("a hallucinating realism")[3] and *Fox Movietone Follies* ("not the slightest hint of an aesthetic in this spectacle")[4]—that placed popular cinema side by side with Picasso and African musical instruments. Europe was perceived as being as worthy of ethnographic study as was Africa and other distant colonial sites. Clifford describes *Documents* as a "subversive, nearly anarchic documentary attitude" that constituted "an epistemological horizon for twentieth-century cultural studies" (134). Its techniques of collage and juxtaposition and its transgression of cultural purities involved the recognition, on the one hand, that nothing was uncollectible, and on the other, that the values implicit in classification and categorization were entirely arbitrary. In many ways, *Documents* is the originary moment of subversive cultural criticism. Just what this type of criticism might be, and how the avant-garde has evolved out of its moment, is what is at stake in the exploration of experimental ethnography.

Although *Documents* was somewhat removed from any actual film practice, the cross-fertilization of artifacts and aesthetics, documentary and art, was occurring simultaneously in the contemporaneous series of "city films" being produced around the world. Dziga Vertov's *Man with a Movie Camera* (1928), Ruttman's *Berlin: Symphony of a City* (1927),

Jean Vigo's *A Propos de Nice* (1929), Cavalcanti's *Rien que les Heures* (1926), *Sao Paulo: Sinfonia de uma Cidade* (1928), and Joris Ivens's *The Bridge* (1928) and *Rain* (1929) are examples of the many poetic documentaries that were produced at the end of the silent period. These films all exhibit the intermixing of photo-realism and montage effects of the *Documents* aesthetic, even if they cannot be described as surrealist works. Ethnographic surrealism was a short-lived moment, out of which ethnography, art, and surrealism "emerged as fully distinct positions" (Clifford, 134). And yet their blurring constitutes a crucial historical conjunction. Its disruptive potential is both a reorientation of the avant-garde toward everyday life and a reorientation of ethnography toward cultural pluralism and hybridity.

The filmmaker for whom *Documents* provided the most immediate backdrop is Luis Buñuel, who brought a surrealist perspective to an early instance of ethnographic film in *Las Hurdes* (1932). In this chapter, I will discuss this text as an exemplary instance of experimental ethnography and juxtapose it with a much more recent film that is suggestive of how a surrealist aesthetic can still be operative in experimental ethnography in the late twentieth century. Tracey Moffatt's film *Night Cries: A Rural Tragedy* (1990) updates the surrealist project to embrace a critique of colonialism, and to delineate a postcolonial subject position, both of which are radically absent from Buñuel's film.

Las Hurdes: Posthumanism

In 1932 Luis Buñuel shot one of the most shocking ethnographic films ever made. Variously titled *Land without Bread, Unpromised Land,* and *Las Hurdes,* it is shocking because of its profound lack of sympathy. Images of the Hurdanos, a destitute population settled in a remote region of Spain, are accompanied by Brahms's Fourth Symphony and a voice-over commentary that is condescending, sarcastic, and brutally blunt. Perhaps the only true example of a surrealist documentary, *Las Hurdes* tends to be marginalized in most accounts of Buñuel's oeuvre, as well as most accounts of surrealist cinema, documentary cinema, and experimental cinema. As a completely idiosyncratic and anomalous film, it makes an ideal entry point to experimental ethnography in the cinema, a point that is by no means an origin. *Las Hurdes* refers back to thirty years of protodocumentary filmmaking, as well as forward to a subsequent history of collusion between the avant-garde and anthropology.

The *Documents* group represented a splinter group of the surrealist cadre, and Buñuel himself had an uneasy relationship to the surrealist project. James Lastra has situated Buñuel and *Las Hurdes* within the historical context of divisions within the surrealist movement and concludes that his strategies of representation come closest to Bataille's heterology. That is, Buñuel develops "a form that respected the materialist and heterogeneity of Hurdano life without recuperating it for reason, nationalism, or even humanism."[5] In 1931 the surrealists in France mounted an anticolonial exposition in France, deploying many of the same tactics as the *Documents* journal. Neither project was, however, free of an Orientalist tendency to idealize the Other as a site of alterity. Lastra argues that Buñuel aimed to counter this approach with a text that could not be recuperated in any way.[6]

Las Hurdes was originally screened in Madrid in 1933 with Buñuel delivering the narration "live" in the manner of a silent-film lecturer.[7] In the various versions of the extant film in English, the narration has been recorded slightly differently, and the version currently available on video has toned down what was originally described as a combination of "insolent indifference" and "apparent objectivity."[8] The newly recorded tone of voice adopts the conventional soft edges of contemporary documentary style, but this tone has made it more difficult to read the film's ironies. *Las Hurdes* is an extremely ambivalent and ambiguous film that has provoked at least one recent critic to say, in an article in *Third Text,* against the dominant critical grain: "I suggest that *Land without Bread* is distinctly colonialist in its reduction of a hinterland people to the status of freakshow exhibits for the Parisian avant-garde and that this is because, rather than in spite of, its ethnographic and surrealist character."[9] This reading is not simply a response to the toned-down narration; it is a very literal interpretation that is certainly warranted by the film. *Las Hurdes* was first received by an extremely displeased audience, which of course was precisely the response Buñuel was aiming for. Its exemplary status is not its correctness but its shocking transgressions of the humanist mode of colonialist ethnography.

A necessary context for *Las Hurdes,* in addition to the surrealist one, is that of the transition to sound that the cinema was completing in 1932. Although neither music nor commentary was recorded on the film until 1937, it was essentially Buñuel's first sound film, and as such, it constitutes a remarkable parody of the voice-over documentary that did not yet exist. Buñuel may have been working with the conventions of the travelogue lecture, but he delivered his original monologue from the projection booth rather than a podium.[10] Like most travelogues, the film is framed by the arrival and departure of the narrator-adventurer-ethnographer, marking off very clearly the boundaries between here and there, us and them.[11] The narrator's attitude of condescension and matter-of-fact description is very much that of the tourist displaying the sights of his travels.

Like the illustrated lecture, Buñuel's voice-over is "impersonal" in its lack of empathy with the Hurdano culture, and yet it is authorized by the "person" of the traveler-ethnographer: he who has been there. The narration, furthermore, adopts the first-person plural "we," referring perhaps to the film crew, but invoking the familiar dualism of "us and them." In *Las Hurdes,* the voice, perhaps for the first time, is disembodied. The voice of God has not yet been officially born, so Buñuel invents him, along with his infinite powers of making meaning. It may be fair to say that the film could not have been made much later than 1932, and even then, the parody was horrifying in its blatant abuse of discursive power.

Caught within the imperious, disembodied discourse of the narrator, the bodies of the Hurdanos are furthermore photographed in the most submissive manner. Not only are they objectified by the camera in their various poses, but Buñuel's montage makes no attempt to develop a realist, diegetic narrative space. The ordering of quick-paced shots has been compared to a slide show, which is indeed the precursor of the cinematic travelogue.[12] What movement there is, in the profilmic, and of the camera, is minimal. With very little depth of field, even the landscape shots appear cramped in a very flat pictorial space. The effect is one of extreme fragmentation, a series of glimpses of people, animals, landscape, and architecture, each shot subject to the narrator's cursory explanation.

Music, like spoken commentary, was an integral part of silent film, and since 1927, soundtracks had begun to be physically attached to films, becoming an important component of the text. In *Las Hurdes,* the role of music in the fixing of meaning and the production of knowledge is made evident through its failure. The function of Brahms's Fourth Symphony is to provide a radical juxtaposition of a classical, highly developed culture with the primitivism of the Hurdanos. Its transcendent, triumphant, major-key hyperbole is completely incongruous with the ethnographic imagery. Together with the commentary, this soundtrack may be one of the most successful instantiations of the famous 1928 Soviet manifesto on sound in which the contrapuntal use of sound is advocated for avant-garde cinema.[13]

Buñuel uses the soundtrack as a "montage element," building the film on three separate discursive levels — music, image, and narration — realizing that film is an audiovisual medium. The power of the soundtrack, the impact of narration on the way images are read, and the effect of music on how they are "felt" are laid bare in *Las Hurdes.* Most critics and commentators on the film — and there have been many perceptive and articulate ones — agree that the film foregrounds and throws into relief some of the basic prejudices and conceits of anthropological cinema. As Vivian Sobchack says:

We can see neither as an Hurdano nor as the narrator — nor even as our once unselfconscious selves. Rather, we are led to question our own devious prejudices always ready to surface and distort the world in every glance. Even though we are doomed to failure, we are asked to strain and squint and peer through our own history, our own culture, to get a glimpse of some adorned and shadowy reality which can never be made clear and visible but which will forever lurk in our peripheral vision.[14]

As an exemplary instance of experimental ethnography, the film engages with quite a number of issues that go to the core of the politics of representation in anthropological cinema. In addition to the strategic use of the soundtrack, three further aspects of the film need to be identified: the (un)reliability of visible evidence, the discourse of primitivism, and the role of sacrifice and death.

The first point is related to the tension between voice and image. For example, over a shot of a woman who looks about seventy years old, the narrator says, "this woman is thirty-two years old." Doubt immediately enters the contract between narrator and viewer, a doubt that spreads insidiously throughout the entire film. Can we believe anything he says? Can we believe that he could be deceiving us? And if he is telling the truth, of what use is truth to the woman or to the viewer? The doubt is compounded by sarcasm: the narrator says, over a shot of the interior of a village home where a few unidentified objects are tacked on the wall: "Note the flair for interior decorating."

Still from Luis Buñuel's *Las Hurdes* (1932). "This woman is thirty-two years old."

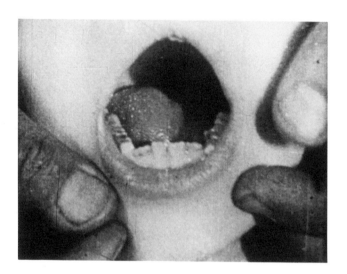

Still from Luis Buñuel's *Las Hurdes* (1932).

Despite its authority, the voice-over does not completely close down the "meaning" of the images. In a key sequence in a schoolroom, when the music has momentarily died away, our attention is drawn to a picture of an *infanta* on the wall. The narrator says, "What is this fair lady doing here?" These comments on representation break the more objective matter-of-fact mode of address that dominates the film, puncturing the veneer of authority and inviting the viewer to participate intellectually.

The commentary on visible evidence in *Las Hurdes* is extended to a demonstration of ethnographic cinema as a scientific instrument. In one of the early sequences, a young girl is examined by a member of the film crew as the narrator explains that she has a mysterious illness that afflicts many of the Hurdanos. A close-up of her open mouth underlines the role of the camera as a tool of examination and penetration, with the cool detachment of a medical instrument. The narrator says, after the cut to the next image, that "we were told that the girl died two days later." At another point, illustrations from a scientific book on mosquitoes are inserted as the narrator explains that the Hurdanos suffer from malaria. The scientific drawings are followed by a man shaking (apparently) from the disease, so that the anthropological and entomological discourses are suddenly aligned. Malaria, like the anopheles mosquito, is "easily recognized," but not by the Hurdanos.

The alignment of visible evidence and scientific method is also their failure, though. The Hurdanos keep dying, in a persistent resistance not only to the interventions of science but equally to the ethnographic impetus toward abstraction. The narrator's rhetoric consistently refers to individual Hurdanos as "typical" of the various social and medical disorders with which the film is obsessed, a common strategy of ethnographic film by which the individual social actor becomes an illustration of an ethnographic principle.[15] These people may be "typical," but they are contradictorily individuated by their deaths. The failure of the film is its failure of aesthetic redemption, compounded by the failure of scientific discourse, to save — or even help — the Hurdanos. In aligning these two failures, Buñuel also aligns the structures of visual culture with those of social science as discourses of power and subjugation.

Bill Nichols has suggested that the desire for knowledge that governs ethnography is a desire that parallels pornographic desire; both demand a certain diegetic coherence in the representation of the Other. The viewer needs to be able to fantasize his or her participation into the spectacle as one of mastery,[16] so the codes of narrative cinema are often deployed for the creation of a closed diegetic space, from which the viewer is categorically absent. *Las Hurdes* eschews any pretense of transparency, addressing the viewer directly as a voyeur for whom the Hurdanos are being presented as specimens. The great gap between the known and the knower, the viewed and the viewer, is the shock of *Las Hurdes.* Its greatest transgression is in its inhumane refusal to even try to close the gap or cover it up, and this is very closely tied to the film's failure to create a closed diegetic space.

The disjunctive cutting of *Las Hurdes,* within scenes and between scenes, prevents any kind of spatial orientation for the viewer. Despite the premise of the entry and exploration of the Hurdanos' villages and environment, Buñuel has respected few conventions of continuity editing. In conjunction with the double-layered contrapuntal soundtrack, the film might be described as an "open" modernist text. And yet this formal playfulness is inappropriate to its subject of lived poverty. He has radically overstepped the boundaries of avant-garde "art" and taken its strategies into the realm of social science. The subversive quality of *Las Hurdes* has everything to do with the expectations of "appropriateness."

Las Hurdes has an equally "inappropriate" view of primitivism. The film's inversion of ethnographic conventions reveal the ideological and representational structures that are embodied in the myth of primitivism. It has been pointed out that although the Hurdanos are very likely descendants of Jews fleeing the Spanish Inquisition,[17] Buñuel makes no mention of their ethnicity. The Hurdanos are represented not as victims of history but as a regressive enclave, an exotic curiosity. The narrator's explanatory commentary implies an infinitely regressive cultural process, so that the Hurdanos come to represent an inverted modernism, in which their relations with nature and government are increasingly devastating. Every cure, every attempt at bettering their lives, makes them worse. Death is the logical and inevitable outcome of every endeavor and haunts the film as a recurring event with no redemptive power.

The rhetoric and diction of the narration is largely responsible for the sense of regressive social decay. For example, "Although the Spaniards are naturally given to song, never once did we hear anyone singing in these dreary streets." Or, over shots of children eating bread, "Until very recently bread was unknown to the Hurdanos. The bread these children are eating was given to them at school. The master usually makes them eat it in front of him for fear that it will be taken from them by their half-starved parents." Over a two-shot of a man and a woman eating some berries, we are told: "May and June are the two hottest months of the year for the Hurdanos. By that time the stock of potatoes has long been exhausted. They have nothing to eat, nothing but these unripe cherries. If they wait till the cherries ripen, they will starve, so the Hurdanos have no choice but to eat them and so they suffer from chronic dysentery." Another passage concerning the search for food is illustrated by a series of images that move from observation to analysis to confrontation:

Here at last are the precious strawberry trees [triumphant music, landscape], but their trials are not yet at an end [a woman fills a sack held by a man], for this apparently harmless plant is the haunt of the deadly adder. The peasants are frequently bitten [frontal close-up of a man holding up his bandaged hand for the camera]. This is seldom fatal in itself, but [extreme close-up of the hand] the Hurdanos generally infect the wound by their unhygienic efforts to cure it [close-up of man's face, glancing up at the camera and back at his hand].

In each of these examples, the mode of address uses the referential language of the lecturer's pointer: "these children," "these unripe cherries," "here at last." The man's glance in the last example plays a similar role, pointing to the hand proffered to the camera. The effect is one of layers of discourse, in which the image is at once prior and inert. As a mode of primitivism, the regression is implicit in the cinematic medium: the logic of documentary realism pushes the referent back historically, precluding any possibility of "catching up." If ethnography and the cinema are two aspects of a single culture of colonial modernism, one of the key features of experimental ethnography in the cinema is a deconstruction of the logic of primitivism that has tied them together.

As an ideology, primitivism is a construction of Western modernism, arising in conjunction with an industrialized society that began to see itself in terms of a loss of innocence. Primitivism denotes a highly conflicted desire to retain a sense of the premodern without losing faith in the principles of "civilization." Other cultures become fetish objects that represent the childhood of humanity. Only in their infantilized form can these others be linked to the colonial form of "us," the human race. However, "the myth of primitivism" also has a utopian aspect and represents a progressive impulse of modernism insofar as it challenges the norms of industrialized society. If postcolonial theory has focused on the ideological effects of primitivism, the avant-garde has been preoccupied with the latter, progressive, impulse. One of the tasks of experimental ethnography is to trace the transformation of primitivism in postmodern culture. This surrealist ethnography suggests that it may only be in a posthumanist culture that the heritage of colonialist anthropology can be left behind.

In *Las Hurdes* Buñuel effectively deconstructs the two-sidedness of primitivism, foregrounding the "unhygienic conditions" of the Hurdanos as both symptom and cause of their misery. The only happy Hurdanos are the group of village idiots who stare down the camera in a brief challenge to the film's caustic and condescending gaze. Whereas this brief lapse into the irrational may be the film's most obvious nod to surrealism, Buñuel's strategies echo many of Bataille's in the pages of *Documents*. Dennis Hollier describes the confluence of ethnography and surrealism as an uneasy alliance, in which topics, such as spitting, had different significance for different writers. For the ethnographers, "Dirtiness is proper to man, from which it follows that the less a thing is clean, the more human it is." But the impoverished conditions of the Hurdanos embody a principle of excess that was especially significant for Bataille. As Hollier explains, "Everything must be said, yes, but on the condition that not everything can be said. . . . The avant-garde has no use for the right to shock proffered by the ethnographers: where, if anyone takes offense, one simply shows one's permit. Ethnographer's license? But what would a sacrilege be within the limits of mere reason?" [18]

The ethnographic perspective of *Las Hurdes* defies reason, pushing its shock value beyond the limits of humanism. Buñuel takes advantage of his "license" as a filmmaker, but he also maintains a strict separation between "reason" and "reality." The regression of the Hurdanos is unspeakable and unknowable except as a shock to the system of civilization. The sheer hopelessness of their situation situates the Hurdanos as not just stuck in the past like most "primitive" cultures, but as an inversion of human progress. Their future of infinite decay and regression is the mirror image of modern progress, an inversion that is implicit in the contradictory myth of primitivism.

It is not incidental that the Hurdanos are a European people. The film exemplifies Trinh Minh-ha's observation that "there is a third world in every first world," [19] and in 1932 this would have been an especially striking subversion of ethnographic otherness. The Hurdanos are an extreme instance of an impoverished peasant class hidden within industrialized Europe. Lastra has argued that Buñuel's anticolonialism is an attack on "a kind of 'colonialism' *internal* to certain societies — a suppression of difference in the interests of national identity." [20] Surrealist ethnography is a means of resisting cultural imperialism — the subsumption of all cultural differences within a standard of "the same." If the specific intervention of *Las Hurdes* pertained to the Spanish nation-state, its formal innovations are equally significant to the ideology of humanism. As an anthropological method, humanism also embraces otherness as a means of transcending cultural difference — as Roland Barthes pointed out in his critique of "The Family of Man." [21] *Las Hurdes* proposes an otherness that cannot be recuperated.

Cultural difference is announced in the opening titles, which evoke the "first-contact" mystique of ethnographic purity, along with the romance of survival that Flaherty had exploited ten years earlier with *Nanook of the North:* "The Hurdanos were unknown, even in Spain, until a road was built for the first time in 1922. Nowhere does man need to wage a more desperate fight against the hostile forces of nature. . . . In light of this, the film may be considered as a study in 'human geography.' " This introduction is followed by a voice-over and a map of Europe indicating the so-called primitive communities (Tchecoslovaquie, Savoie, Italie, Espagne), which is then dissolved into a map of Spain with major cities marked, and then to a more local map of Las Hurdes and its surrounding towns. The narration posits the Hurdanos themselves as being typical of an antithesis to "civilized" society: "In certain hidden and little-known parts of Europe, there still exist remnants of the most primitive type of human life. A typical example is to be found in Spain. Only sixty miles from Salamanque with its old university, famous for its literary and scientific traditions, live the Hurdanos. They are cut off from the rest of the world by a lofty range of mountains. To reach the Hurdanos we were forced to pass through the village of Alberca."

By withholding the history of the Hurdanos and refusing to acknowledge their ethnic or cultural specificity, the film apprehends them as an element of the Spanish national unconscious. Indeed, the layering of discursive registers in *Las Hurdes* replicates the Freudian structure of consciousness. The imagery of the Hurdanos, gathered in glimpses, is a return of the repressed inequities within a manifestly democratic and ethnically coherent culture. Where the Brahms represents the most systematic formal aesthetic language, the Hurdanos are depicted as grotesque and monstrous and are manifestly without form. Bataille attacked architecture as a straitjacket that could be escaped only by way of a path "traced by the painters—toward bestial monstrosity."[22] And if the Hurdanos are being "used" in this avant-garde enterprise, they are not contained by it. As "an aesthetic of the irretrievable," *Las Hurdes* renders the cultural otherness of the Hurdanos as monstrous and therefore unrecuperable as Jewishness or as victims of history. They are not the primitive "other," but the primitive within.[23]

The third and final point to be made about *Las Hurdes* as an exemplary instance of experimental ethnography concerns its discourse of cruelty. At the heart of the film is a scene in which a goat falls to its death from a rocky cliff. The narration seems to precipitate the accident by saying, "Goat meat is only eaten when this happens," and the film cuts from a medium shot of a goat on the cliff, just when it is about to jump or slip; to a long shot in which the goat falls, striking the rocks on its way down; to a third shot of it falling past the camera and rolling down until it finally stops dead. In the second shot, a puff of smoke can be detected on the right side of the frame. The last shot is taken from a camera position located somewhere on the cliff itself. The scene is obviously set up—in terms of montage, narration, and even within the profilmic. Conley has described this sequence as a "photographic ritual and an exemplary sacrifice."[24] The goat is effectively murdered for the film, in the same way as a rooster is decapitated earlier in a village ritual (censored from most prints of the film).

The giveaway puff of smoke betrays the documentary contract of authentic reality. Not only have the filmmakers intervened, but their actions are murderous.[25] As a spectacular sacrifice, it may evoke Bataille again, who identified sacrificial ritual as a transgression of the bourgeois sense of self.[26] The ritual sacrifice of animals has come to be a familiar trope of ethnographic film. Death plays a crucial role, both as narrative event and as indexical marker of cinematic truth, an irreversible sign of the once-only of documentary realism. The camera as witness of ritual sacrifice binds the filmmaker to "the field" and authenticates the realism with a historically specific event. However, it is difficult to see any redemptive power in this sacrifice in *Las Hurdes*. The film spectator is hardly the "collective," and as Tom Conley notes, the Hurdanos are not represented anywhere in the film as a real mass or collective.[27] One could even argue that the cinema deadens the redemptive potential of any ritual sacrifice by making it infinitely repeatable. Death on film was an "obscenity" for Bazin because it reversed the irreversible.[28] By staging such a ritual sacrifice, Buñuel renders spectatorship a matter of witnessing without the erotic charge of the religious ritual and identifies a particularly sadistic aspect of colonial culture.

The killing of the goat in *Las Hurdes* is a shock of the order of Walter Benjamin's dictum that "there is no document of civilization which is not at the same time a document of barbarism."[29] By 1940, when Benjamin had come to this conclusion, the progressive project of the surrealists had long since dissipated. Many of Benjamin's most important essays were written contemporaneously with the *Documents* journal and with *Las Hurdes.* He seems not to have commented directly on either of these enterprises; nor was he interested in the emerging field of ethnology. And yet his remarks on surrealism and on cinema are extremely pertinent.

Shock, for Benjamin, was a condition of modernity that needed to be mobilized by the avant-garde. Surrealism came close to realizing the potential of shock as an awakening from history, but Benjamin also criticized its nihilistic inability to "bind revolt to revolution."[30] *Las Hurdes* may ultimately fall to the same critique, and yet it exemplifies Benjamin's observation that the revolutionary potential of surrealism lies in its blasting open of the image sphere. In the aftermath of "such dialectical annihilation—this will still be a sphere of images and, more concretely, of bodies."[31] Benjamin saw in surrealism a means of "awakening" a Marxist materialism in danger of becoming a stale orthodoxy in 1929. His description of surrealism as "profane illumination" distinguishes its redemptive power from that of religion and grounds surrealism in "a materialistic, anthropological inspiration" (179). Benjamin's own study of the Paris Arcades constitutes a form of surrealist ethnography and was indeed inspired by their collecting of urban phenomena. The textual strategies of *Las Hurdes* indicate the significance of the surrealist project to ethnography in its radical ambivalence and equivocation, its absolute refusal to accommodate the Hurdanos into any aesthetic or ideological system of thought. The film's materialism consists of a rejection of humanist models, and a reduction of cinematic representation to a collision of competing discursive voices.

Las Hurdes is shocking because its antihumanism allows no position from which to judge; it appears to have no "ethical" perspective within the film. There is no "we" with which the viewer can identify, no comfortable subject position. The film belongs to a very specific moment in history when the surrealists mobilized such social transgression for a politicized aesthetic practice. Benjamin realized early on that this was really only a matter of playing with bourgeois codes of morality and changing the rules. As the only cinematic example of surrealist ethnography produced in this period, *Las Hurdes* goes beyond this play with decorum and pushes its transgressive practice onto a materialist plane. "The study in human geography" shows how the construction of cultural difference is a sadistic colonial practice. Its use of a modernist technique of fragmentation exploits the potential of the shock effect in a horrifying depiction of social decay. The imagery and references to death that haunt the film are inseparable from the uncanny familiarity of its structure. The exploitation of the Hurdano people resounds as the repressed memory of "civilization" surfacing in the form of a scientific object.

Buñuel's modernist techniques of fragmentation and textual discursiveness cut through any conception of lost aura. His irony is Benjamin's allegory, insofar as the authenticity of the Hurdanos, sealed only by their deaths, is inaccessible to the medium of cinema. The Hurdanos are surrounded by references to Christianity that are traces of a luxury unavailable to them, mere spiritual commodities in Buñuel's treatment. Neither ritual value nor cult value can be attached to the images of these people; the failure of such aesthetics is only underlined by the killing of the goat. Phenomenological perception and its corollary of "exhibition value" are both cause and symptom of the horrors of *Las Hurdes*.

Night Cries: Another Colonial Horror Story

Surrealism as an aesthetic movement belongs to the particular conjunction of European cultural and political history between the First and Second World Wars. To describe contemporary filmmaking as "surrealist" implies a slightly different meaning of the word: it is necessarily more of a description than an identification, motivated by Clifford's aim "to recapture, if possible, a situation in which ethnography is again something unfamiliar."[32] It may be a particular reading of surrealism that illuminates recent examples of experimental ethnography, and it is that sense of a two-way street, of mutual correspondences across history, that I want to access by invoking surrealism in the context of a film made by Australian Aboriginal filmmaker Tracey Moffatt.

Moffatt, a film school graduate, claims "the right to be *avant-garde like any white artist*,"[33] but her version of avant-garde cinema is not what one might expect. The only real experimental antecedent is Maya Deren's *Meshes of the Afternoon*, as *Night Cries: A Rural Tragedy* draws on fictional genres of the melodrama and the horror film rather than documentary or experimental aesthetics. The sixteen-minute film is staged on a studio set that is lit like a Hollywood melodrama; in fact, it is introduced by an epigraph from an American melodrama called *Picnic* (Logan, 1955). The relationships with which Moffatt's film is concerned emerge as historical, a history that turns on the bodies of the two central figures, a young Aboriginal woman caring for her adoptive white mother, now terribly aged and helpless.

Night Cries explores the contradictory emotional bonds that have developed within the Australian forced adoption and assimilation program, although the details and history of that practice are not given in the film. Its stylized setting is a rendering of the homestead of *Jedda* (Charles Cauvel, 1955), one of the first big Australian color widescreen films. Moffatt's project is a "resurrection" of the young Aboriginal girl who is thrown off a cliff and killed in the 1955 film. To rethink and revise the discourse of primitivism within the 1955 "classic," she returns to the film's prologue, writing out the men in the film, and focuses on the mother-daughter relationship as a way of reframing the Aboriginal girl's identity.[34]

Most striking about *Night Cries* is the rendering of the Australian outback with a bright, shiny, fake landscape shot entirely in studio. This dreamscape is typical of Moffatt's signature style as a total elimination of nature.[35] Like Oshima's banishment of green from his films, the explicit turn to artifice refutes any naturalization of cultural processes.[36] The scenes that are played out in this garish setting are disconnected, without dialogue, as if they were glimpses into something that has been going on for a long, long time. The younger black woman nurses the older white woman, washes her, and smokes patiently while waiting outside the outhouse. She writes a letter, hears a whip cracking outside the window, and flashes back to a time when their roles were reversed, when, as a child, her mother brushed her hair. She also recalls a terrifying outing at the beach when her light-skinned mother turned her back

Still from Tracey Moffatt's *Night Cries: A Rural Tragedy* (1990). *Courtesy of Women Make Movies.*

on her brown-skinned children. In the final scene, mother and daughter lie side by side on a pier, the older woman apparently dead and the younger one shaking with sobs. A child's crying seems to emanate from her body. With no dialogue, the film relies on the discourse of spectacular excess and the nonlinguistic signifiers of *mise en scène* and sound for its melodramatic mode of expression.[37]

The soundtrack of *Night Cries* is filled with the shrieks of a horror movie, creating an eerie sense of isolation around the homestead in the outback. The dream imagery of two black children and a young white mother on some kind of seaside outing is dominated by the nightmarish violence of sea crashing on rocks. Like *Las Hurdes,* this film draws on the uncanny structures of the horror film, and Moffatt also evokes a scenario of decay, although here it is the decay of colonialism. The old white woman is crippled with arthritis, her fingers hooked up to some kind of mechanical apparatus. The women's relationship is a melancholy one in its pathetic routines, but also one of strength, transcending the cultural roles that each has been assigned. In keeping with the tensions of the Hollywood woman's film, psychological struggle is diverted into aesthetic excess; the contradictions of the family drama are not resolvable, but are diverted into pathos.

By retreating entirely to the realm of artifice, Moffatt abandons "the real" along with referentiality as an epistemology. And yet this is not fiction, either. In this case, "family drama" extends to the larger cultural family of Australia and the colonial program of forced adoption of children with mixed blood. The bodies of the two women, furthermore, suggest the terms of a cultural renewal, even if it will be one forever haunted by colonial ghosts. The imbrication of colonial and familial relationships conveys a sense of the symbiotic aspect of the production of otherness. Scenes and sounds of whipping, along with an overwhelming sense of entrapment, accompany the emotional bonds between mother and daughter to articulate the complex psychological structure of dependency.

One of the effects of Moffatt's startling *mise en scène* and elliptical narrative is a sense of textures and physical experiences. Scenes of washing, sea spray, and cooling down with a hose constitute a discourse of sensual memory, drawing the viewer into the film on an affective, evocative level. Is this ethnography? As a study of a culturally specific situation, *Night Cries* demands an expansion of the idea of ethnography. Along with the banishment of nature is a complete transformation of the terms of the documentary contract with reality. Veracity applies only to the emotional pathos of the colonial relationship played out in this film. Moffatt lingers on her theatrical tableaux, allowing the waiting to register with the viewer; waiting for the old woman to die, waiting for history to fulfill the promise of the landscape. In a couple of close-ups of Marcia Langton, who plays the Aboriginal daughter, she seems to return the look of the camera, gazing out of her fictional confines to briefly address the spectator. As Langton is a well-known Australian writer, she provides an intertextual point of reference, interrupting the veneer of fiction with the body of a historical subject.[38]

The other important historical subject in this film is Jimmy Little, an Aboriginal pop star of the 1960s. Moffatt includes clips of him singing (in suit and tie) his hits "Love Me Tender" and "Royal Telephone," the only instance of a synchronized voice in the film. In the context of *Night Cries*, Little signifies the deep cultural ambivalence of assimilation, the structures of mimicry and camouflage by which the colonized assumes the identity of the colonizer. Little's performance is a kind of ventriloquism of a tradition "which is not his, but which he sings as his own."[39] Onto the drama at the homestead, it casts the shadow of colonial history against which the women's story needs to be read, a history that is not "factual" but cultural and textual.

Night Cries is exemplary of a new mode of documentary film that Bill Nichols calls "performative." Evolving out of the reflexive documentary style, performative documentaries stress "subjective aspects": They "rely much less heavily on argument than suggestion; they do not explain or summarize so much as imply or intimate."[40] They also present a major disturbance to the way that ethnographic film traditionally makes meaning: "Performative documentary suspends realist representation. Performative documentary puts the referential aspect of the message in brackets, under suspension. Realism finds itself deferred, dispersed, interrupted and postponed."[41] For Nichols, the possible limitations of this mode of representation include the fact that the "loss of referential emphasis may relegate such films to the avant-garde," and they may have an " 'excessive' use of style" (95). I would suggest that it is precisely the recourse to the avant-garde, and the adoption of an experimental style, that is behind this tendency in documentary.

In freeing ethnography from its documentary pretext, *Night Cries* relies on another kind of knowledge, beyond the rationalizations of anthropological cinema. This is where it advances onto the terrain of surrealism, deploying the logic of the dream in place of that of explanatory rhetoric. Performative documentary is not simply a recourse to fiction, but an embrace of the fundamentally allegorical structure of cinema. It renders cinematic transparency as a receding memory of a more primitive form of representation, before the "fall" of mimeticism to modernist fragmentation: Benjamin's " 'orchid' in the land of technology."[42] Memory and fantasy are conjoined in the fabrication of this transparency, this spectacular image from which tactile and olfactory senses are banished.

In its invocation of the utopian discourse of desire implicit in film melodrama, *Night Cries* is exemplary of Stephen Tyler's transcendent form of postmodern ethnography: "Evocation is neither presentation nor representation. It presents no objects and represents none, yet it makes available through absence what can be conceived but not presented. It is thus beyond truth and immune to the judgment of performance. It overcomes the separation of the sensible and the conceivable, of form and content, of self and other, of language and the world."[43]

Patricia Mellencamp points to similar aspects of *Night Cries* to position it within a new development in women's cinema that she calls an empirical avant-garde: "The empirical avant-garde destabilizes history through the experimental, granting women the authority of the experiential. . . . The focus is on *becoming,* on *relations,* on what happens *between* experience and thought, between 'sensations and ideas,' between sound and image, between cultures, between women." [44] All three of these contexts—the performative, the postmodern, and the empirical—would adequately describe the dynamics of Moffatt's film, and indeed of much of contemporary experimental ethnography. Locating the film within a surrealist aesthetic, however, may help to show how its unusual strategies of representation function as a form of cultural critique.

Autobiography operates in this film as a form of "convulsive identity." [45] Moffatt herself was adopted by a white mother, although this biographical fact is not alluded to in the film.[46] What is at stake in her re-visioning of *Jedda* is identity—the identity of the postcolonial Aboriginal subject. The film effectively sets up a complex interface between colonial history, family trauma, postcolonial identity, and cinematic representation. A discourse of the self is inscribed in cultural history to produce a "microhistory," which is nevertheless distanced from the author of the text. Moffatt's identity, like Langton's, her alter ego in the film, is available only by way of intertextual references. *Night Cries* is deeply embedded in a contextual network of social history, and yet it is also violently removed from that history. It is cut off from all origins, all foundations, even while it reconfigures its sources—autobiographical, historical, and referential—as discourses of imagination, fantasy, and creative memory.

The use of film genres in *Night Cries,* specifically melodrama and the horror film, is further means of employing intertextuality to cut into and across a particular cultural history. Narrative genres offer mythic structures of desire that are much more overt, and more legible, than some of the more invisible narratives that conventionally structure ethnographic film. Moreover, Moffatt's treatment of these intertexts, exaggerating and stylizing their photographic qualities, is a means of evoking the *mise en scène* of colonial identity through the sheer power of the image. It is a history of images and a history in the image, in the very illumination of her deeply saturated colours, in which the trauma of her own history is displayed.

Hal Foster suggests that the lack of "foundations" in the surrealist aesthetic constitutes a subversive style. In Moffatt's case, "nonfounda-tional" refers not only to her intertextuality but to the simulacral status of the image itself. Her ethnography involves a crucial transformation of the photographic image as historical signifier. For Benjamin, the historical form of the photograph is an evacuation of history, of the impossibility and irretrievability of the present tense, which is merely a flash between the past and the future.[47] He claims that "to articulate the past historically does not mean to recognize it 'as it really was.' It means to take possession of a memory as it flashes up at a moment of danger."[48] Benjamin's theory of history is in many ways embedded in photography—as a cultural form and as a medium that, as many others have also pointed out, is closely tied to memory and death.

If the referent of the photograph is in this sense always vanishing, and a sign of historical time, Moffatt's indulgence in a manifestly fake image dissolves the present into a fantastic scenario linking past and future. Her "possession of a memory" renders her own origins—in Australia's forced adoption program for example—a fantastic scenario. Not to be forgotten, its danger is tempered by a forgiveness that is not in the least sentimental, but filled with the passion of redemption. Moffatt's un-canny *mise en scène* suggests that the memory is already colonized, by imagery as diverse as *Picnic, Jedda,* and Jimmy Little. But the drama that takes place there, in memory, begins the task of decolonization by introducing the postcolonial subject, Langton-Moffatt, into the scene of historical horror.

Ethnography and/as Trauma

Hal Foster claims that "the political in surrealism lies less in its stormy party affiliations and isolated anarchistic gestures than in its uncanny ability to oppose to modern rationalization its other face."[49] Foster may be referring to industrial mechanization, and yet "modern rationaliza-tion" is equally characteristic of colonialism and its various techniques of domestication and assimilation. If, moreover, "the usual definition of the Surrealist image as a coupling of different elements in space can be read in terms of a working over of different memories and/or fantasies in time, a working over of trauma" (159), the "other face" of colonialism is indeed traumatic in Tracey Moffatt's treatment.

Like Buñuel, Moffatt evades the totalizing, essentialist gesture of hu-manism, and yet she allows for a dimension of "affect" to sneak back into the ethnographic spectacle by incorporating a feminist discourse of maternal melodrama. The benevolence of humanism is ultimately a condescension toward the Other,[50] and it is this convention of anthropology that is challenged in these two very different films. Surrealist ethnography might therefore be a means of denoting the strategic roles of ambivalence, cruelty, *and* empathy in refiguring the ethnographic relationship in postcolonial culture.

Night Cries uses the horror film to address the horrors of colonial culture, a generic treatment that *Las Hurdes* also seems to anticipate. Buñuel evokes the dangers of the photographic image and its implicit historical structure, marking the deep divide between those "out there" in the real, and those who watch in here, in the auditorium. Once the realism of ethnography is displaced by the simulacrum of Moffatt's *mise en scène,* the very structure of historical memory becomes surreal, "a signifier of an involuntary memory, a traumatic fantasy."[51] As a postmodern, performative ethnographic text, *Night Cries* transposes the cruel ironies of *Las Hurdes* onto another register. Its surrealist strategies are techniques of mobilizing a subject position within the traumatic landscape of colonial culture. Technologies of representation become the means by which memory takes on the pathos of melodrama and becomes a scene of desire and despair. If Benjamin saw the potential of the surrealist project as the need "to win the energies of intoxication for the revolution,"[52] here that intoxication is inspired, precisely, by the pain of colonial history. The body of the Aboriginal subject becomes the site of memory and emotion, dream and history.

II

DOCUMENTARY BEFORE

DOCUMENTARY

Still from the *Living Canada* series (1903), produced by
Charles Urban's Bioscope Company of Canada for
the Canadian Pacific Railroad.

3 The Body as the Main Attraction

History breaks down into images, not into stories.

—WALTER BENJAMIN, *Passagen-Werk*

Early cinema is a key moment in the cartography of modern culture, not as a point of origin, but as a point of indeterminacy, a period in which cinema, along with so many other practices and technologies, "was an invention without a future." As such, it has become a point of return, a place where the human body was last seen before its future alienation in mechanical reproduction. Although many of the historical debates and much of the theory that has emerged concerning this early period is preoccupied with narrative and the different forms of storytelling that circulated in film culture, the dominant mode of film practice before 1907 was the actuality.[1] Actualities were short films shot around the world, nominally "unstaged," although many were documents of performances, dances, processions, and parades.

Actuality cameramen were drawn to a wide range of subjects as "attractions"—from royalty to children, from native cultures to military conflicts, from activities of everyday life to landscapes and urban panoramas. The cinema provided its own logic of the spectacle: whatever it captured became an attraction by virtue of being filmed. Often the camera position was itself a function of the attractions of modern life: thus the popular "phantom rides" in which the camera was placed on the front of a moving train or streetcar. The traveling cameraman shot the world in motion, gathering the momentum of "progress" into the machine of representation. Within this image culture, a new form of experience was developed, one with specific effects on the human body. As Tom Gunning describes it, "The body itself appeared to be abolished, rendered itself immaterial, through the phantasmagoria of both still and motion photography. This transformation of the physical did not occur through the sublimation of an ethereal idealism. The body, rather, became a transportable image fully adaptable to the systems of circulation and mobility that modernity demanded."[2]

Among the subjects of early actuality filmmaking, native peoples were extremely popular. The spectacle of "the primitive" emerged directly from the display of indigenous people in world fairs where "native villages" were "part human zoo, part performance circus, part laboratory for physical anthropology."[3] Early films took over these functions, eventually replacing imprisonment with visual objectification. No longer reliant on techniques of captivity and faux environments, the display of other cultures began to include urban scenes from Asia and the Middle East, and a greater variety of cultural spectacle became available to metropolitan audiences in Europe and elsewhere. The body is effectively replaced in many of these films by costume, and in the favored format of the long shot, faces are a minor detail. Even European monarchs joined the procession across global screens, also adorned with finery and surrounded by crowds. Thus in early cinema, as the real body is released from captivity, the simulacrum of the body becomes a fetish, and "culture" becomes a spectacle of ritualist activities.

By the centenary of cinema in 1995, the great wealth of early cinema had begun to be available on video. In its new incarnation, it has become a kind of optical unconscious of modern culture. Whereas the avant-garde of the 1960s and 1970s used techniques such as optical printing, loop printing, and reversals to mediate the imagery of early cinema, on video, the films are already "found" and subject to extensive manipulation. The grain of the electronic image, and indeed the intervention of a machine that was not even imaginable at the turn of the century, places these small texts at one remove. It enables us to see how people saw as well as what they saw, historicizing the medium of representation along with its contents. This doubleness is the allegorical potential of experimental ethnography; the referent is retrieved from the memory of the technology for which it was once exhibited. Actualities, seen as fieldwork, designate moments in historical time when bodies encountered machines. The breakdown of time offers a kind of prism through which the present and the past might suddenly correspond in unforeseen ways: "The continuum of history," in Walter Benjamin's words, "might be blasted open."[4]

Filmmakers and theorists since the 1960s have noted a crucial affinity between early cinema and modernist aesthetics. In keeping with Benjamin's theory of history, this parallel enables a certain form of dialectical materialism, the utopian potential of which lies in the crystallization of time, the "constellation" of historical moments:

Historicism contents itself with establishing a causal connection between various moments in history. But no fact that is a cause is for that very reason historical. It became historical posthumously, as it were, through events that may be separated from it by thousands of years. A historian who takes this as his point of departure stops telling the sequence of events like beads of a rosary. Instead, he grasps the constellation which his own era has formed with a definite earlier one. Thus he establishes a conception of the present as the "time of the now" which is shot through with chips of Messianic time.[5]

The cinema before 1906 was given the label "primitive cinema" by Noël Burch, not because of its content, but because of its formal characteristics. The term was not meant to be derogatory, but distinguished early cinema from the "bourgeois" narrative cinema that came to dominate film practice.[6] For the first ten to fifteen years of the cinema, narrative closure, spectator positioning, and other mechanisms of bourgeois ideology had not yet been codified in film language, and filmmakers and film viewers may have been more "free" to use film in what are retrospectively radical ways. This is the myth of primitive cinema. Of course, neither early cinema nor native cultures were free of ideology, and yet the fantasy of other, alternative, cultural forms is an important component of historical imagination. If the convergence of primitive cinema and ethnographic primitivism can be mapped historically, perhaps the utopian historiography of the primitivist discourse can be redeemed allegorically, outside the colonialist, modernist anxiety about essences.

In the 1960s and 1970s, avant-garde filmmakers began to return to early cinema as an archival practice and as a prehistoric site of alterity. Once their work is resituated within a historical perspective, it may provide a model for mobilizing the historiography of primitivism within the terms of visual culture. Even if the mythology of a pure, "uncorrupted" cinema informed their interest in the cinema before Griffith,[7] their tactics of appropriation tended to be marked by the signs of historical distance and difference. Modernist aesthetics of minimalism, repetition, and medium specificity are superimposed onto film fragments salvaged from an earlier era. In this chapter, I will discuss one such textual appropriation of early cinema, David Rimmer's *Seashore* (1971). I am interested in not only the ethnographic body itself but the layering of gazes within the techniques of appropriation. It is a topic to which I will return in chapter 9, but for now, it is important to point out that my reading of early cinema as an ethnographic cinema is informed by its status at the end of the twentieth century as an archive. The examples of *From the Pole to the Equator* (1987) and Eadweard Muybridge's photographic motion studies in this chapter are not simply explorations of the ethnographic aspect of early cinema practices but are suggestive of how those practices can be re-presented and reread in cinematic and critical forms.

Tom Gunning has described film before 1907 as "the cinema of attractions," emphasizing the exhibitionist quality of both story and actuality films.[8] To consider the cinema of attractions as an ethnographic cinema is to explore an alternative documentary practice, and to foreground its subject matter, and its choice of bodies to film, within this emergent culture of the spectacle. Filmmakers and audiences at the turn of the century may not have perceived these films as "alternatives" to an institutionalized norm because such a norm had not yet developed. However, in its fascination with exotic and erotic subjects, the cinema of attractions did represent an alternative way of seeing. The cinema was intimately bound up with the expanding horizons of modernity and enabled people to see more, and to see differently. It is in this sense that early cinema can be described as experimental.

Gunning's use of the term "attraction" is inspired by the 1920s avant-garde, for whom the cinema had already lost some of its radical potential.[9] The exhibitionist character of early cinema binds it to the fairground and vaudevillian context in which it actually circulated. For Eisenstein, the status of cinema as an "attraction," furthermore, included its physical stimulation. Like Benjamin's "shock effect," the radical potential of cinema was its direct address to the spectator — meaning the return of the glance (which is a frequent occurrence in early cinema) *and* the disjunctiveness of its montage. Anticipating the effect of Eisenstein's dialectical editing, early cinema programs were composed of heterogeneous series of short films, both actualities and protofictions, some as short as ten seconds, which were spliced together by exhibitors.

The only fixed point in this cinema that lacked both diegesis and closure is the spectator himself or herself, to whom the display is directly addressed.[10] With no illusion except the magic of mimetic reproduction, the cinema of attractions rendered cultural difference as an encounter and an uninhibited display of bodies. The absence of an aesthetic of realism entailed what Miriam Hansen has described as "another kind of voyeurism" in which theatricality and peep show perspectives merged in an ambiguous form of address.[11] Although much of the critical work on early cinema has helped us to understand the dynamics of spectatorship during the period in which the films were made, I am interested in the dynamics of historically dislocated spectatorship.

By the term "documentary before documentary" I want to suggest that the "ethnographic" aspect of early cinema, seen from a postcolonial, postmodern perspective, can be read differently, as a return of the colonial repressed. In other words, I want to develop the analogy of primitivism that linked modern aesthetics with anthropological time into a dialectics of spectatorship. As a form of experimental ethnography, early cinema offers a model of textual "openness" in which meaning is not closed down. Depending on how it is appropriated by critics and filmmakers, the cinema of attractions can offer an amazing insight into how the body became a cultural sign within an apparatus that had not yet distinguished the language of science from that of art.

The cinema of attractions did not disappear with the emergence of narrative, and Gunning stresses that "the radical heterogeneity" of early cinema should "not be conceived as a truly oppositional program, one irreconcilable with the growth of narrative cinema."[12] Especially when this period is considered from an ethnographic perspective, the tendency in early cinema to put otherness on display, to stare, and to covet the best possible view, remains a constitutive feature of visual anthropology. With the development of diegetic codes of narrative realism, the "attraction" of otherness simply becomes better masked. The ideology of humanism demands that the fascination is hidden within a scientific discourse of reason, but in the cinema of attractions, the mask has not yet been conceived.

One of the first conjunctions of cinema and ethnography was Félix-Louis Regnault's 1895 application of Jules Marey's chronophotography to the study of native bodies. The techniques of stop-motion photography enabled Regnault to compile a visual archive of information for the taxonomic comparison of peoples according to physiognomy. Fatimah Tobing Rony argues that Regnault's experiments invented race as a visual spectacle. Within the evolutionary paradigm of Regnault's anthropology, "History was a race: those who did not vanquish would vanish. . . . Time was conceived in evolutionary terms, with race as the key factor, and the body as the marker of racial and thus temporal difference."[13] Although race had been an object of study for decades, and the racial body had been excessively visualized in popular (and "high") culture, Regnault inaugurated the visual *proof* of racial difference using the camera as a scientific instrument.

Regnault's use of protocinema technology privileged a discourse of detail — as document, as ornament, and as index. It recorded the excess that signified savagery and decadence, and it also referred to the indexical record of anatomical and physiological detail made possible by the photography of movement.[14] Regnault's experiments were carried out in Paris, his African subjects borrowed from the fairground exhibit; and so, as Rony points out, "it was the *body* that was authentic." Moreover, the ethnographic (black) body "represented a purer, authentic, and healthier man than the overstimulated, nervous and weakened modern urban citizen."[15]

Of all the contradictions embedded in the myth of primitivism, "the noble savage" is perhaps the most familiar. If primitivism is a fetishistic means of representing the absence of "aura," or authenticity, in modern life, the body of the Other serves as the vehicle of this denial. The failures of modern progress are displaced onto the spectacle of the body of the Other, collected and preserved within the technologies of modernity. But for the body to be an attraction, it has to be all covered with headdresses, robes, paint, turbans, and feathers. The fetish is a substitute for the missing part, which in this case is the body, missing from the screen (hence its lack of aura) and fragmented and torn apart in modern culture. Non-white skin color constitutes part of the decorative exoticism of the spectacular body.

That Regnault's experiments were put in the service of military training indicates the affinities of the ethnographic abstraction of the human body to modern practices of war. The ethnographic inscription of race was developed in the context of nation building, as the idea of culture was closely bound to physical and hereditary appearance.[16] In the emergent visual culture of the late nineteenth century, physiognomy became a sign system, a form of writing. Early cinema is thus an important point in the emergence of the racial stereotype in visual culture, a point where it becomes standardized as a fetish. Homi Bhabha has suggested that the fetish character of the stereotype can be read as a deconstruction of racist discourse: "By acceding to the wildest fantasies (in the popular sense) of the colonizer, the stereotyped other reveals something of the 'fantasy' (as desire, defense) of that position of mastery. . . . It is recognizably true that the chain of stereotypical signification is curiously mixed and split, polymorphous and perverse, an articulation of multiple belief."[17] Bhabha's privileging of the ambivalence of the stereotype is motivated by the need to analyze the fantasies of colonial discourse. The Other appears in the cinema of attractions as a fetish object, but it is a stereotype that is embedded in a dialectical image. As the image becomes an allegorical form of colonial discourse (as it does from the perspective of a century), it renders otherness both desirable and different, and always *prior* to the time of viewing.

Benjamin, we may recall, compared the work of the filmmaker to that of the surgeon. In penetrating reality, the cinema constitutes a kind of optical unconscious, in which the residues of the past are preserved as the traces of experience. Benjamin characterizes cinema, and modernity in general, as a culture of fragmentation. Like the surgeon who cuts into the body, the picture obtained by the cameraman "consists of multiple fragments which are assembled under a new law."[18] If that body is understood as a colonial body, the "new law" encompasses an emergent form of visual anthropology. It is significant that in the fetishization of the Other in early cinema, the body becomes a fantastic image, an "impossible image." Submitted to the view, the ethnic body is always dramatized in its ethnicity, supplemented by cultural paraphernalia and put on display. Its separation from the viewer is thus overdetermined as it enters the regime of desire.

Michael Taussig has developed Benjamin's notion of the optical unconscious within the context of anthropology. For Taussig, Benjamin theorized "a surfacing of the primitive within modernity as a direct result of modernity."[19] Mechanical reproduction (film and photography) constitutes a conflation of the copy with "a palpable, sensuous, connection between the very body of the perceiver and the perceived" (21). Taussig describes the indexical quality of cinematic representation as a kind of contact. In the photographic "copy" there is always the trace of "contact": the presence of the filmmaker in the same field of vision as the person, object, or scene filmed. "Copy and contact merge with each other to become virtually identical, different moments of the one process of sensing; seeing something or hearing something is to be in contact with that something."[20]

The cinema is fully implicated in colonial culture in its obsession with contact and the mystical properties of mimeticism. Nowhere are the colonial dimensions of mechanical reproduction more clearly delineated than in the early travelogues and actualities that were collected around the world. In the burgeoning of visual knowledge at the turn of the century, the cinema is a privileged site through which social knowledge becomes mapped onto physical, spatial, and tactile relationships. As an archival cinema, early film potentially brings colonial relationships into view. The double structure of copy and contact is an allegory of the distancing of (lost) auratic experience that is so central to Benjamin's conception of the twentieth-century artwork. History and memory conspire in an act of redemption that transcends conventions of knowledge and fetishization. The aura of contact — the mimetic magic of the machine — is inscribed in the phenomenon of the attraction: the cinema was itself on display in its first decade.

In the reappropriation of early cinema as an archival cinema, this allegorical structure is potentially writ large. "The third eye" that Rony describes as the critical perspective that intervenes between colonized and colonizer in ethnography is a form of allegorical appropriation. She is able to imagine what the Africans in Regnault's chronophotography are thinking[21] precisely because, one hundred years after those images were made, the body can be distinguished from the image as something that preceded it and exceeds it. The image is "in ruins" when it is no longer transparent; early films of native peoples become legible as documents of colonialism, not documents of native peoples. As allegories of the colonial gaze, these films and protofilms enable us to read the body as a fetish constructed within the "time machines" of anthropology and cinema.[22]

Ethnographic Spectacle

One of the most extensive excavations of the colonial aspect of actuality filmmaking by way of an experimental praxis is *From the Pole to the Equator* (1987), by two Italian filmmakers, Yervant Giankian and Angela Ricci Lucchi. The ninety-six-minute film consists entirely of footage that was originally shot by Luca Comerio between 1910 and 1915. Even though this is a little later than the period designated as "early," or primitive, cinema, Comerio's footage is a good example of how that style went "underground" with the advent of narrativity. Appropriated,

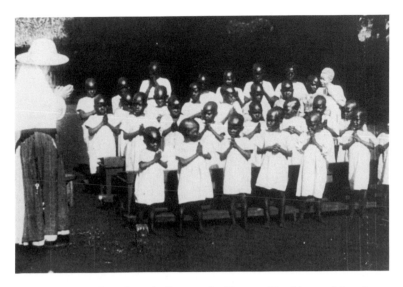

Still from *From the Pole to the Equator,* by Yervant Giankian and Angela Ricci Lucchi (1987). *Courtesy of the Museum of Modern Art.*

found, recombined, and reframed seventy years later, Comerio's footage is not redeemed but remains testimony to the cruelties of the colonial gaze. *From the Pole to the Equator* is in this sense a counterexample to the subversive potential of experimental ethnography, failing to realize the allegorical inscription of the ethnographic body. Its failure is, however, instructive.

Giankian and Ricci Lucchi subject Comerio's imagery of colonial power to extensive rephotography: they have slowed it down, tinted it, and added a soundtrack of elegiac melancholy. Several richly symbolic shots of landscape filmed from a train in the Alps—"phantom ride" footage—convey the sense of traveling back in time. But the trip back is horrifying. The salvaged imagery depicts the worst atrocities and forms of subjugation carried out in the interests of empire building, including brutal killings of people and animals, comparisons of European leisure classes with rural Africans and Asians, people performing native dances for the camera, and scenes of military battles, casualties, and marches. This material is edited together without narration or intertitles.

Comerio had aspirations to be Mussolini's official filmmaker,[23] and his cinematography aestheticizes his subject matter in keeping with Benjamin's observation that in fascist aesthetics, the self-alienation of mankind "has reached such a degree that it can experience its own destruction as an aesthetic pleasure of the first order."[24] Comerio was particularly fascinated with the military and missionary submission of colonial peoples, including their mobilization in uniform. Benjamin quotes Marinetti's manifesto on the Ethiopian colonial war—the one that Comerio filmed—as an example of the fascist aestheticization of politics: "War is beautiful because it establishes man's dominion over the subjugated machinery by means of gas masks, terrifying megaphones, flame-throwers, and small tanks. War is beautiful because it initiates the dreamt-of metallization of the human body."[25] To this litany, Comerio's footage incorporates the cinema as an instrument of subjugation, and it furthermore designates the body that is mechanized as the conquered, colonized body of color.

Giankian and Ricci Lucchi's treatment of the archival imagery exaggerates the historical distance by layers of mediating grain, burying it under the signs of celluloid degradation. And yet these effects also make the footage more beautiful.[26] Antiwar films rarely evade the spectacle of violence, and this film is no exception. Chris Jenks, following Guy Debord, notes that "social life is degraded rather than honoured by its transformation into the realm of 'the spectacle.' . . . The spectacle indicates rules of what to see and how to see it, it is the 'seeness,' the (re)presentational aspect of phenomena that are promoted, not the politics or aesthetics of their being 'see-worthy.' From within this critical concept the *flâneur* can deduce, and thus claim distance from, the necessity of objects-to-be-seen as appearing in the form of commodities."[27]

In *From the Pole to the Equator,* Comerio's footage becomes a seamless, continuous movement through time and space, with little space for *flânerie.* The spectator is drawn into the spectacle of history. The fragments have lost their fragmentary status, and under the influence of the musical score, they have also lost their status as commodities. If the commodity status of early films allows us to see how images circulated as objects in visual culture, that commodity status constitutes their allegorical potential. We may be able "to *see*" the Comerio materials, but we are not able "to *see through* them,"[28] because in place of analysis, we get only aestheticization. The images are not, in other words, rendered textual, merely ephemeral and mysterious. Titles announce at the beginning of the compilation that Comerio died in 1940 "with amnesia," but the filmmakers have recovered his memory as a form of nostalgia that incorporates, rather than allegorizes, the gaze of imperialism.

From the Pole to the Equator, despite its use of found footage, replicates the stylistic strategies of the contemporaneous *Koyanisquattsi* (1983) and *Powaqqatsi* (1988). Godfrey Reggio's two feature-length thirty-five-millimeter films, scored by Philip Glass, draw on the power of the spectacle for their experiments in ethnography. Also lacking any verbal or written textual supplement, the imagery of "culture," landscape, and technology bears the full weight of meaning. Reggio's films convey an unambiguous moral message: that industrial technology has threatened Third World people's mode of existence and has alienated humanity from itself. But because this message is packaged in a display of virtuoso audiovisual technology, the two films nevertheless participate in the very tendency they seek to critique. It is the cinema itself on display, with its ability to organize and control the fetish of the human body.

Koyanisquattsi and *Powaqqatsi* are good examples of what Trinh calls the "humanism of the commodity" and its "totalitarian monologue" that insists that we all agree with its vision.[29] The display of images of other peoples, within a humanist perspective of global endangerment, diffuses cultural difference into a closed system. Despite Reggio's use of experimental techniques such as slow motion, pixilation, and long takes, the films lack any extrinsic or intrinsic commentary on the filmmaking practice. The technical effects may break the illusion of reality, but they merely enhance the illusion of mastery through vision in this new version of "the cinema of attractions." Insofar as everything becomes visible, and nothing escapes the surveillance of the witness, these films confirm Trinh's critique of the power relations of meaning: "The totalistic quest for the referent, the true referent that lies out there in nature, in the dark, waiting patiently to be unveiled and deciphered correctly. To be redeemed" (50).

In the case of Comerio's footage, returned to seventy-five years after the fact, the referent is not redeemable. The referent is merely a ruin of visual culture, whereas the film itself still circulates. Because the makers of *From the Pole* have closed the gaps between the found films, their status as cultural commodities is obscured, and their referents are not quite dead. They are still waiting for redemption, but given their insertion into the machinery of domination, it will not be soon in coming. The people, like those in Reggio's films, are victims of the technology of visual culture.

The lack of any information, narration, or titles in *From the Pole* is one of the recurring features of experimental ethnography, and it is an important means of deflecting the scientism of conventional ethnographic practices. And yet the reduction to sheer image and spectacle always runs the risk of aestheticization, of turning the Other into a consumable image. *From the Pole* engages in a deliberate aestheticization of the colonial image bank, deploying a gamut of effects including color tinting, slow motion, and electronic music to create a sensual, affective viewing experience. The inappropriateness of such a treatment to the scenes of cruelty and subjugation is not only disturbing; it transposes the archive into a fantastic scenario that privileges the pleasure of the image over its role in constructing history and memory. The colonial scene is distanced to some remote time and place from which the contemporary viewer, and the 1980s filmmakers, are infinitely distanced.

Trinh's alternative to the quest for "total meaning" is "an imagination that goes toward the texture of reality . . . capable of playing upon the illusion in question and the power it exerts" (50). Neither *From the Pole* nor Reggio's two films explore "the texture of reality"; instead they make a fetish of the means of representing reality. Their reflexive use of techniques remains a technique of getting a better look, and not means of analyzing the structures of illusion and power within that look.

From the Pole may be one of the most significant cinematic recyclings of the colonialist cinema of attractions, and yet it fails to realize the dialectical potential of the archive. Comerio's footage is exceptional actuality material because it was so deeply informed by a particular colonial mandate. We can see in it how the body of the colonial subject functioned in the early part of the century as a spectacle in "modern" culture. Giankian and Ricci Lucchi return to this period in the spirit of a nostalgic longing, as if there were a logic to colonial history, an inevitability of its unfolding before a camera, as if Comerio was not complicit in this horrific cinema of attractions; as if, in Benjamin's words, there were no correspondence between then and now.

Minimalism and Ethnographic Analysis

To find a more analytical appropriation of early cinema, we need to turn to the structural filmmakers' use of early film.[30] The appeal of the actuality to the avant-garde of the early seventies included its anonymity, its one-shot format, and its construction of space.[31] "Primitive" films, shot from a single camera position with little sense of off-screen space or composition in depth, tend to be organized around a frontal performance frame and thus have a flattened effect. These one-shot actualities serve as the foundation for experimental films such as *Gloria!* (Frampton, 1979), *Eureka* (Gehr, 1974), *Lumière's Train (Arriving at the Station)* (Razutis, 1979), and David Rimmer's *Seashore* (1971). The analysis of form, perspective, light, grain, and composition gradually removes "content" from referentiality. The image itself is subjected to analysis to see how it was seen, and how it can be seen differently.

Structural filmmakers' preoccupation with early film was part and parcel of the introspective "purification" of the medium. The stripping away of institutional and narrative codes led numerous filmmakers back to cinema's origins, where pictorial composition, montage (or the lack thereof), and address might be found in their raw state, uncontaminated by "bourgeois" narrative codes. Bart Testa describes these films as "pedagogical interventions, as works that allow us to see cinema again, in places and at levels where we had ceased to see it." [32] In the search for pure cinema, structural filmmakers often, if inadvertently, stumbled into ethnographic representation.

One example of the avant-garde's turn to early cinema for a reinvention of cinema is David Rimmer's *Seashore,* which exhibits the attention to detail characteristic of this film form. The fragment of film on which Rimmer works in *Seashore* has been related by Testa to "the many picturesque views of the sea, boats and the shore in the first years of film production . . . its composition in large measure defined the visual code of the extreme long shot." [33] The fragment consists of four groups of figures: three women in the center tentatively wade into the sea, a couple of bathers screen right play in the waves, a group of men and women stand fully dressed on the shore screen left, and a group of bathers waist deep in the middle distance stand off a rocky outcrop completing the curve of the beach. Although the source of the image is unknown, the bourgeois settings and costumes, the composition in depth, and the quotidian action are highly evocative of the Lumières' style and era.

Neither characters nor documentary subjects, the people in *Seashore* are visually explored and examined with an intensity and epistemological distance equal to that of the ethnologist. Text becomes texture, and the reference to reality gives way to a history of the referent. It is a complex image with a number of rhythms, including the movement of the water. In its brevity—the loop is only a few seconds long—the image hesitates between film and photography, marking their proximity and

Still from David Rimmer's *Seashore* (1971). In this frame enlargement, the image is flipped, and the screen direction is a reversal of the main orientation of the image in the film. Courtesy of Canadian Filmmakers Distribution Centre.

also their radical difference with respect to movement. When the loop is shortened, the smaller movements and gestures appear automatic and mechanical; when the fragment is flipped and superimposed on the original screen direction, the image becomes symmetrically framed. A total fragmentation of the image occurs with the reproduction of projection flaws: white leader, frame lines, and flicker.

All of these formal devices, added to the pattern of surface flaws on the film emphasized by freeze-frames, distract the viewer from the original image. With the destabilization of the composition, the recorded event becomes more indistinct and more distant, a distance that is historical before it is ethnographic. Rimmer's rephotography of found footage is allegorical in the sense that its signified content lies elsewhere, in another movie in another time.[34] That "other time" may be a mythic time in film history, but the historical referent has the specificity of the singular moment captured by a seaside photographer.

A film such as *Seashore* might, on one level, be a purely formal exercise in deconstructing codes of perception, and yet it is more difficult to ignore the people who populated early cinema when they cross your field of vision and cross it again and again and again. The almost accidental emergence of a trace of history — real people doing real things — is the obverse of the salvage paradigm, which tends to endow the historically and culturally specific with meanings well beyond the documented experience (meanings of primitivism, of anthropological humanism, of pastoral romanticism, and so on). Instead of "bringing culture into writing,"[35] *Seashore* discovers culture already written and investigates the structure of this representation. It reproduces the allegorical structure of ethnography in such a way that writing — the language of representation — is shown to destroy and violate the referent.

The brevity and anonymity of the fragment of history that is glimpsed in *Seashore* might seem to compromise its epistemological value. And yet its connotative meaning is rich precisely because it is "foreign" and difficult to decode. What are the relationships between the different groups of people? Is the group on the beach crowded into the frame because they are posing? Are the bathers in the water male or female, young or old? Is this a typical leisure activity of this period, whatever period it is? In this country, whatever country it is? Precisely because these questions have no answers, a level of inquisition is denied, as is even a passive attitude of observation. The privilege of looking into history is itself finally taken away in the reduction of the image to light, line, and form.

In *Seashore*, repetition functions as a vehicle of amplification for a fragment of film that is only "meaningful" insofar as it is different from our own cultural and historical experience. As in the many other examples of found footage throughout Rimmer's work, the anonymity of the people filmed is made mysterious.[36] The images tend to evoke a sense that Roland Barthes has described: "Since every photograph is contingent (and thereby outside of meaning), Photography cannot signify (aim at a generality) except by assuming a mask."[37] Photographic contingency "immediately yields up those 'details' which constitute the very raw material of ethnological knowledge" (28). And yet Rimmer never allows us the time for contemplation necessary to the pleasure of the photographic text. The movement, repetitions, and fragmentation of the image provoke a desire for a look that is always denied by the filmic appropriation of the photographed scene.

In the repetitions of *Seashore*, surface flaws on the degraded film stock become signs of historical distance, but they also foreground the random, contingent aspect of early film. Dai Vaughan has described the "spontaneity" of a Lumière film, *A Boat Leaving the Harbour*: "The unpredictable has not only emerged from the background to occupy the greater portion of the frame: it has also taken sway over the principals."[38] If early audiences were occasionally compelled to prod the screen to test the reality effect, Vaughan says it is testimony to "an escape of the represented from the representational act." Rimmer's film reenacts this "invasion of the spontaneous" into the art object of minimalist filmmaking. Behind the play of surface flaws, a profilmic space unfolds around the movement of water and bodies, a space in which people are free of meaning, allowed to wade in the waters of their own time. This is exemplary of a Benjaminian redemption because it realizes the dialectical potential of the photographic image as an inscription of historical difference.

Seashore, like many of Rimmer's films, appropriates "found" imagery and modifies it through serial repetition. One of the more well-known instances of such a treatment of early cinema is Ken Jacobs's *Tom Tom the Piper's Son,* which appropriates a short 1905 narrative film. David James describes the effect of Jacobs's deconstruction: "Jacobs's metafilmic scrutiny of the object text discovers not a stable meaning, but only multiplicity and change, a text centrifugally dispersed, constantly reformulating itself in a new configuration."[39] In the decomposition of the "primitive narrative," the body emerges as an entity prior to character, and historically prior to documentary. Through the mediation of the avant-garde, early cinema emerges as an ambiguous realm of representation, in which the historical body is caught up in a visual language. In fact, the prototype of this conjunction of analytical repetition and ethnographic documentation predates early cinema itself.

Muybridge's Motion Studies: Ethnography and the Everyday

If analysis is one of the themes of experimental ethnography, scientific and formal analyses need to be recognized as being intimately bound together. One of the primary sites of such a collusion is Eadweard Muybridge's motion studies, a critical moment in the complex history of cinema's invention, and also a primal scene for numerous avant-garde filmmakers.[40] Muybridge's serial photographs of the human figure in motion were shot in 1884 and published in 1887. Although his project was mainly intended as a scientific one, and was funded as such, it is also described in the 1955 edition of *The Human Figure in Motion* as "one of the great monuments of 19th century photography" and an unsurpassed "source-book for artists, students, animators and art directors."[41] As a study of the human body, it seems to have had more of an impact as a formal and aesthetic study than as a scientific one. It certainly exemplifies the way that modern visual culture combined aesthetic form and ethnographic observation in a single gesture.

Muybridge's motion studies inaugurated a number of aesthetic techniques that have become associated with the avant-garde. And yet the repetition and gridlike structure of the images are also the means by which the body enters into the mechanics of industrial society. What Benjamin described as a loss of "aura" has been theorized by Rosalind Krauss as the disappearance of the "originality" of the avant-garde. She discusses the many gridlike structures throughout modern art as a means by which the originality of authorship (the genius of modernism) is deferred and displaced: the grid in modern art reveals the postmodern lurking within the modern. "The absolute stasis of the grid, its lack of hierarchy, of center, of inflection, emphasizes not only its anti-referential character, but more importantly — its hostility to narrative." The attraction of the grid motif is its "sense of being born into the newly evacuated space of an aesthetic purity and freedom . . . the grid-scored surface is the image of an absolute beginning."[42]

As a documentary study, Muybridge's grids may depend on an absolute referentiality, and yet that referent — the human body — is radically transformed through repetition, as if it too were made anew. The body does not become a character, and the models are not named. The body becomes a sign in a sign system that refers back only to itself. Because Muybridge shot the successive stages of physical activities from two or three different angles, and printed the photographs above each other on each plate, the study has the effect of decentering vision. There is no ideal point of perspective; the photographer as artist is effaced by the vision of the machine that sees from three different points simultaneously. The bodies themselves, against a backdrop of another grid, are submitted to vision, to close examination. Above all, the analysis is the photographic recording; the photos are not the data for another level of analysis. In this conflation of photography and science, the body enters into visual language as the sign system of "man."

The nakedness of the models may be appropriate to the athletic shots with which the study begins, but the images of naked men engaged in activities such as swinging a scythe or a pickax, digging with a spade, sawing, bricklaying, and performing various blacksmith and carpentry

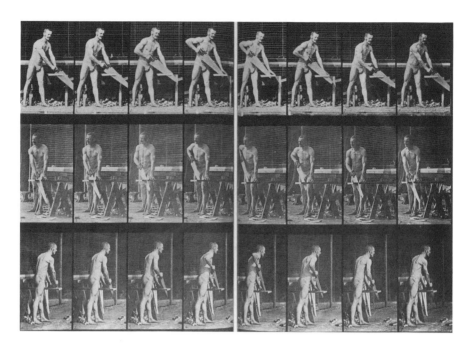

Carpenter Sawing, plate 83 from Muybridge's *The Human Figure in Motion* (1887).

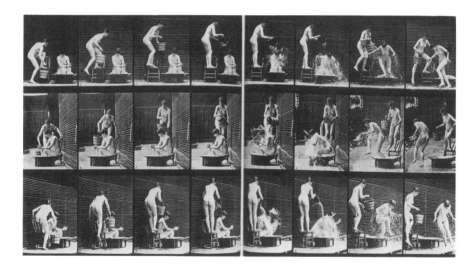

Woman Emptying Bucket of Water on Seated Companion, plate 160 from Muybridge's *The Human Figure in Motion* (1887).

skills are strikingly denaturalized. Thus, the Muybridge photo-analyses also prefigure the surrealist aesthetics of defamiliarization. The combination of nudity and everyday activities resembles a kind of dreamscape.

These experiments, however, brought together the "heroic/athletic" and "workingman" physiques on the single plane of science. They fed directly into the factory management techniques of Taylorism by rendering the body as a mechanical apparatus.[43] The incorporation of physical labor into the study of physiognomy — alongside the conventional, classical athletic poses — introduces a new materialist sense of the human body. Ethnography in the late nineteenth century was, for the most part, still in its Darwinist phase, in which the empirical study of "otherness" was of other bodies, not other cultures. It was intended to position Others within a hierarchy of the human species. With Muybridge, the body of the white man is likewise subjected to a series of empirical tests, but the extensiveness of the visual "testing" is in the interests of a slightly different conception of "man."

One of the most striking features of Muybridge's study of the human figure is the different ways that men, women, and children are posed and photographed. Whereas the men are engaged in simple actions, athletics and physical labor, the women are drinking, smoking, playing, praying, dressing, undressing, and doing a few household chores. Like the men, the women are performing all these activities in the nude. For Linda Williams, Muybridge's treatment constitutes a "gratuitous fantasization and iconization of the bodies of women. . . . At a time when the cinema was much more a document of reality than a narrative art, women were already fictionalized, already playing assumed roles, already *not there* as themselves."[44] Images of women are standing in for women, whereas the photographs of men are photographs of bodies in motion. The woman's body has no empirical, indexical meaning outside of a diegetic frame of reference. Her "motions" need to be codified within cultural narratives of domesticity, sexuality, and "society."

The gender differences in Muybridge's motion studies point to the way that the study of "man" tends to become the study of "culture" as soon as it is submitted as visible evidence. The classical poses that open the study have a scientific potential of demonstrating human anatomy in action: fit young men with rippling muscles running, jumping, lifting, and throwing. These images introduce a certain body as being "typical" of man as a species and can easily be compared to Muybridge's studies of animals. In the male section of the study, the only exceptional bodies are deformed or debilitated: "Elderly Man Walking Upstairs," "Amputee Walking with Crutches," "Legless Boy Climbing In and Out of Chair." The entire male part of the series lends itself to a level of abstraction and physical, empirical typicality that is available only to the white man in Victorian culture. And yet even the men's activities are ultimately rendered culturally specific with the final three plates: "Man Standing at Rifle Drill," "Man Assuming Kneeling Position and Aiming Rifle," "Man Falling Prone and Aiming Rifle." The result of combining the athletic with the working body is a militarized body in the machine of empire.

One has to wonder what the scientific merit is of demonstrating the stages of movement of "Woman Turning, Throwing a Kiss, and Walking Upstairs," or "Woman Sitting in Chair, Drying Her Feet," or "Woman Sitting Down in Chair Held by Companion, Smoking Cigarette." Williams notes the erotic investment of many of these images, especially those of dressing and undressing, and those featuring two nude women interacting with each other. The prurient gaze of the "women's" section of the study continues into the short section on children, in which women appear again nude and seminude, as in "Girl Walking towards Woman, Carrying Flower." A tension is set up in these photos between the indices of measurement, accuracy, and precision of the grid, and the quotidian, unregulated activities of women and children. The titles do not classify the images according to empirical principles, but by descriptions of "everyday behavior."

The women's bodies are of an entirely different order of "evidence": they are observed but not measured. Their physique is constantly slack, with hunched shoulders, and only one model shows any musculature. Women's work in these photos is represented through poses and props, not as a matter of physical strength. Moreover, the cigarettes, the scenes of washing, and the dressing and undressing designate a very specific kind of woman. Whereas the male models were professional athletes and university professors of "physical culture," Muybridge's female models were all professional artist's models. In the Victorian production context, only such models would have performed nude, and thus Muybridge has them perform "everyday activities" of that kind of ("loose") woman.[45] The woman therefore enters the age of mechanical reproduction as an exhibitionist. The professional female model's independence from Victorian morals announces her novelty, and thus her

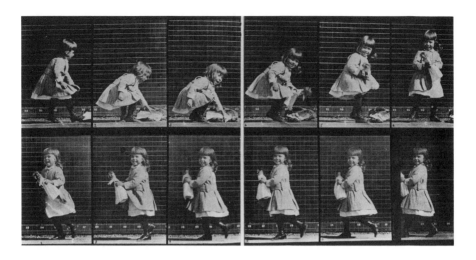

Girl Picking Up Doll from Floor and Carrying It Away, plate 193 from Muybridge's
The Human Figure in Motion (1887).

affinity with the technology of reproduction. Her inclusion in this particular "monumental" study indicates the necessity of such exotica to
feed this new way of looking at people: measuring is no longer enough.

Children appear in a short section at the end of *The Human Figure in
Motion* both clothed and unclothed, mainly engaged in various forms
of play. In many of these photos, the children look back at the camera,
coyly acknowledging their performative role in the nascent apparatus
of attractions. Because of their playfulness, these images underline the
way that Muybridge's project produced a kind of temporal excess, a
loss, an effect of representation as inadequate to the historical real of
lived experience. The absurdity of the project of measuring human behavior is evident in the inability to "contain" the children's activities.

Throughout the Muybridge study of the human figure, a tension
exists between the theory of "the moment" and the actual spontaneity
of everyday life. As Leo Charney has pointed out, Muybridge's experiments proved that movement could not be captured, that it had to be
broken down into "series of moments and fragments, as an illusory
continuity."[46] Once the "bond to the real introduced by photography became representation," the illusions of cinema became possible —
and gaps in reality became apparent, between the discrete fragments,
between the moments that could be captured. As a realist discourse,
Muybridge anticipates the necessary fictions of cinematic representa-

tion. He does this on the level of form, but equally with his choice of activities and movements to photograph. The theory of "man" ultimately breaks down to a naked man performing a military drill: lacking a uniform, the body itself is militarized, mechanized, and drained of its individuality and spontaneity. Without some kind of regulated movement, "man" cannot be studied scientifically. And only the white man can be as perfect as a machine.

If it is impossible to capture movement, if reality in fact evades the camera, the possibility of hidden aspects of reality takes on new significance. Not everything can be seen. Williams has theorized the woman's role in this study as a fetish, and the supplementary diegetic references—props, titles, and so forth—act on a psychoanalytic level to conceal the threat of castration that the serial photography has opened up. Woman represents difference (she is her difference), and although Muybridge "exerts a form of mastery over that difference," the representations of women "perpetuate the nagging fear of the lack she represents" (522). Moreover, the difference of women points to a shift in ethnographic representation—from empirical measurement to vérité social observation. That it occurs by way of the woman's body suggests that what was becoming visible needed to be controlled. The "lack of mastery" was not only over the representation of reality but over a rapidly changing urban culture, including the increased public presence of women.[47]

Both men and women perform activities that would have been associated with the working classes, with the exception of some of the male athletics. Male and female bodies are posed according to the aesthetic tradition of the nude, and in this conjunction of art and science, the working-class body is idealized, but only as a cog in the machine of modern industrial culture. The contradictions implied in the photos of women and children, whose productivity is "natural" rather than industrial, suggest that their "threat" is one of spontaneity and contingency, an excess of the referent (rather than "lack" in the psychoanalytic paradigm). Even in the laboratory setting, another temporality is inscribed in their image.

In many ways, Muybridge's motion studies evoke the panoramic literature of the 1830s that so impressed Walter Benjamin. Margaret Cohen has described these texts as having an "epistemological project allying them with the nascent social sciences": "The phenomena to come under the panoramic text's panoptic gaze range from typical people and places to customs and habit, likes, dislikes, quirks, and memories."[48] Panoramic literature mixed a range of different narrative forms, by different authors, capturing different facets of Parisian reality. "No overarching subjectivity, however, steps forward to guarantee the referential veracity of the panoramic whole," says Cohen. Anticipating Muybridge's diffracted point of view, panoramic literature was illustrated by lithographs that provided continuity where the written text threatened to splinter into fragments. Cohen argues that this use of visual imagery inaugurated an image standard that came to structure the "modern everyday" through the cinema. It provided "a common currency unifying the discursive chaos that characterizes the abstract and complex social formations of modernity" (245). With Muybridge, it becomes clear how this fragmentation is at once a structure of time — in which reality is broken down into pieces — and one of social roles and types.

Burch notes that the photos were perceived as being "ugly" by their first viewers,[49] and it is precisely the awkward union of art and science that allows us to see these motion studies as experimental ethnography. Because the photos were produced outside the domain of social science — which hardly existed at the time — the discourses of science, abstraction, and empiricism are thrown into the light, where they react badly with the contingency of referentiality. Muybridge's goal may have been to produce a photographic image standard, an authoritative guide to the representation of the human body, and yet once that body enters the sphere of the technological gaze, the panoptic attempt to see everything, the body behaves quite differently. It cannot behave like a mute object of study but becomes textual, linguistic, discursive, always alluding to an experience outside the text, prior to its effects of alienation.

One can perhaps see in these motion studies a fading ritualistic aspect of everyday life, embedded in the routines of play, work, and sport. The repetitious quality of the everyday is alluded to by the framing discourse of typicality that situates these photos on the cusp of the age of mechanical reproduction. They illustrate perfectly the emergent form of the shock experience of modernity. Benjamin notes that "the unskilled worker is the one most deeply degraded by the drill of the machines. His work has been sealed off from experience; practice counts for nothing there. . . . The shock experience which the passer-by has in the crowd corresponds to what the worker 'experiences' at his machine."[50] The link between visual stimulation and alienated labor constitutes a new historiographic potential for Benjamin. In the experience of the "moment," the sensation of the present tense is so fleeting that it constitutes a jolt of history. Past and future meet in the moment of shock. In Muybridge's motion studies, the transformation of ritual into mechanized labour (for the men) and exhibitionism (for the women) is made visible.

Indeed, in the great gender divide of *The Figure in Motion,* two different notions of experience emerge. For the men, the body experiences the shock of the production process and is inserted into the machine of modern "progress." The same might be said of the designated male viewer of the "female" section of the study. For the women, the experience of time passing in everyday activities aligns them with the *flâneur* on the margins of the crowd, outside the production process. Their role is to shock and to attract, and yet they gently resist this role in the performance of everyday activities. Those of washing and mothering, especially, allude to a ritualistic experience in which "the disintegration of aura" is palpable. Insofar as Muybridge included both sets of photos in his total study, one may look at them as two parts of a single attempt to capture modern experience. The structure of serial photography becomes a means of bringing together divergent modern experiences, and divergent conceptions of "the moment" and its historiographic potential.

The Aura of Origins

As one of the mythic origins of cinema, Muybridge's motion studies have attracted the avant-garde because of the particular problems of authentic representation that they produce. My reading of Muybridge is possible only from a perspective of postmodernity, when "the signifier cannot be reified." Krauss notes that "the theme of originality, encompassing as it does the notions of authenticity, originals, and origins, is the shared discursive practice of the museum, the historian, and the maker of art."[51] The body as sign system is the greatest challenge to the theme of the grid as absolute origin of antireferentiality. A film such as *Seashore,* which works within the interstices of referentiality and the "pure form" of serial repetition (and is thus neither strictly modern nor postmodern), enables us to see the ethnographic as the discourse of the body in modernity.

The example of *From the Pole to the Equator* is suggestive of the pull of early cinema to be salvaged in new forms. But when the attraction of history is precisely the spectacle of the colonial body, as it is in a great deal of early cinema, we cannot "entrust the archive to expose its own secrets and agenda."[52] Modernist strategies of analysis, fragmentation, and disruption are necessary to break down the hold of the desiring gaze through which the body entered modernity. As Reggio's films indicate, the structure of the cinema of attractions is still with us today. Early cinema may have the aura of origins, but it is only the beginning of an anxiety over loss that inspired the copy-contact nexus of salvage ethnography. The fetish of the body in the burgeoning society of the spectacle is constitutive of its removal from the everyday. Once the trace of contingency, of lived history, can be read back into the image, we can begin to imagine the body outside the archive, before the institutional gaze. This is the potential of dialectical images as a form of experimental ethnography, to deflect origins and authenticity into the profilmic space of the Other, outside and beyond techniques of representation.

4 Ethnotopias of Early Cinema

The theory is meant to orient, to provide the roughest sketch for travel,
by means of moving within and through a relentless artifactualism, which
forbids any direct si(gh)tings of nature, to a science fictional, speculative
factual, SF place called, simply, elsewhere.

—DONNA HARAWAY, "The Promises of Monsters"

Travel is a powerful metaphor for experimental ethnography, embracing a number of key tropes including cross-cultural encounter, subject formation and identity, displacement, homelessness (and its corollary inscription of absent, new, and temporary homes), geography, and literature. James Clifford has proposed "travel" as a means of rethinking and revising the essences of cultural anthropology as "constructed and disputed *historicities,* sites of displacement, interference, and interaction."[1] Ethnographers have always traveled, producing field notes that often double as travel diaries, Lévi-Strauss's *Tristes Tropiques* being an exemplary instance of such writing. Filmmakers, too, have always traveled, and one of the most important cultural ramifications of early cinema was the exchange of images made possible by traveling cameramen and exhibitors.

Although there are a number of different ways that "travel" operates as a form of experimental ethnography, some of which will emerge in subsequent chapters, here I am particularly interested in the utopian aspect of travel. Ethnography and science fiction may seem to be strange bedfellows, and yet both are means of representing culture as historical and as "topos"—mappable. If ethnography as a human science devolved from geography,[2] it traditionally maps culture backward in time, focusing on cultural origins, "vanishing" cultures, and the nature of (uncorrupted) culture. Science fiction maps the future of culture, but like ethnography, it is firmly rooted in the experience of the present. The reflecting mirrors of ethnography and science fiction share a utopian thrust toward historical change and transformation: the pastoral image of primitivism finds itself only slightly altered in the techno-fantasies of parallel universes. Both utopias, however, need to be traveled to, whether by the starship *Enterprise* or the *Kon-Tiki* or into the highlands of Papua New Guinea.

This chapter brings together three film texts that indicate how the utopian imagination informed early cinema, and how, by way of early cinema, it plays a role in experimental ethnography. In this second foray into documentary before documentary, I will discuss a series of actualities that portrayed Quebec as an exotic culture to potential European immigrants at the turn of the century. Second, Georges Méliès's *Voyage dans la lune* (1903) may be the antithesis of the early nonfiction film, but its fiction is based precisely in the narrative of colonial exploration through which films such as the Quebec series were produced. The final example is a 1988 Brazilian film called *Uaka,* in which excerpts of the Méliès film are intercut with an ethnography of the Kamauirá Indians. An implicit analogy is drawn between primitive cinema and a "primitive" people, as a discursive constellation of history, the occult, and eternity. These three texts evoke a historical perspective by way of science fictional tropes of time and space.

The quest-driven narrative of travel is a model of ethnographic textuality as science fiction, the utopian aspect of which I am calling ethnotopia. The term "ethnotopia" is used by Bill Nichols in a slightly different sense from how I want to use it here. For him, it refers to an ideal of limitless observation, the desire behind the fascination with the Other: "It is a world in which We *know* Them, a world of wisdom triumphànt."[3] Such ethnotopian desires can be ascribed to a few generations of ethnographers whose faith in the principles of social science still takes them around the world. Another kind of ethnotopian desire informs the ethno-fictions of Jean Rouch and his advocacy of "shared anthropology"—or participatory anthropology. What he described as science fiction[4] was an ethnotopian form of filmmaking that freely deployed narrative and dramatic techniques, in conjunction with (scientific) anthropological material, to offset the apparatus of fascination and epistemological possession referred to by Nichols. It is not coincidental that *Jaguar*, the film that most overtly developed this ethnotopian form, is a film about migration and travel.

Jaguar may indeed be described as science fiction, and it points to the way that the discourse of authenticity has been experimented with in ethnographic film. The voice-over commentary and dialogues, recorded in a studio by Rouch and the principal actors many years after the film was shot, is a fascinating instance of historical disjunction and subjective splitting. The liberating potential of lightweight sixteen-millimeter film equipment enabled Rouch to share the migratory journey with his African subjects, and this undoubtedly provoked the technological fantasy implied in the science fiction epithet. Moreover, as a travel film, it also points to the interrelated themes of fantasy, quest, and home/homelessness that link ethnography and science fiction as narrative genres. Rouch's conception of a truly "participatory cinema," in which the barriers between subjective and objective roles would completely break down, was indeed science fiction. This is the utopian project of ethnography that remained unrealized by Rouch himself.[5]

If the ethnotopian impulse is toward an elimination of the self-other paradigm of cultural knowledge and representation, it imagines the dissolution of the ego and the I, and the transcendental perspective. Writing in a science fiction mode, from the (fictional) year 2029, Christopher Pinney argues that virtual reality has transcended the frame of the voyage and the journey that once installed the "I" of the traveler at the center of every journey. The fantasy of VR and cyber-culture is the utopian dream of "total cinema" taken to extremes unforeseen by Bazin, a total eclipse of subjectivity. Pinney argues that without the frame of the journey, the subject of perception potentially sheds his or her identity. The temporal frame of the journey is the means by which travel "made meaning" with reference to the traveler as having a "depth" of consciousness, inwardness, and coherent subjectivity. The effect of new technologies at the end of the twentieth century is the ability to imagine the dissolution of that temporal frame and its corresponding subject effects.[6]

Pinney's SF theorizing of the new subjectivities created in cyberspace and VR technologies is overtly utopian. His claim that "whereas time travel blurred parent and child, virtual reality's distance-travel has blurred self and other," ironically echoes Rouch's version of ethnotopia. With the end of geography and physical travel, the new forms of travel "undercut the position of the subject. . . . We always arrive without setting out, and we are catapulted, disorganized, unpositioned, and *split*" (424). The utopian thrust of Pinney's discourse, which of course dismisses any economic or political arguments against cyber-culture, confirms Fredric Jameson's observations regarding the utopian text. Its true vocation, in Jameson's opinion, is "to confront us with our inability to imagine Utopia."[7] The repression of the negative constitutes an inversion of representation such that the attempt to visualize "progress" in science fiction results in an eternal present tense, without history. We find ourselves once again with the mirror image of primitivism. Pinney could be writing about Hales Tours, a fairground film exhibition of 1905 in which spectators watched "Tours and Scenes of the World" projected in a slightly rocking train car.

In keeping with Benjamin's theory of history, Jameson also notes the potential of utopian fiction to transform the present "into the determinate past of something yet to come" (245). Jameson has elsewhere insisted on the necessity of retaining utopian forms of thought, even as inscribed in romance genres, for their conjunction of desire with historical temporality.[8] The ability to imagine qualitative social transformation depends on the memory of the past as historically different. Thus the shift indicated by Pinney at the end of the twentieth century from temporal to spatial utopian forms is for Jameson detrimental to historical thinking.

Returning to primitive cinema at the end of the twentieth century and rethinking it as experimental ethnography is an attempt to realize the utopian impulse of science fiction for anthropology. The particular conjunction of visual culture and colonialism at the last *fin de siècle* produced a number of different ethnotopias. If utopian narratives are about the struggle to imagine the difference of the future, the designation of early cinema as having a different relation to modernity (than the subsequent forms of modern visual culture) provides a valuable model for the ethnotopian imagination.

In the culture of nostalgia, historical time loses its necessity, but nostalgia is not the only form of postmodern memory. Benjamin's conception of history leaves open the possibility of dialectical images — of the recovery of temporality within the image itself. History becomes inscribed in spatial relationships with the advent of photography and its representation of the impossible distance between the referent and its viewer. The dialectical image is a monadic crystallization of past, present, and future, which Benjamin describes in utopian terms: "Progress does not reside in the continuity of temporal succession, but rather in its moments of interference: where the truly new first makes itself felt, as sober as the dawn." [9] The ethnotopian imagination is thus a desire not only for the dissolution of the self-other structure of representation and visibility, but equally for the difference of historical time. For Benjamin, these two desires are intimately linked. In "The Storyteller," he describes a narrative form grounded in "eternity" rather than teleology, and a historiography that is independent of the subject's journey through time. [10] The cultural memory that one finds inscribed in early film may be such a historiography, offering traces of experience, fantasy, and travel, grounded in forms of collective fantasy.

Winter Sports in Quebec: Ethnographic Space

The Lumière brothers' films are exemplary of the modern everyday as a genre of representation at the turn of the century, but the entire cinema of attractions constitutes what Margaret Cohen describes as "an epistemological twilight zone." [11] Actualities combine an empirical form of knowledge with the magic of cinema, its tricks of decoupage and representation. Combined with protofiction films, trick films, and live vaudeville acts, early film programs linked glimpses of a wide range of disparate places and activities. The example of films shot in Quebec, where there was no indigenous film industry until decades later, is perhaps exemplary of many parts of the world outside the metropolitan mainstream that fed the exotic appetite of the cinema of attractions. Edison's catalogs are filled with titles of various winter sports photographed in Quebec and other parts of Canada. Among them are a handful of films made by a British photographer named Joe Rosenthal as part of a British series called *Living Canada*. [12]

Most actualities from this period remain relatively unauthored, as the products of the cinematic operation itself, indices of its techniques of mechanical reproduction. Although they were shot all over the world, these novel forms of "armchair" travel often lacked the frame of the journey, as they were fragmentary products of film companies. Rosenthal's films were exhibited in programs that combined the work of many different cameramen and companies, and yet the local Montreal press singled him out: "In the pursuit of animated photographs of a novel character, Mr. Rosenthal has had many adventurous experiences," the most spectacular of which was his action photography of the Boer War.[13] Thus, a narrative of individual travel is supplied by the press to supplement the films that, in themselves, lack a "subject position," or human point of origin.

The *Living Canada* series was sponsored by the Canadian Pacific Railway (CPR) to encourage British immigration, and the story goes that the filmmakers were instructed not to show any winter scenes for fear of discouraging potential immigrants.[14] Despite this directive, Rosenthal shot a number of films in 1903 of winter activities in and around Montreal, scenes that portray a world of continuous fun and games, a world where men, women, and children frolic in wide-open spaces, impervious to any hint of cold weather. The setting is primarily urban, and the activities are more or less organized, in some cases as clubs, suggesting that these winter sports are the leisure activities of an industrial, modern culture. The films thus represent a utopian colonial society, in which the snow and ice work to transform the urban environment into an amusement park.

These images of everyday life are not necessarily typical of the cinema of the period and were in fact shown in Montreal on a program that included scenes of the Durbar at Delhi, panoramic shots of Western Canadian landscape, the queen reviewing troops in England, and so on.[15] Local scenes of tobogganing were interspersed not only with other nonfiction attractions but also with trick films and early narratives such as *Ali-Baba and the Forty Thieves* and *Voyage dans la lune*. The program, compiled by the Palace Theatre in London, ran for two weeks at Windsor Hall in Montreal, advertised as "the sights, march and progress of the world." The English press attributed the popularity of the Canadian imagery to its depiction of "the links that unite the Empire." The Montreal spectators would have been able to see their own community as an integral aspect of modern progress, of which the motion picture was of course an equally important component.

The conjunction of the cinema and empire building produced what I want to develop as an early form of ethnographic representation. Of "the view aesthetic" in early nonfiction cinema, Tom Gunning says, "The voyeurism implicit in the tourist, the colonialist, the filmmaker and the spectator is laid bare in these films, without the naturalization of dramatic structure or political argument. These 'views' stage for us the impulse toward 'just looking' so important to our modern era; and we have learned in the work on visual culture over the last decade that

Still from the *Living Canada* series (1903), produced by Charles Urban's Bioscope Company of Canada for the Canadian Pacific Railroad.

Tossing the Photographer, still from the *Living Canada* series (1903).

'just looking' is never *just* about looking."[16] In fact, early films made by roving cameramen subscribed to a few conventions, mainly techniques of getting a better look. Livio Belloï describes the prominent genre of the sports view in the Lumière archive. This view, he says, "is often founded on a cleaved space; [a] double space, shared between the area of the game (that of the participants) and the area of spectating."[17] Belloï goes on to describe the complex role of the many onlookers in the Lumière films to conclude that Lumière needs to be recognized as a *sociologist* because the Lumière view "involves a thought of the *space of interaction,* of its place, practices and uses." The early nonfiction filmmaker is an orchestrator of the look, and the view is often a "double observation" — of the attraction in the profilmic, and of the divided attention of the onlookers for whom the camera is itself an attraction.

In the 1903 films of winter sports in Canada, onlookers are constantly interfering with the view of the main attraction, to the point where their proliferation makes a virtual carnival of the ostensible hierarchy of looks. The constant intermingling of people lends the films a sense of community, and the photographer's eye-level camera angle draws his gaze into the crowd, on the level of the body. And yet there remains a strict separation of body and machine. One of the films, *Tossing the Photographer,* even has the photographer in amidst the members of the Blue Toque Snowshoeing Club, leaving his camera either unattended or in the hands of an uncredited assistant. In a second shot, the snowshoers file off into the distance, waving good-bye to the camera and its operator, presumably back at his post.

The photographer's brief abnegation of his place at the origin of the view is symptomatic of the disorienting *mise en scène* of these films. The winter landscape, unlike the more typical urban and seaside settings of early films, has few cues to perspective with which to frame the view. Often in these short films, the blank background is framed almost randomly, rendering the "view" superfluous to the activity, as a supplementary point of excess. Sometimes the orchestrated view of an organized activity dissolves into a chaotic sight, and the camera's gaze is rendered banal and redundant. In the scenes of iceboating, the white sails fill the screen and literally empty the view.

Within the different scenes of *Living Canada*'s winter sports are many examples of in-camera editing that enable a continuous "best view" without any concern for spatial continuity.[18] Most typically, the camera will be positioned in front of a ski slope or toboggan run, and a series of discontinuous shots will match-cut different skiers, sledders, and dog-sleds in frame. With the speed skaters, the group of skaters is repeatedly center frame, but the background constantly changes as the skaters move around the photographer's position in the center of the ice. The view is further obstructed by other figures on the ice, through whom the skaters weave a path, skating backward and forward. In the parade scenes and in some of the races, movement in opposite directions is edited together. Rosenthal, like many early actuality cameramen, fragments the scene into short, discontinuous pieces. His single viewpoint, and its potential for articulating a subject position, is thus destabilized, and the role and position of the camera are rendered indeterminate.

The "tossed" or decentered view in these films may or may not be a radical instance of a film form that is already unconventional with respect to the documentary film as it subsequently developed. My point is not to privilege these films as formal departures from a norm but to suggest the ways in which "the view" in early nonfiction film is a structural element of each scene. The camera cannot be said to compete with another attraction, although it is often positioned as a kind of obstacle into which toboggans and sleds are in danger of slamming. It takes up space within the crowds. The low angle of many of the shots, and the depth created by the figures in the medium-long shots, situate the view within a physical, tactile space of figures. The single viewpoint is certainly privileged, but it is coextensively marked as a point in a distinctly social space.

The attraction of and in these films is not the pageantry of monarchs or the contours of exotic landscapes, exhibitions, or peoples. Instead, the details of daily life are displayed for a camera that incorporates them into its play. The grace of the skaters, like the chaotic scene of the snowball fight, are moreover transcendent moments within the context of everyday life. The athletic bodies, along with the fully dressed pleasure skaters and the scruffy children on sleds, are the main attraction of these short films. Against the white backdrop of the snowscapes, the figures attain a kind of autonomy and integrity that is unusual in visual culture of any period.

The parallels with *cinéma vérité* and its techniques of *in medias res* perspective are, in this case, somewhat ironic. One of the inaugural films of the *cinéma direct* movement in Quebec is a film called *Les Raquetteurs* (*The Snowshoers*), by Gilles Groulx and Michel Brault (1958), which returned to winter sports for a depiction of "les Québécois" in a very different political climate. The *vérité* representation of social rituals was a key contribution to the language of cultural identity that was developed during Quebec's "quiet revolution" of the 1960s.[19]

At the turn of the century, the *Living Canada* series was very much part of an imperial culture, in its role in encouraging British immigration. If in the western provinces this meant the displacement of native cultures, in Quebec it was important in maintaining British domination over the French. In 1901, British immigrants represented only 17.6 percent of the population of Quebec (only slightly higher than today) but held most of the economic and political power.[20] The Canadian context may thus help to define the colonial gaze as the construction of an imaginary social space outside the fragmenting experience of modern industrial culture. In early colonialist cinema, the relation of the human figure to the technology of mechanical reproduction constitutes a kind of translation of the auratic body into industrial society, thus producing a particular form of the colonial body. It may not be a native or indigenous population that appears in these films, but it is nevertheless a colonial culture, depicted as close to nature, enjoying the freedom of the New World.

In the *Living Canada* films, the transformation of everyday activities in Quebec into a spectacle is achieved through the foreigner's look, a look that renders the social body visible. In early nonfiction cinema, the aura of experience in mechanical reproduction might be regarded as the transformation of the social body. Offered up to the gaze as a phenomenological sight, just as mechanical reproduction begins to tear it apart, the social body is a sensual, textural entity. The gaze of a *flâneur* such as Joe Rosenthal, on the margins of the social body, is still an appendage of that body, a sign of its modernity, but not yet coded as a subject of perception.

As a form of ethnography, early nonfiction film differs from the scientific gaze of subsequent Griersonian documentary, but also from the humanist gaze of Flaherty and the vérité filmmakers. The "view" aesthetic is not a human gaze, and even in these Quebec films, the participatory camera is still rendered as a technical apparatus. Benjamin says of photography in general: "It is indeed a different nature that speaks to the camera from the one which addresses the eye; different above all in the sense that instead of a space worked through by a human consciousness there appears one which is affected unconsciously." [21] In early nonfiction film, the camera has not yet assumed the guise of the eye and enables what Benjamin calls the "physiognomic aspects of pictorial worlds" to become visible. Along with the winter sports films in the Bioscope presentations at Windsor Hall in 1903 were a series of microscopic views that enabled audiences to see how blood circulates, to see microbes in a morsel of cheese, and to see various other images of "the unknown world." The views of people likewise suggested a penetration of space, made possible by the journeyman cinematographer.

As a simple illustration of the difference between nonfiction cinema at the beginning and at the end of the silent period, the 1903 films might be compared to a 1927 British film called *Tour of the Dominions,* which, as the title suggests, is also an example of a colonial text. It provides a good indication of the way that the documentary gaze becomes increasingly removed from its object, adopting a scientific, omniscient perspective. A skating scene is included in the later film, but only from a very high angle that renders the skaters as tiny ants moving within a circumscribed arena. Whereas the "bird's-eye view" was another staple of the cinema of attractions, the attraction in the early period is the angle itself, a liberation of the body from earthly restraints. In *Tour of the Dominions,* people are almost completely absent, and the view is not that of a bird but that of an overseeing authority. Most of the 1927 "tour" of Quebec consists of visits to monuments and panoramic views of cityscapes, whereas the gaze of the 1903 films constitutes itself as a form of social observation. The early films are densely populated, and the human figure is always central as the main attraction.

In the cinema of attractions, the privileging of the single viewpoint often involves a negotiation of the gaze, in which the camera itself occupies the central space. The optical unconscious of early cinema is also the optical unconscious of colonialism, insofar as the gaze is a mechanism of dividing and conquering, of preserving and possessing. At the same time, we can occasionally see in early cinema the paradox of colonial culture laid bare, in its excessive mimeticism, its display of technology as what Taussig calls "white man's magic," a constellation of copy and contact.[22] The video medium that has only recently freed these films from the archive gives them what Benjamin would call a "second nature," making them the textual allegories of films on the verge of disappearing.

To understand early nonfiction film as ethnographic is to recognize another form of visual knowledge. Although these films would originally have been accompanied by a verbal lecture in which their geographic and ethnic specificity would have been fixed, they are now much more open. To identify the Montreal setting of the *Living Canada* series demands an experience of place, a kind of knowledge that expresses itself, in Benjamin's words, as a "flash of recognition": "What differentiates images from the 'essences' of phenomenology is their historic index. . . . These images must be thoroughly marked off from 'humanistic' categories . . . for the historical index of the images doesn't simply say that they belong to a specific time, it says primarily that they only came to legibility at a specific time."[23]

From our perspective nearly one hundred years after these films were shot, the depiction of Quebec as a utopian playground becomes exemplary of Benjamin's dialectical image in which "the past and the present moment flash into a constellation."[24] This social body has a particular resonance insofar as the cameraman and the written signs within these films point to an Anglophone society, of British descent; as was the ideal audience of potential immigrants. Of course the actual bodies in the films transcend linguistic divisions, and the series was seen by French as well as English audiences,[25] which amplifies its utopian dimension. Today in Quebec the history of the English is the history of the oppressor, and its collective memory is heavily repressed. And so a particular social body is legible here in these films as a colonial fantasy, in an ethnographic form of the optical unconscious.

It would seem as if the time has finally come when the imagery of early nonfiction film has suddenly become legible. This prehistory of the documentary has been repressed because of its overt inscription of the gaze,[26] but also because of its coextensive form of a strictly visual epistemology. In the surviving fragments of early nonfiction cinema, meaning is something that, in Trinh Minh-ha's words, "remains fascinated by what escapes and exceeds it."[27] The optical unconscious is an apparatus of fascination overlayed with the fragmented experience of modernity, and if we are able to see the leisure activities of an urban colonial culture, we are also able to see how these activities might have functioned as an attraction. The alternative public sphere of early cinema thus pertains not only to a new form of spectatorship[28] but equally to another form of ethnographic representation, one that predates the aesthetics of objectivity.

If winter sports in Quebec once offered Europeans and Americans a virtual trip to Canada, these films now offer us a virtual trip into history. The construction of space even presages some of the effects of contemporary forms of virtual reality: the decentered, frameless experience. Another filmmaker whose films look oddly familiar one hundred years after they were made is Georges Méliès. One of the pervasive myths of early cinema is the Lumière-Méliès dualism of realism and fantasy. Most histories of ethnography trace its genealogy back to the Lumière brothers' documentation of everyday life. Without denying the evident ethnographic character of the Lumière actualities and the genre that they spawned, we should not write Méliès out of the history of ethnographic film. If ethnographic realism has led to an epistemological impasse, it has been at the expense of understanding the ethnographic fantasies of cultural difference, travel, and spectacle.

Méliès's signature style of the trick film brought magic and cinema into close alignment, and in *Voyage dans la lune* (1903), the techniques of montage and stop action are brought to bear on the encounter with colonial otherness. On the moon, the five astronomers are attacked and captured by a horde of "Selenites" — men dressed in skeleton costumes. The Selenite court and the Selenite king, before whom the astronomers are brought, are decorated with African motifs, including masks and spears. But these Africans are easy to kill: hit with an umbrella, they simply explode in a puff of smoke. The ability to manipulate reality becomes an instrument of mastery and destruction for Méliès, a means of countering the threat of the Other. *Voyage dans la lune* was produced at the height of colonial exploration and expansion, and the themes of territorial conquest, savage rituals and governments, and genocide and adventure are directly related to ongoing colonial exploration and imperialism.

Méliès's film is loosely based on Jules Verne's novels *De la Terre à la lune* and *Autour de la lune,* originally published in 1865 and 1869 in serial form, with lithographic illustrations. In Verne's stories, the scientists don't actually land on the moon but orbit it and return to earth without seeing any Selenites. The voyage in Verne's account is the product of American New World ingenuity, with "every known nation in the world" showing support—including voices from Turkey, China, India, and Egypt. It is a global effort, representing the ultimate triumph of

Still from *Voyage dans la lune,* by Georges Méliès (1903).

man over nature. Méliès's image of the bulletlike projectile is taken directly from Verne, whose fictional scientists, members of a post–Civil War gun club, desire a more peaceable application for military science.

Jameson describes Verne's science fiction as inaugurating a new form of historical imagination based on the depiction of the future rather than the past.[29] Méliès not only shifts the colonial focus from the New World to the "undiscovered" world but tempers Verne's scientific discourse with imagery of the occult and the magical. Verne's futurism is thus thoroughly mixed with a discourse of primitivism in its translation to cinema. The moon is no longer an inert mass to be mapped but a site of savagery and mystery to be colonized. If Verne's account marks the limits of colonization and announces the "new frontier" of technology, Méliès turns all of Verne's optical instruments backward and in on themselves in the cramped space of his studio sets.

The astronomers themselves are initially dressed like magicians or alchemists, until the scene shifts to the production of the rocket ship, and they change into the "everyday" clothes of Victorian gentlemen. The scene of the rocket building situates the story against the (painted) backdrop of modern industry as the scientists admire the pouring of molten metal and the accompanying belching of steam. Thus an element of magic is incorporated into the high-tech adventure story as the industrial processes are depicted as part of the fantasy. The cinema is of course the linchpin in the identification of magic and technology, especially the cinema as Méliès configured it. In keeping with Benjamin's theory of cinema, Méliès's utopian discourse is a form of "profane illumination" within the context of industrial capitalism.

In Verne's version, much is made of the launch of the rocket, with the whole world attentive to the event, but Méliès has the astronomers' meeting and their launch decorated with a chorus line of girls wearing shorts and marching in military formation. Linda Williams includes Méliès along with Muybridge as an early filmmaker for whom the female body poses a particular threat. His preoccupation with women is consistently a form of mastery over them, a reduction of woman to *image,* one that is infinitely manipulable.[30] The women are identical robotic commodities produced by the cinema machine, and later the Selenites are also spewed forth, being generated as fast as the astronomers can blow them up, indicating the proximity of colonial otherness to the representation of women in the Méliès universe. In *Voyage dans la lune,* the Selenites are made to disappear—a role often given to women in Méliès's films. Both women and "tribal" others are incorporated as aspects of the fetish of cinema itself. They are nothing *but* image, as their bodies are continuous with the body of the film and its illusion of presence.

By way of the skeleton costumes worn by the Selenites, the discourse of otherness is furthermore linked to death. Allegory, for Benjamin, is exemplified by the death's head, which signifies the impossibility of signification. The iconography of death, skulls, and bones figures in Benjamin's study of baroque drama as emblematic of the failure of resurrection and symbolic representation. Like the ruin, which becomes another crucial allegorical site for Benjamin, the image of bones marks the subjection of history to nature. The transience of material things, including the body, renders representation a failed attempt at salvage: "In the context of allegory the image is only a signature, only the monogram of essence, not the essence itself in a mask."[31] Méliès's version of the cinema of attractions was fully allegorical. Every image fetishized the machine that produced it and flaunted its incomplete status as being manufactured.

As the astronomers sleep in *Voyage dans la lune,* seven stars with women's faces appear above them, framed by the moonscape and a distant view of the earth. They are followed by a group of women and one man perched on stars and planets. These figures constitute a kind of cross between angels and constellations, evoking the science of astrology as dreamed by the tired scientists. In this curious inscription of dreaming within a science fiction narrative, these figures exemplify Benjamin's wish images. In his *Passagen-Werk,* dream images are described as having a revolutionary potential, as hinted at by one of Benjamin's favorite quotations: "Every epoch dreams the one that follows it."

To the form of the new means of production which in the beginning is still dominated by the old one (Marx), there correspond in the collective consciousness images in which the new is intermingled with the old. These images are wish images, and in them the collective attempts to transcend as well as to illumine the incompletedness of the social order of production. There also emerges in these wish images a positive striving to set themselves off from the outdated—that means, however, the most recent past. These tendencies turn the image fantasy, that maintains its impulse from the new, back to the ur-past. In the dream in which every epoch sees in images the epoch that follows, the latter appears wedded to elements of ur-history, that is, of a classless society. Its experiences, which have their storage place in the unconscious of the collective, produce, in their interpenetration with the new, the utopia that has left its trace behind in a thousand configurations of life from permanent buildings to ephemeral fashions.[32]

The romantic iconography of cosmological deities mapped onto the modern adventure in *Voyage* produces a utopian fantasy grounded in "science" as well as an occult conception of fate. The trip to the moon is also a sort of trip to an afterlife, where the astronomers are visited by angels. In any case, their dream evokes a less than scientific conception of space and space travel, endowing the science fiction tale with precisely the kind of collective imagination described by Benjamin, one that falls back on an ur-past of superstition and magic.

On the moon, the astronomers do not find a pastoral alternative to the stimuli of modernity, although this is implied by the wish image of the guardian constellations. The sudden explosions of the Selenites may constitute an instantiation of the "shock" effect of the cinema to delineate a new regime of the momentary, transient present; however, the famous instance of temporal overlap in which the rocket lands in the eye of the moon in an extreme long shot (from the perspective of the earth), and again from another perspective on the moon, is a very different order of representation. This cut is a regressive moment, repeating the momentary instant of contact, falling back and away from the technology of modernity to a pictorial space of figure and ground. The rocket ship is transformed from "figure" in the face of the moon to "ground" in the *mise en scène* of the moonscape as the astronomers exit from its hatch.

The desire for travel, for adventure, for the unfamiliar and strange, is indulged in full in *Voyage dans la lune,* but by way of a distinctly nineteenth-century representational genre. Méliès's cinema is in many ways a transitional cinema, lingering on the threshold of modernity and delineating the shifting conception of time that the cinema brought about. It dramatizes the ethnographic effects of the time machine of cinema by mapping the future onto the past within the narrative frame of the voyage. The "everyday" is completely evacuated in favor of presentational tableaux and stage mechanics, as if the miracles of modern science and technology approximated the magic of native (preindustrial) cultures. In the pictorial space of *Voyage,* the savage, the feminine, and the specter of death constitute a territory to be explored and exterminated by a mastery of space.

If we can see the earth from the moon, exactly in the place in the sky where the moon is seen from the earth, a certain reversal is imagined. Méliès's film attempts to follow through on this early depiction of othering, and one of the imagined effects is a greater proximity to friendly planets. Méliès takes his early-twentieth-century audience into a primitive, pre-Christian astrological cosmology by way of the cinema, an apparatus that sustains a "primitive" sense of magic in modernity. The eclipse of the referent in Méliès's experimental ethnography constitutes the disappearance of the body into the cinematic apparatus; it also suggests that the transformation of experience in modernity is closely bound to the encounter with the Other body of colonial culture.

Time Traveling: Méliès Goes to Brazil

The quotation of *Voyage dans la lune* in *Uaka* (1988), by Brazilian filmmaker Paula Gaitan,[33] indicates the Méliès film's potential as a transient text and its status as a kind of ur-text of experimental ethnography. *Uaka* is a film that draws on both experimental and ethnographic forms and in many ways exemplifies postmodern ethnography.[34] It is about the Kamauirá tribe of the Upper Xingu, in the "heart of the Amazon." Gaitan's photography adopts the attitude of the tourist who has been invited to observe the celebrations of *quarup* and the preparations leading up to the festival, but she has taken the liberty of interfering with these images on several levels. Some of her techniques include rapid camera movements (swish pans), an ironic play with diegetic and nondiegetic sound, and a highly disjunctive editing style. Besides the inserted images of *Voyage dans la lune* are cuts to the high-modern architecture and industrial landscape of Brasília. One image in particular, of tall buildings silhouetted against a darkening sky, is a technological sight/site that looks like a rocket launch (the association is enhanced by a low rumbling on the soundtrack). Finally, in addition to the observational ethnographic footage, Gaitan has had the villagers perform certain activities in a fairly theatrical mode.

The only explanations in the film are provided by the Indians whose voices are occasionally subtitled and carried over the image track. They describe the importance of *quarup*, a festival honoring Navatsunim, a deity who enables the people of Xingu to be eternal. Early in the film, it is explained that the clouds draw figures and messages that help the people to dream of Navatsunim. The fragmentation of the pastoral that takes place in *Uaka* is accomplished with a strong suggestion of travel, not only from place to place, but through history. Images of the villagers traveling, by foot, bicycle, and truck, are filmed in both documentary and theatrical modes. In the former, the Kamauirá people assemble for *quarup;* in the latter, they travel in family groups to the city of Brasília, carrying baggage, against a rear-projected painting of sky and clouds, literally moving into modernity.

The relaxed rhythm of montage and the constant soundtrack of ambient village chatter and music are examples of a form of cinematic evocation that coexists with discursive signification. Gaitan's images, like Trinh Minh-ha's, are aestheticized to produce a poetics of the other culture, suggesting the depth of all that remains unseen and unknown. The fragmentary style and refusal to explain or understand this culture banishes the scientism of ethnology. It resembles Trinh's films *Reassemblage* (1982) and *Naked Spaces* (1985), but absent from this film is the filmmaker's anxiety over representation. Instead of theory-talk, Gaitan has used a number of different filmmaking styles to suggest ways in which the Kamauirás can be imagined as part of modern culture.

Video image of still from Paula Gaitan's film *Uaka* (1988).

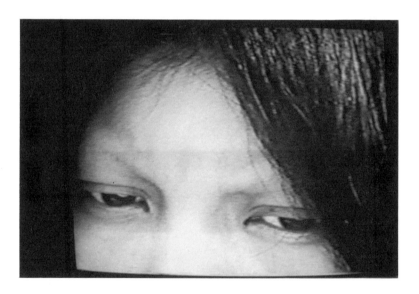

Video image of still from Paula Gaitan's film *Uaka* (1988).

The Indians in *Uaka* have accommodated rock music, cigarettes, and bicycles into their village life while resisting the ideology of "progress." Gaitan's editing suggests obliquely that this life is threatened, but also that it is transient, historical, and conscious of modernity. Certainly the pastoral mode is still there, but what is gained in the absence of Trinh's theory-talk is a conception of ethnographic history, a temporality that subverts the romance of nostalgic forms. The spectacles of the film, especially images of two men with huge horns and the few rear-projection sequences, inscribe a touristic perspective that is not interested in penetrating the mystery of the other culture. What is inside those darkened houses remains safe. The viewer never leaves the "commonsense world" at all.

In *Uaka* anthropological similarities and differences are negotiated through discourses on and about representation, epistemology, and travel. It is important to recognize that this negotiation takes place in the near absence of written and verbal discourse. Silence allows the image to "say" cultural experience without the need for translation. The displacement of the villagers into modern settings, marked by quintessentially modern architecture, constitutes a visual anthropology that deploys vision, imagery, and sound for rhetorical purposes. Performing their own encounter with modernity, the Kamauirá are liberated from the premodern identities with which they are conventionally endowed. Partly because of the many extreme close-ups of people's eyes throughout the film, one senses their sincere grasp on eternity, and one may believe that it is change, not loss, that is taking place in their encounter with history.

Ethnographic allegory here refers not to a lost past but to an unknown and unknowable future. Indeed, it is an overtly allegorical strategy by which this is accomplished. Gaitan represents the villagers' travel across the sky to Brasília in a highly stylized form, departing radically from ethnographic documentary realism for these sequences. The departure from realism becomes a departure from the eternal present tense of cinematic representation and inscribes a discourse of temporal difference onto the images of the ethnographic culture.

Gaitan uses Méliès's film, not simply as an allegory of cinema, but as an allegory of Western primitivism and desire for knowledge, travel, and the sky. The desire for universal knowledge embodied in space exploration is on one level parodied by *Voyage dans la lune* in its archival form and, on another level, historicized and qualified as one epistemology among other possible knowledges. The reference to Méliès is also a reference to representational practices and the "primitive" stage of both cinematic representation and space exploration. The Indians in the film display their own representational practices, which are as closely tied to their imagination of eternity as was Méliès's science fiction a projection of "primitive" cinematic fantasy.

By realizing the occult in First World experience (the desire for the sky, for eternity) along with the banality of the industrial landscape (the "rocket launch"), the Other culture is brought closer without being exoticized, dominated, or penetrated. "We" have "lost" the imaginary of Méliès in the technological conquest of the universe just as surely as the Amazon Indians are threatened by the capitalist thrust of progress. And yet are Méliès and *Voyage dans la lune* really lost if we can see this fantastic science fiction again and again? Would we really be content with a cinema that had not changed since 1903? The montage of *Uaka* raises precisely these questions with respect to the Xingu Indians, who are thereby located within a present tense that has a future as well as a past.

Dreamscapes and Ethnographic Time

The images from *Voyage dans la lune* that appear in *Uaka* are those from the astronomer's dreams, along with the long-shot landing of the rocket-bullet in the eye of the moon. Gaitan's invocation of Méliès's allegorical style is a means of evoking the motivating desires of *quarup:* for redemption, "to have the dead come back to life." Redemption is the allegorical imperative, and its structure is one of historical time, of loss and remembrance. The body as the main attraction in early cinema is a fetishized body: an allegory of its own fragmentation in modern culture. Incorporated into the techniques of mechanical reproduction, the body has lost its aura, it has disappeared in essence, and yet it reappears in a reconstituted form — as a dream image that disavows its own absence. Insofar as the primitive is the emblematic fetish of the Other, denying full personhood in a perpetual cultural childhood, primitive cinema provides the tools to deconstruct this fantasy. Its redemption implies its death. Its loss, however, is the dialectical form of the imagination of a transformed future, and the redemption of experience.

Because of its departure from indexical representation, *Voyage dans la lune* takes on new dimensions in postmodern culture. When the astronomers flee the Selenites across the painted backdrop of the moonscape, they might be figures in a contemporary video game. The resurrection of the film in a popular 1990s music video suggests that it may be a kind of ur-text of postmodern ethnography.[35] Benjamin advocates a "telescoping of the past through the present,"[36] which is precisely the means by which a "primitive" film such as *Voyage dans la lune* can be seen differently. It is also the way that "the primitive" can be understood as a utopian construction; it marks a point where past and future correspond, but it is a point that is visible only from the present. "It is the present which polarizes the event into fore and after history" (61).

The historiography of early cinema provides a unique perspective on cultural representation in the early twentieth century. One can already see the frame of the journey dissolving in the fetish of the cinematic apparatus that renders its operator not a "subject," but an extension of the machine. The exotic landscape of a Canadian winter becomes one more dreamscape within a cinematic practice of imaginary transcendence of the restraints of time and space. Our time traveling is only another variation of the world traveling of earlier spectators; it enables us to realize the desires for cultural exchange and reversal that were awakened with mechanical reproduction. The *Living Canada* films, like *Uaka,* depict a community experience within a dreamscape in which nostalgic and "progressive" desires are fragmented into an ethnotopian temporality that represents historical change as a function of eternity.

My excursion into early cinema, which will continue in the next chapter into the second decade of the twentieth century, is designed as a nomadic journey. The theorization of utopian ethnographic travel narrative is evoked by Deleuze and Guattari as a form of deterritorialized subjectivity.[37] Teshome Gabriel describes nomadic cinema as one that "smashes down boundaries — between documentary, travelogue, experimental and narrative fiction." He uses the trope of the nomad to describe black independent cinema not as an oppositional cinema but as one with "no self-identity. Its films make use of the same reference and language of exploitative cinema."[38] Clearly, we are still in the realm of metaphor and of literary thought, and yet this is the language of ethnography. Freed from its moorings in empiricism, ethnographic representation wanders in and between categories of thought in a utopian deterritorialization of cultural knowledge.

5 Playing Primitive

The Indian thereby driven back into the ghetto, into the glass coffin of virgin
forest, becomes the simulation model for all conceivable Indians *before*
ethnology. The latter thus allows itself the luxury of being incarnate beyond
itself, in the "brute" reality of those Indians it has entirely reinvented —
savages who are indebted to ethnology for still being Savage: what a turn of
events, what a triumph for this science which seemed dedicated to their
destruction!

— JEAN BAUDRILLARD, "The Precession of Simulacra"

In the archives of film history, traces and fragments of disappearing
films occasionally surface in "restored" versions. If experimental ethnography relies "on the use of past texts as sounding boards"[1] for a
revision of ethnographic method, the restoration and recovery of "lost"
films provides a particularly rich site of analysis. In this chapter, one
particular film from 1914 will be analyzed as an instance of retrospective
ethnographic history. *In the Land of the War Canoes* is an authentically
inauthentic text, a restoration of one of the earliest ethnographic films,
a film that observes very few principles of objectivity or reliable fieldwork. It is a rare example of a premodern ethnographic film that anticipates many of the elements of postmodern ethnography. To return to
it as an experimental film, rather than as an anthropological film, is to
trace the effects of fragmentation and historical distance on the representation of culture.

Nonfiction films of the second decade of the twentieth century are in
many ways a caesura in film history. Neither actualities within the aesthetic framework of the cinema of attractions, nor "documentaries" in
the style initiated by Flaherty in 1922, they constitute a wealth of cul-

tural documentation that has only recently begun to be recognized by scholars and archivists. The 1994 Amsterdam Workshop was devoted to this material, and in the published record of the discussion of a program of "Fictional Anthropology," the participants were struck by the way that native peoples appear to "perform" themselves for the camera.[2] With the development of cinema, culture immediately becomes a representation, in which people participate with different degrees of complicity. Performances for the camera can occasionally be read as forms of cultural resistance,[3] especially once this cinema has become an archival text, and the tensions between the body and the machine become tangible. *In the Land of the War Canoes* exemplifies the role of performance in documentaries of this period, although in its particular combination of anthropology and Hollywood melodrama, it is an anomaly of film history.

In 1914, Edward Curtis, in close collaboration with the Kwakiutl Indians on Vancouver Island, attempted to make a "photoplay," or narrative drama, that would be both entertaining and educational. An enormous failure on both counts, the film quickly disappeared. In 1973 two anthropologists, Bill Holm and George Quimby, restored the film in collaboration again with the Kwakiutl, adding a soundtrack and changing the title from Curtis's original *In the Land of the Headhunters* to *In the Land of the War Canoes*. We really have two films under consideration, the first of which, *Headhunters*, is virtually unknown and unseen.[4] Its theatrical run was extremely brief,[5] and by the time the film came to be restored, neglect and fire damage had destroyed entire scenes and numerous frames.[6] My remarks on the original are somewhat hypothetical, based on the fragmentary glimpses made available in the "restored" film. They are also made with a view toward a redemptive form of ethnography inspired by the virtual reappropriation of *Headhunters* by the Kwakiutl people. The 1973 version of the film features a soundtrack of Kwakiutl dialogue, chanting, and singing—none of it subtitled—as well as drumming and natural sound effects of birds and water. Made in consultation with fifty surviving cast members, the "restored film" functions as a kind of prism through which the 1914 film might be glimpsed in fragmentary form.

War Canoes is on one level a kind of repossession of *Headhunters* by and for those whom it was ostensibly "about." However, Holm and Quimby's restoration of the film also destroys the narrative flow of Curtis's original, replacing all of his intertitles with their own, reducing

Still from Edward Curtis's *In the Land of the War Canoes* (1914) showing the effects of deterioration of the original print.

the total from forty-seven to eighteen.[7] Brad Evans, one of the few people to have viewed Curtis's original footage, argues that the reediting of the film destroys its sense of storytelling, "leaving us much more with a 'cinema of attractions' than Curtis ever imagined."[8] The result is a curious hybrid of a "photoplay drama" and primitive cinema, in which the anthropologists have reproduced an earlier cinematic language in the remnants of Curtis's experiments with narrativity. Although Curtis's original film may have had a narrative coherence comparable to the fiction filmmaking of the early teens, in Holm and Quimby's restoration, *War Canoes* still retains the traces of early (pre-1907) cinema.

Curtis's inspiration was the huge success of the Indian film genre, which was most popular between 1908 and 1913.[9] He intended his film to be commercially competitive with the Hollywood-produced Indian film because it would be more authentic, featuring actual Indian actors and real props, customs, dances, and activities. The vehicle of this authenticity, however, was a convoluted narrative of romance, intrigue, and adventure, which Curtis wrote and had the Kwakiutl act out. In *War Canoes*, the anthropologists have added intertitles that are elliptical and highly condensed, making the story absolutely impossible to follow.[10] The plot has become an odd supplement to the images, which bear little resemblance to the narrative events announced in the titles. It is possible that in the 1970s the Hollywood photoplay was felt to be an inappropriate vehicle for ethnographic documentation, and so in the interests of social science, the narrativity of the original was dismantled. The effect is a radical separation of the text of the performers and the text of the author-filmmaker. The Kwakiutl, now dubbed in on the untranslated soundtrack, seem to have one film, and the anthropologist and non-Kwakiutl spectator have quite another.

In the attempt to provide an "authoritative" text of visual evidence, the anthropologists may have been less interested in narrative continuity than in preserving images of Kwakiutl culture, and yet they actually reshot one spectacular death scene in which a dummy body is thrown off a cliff after a dramatic struggle (echoes of *The Great Train Robbery*).[11] With very little cutting within scenes, and infrequent close-ups, most of the action unfolds uninterrupted in front of single static camera setups. Besides many instances of mismatched screen directions, *War Canoes* includes a vision scene, a popular convention of early cinema. Small camera movements are occasionally used to reframe action, but the frame serves for the most part as a static proscenium with little depth of field. The restored film includes Curtis's still portraits of the lead actors in costume as a means of introducing the characters, but these were not used in the original, and there are few close-ups to maintain character identification. All of these characteristics of *War Canoes* link it to the period that Noël Burch calls "primitive," before the fall of cinematic language to the limited conventions of narrative realism.

The 1973 version is designed to show off as much ethnographic data as possible about Kwakiutl life, and it is very much a process of "showing and telling," which André Gaudreault has identified as the privileged narrational form of early cinema. In the absence of Curtis's dialogue titles, the native actors lose a great deal of their characterization and become objects to be seen.[12] If for Curtis the all-native cast was a sign of the film's authenticity, in the restoration, the anthropologists have stamped the film with a different sign of authenticity. A long string of credits notes all of the institutional and museum personnel involved, as well as all the native informants and cast members. They have also privileged the canoes as the centerpiece of the film, in order to downplay the savagery implied in Curtis's original title.

The exploitation of "head-hunting" in Curtis's title and story line aligns even the original film to some extent with the cinema of attractions. Among the actualities of early cinema, one can find a whole range of "Indian pictures" with titles such as *Teasing the Snakes* (Edison, 1901) and *Circle Dance* (1898) in which exotic images of Native Americans were exploited for white audiences. Curtis's early motion picture footage entered mainstream circulation in this manner, as an extension of his pursuits in commercial photography.[13] Despite Curtis's ambitions for a theatrical release for *Headhunters,* its narrative interruptions of ceremonial dances and displays, along with the other traits of early cinema, suggest that it combined the "attraction" of the spectacle of otherness with dramatic narrativity. The incorporation of a museological gaze may help to explain the film's failure at the box office.

In all his various photography, film, and research activities, Curtis took it upon himself to document the native cultures that he saw as dying, and he perceived his work as an urgent task. His photography of Native Americans is consistently tinged with a romantic sense of loss, but that sense of inevitable decay is significantly absent from *Headhunters,* although to make the film, he undertook a massive recovery project of traditional Kwakiutl culture. All of the architecture, totem poles, masks, and costumes were prepared specially for the film. All signs of nonnative culture were carefully eliminated from the *mise en scène* to create the impression of an untainted Indian culture.

The collecting of trophy heads in war had not been practiced by the Kwakiutl for several generations, but within this version of the salvage paradigm, the Indians were depicted as full-fledged savages. Not only do they triumphantly wave fake trophy heads around, but a couple of scenes also feature human skulls decoratively arranged in the lair of an evil "sorcerer." Given the theatricality of these scenes, in terms of both performance and *mise en scène,* the head-hunting can be perceived as a narrative device, a practice performed only allegorically by the Kwakiutl descendants of ancient warriors. And it is in terms of allegory, in the way that the Kwakiutl perform their culture and their traditions, that the film constitutes a resistance to ethnographic authority. Underscoring the savage violence is a violence of representation that challenges the colonialist mandate of the film. *Headhunters* is not a text of mourning but a text of the triumph of good over evil, in which the repressed violence of Curtis's noble savage photography is unleashed.

The inauthenticity of the film's ethnography is not simply due to the incorporation of script, performance, and props. Curtis freely invented names and mixed elements of different rituals and ceremonies together.[14] He spent four years preparing for the film and from his fieldwork produced one volume of his mega-opus, *The North American Indian,* on the Kwakiutl. He did make an effort to reproduce all of the masks, totem poles, canoes, and other objects of Kwakiutl life quite faithfully, and yet the requirements of the photoplay demanded an imposition of a foreign narrative form and a blatant disregard of the subtleties of Kwakiutl culture. The difference between Curtis's meticulous research and his carelessness in film production is indicative of a faith in cinematic representation as a transparency—based partially in the aesthetics of the actuality and partially in those of the new narrative realism. It was presumably enough that the Indians were played by Indians and that the props were made by them for the film to be "authentic."

In 1912 Curtis had assembled his photographs and early motion picture footage together as an illustrated lecture that he toured with orchestra, under the title "The Vanishing Race."[15] Curtis's ethnography was produced on the margins of academic anthropology, as a sideshow informed equally by the entertainment market for exploitation curiosities and by a serious sense of commitment to cultural documentation. Curtis was notorious for supplying costumes and props to create a noble savage effect for native peoples long since separated from their ancestral heritage.[16] The sense of urgency behind Curtis's project was produced within a romantic sensibility that entitled him to take artistic license of some scope in what he called his photographic art-science. To his credit, at least he represented an embodied culture and linked native peoples with the signs of their ethnicity, even if his pictures are inflected with a melancholy sense of loss. Only seven years after *Headhunters* was released, the Kwakiutl potlatch ceremonies, outlawed since 1885, began to be raided, and the ceremonial artifacts confiscated by the National Museum in Ottawa.

Curtis's own description of his intentions in *The North American Indian* is telling. His twenty-volume photographic record "represents the result of personal study of a people who are rapidly losing the traces of their aboriginal character and who are destined ultimately to become assimilated with the 'superior race.' " [17] The last two words may be in quotation marks, but Curtis's fascination with native peoples was firmly based in the racist presumption that cross-cultural encounter was necessarily a contest subject to evolutionary laws of survival. By insisting on the otherness of native peoples in his photographs, he cultivated a mystique of Indianness that could only contribute to the racist preclusion of cultural diversity. Otherness could only be valued in its specificity on the verge of its extinction. The exotic value of Indian pictures was in direct proportion to the elimination of lived native cultures. In the frame, on the page, and on the screen, Native Americans were made safe, a process that Edward Curtis, with the benevolent support of Theodore Roosevelt, was instrumental in aestheticizing.

The Northwest Coast native peoples played an important role in the ideology of "vanishing races." [18] Curtis was not alone in being attracted to a culture that, in the early twentieth century, was still quite isolated from European society and had retained many indigenous arts and customs.[19] The Kwakiutl figured prominently in Franz Boas's anthropology, a body of work that was far more significant than Curtis's in altering racist views of native peoples. Curtis acknowledges Boas in his introduction to his own Kwakiutl ethnography, but the more important link between these men is their mutual "informant," George Hunt.

The son of an Englishman and Tlingit Indian, Hunt was trained as a field-worker by Boas and guided both men through the Kwakiutl culture and language in which he grew up. Jeanne Cannizzo has argued that "George Hunt is one of the most important originators of our current view of 'traditional' Kwakiutl society; he is a primary contributor to the invention of the Kwakiutl as an ethnographic entity." [20] Hunt played an instrumental role in the production of *Headhunters.* Not only were most of the actors Hunt's own relatives, but photographs of the shoot suggest that he was Curtis's assistant director, holding a megaphone and instructing the performers.[21] This figure of the informant as assistant director may be an instance of what Trinh Minh-ha calls the "Inappropriate Other," [22] or what James Clifford describes as an exemplary cultural traveler.[23] Unlike the ethnographers Curtis and Boas, Hunt is neither insider nor outsider, but a slippage between positions that unfixes them both. As assistant director, his role as translator and interpreter is revealed as one of anthropological creation and, literally, direction.

Both Boas and Curtis were engaged in totalizing, exhaustive documentation enterprises that were necessarily doomed to incompletion.

Curtis's work was explicitly framed as art-science but fell in between both camps, into the realm of popular culture.[24] Boas's work was equally problematic as a "science," though. James Clifford notes that while Boas may not have subscribed to the "vanishing race" theory of cultural evolutionism, his conception of culture was nevertheless one in which "culture is enduring, traditional, . . . a process of ordering, not of disruption. . . . It does not normally 'survive' abrupt alterations."[25] Like Curtis, Boas "wrote out" of his account all signs of Kwakiutl adaptation to European culture, attending only to the pure elements of traditional life.

Boas introduced methods of fieldwork that were designed to be "as free as possible from the certain self-contamination of the data by the ethnographer himself." To understand culture on its own terms, to "present Kwakiutl culture as it appears to the Indian himself,"[26] one can do little more than transform it into "data." Helen Cordere notes that "Boas has been charged with being indifferent or hostile to the proper scientific goal of formulating scientific laws . . . that his ethnography is an arid accumulation of fact upon fact."[27] Boas himself filmed the Kwakiutl in 1930 but never edited the footage. Rosalind Morris has suggested that the "raw footage" was in fact more in keeping with Boas's ethnographic method: "For much of Boas's written ethnography reads like the footage for [a film]: numerous sequences of detailed images strung together one after the other with only minimal theorization. Moreover, while he occasionally discussed anthropological uses for the footage, these did not include the production of an edited 'film.' "[28]

To make "a film" from raw footage necessarily implies a narrative structure or form, which Boas may have been reluctant to impose.[29] Curtis, on the other hand, by using the narrative model closest at hand, that of the Hollywood photoplay, forces the natives into the twentieth century. Boas's ethnography may have been an important step toward the eradication of scientific racism, and yet in objectifying culture, it leaves little room for the subjective space of native peoples. It is a far cry, in other words, from "how culture appears to the Indian himself." Boas's contribution to ethnography was instrumental in transforming the stereotype of the primitive, and yet Curtis's profoundly primitive attempt to dramatize Kwakiutl culture represents on some level a recognition of native subjectivity.

The myth that Curtis devised for *Headhunters* is composed of Oedipal desires, repressions, conflicts, and triumphs. In the original scenario of the film, the hero, Motana, transgresses a "divine" law by dreaming of a

Still from Edward Curtis's *In the Land of the War Canoes* (1914). Motana, the hero, sneaks into the enemy's home to rescue the princess, Naida.

woman when he is supposed to be fasting; a rival suitor steals a lock of Motana's hair, but Motana fights the magic spell and beheads the evil sorcerer to win the maiden, Naida. After a series of adventures, battles, kidnappings, and rescues, Motana triumphs over evil and takes the place of Naida's father, the chief.[30] Instead of a monotonous collection of "data" that was the downfall of the contemporary travelogue, Curtis positioned the natives within a discourse of desire. Clearly modeled on the contemporary photoplay scenario, which might be considered a powerful mythology of middle-class America, the story nevertheless, in principle, allows the native character to assume the Oedipal role.

In the film as it has come to us via *War Canoes,* an allegorical subjectivity is produced through a multilayered performance style. Curtis says that he was attracted to the Northwest Coast Indians because "their ceremonies are developed to a point which fully justifies the use of the term dramatic."[31] The Kwakiutl had a whole range of dances and roles that individuals and families exchanged ceremonially. The potlatch system involves the distribution of wealth, and this economic structure is closely bound up with a dramatic structure of mythologically based costumes, masks, songs, dances, roles, and even dialogue. The winter ceremonial that occurs toward the end of *Headhunters* is an annual event that Boas describes as a "great impressive ceremony of sanctifying the tribe." He also notes that the Kwakiutl name for the ceremony, *ts!e'ts!equa,* means "to be fraudulent, to cheat." [32]

The Kwakiutl, in other words, were experienced actors, which may explain the ease with which they were able to follow directions without having seen a motion picture themselves. The acting in the film ranges from naturalistic performances of activities such as canoeing and clam digging to melodramatic hysteria and, given the prevalence of long shots, can be readily compared to primitive cinema's reliance on gesture, costume, and setting for characterization. Curtis had all the actors wear wigs and costumes, which enabled them to pose as their ancestors rather than themselves, even when performing the nonceremonial activities such as hunting and paddling. The actors do not completely fill their assigned roles, partly because the characters are so clearly foreign to their culture, and partly because of their histrionic performance style. The integration of their own ceremonial dances, in which people are dressed as animals and birds complete with masks, furs, and feathers, only enhances this sense of the doubleness of the performance style.

If allegory is one of the principal means of inverting the salvage paradigm that informs conventional ethnographic praxis, performative doubling is a valuable cinematic technique. Realist aesthetics demand a disappearance of the social actor into his or her "role" in the film; the veracity of the aesthetic precludes any indices of "acting." Performative strategies that enable social actors some distance from their "image" are means of pointing to another reality outside and beyond the discourse of visual knowledge. The Kwakiutl performances in *War Canoes/Headhunters* constitute a rare display of the allegorical structure of native performance and might be described as a form of postcolonial translation, as proposed by Homi Bhabha: "The power of the postcolonial translation of modernity rests in its *performative, deconstructive* structure that does not simply revalue the contents of a cultural tradition, or transpose values 'cross-culturally.' . . . It is to introduce another locus of inscription and intervention, another hybrid, 'inappropriate' enunciative site, through that temporal split — or time-lag . . . for the signification of postcolonial agency." [33] *Headhunters* (as seen through the prism of *War Canoes*) challenges the purist implications of primitivism because it is designed so clearly as a spectacle of the primitive. Its allegorical fantasy of otherness seems to be modeled on nothing less fantastic than *Voyage dans la lune.*

Ethnography and Silent Film History

Within the history of film, the allegorical style of *Headhunters* needs to be recognized as being somewhere between Georges Méliès's *Voyage dans la lune,* made twelve years earlier, and Fritz Lang's Niebelungen films, made ten years later. The proscenium-framed ceremonial sequences and the crowding of the frame by rows of agitated, costumed people are reminiscent of the opening shots of *Voyage dans la lune,* and the prominence of skulls and trophy heads as decor and fetishes also echoes Méliès's overdecorated and prop-laden *mise en scènes.* The primitivism of Curtis's visual style translates Kwakiutl exoticism into the language of magic and adventure initiated by Méliès, and as we have seen, Méliès's science fiction is itself an ethnographic cross-cultural fantasy articulated in the language of colonialism and tribalism.

The parallel with *Siegfried* (1924) and *Kriemhild's Revenge* (1925) is a little more oblique, and I certainly do not want to suggest that Lang may have in any way been influenced by Curtis's film. Lang was immersed in the European modernist discovery of primitivism and incorporated many tropes of African art into the expressionist sets and costumes of these films. Although he uses far more close-ups, Lang's characters are just as completely enveloped in costumes, wigs, and headdresses as are the Kwakiutl in *Headhunters.* Both Lang's and Curtis's films feature monumental proscenium-framed sets, and the action is often staged either in front of stylized architectural facades or in pastoral nature settings. The Niebelungen films are also about romance, power struggles between families, revenge aided by magical powers, marriage ceremonies, savage tribes (the Huns in *Kriemhild*), and tests for the hero to undergo.[34] The parallels are testimony to Curtis's imposition of European culture onto the Kwakiutl, but at the same time, they indicate the strength of the "primitivist" analogy in experimental film praxis.

Whereas comparing *Headhunters* to the work of Méliès and Lang is an important means of indicating the ethnographic discourse latent in the history of experimental fiction filmmaking, comparing it to Flaherty demonstrates the subversive potential of experimental ethnography. In 1915 Robert and Frances Flaherty met Curtis in Toronto and had a private screening of *Headhunters.* Flaherty also screened his 1914 footage of the Inuit, his first motion picture attempt that was destroyed by fire before *Nanook of the North* was made. In Frances's comparison of the two films in her diary, she says that Flaherty's images "in all their crudity . . . stood out human, real, convincing and big in contrast to the spectacular artificiality of Curtis's. . . . As Mr. C. himself said of our pictures, there was an intimacy about them; but he also criticized them as monotonous." [35] In 1914 Flaherty's footage was shot and assembled in the travelogue mode popularized by expedition films such as Herbert Ponting's 1911 film of the South Pole, *The Great White Silence,* although even Flaherty's first Inuit footage featured a single protagonist and his family. [36] From Curtis, Flaherty learned the importance of narrative and the commercial doors it might open as a means of financing ethnographic filmmaking. Frances Flaherty also notes that Curtis was having trouble marketing his film because it was regarded as too "highbrow." Ironically enough, by replacing Curtis's "photoplay" melodrama with an existential drama of human survival, Flaherty was able to reach the audience that Curtis himself missed.

The difference between *Nanook* and *Headhunters* lies not only in the kind of story but more crucially in the narrative form in which the story is told. The vehicle of Flaherty's humanist intimacy is a tightly edited narrative in which close-ups individualize the natives as characters, and extreme long shots locate these characters in the picturesque and radically foreign Arctic setting. A careful integration of titles and images naturalizes the narrative and cloaks the colonialist perspective with a tone of familiarity. In the full-fledged "institutional mode" of the narrator system, or interiorized film lecturer, [37] Nanook's story appears to tell itself. It may well have been progressive in comparison with the "curio" approach of contemporary travelogues such as those of Martin and Osa Johnson, and indeed Flaherty was quite conscious of wanting to create a more "intimate" portrait than had been done in any other ethnographic motion picture. [38] The subjectivity that Flaherty creates for his characters is, however, extremely limited. The simplicity of the raw struggle between man and nature in *Nanook* imputes an existential simplicity to the performers, who are identified completely with the roles they were asked to play.

Both Curtis and Flaherty chose to depict their respective native communities in the eternal present tense of the ethnographic "salvage paradigm." Flaherty was perhaps motivated less by an ethnographic concern to document the ways of a "vanishing race" than by a concern for dramatic content. The early scenes in the film that juxtapose the Inuit with the white man's world of gramophones and cod-liver oil do more to primitivize the Inuit than any of Curtis's head-hunting, precisely because of the heightened realism of Flaherty's visual style. It is *because* of Flaherty's naturalized narrative realism, created through his "mastery" of film language, that he could be charged with faking scenes, a charge that only authenticizes the realist context of the staging. This realism is promoted by the performances of the Inuit, as well as the drama of everyday life that they were asked to enact.

With the removal of all signs of acting and theater, *Nanook* could be more fully accommodated into the aesthetic realm of cinematic realism and, through John Grierson's endorsement, become instrumental in the development of documentary codes of authoritative authenticity. Flaherty's still photographs of the Inuit are in much the same style as Curtis's Indian photography, but that romantic stylization is more acceptable as realism when the still pose is animated in "moving pictures." *Nanook* is in a sense the cinematic equivalent to Curtis's photographic romanticism in its stylized aestheticization of native life. It completely fulfills the modernist predicament of recognizing the cultural purity and integrity of the ethnographic other while keeping that culture at a safe distance. The distance is made safe by representing native culture as outside of history, stuck in an eternally present tense. Both *Nanook* and *Headhunters* blur the distinction between the native performers and their ancestors, and yet the failure of *Headhunters* as narrative realism invites that historical difference to be read back into the film.

Headhunters is a film that forces ethnography into a wider discussion of film history. The theatrical aspect of *Headhunters* supplements narrativity with a discourse of the ethnic body ("tribalism") that can be traced to many other films of the first thirty-five years of film history, including the Hollywood Indian pictures that were Curtis's inspiration.[39] *Nanook* has become a privileged instance of art cinema precisely because its universal humanism subjugates the ethnic subject to the authority of realism. In *Headhunters* the stereotype of the primitive redeems the ethnic subject in a discourse of specificity and historicity. Its peculiar mix of art and science needs to be recognized as a prototypical experimental film with a complex spectatorial address.

The Kwakiutl dances and ceremonies in *Headhunters,* like Curtis's earlier actuality footage of Navajo and Hopi Indians, are shot from a single
camera setup with no editing within continuous actions. Compared to
the actualities, the Kwakiutl are much more exhibitionist in their presentation of their culture. This theatricality, both in their performances
of Curtis's melodramatic characters and in their own mythical characters, is what makes the film such a different form of ethnography. The
address to the spectator is thus somewhat different.

The sets where the ceremonial dances are staged are designed as
proscenium-framed platforms, with totem poles on each side and a curtain behind the performers. In one scene, the curtain drops to reveal
another row of costumed dancers. In another, a front row of dancers
face the camera, a second row have their backs to the camera, and behind them a row of painted boards are raised and waved about. Holm
and Quimby say that these boards "represent a supernatural being, and
are described as being dangerous to look at."[40] Their explanation is
surprising because the film lacks any sense of supernatural or mystical
forces. The presentational aspect of these ceremonies and their indication of the theatricality of Kwakiutl culture suggest that they were
designed precisely "to be looked at," but not by the camera, or by the
white ethnographer and his audience. Curtis's single wide-angle lens
cannot even represent the depth of field necessary for the full effect of
the spectacle. Again, the image is an allegorical one, slightly distanced
from the "magic," precisely because of the structure of the "attraction"
that keeps spectacle and spectator very separate. The sacred aspect of
the ritual is essentially protected from filmic appropriation.[41]

Curtis claims that he had to enter into intensive negotiations in order
to cast the film, as it had to be determined that each actor and actress
was "entitled" to play his or her designated part.[42] In the end, Motana
was played by George Hunt's son; three different women played the
female lead, Naida; and one actor played two of the principal male leads.
When Holm and Quimby screened the unedited remains of Curtis's
film in the 1960s, some Kwakiutl spectators who recognized actors and
actresses could not follow the story line, which arbitrarily identified
individuals as characters. They likewise saw locations as familiar places
rather than as the places named in intertitles.[43] Insofar as the Kwakiutl

spectators read the images indexically rather than symbolically, theirs is a resistant reading, against the metaphoric grain of the text.

Instead of a "photoplay," Kwakiutl audiences may well see a documentary of their performance in a white man's movie. The film constitutes a living memory of both the traditional practices and the colonial containment activated by the rigorous framing and "photoplay" conventions. As a text of cultural memory, the film is formally allegorical, enacting several layers of representation. The contact between the 1914 performers and the 1972 soundtrack is in itself a vibrant historical correspondence, an inscription of the distance between generations, and the echoing sense of community between them. The peculiar mix of fiction and documentary that is *War Canoes* invites a broad spectrum of readings and meanings. The fictional aspect enables the documentary to be read differently, to be "displaced" and made ambiguous, giving the viewer more control. Dai Vaughan argues that once the boundary between fiction and documentary is perceived as being more fluid, ethnographic film style can and should be wide open: "Superficially reasonable demands that our films be comprehensible are often in effect demands that the viewer be browbeaten into sharing *our* understanding of them. Documentary's images are, ideally, not illustrative but constitutive. They are constitutive of the viewer's meanings, since it is the viewer who constitutes them as documentary." [44]

It is only recently that *Headhunters* became a documentary through its second life as *War Canoes*. Originally, it was apprehended as a fiction, constituted by quite a different audience than that of the anthropology and native communities. In *Moving Picture World* in 1914, Stephen Bush enthusiastically described the film as "a gem of the motion picture art." He praised its epic quality and compared it to Wagnerian opera. [45] Film theorist Vachel Lindsay described the representation of the Indians as "figures in bronze." [46] These critics confirm the affinities of ethnological primitivism and modern art that were so prevalent during this period, but they also point to the highly allegorical nature of the film. Even for these viewers, the actors represent their own nobility, savagery, and spirituality without becoming fully identified with the primitivism they enact.

Nanook of the North has also lent itself to reappropriation by the Inuit community. Zacharias Kunuk's *Quaggiq* (1989), a videotape made for the Inuit Broadcasting Corporation, is a kind of remaking of *Nanook* by and for Inuit actors. The community television aesthetic and amateur acting retains exactly the sense of doubleness conveyed by the histrionic performance style of *Headhunters.* Claude Massot's documentary *Nanook Revisited* (1990) features contemporary Inuit audiences laughing at and critiquing *Nanook,* but also exhibiting a certain fascination with its romanticism. The apparent persistence of *Nanook* in Inuit culture as a site of re-viewing, remaking, and rereading suggests that while the salvage paradigm is an ethnographic allegory of colonialism, it may also preserve a utopian form of memory of some historic value to native communities.

War Canoes and *Nanook* represent exceptional moments in film history because they are already so highly intertextual, representing the salvage paradigm as a form of narrative desire. The ideal of cultural autonomy and integrity is represented in these films as an ideal, and on some level, they do answer to the narcissism of film spectatorship, to see oneself or one's ethnic group on-screen, occupying the space of a privileged subjectivity. Despite the imperialist paradigms in which these silent ethnographic films were made, native viewers need to be credited with the ability to read against the grain of colonialism. In the attempts of native communities to maintain cultural identity through traditional languages and activities, the films offer a unique image of the previous generation's attempt to do exactly the same thing.

Interviewed in *Box of Treasures* (Chuck Olin, 1983), Gloria Cranmer Webster, a Kwakiutl museum curator, points to the monumental canoes in motion as the most valuable aspect of the film, which to her is otherwise "hokey." Obviously, we cannot impute readings or viewings to native audiences, and the playfulness that for me raises the film far above the hypocrisy of so much scientific and aesthetic ethnography may ultimately be just another academic argument. And yet Webster's explanation for why the Kwakiutl so eagerly took part in Curtis's film is that it was, quite simply, a lot of fun. If the film can teach us anything about postmodern ethnography, it might be in the very perversity of the "photoplay" intertext of entertainment and the "primitive" cinema of attractions. As an antirealist discourse, it frees ethnography from the burden of authority and from the weight of a historiography of loss. *War Canoes* is a many-layered film about a vibrant, living, native community with strong ties to both its colonial and precolonial past. The film, in its many layers and fragmentary survival, is a unique example of a postmodern document of cultural memory. Instead of representing a dying culture, Curtis's film inscribes death into the reenactment of a culture whose cinematic documentation becomes a form of redemption.

Primitive Cinema and "Free Play"

Within the history of ethnographic film, *Headhunters* may be the primitive moment, the primal ethnographic style that is so politically incorrect that it is perfectly legible as an allegory of colonialist practice. The beauty of the film is in its perverse inauthenticity, its stylized artifice and theatricality. Its allegorical structure points to that which cannot be represented, that which lies outside the domain of the white man's camera. Curtis's artistic aspirations were far more commercial than those of the avant-garde that came to identify with early cinema, and yet it was his artistic license that enabled him to challenge the fiction and travelogue conventions of his day. Especially in its contemporary form, as an archival text, the film can be aligned with the avant-garde and its rereading of primitive cinema. However, *In the Land of the Headhunters* is best situated somewhere between Buffalo Bill's Wild West Show and Josephine Baker in its attempt to capitalize on Curtis's ethnography by means of Hollywood film conventions. In the sheer perversity of the project, the film may provide a model for a postcolonial, postmodern form of ethnographic representation.

The affinities between the American avant-garde and early cinema lie in the discovery and rediscovery of film as a language of representation. From the perspective of gender relations, Judith Mayne has suggested that the alterity of "primitive" cinema has been a rich source of inspiration for feminist film practice. She points out that "the inquiry into 'primitivism' is very much connected, not to the dismantling or bracketing of narrative, but to its reconceptualization."[47] In the case of primitive ethnography, we have a similar opportunity that might restore the utopian thrust of primitivism to a postcolonial narrative. Although Curtis's original film may have moved beyond the forms of early cinema and included some of the devices of continuity editing associated with the nascent codification of narrative realism, the "restored" version of the film interrupts that narrativity and displays it as an archival series of fragments. Despite the different terms of authenticity informing the original and the remake, the Kwakiutl survive their cinematic (mis)treatment as performers. If Curtis's still photography preserved native people in a perpetual perspective of disappearance, his turn to melodrama repositions the native in the role of agency and desiring subjectivity. In its present state, as a film that is neither a documentary (because it is so inauthentic) nor a fiction (because the narrative is so incomprehensible), *Headhunters/War Canoes* is a key instance of the survival of a "cinema of attractions" beyond the parameters of early cinema. The imbrication of cinematic and ethnographic primitivism ultimately produces an excessive discourse of native subjectivity.

III

THE UNDISCIPLINED

GAZE

Still from Bill Viola's video *I Do Not Know What It Is I Am Like* (1986). Photo by Kira Perov.

6 Zoology, Pornography, Ethnography

A man attending a slide show on Africa turns to his wife and says with
guilt in his voice: "I have seen some pornography tonight."
— TRINH T. MINH-HA, *Reassemblage*

The Panopticon functions as a kind of laboratory of power.
— MICHEL FOUCAULT, *Discipline and Punish: The Birth of the Prison*

The title of Bill Viola's videotape *I Do Not Know What It Is I Am Like*
(1986) halts the quest for knowledge before it even begins, announcing
a kind of failure of knowledge and a quest for identity. As representations of consciousness, the different parts of the tape involve looking at
various things, species, and people with an intensity that has been described as a series of "zoological observations."[1] The limits of vision
are strongly implied in footage shot in the San Diego Zoo, in which
the video frame replaces the cage. Although the signs of "the zoo" are
absent, the effect of containment and restriction is reduced to an effect
of vision and the technological apparatus of the gaze. The electronically
reproduced silence echoes the profound failure of communication that
is intimately bound to the exotic character of endangered species. In
long, ponderous shots, individual birds and fish sit as if suspended in
time, as if you could see the cumulative history of their species dependent on their survival. In close-up, their features are grotesque and unfamiliar, and their eyes seem not to blink. "The Language of the Birds"
is that of cultural marginalization.

Most striking about the birds and fish in *I Do Not Know* is the failure
of the animals to return the gaze. They look without seeing. We cannot
know what they are thinking, if they are thinking; the eye becomes a

mask. Viola may catch his own reflection in the eye of an owl, but nothing and no one looks back at him with any interest. The naked stare that Viola develops strips the gaze down to its scopophilic structure: the desire to see, which is indulged fully, but is always unsatisfying, always leaving a gap of unknowing, of desire that sustains itself through lack.

In Viola's portraits of birds, fish, and animals, the gaze functions as a form of containment and a site of excess. The absolute passivity of the creatures in Viola's apparatus of seeing finally gives way to an eruption of unconscious dream forms of surrealist ethnography. Ethnography, zoology, and pornography share a common disciplinary technology of vision that seeks to control, contain, and master the field of the Other, but in doing so, they produce a supplementary discourse of violence and wildness. The field of the Other is rendered exotic and erotic precisely by virtue of the apparatus of vision. Viola's aesthetics tend toward the mystical, but despite my reservations about his overall project, this tape encompasses some key thematics of experimental ethnography, including a discourse on the gaze, found footage, and possession rituals. I will return to *I Do Not Know* in the two subsequent chapters, to more fully address the significance of the tape's Orientalism, minimalism, and discourse on technology. This chapter will be concerned with the disciplinary apparatus of the cinematic gaze.

The films that are analyzed in this chapter bring together the safari film, the educational film, and the avant-garde. *Unsere Afrikareise* (Peter Kubelka, 1966) disperses the gaze through an explicit and horrifying collision of ethnographic, zoological, and pornographic gazes. The colonial practice of big game hunting is represented in Kubelka's film as an extension of these discourses of power that converge in violence. *Microcultural Incidents at Ten Zoos* (Ray Birdwhistell, 1969) and *Simba: The King of Beasts, A Saga of the African Veldt* (Martin and Osa Johnson, 1928) are examples of the failures of the ethnographic gaze, instances in which it breaks down in its own "frenzy"—its own impossible desires. *Hide and Seek* (Su Friedrich, 1996) is an example of an avant-garde work that appropriates the ethnographic gaze for its own purpose—in Friedrich's case, for an articulation of lesbian identity. In all of these texts, the will to knowledge and the desire to see (scopophilia) are imperfectly aligned, and the gaze is thus inscribed as a structure of social relations in which possession, knowledge, and sexuality constitute overlapping and conflicting discourses.

One of the main contributions that film theory has made to the understanding of visual culture is the analysis of "the gaze" as an ideologically constructed apparatus. What became known as "apparatus theory" dominated film studies in the 1970s in an effort, in part, to "discipline" the field with the scientific methods of structuralism and psychoanalysis. Through the work of Laura Mulvey, Christian Metz, Jean-Louis Baudry, Stephen Heath, and others, the cinema was theorized as an apparatus structured around *a* gaze, which was defined as bourgeois and male. Transcendental and ideal, the vanishing point of the image and the cone of the projector beam and camera lens fixed the spectator as the source and desiring subject of the spectacle on the screen.[2]

Twenty years later, many of the tenets of apparatus theory have come into question. A diversity of "viewing positions" have been posited, and the "unitary spectator" has been dislodged.[3] The limitations of apparatus theory concern its totalizing effect and its inability to theorize other pleasures than those suggested by Lacanian psychoanalysis. The gaze, however, remains an important structural component of the cinema experience and a means of understanding the relation between films, spectators, and people filmed. "Gaze theory" addresses the pleasures and powers of the viewing experience, which is not necessarily specific to cinema but links the cinema to other media, such as photography and video. In conjunction with a more plural notion of spectatorship and a more flexible notion of textuality, the gaze can be thought of as a site of power *and* resistance. If apparatus theory depended on a very limited idea of narrativity — an illusionist, closed, diegetic space — gaze theory might be better developed in the context of other modes of film practice, such as experimental ethnography.

The theorization of the gaze as a form of epistemological inquiry was of course further confirmed by Foucault. Apparatus theory and panopticism are discourses that make a number of common assumptions about representation, power, and knowledge but never really converge in theories of narrative cinema. For Foucault, the cinema would be one of many panopticonic discourses and lacks the specificity attributed to it in apparatus theory. Moreover, in Foucault's schema, panopticism is a discursive practice and is thus subject to historical change, depending on its application. As Teresa de Lauretis points out, Foucault's conception of power as a function of discourse suggests that we "abandon the idea of cinema as a self-contained system, semiotic or economic, imaginary or visionary."[4]

The difference between Foucault's panopticon and the model of Plato's cave proposed by Jean-Louis Baudry for the cinematic apparatus is the embodiment of actual prisoners who *are seen* in the panopticon. Baudry's prisoners are the seers, who mistake the shadows on the wall for reality.[5] The camera obscura model of vision, which informs apparatus theory, insists on a transcendental, invisible, abstract viewing position, one that psychoanalysis has further associated with the voyeur. In Foucault's model of the disciplinary gaze of power, the viewer is specifically a representation of power, as the prisoners are continually "under surveillance."[6] In the panopticon, the content of the image, which apparatus theory failed to analyze beyond gender codes, is not only rendered as "other" but represented as entrapped and incarcerated. If "visibility is a trap," viewer *and* viewed are drawn into a relation of power and subjugation. Unlike the imaginary, regressive situation posited by Baudry, the panopticonic relation is a fully conscious one of regulation and control.

Pornography is a privileged model of the gaze, for it is a cultural practice that produces its object, sexuality, by enacting imaginary means of possessing the image. The parallels between pornography and ethnography have been most thoroughly explored by Bill Nichols.[7] He suggests that ethnography is subject to a certain discipline that proscribes against the eroticization of the Other, although its gaze is in many ways like that governing pornography. The structural qualities shared by pornography and ethnography are those that articulate their respective scopophilic intentions while keeping the Other at a safe distance (223–26). Nichols's analogy between pornography and ethnography is based on their shared economies of pleasure and knowledge. Both modes of representation are governed by a desire to see Others and have developed codified systems of controlling this fascination. The body of the Other is held up to the gaze in both cases, but the limits of visual pleasure and the limits of knowledge need to be masked (226).

The exoticism of animals lies somewhere between the excitement of the sexual spectacle and the otherness of the ethnographic subject. The zoo is an intermediary zone that lies between the pornographic and the ethnographic gazes, in a triangular relation with them. It is a space where "epistemological inquiry" meets that of entertainment and exploitation in full view, without its mask of humanism. Zoology may be a branch of biology, but the zoological gaze also belongs to popular culture — encompassing TV nature programs, Disneyland, water worlds, and of course the zoo itself. Its discipline is literally that of the cage, the container or the frame. As a form of representation, the zoo is a technology of vision; the zoological gaze is an apparatus that is also a cultural practice in which the Other (species) is brought close and yet kept apart, at a safe distance. The zoo as a "discipline" in Foucault's sense is a form of knowledge that is produced in and through technologies of vision: " 'Discipline' may be identified neither with an institution nor with an apparatus; it is a type of power, a modality for its exercise, comprising a whole set of instruments, techniques, procedures, levels of application, targets; it is a 'physics' or an 'anatomy' of power, a technology." [8]

The zoo emerged in colonial culture in tandem with ethnographic practices and even overlapped them. The ethnographic showcases that proliferated in world fairs from 1870, even until 1930, promoted the Darwinian analogy between 'primitives' and apes. The motto of the 1893 World's Columbian Exposition in Chicago was "To See Is to Know" — indicating the coextensive discourses of science, visuality, imprisonment, and imperialism that governed the display of native peoples.[9] The display of animals likewise demonstrated the plunder of the "civilizing process" — the taming of wild beasts and the wealth of knowledge and multiplicity produced through colonial power. John Berger has further suggested that the zoo exhibits the marginality of animals in industrial society.[10] The zoo thus constitutes another instance of the salvage paradigm: it emerges at the moment when animals begin to disappear from daily life, and species become extinct. It idealizes them as a form of loss while, of course, contributing to their very disappearance by "collecting" them out of their natural habitat.

Humanist ethnography has endeavored to keep the zoo and ethnography quite separate, as the science of "man" endeavors to extract culture from nature. And yet, as Donna Haraway has argued, the natural sciences are constructed around a nature-culture dualism that is mapped onto many of the same dualities that inform ethnographic thinking: "Simian orientalism means that western primatology has been about the construction of the self from the raw material of the other, the appropriation of nature in the production of culture, the ripening of the human from the soil of the animal, the clarity of white from the obscurity of colour, the issue of man from the body of woman, the elaboration of gender from the resource of sex, the emergence of mind by the activation of body." [11]

Zoology, Pornography, Ethnography **123**

As a technology, the panopticonic gaze at animals and people is founded, as Haraway suggests, on a discourse of sexuality. The disciplinary context of the voyeuristic gaze is what Foucault calls *scientia sexualis*, "a hermeneutic of desire aimed at ever more detailed explorations of the scientific truths of sexuality."[12] Linda Williams has developed Foucault's analysis of the discourse of sexuality in the context of filmic pornography. What she describes as a "frenzy of the visible" "is neither an aberation nor an excess; rather, it is a logical outcome of a variety of discourses of sexuality that converge in, and help further to produce, technologies of the visible."[13] If in the zoo the logic of "to see is to know" prevails, in pornography "to see" extends beyond "to know" to forms of possession and domination that are transgressive, imaginary, and fantastic.

To see, after all, is not to know or possess the Other, but both pornography and ethnography embody a utopian desire to transcend and eliminate this contradiction. Both imply a mastery of vision that passes for possession and knowledge, apparently triumphing over the repression of sexuality and racial difference by bringing them into the regime of the visible. If we add zoology as a third term to this pairing of ethnography and pornography, the desire for pleasure and knowledge is mapped onto a desire for control and mastery. The cage and the hunt render the limits of the gaze very literal; the killing of wild animals further introduces an element of death into the apparatus of vision that links these different cultural practices.

Pornography and ethnography converge most explicitly in the image of the bare-breasted woman that appears in so many ethnographic films. The body of the woman becomes the site of "primitive sexuality," a sign of the uncivilized ideal and object of desire within a discourse of colonial mastery. However, as Trinh's film *Reassemblage* demonstrates, the naked breast can also be seen differently, within a different organization of looks. Her approach in that film is to shoot from a range of different angles and distances, so as to destabilize the position of the viewing subject. Women's breasts are thus seen, but not from the position of the voyeur or that of the "knower" or social scientist. Trinh declares that hers is not an "anti-aesthetic" stance; nor does she want to be included within a tradition of "experimental film." Indeed, *Reassemblage* does not "subvert" the gaze. It is also open to the more prurient look of the *National Geographic* voyeur; it offers no real protection against a scopophilic gaze.

The films to be discussed in this chapter are like *Reassemblage* in that they are not necessarily "alternatives" to the disciplines of the gaze, but they deconstruct the apparatus of power that informs the will to knowledge. Formal techniques are generated by the demands of the content, in that they foreground the ambivalence and unknowability of the Other. The dismantling of power is not, however, always accomplished by the texts alone but is achieved through their recontextualization and misreading by another viewer than the one they might have initially addressed. The dispersal of the gaze takes place through the slippages of history and of disciplines, and through the eyes of an observer who watches the films and watches how they work. Looking at the discursive overlap between ethnography, pornography, and zoology is a means of analyzing the gaze not as a psychoanalytic category but as a technique that plays a role in a variety of disciplines. The gaze can produce tensions between different discourses of looking, and it is this friction that I want to trace through the following films.

Unsere Afrikareise: Desiring Machines

The African safari, the scene behind the zoological spectacle, is a crucial site of the discipline of looking as an explicitly colonial practice. We turn now to a dystopic configuration of the ethnographic gaze, one that situates it on the cusp of zoology and pornography. For the Austrian experimental filmmaker Peter Kubelka, death is the endpoint of a gaze that links cinema most explicitly with hunting. In *Unsere Afrikareise* (translated as "Our Trip to Africa"), a treatise on the cinematic gaze emerges in which the cruelty of colonialism is articulated as a function of cinema. In the dystopian world of the African safari, the cinematic apparatus becomes a technology of power, implicating the viewer in a structure of voyeurism, violence, and subjugation.

Kubelka is a filmmaker whom Sitney includes among the structural filmmakers.[14] In works such as *Mosaik* (1954–1955) and *Schwechater* (1957–1958), ten years before the American avant-garde, Kubelka worked with "essential elements" of cinema—editing according to mathematical patterns of frames and reducing "image" to rhythms of light on the screen. One of his theoretical concepts was the "synch event": the meeting of sound and image that marked a moment or instant in time and experience.[15] His conception of cinema was as an audiovisual medium with the spectator as its experiential focal point.

Another of Kubelka's projects, which was never realized, was the construction of an "invisible cinema." This would be a "womblike, egg-shaped room. . . . Each seat would curve around the head of the spectator shutting off neighbors and heads in front. In this black box even the size and distance from the screen would have indeterminable dimension. For as long as the film were to last, it would be the world. It would be perfect."[16]

Within the history of avant-garde filmmaking, *Unsere Afrikareise* is something of an anomaly. What was an experimental filmmaker doing in Africa in the 1960s? The film seemed to be a critique of the safari that Kubelka was commissioned to shoot, but it lacked the political rhetoric of anticolonialism. From 1961 to 1966, Kubelka edited down three hours of film and fourteen hours of sound into a thirteen-minute film with an average shot length of four seconds. The film ostensibly continued Kubelka's ongoing project of metrical montage, distilling the essences of cinema into their most pure form. But it seems to have put an end to that project, as Kubelka has made only one short film (*Pause,* 1976) after what became known as his "African film." In 1972 one critic said of the film that Kubelka "asks us to make abstractions from what is conventionally less taken for abstract form."[17]

For a long time, viewers and critics did what Kubelka asked, but what if we no longer made these abstractions; what if we actually saw the German tourists with their guns and servants, the dead animals and the naked Africans? Kubelka's exercises in cinematic articulation and grammatical configuration are performed on imagery that in fact speaks loudly and strongly on the level of the shot alone. If he banished content completely in one of his earlier flicker films (*Arnulf Rainer,* 1960), it returns here with a vengeance, although the film offers no subtitles or explanatory voice-over. Kubelka's aim in *Unsere Afrikareise* was to "try to tear the emotions loose from the people, so that they would gain distance to their emotions, to their feelings." The images and sounds that he captured in Africa serve as the vehicles for emotions that Kubelka then tried to reduce to "mechanisms."[18]

To return to *Unsere Afrikareise* now, in light of postcolonial theory, is to understand Kubelka's project as a struggle between modernist aesthetics and the demands of documentary "content." If the modernist project can be understood as a discourse on the optical unconscious, as Rosalind Krauss has suggested,[19] in the cinema this structure is closely bound up with the regime of the visible and its various pleasures and

Still from *Unsere Afrikareise* (Peter Kubelka, 1966).

powers. The discourse of the avant-garde is one of subjectivity, and Kubelka enters the regime of visual knowledge as an artist, as a subject endeavoring to position himself within the technology of the gaze. His failure to locate himself displaces the spectator as well, and the most frightening thing about *Unsere Afrikareise* is the lack of a way in or out of the film.

The disappearance of subjectivity casts the cinematic gaze adrift in Africa without support and without release, forcing the viewer to confront the Other in all her nakedness and to meet her gaze. Although the film relies on montage and the aesthetics of collage for its effects, Kubelka uses travel footage that adds an "aura" of having been there. It is this "evidentiary" quality that it shares with pornography and ethnography, both of which imply the presence of the filmmaker at the scene. In *Unsere Afrikareise,* a pornographic gaze is distilled within the ethnographic spectacle, and in the process, a different relation to the Other is ironically produced.

I do not want to suggest that *Unsere Afrikareise* is a postcolonial solution to the problem of cultural representation, or an alternative form of either ethnography or pornography. Its systematic inversion of porno- and ethnotopias is articulated within an entirely different domain of cultural practice. In the art world of the American avant-garde that embraced Kubelka,[20] a different kind of mastery presides. Kubelka especially embodies the persona of the great modernist artist, with all of his musical analogies, the rigor of his practice, and his insistence that his films be viewed and reviewed until their patterns and purpose are fully understood.[21] Instead of a will to knowledge, a will to abstraction informs his excessive formalism that pits the filmmaker against "content."

The film was commissioned to be a mirror of sorts, by the Austrian hunters whom Kubelka accompanied to Africa, but it becomes a fun-house mirror, horrifically distorting their image. The montage is consistently marked by rifle shots on the soundtrack, extending the cause and effect of killing to other rhetorical transitions. The horror of the film is not only the merciless killing of wild game but the intercutting of this imagery with supplemental footage of Africans, many of them bare-breasted women. Match cuts equate, through substitution and metaphor, African bodies with the animal targets. Shots of the hunters looking through binoculars and telescopic rifle sights inscribe a voyeuristic *dispositif* within the film, and a voyeuristic gaze is equally implied in the footage itself, which is consistently marked by a depth of field and frames within frames. The hierarchy of vision is articulated as a system of victimization and cruelty, but it is also strategically reversed and turned back on itself. Instead of the "fishbowl realism" of the conventional scientific and erotic gaze,[22] every image becomes a potential target. This is especially true of the Austrians themselves. The hunters are almost always wearing dark glasses, or their eyes are hidden in shadow. They are figured as ideal voyeurs, masters of the panopticon of colonial vision, hidden within their apparatus of power. At the same time, though, they are blind. Glimpsed briefly naked, or eating, they are vulnerable to our gaze in a way in which the Africans are not. In fact, a recurring image in the film is of African women returning the gaze of the camera. One woman is repeatedly seen slowly turning her head, as if she were dancing, keeping her eyes steady. When she lowers her eyes, Kubelka cuts away.

Free of the scientism of ethnography, and outside the commercialism of pornography, the gaze in *Unsere Afrikareise* wanders into uncharted territory, only to be thwarted by a documentary realism that it is unable to control. In Kubelka's disturbing thirteen-minute film, the four features that Nichols understands as linking pornography and ethnog-

Still from *Unsere Afrikareise* (Peter Kubelka, 1966).

raphy are inverted.[23] The voyeuristic gaze is foregrounded, excess is indulged in, the profilmic event is constantly interrupted, and instead of expository or narrative realism, there is only the indexical realism of documented death. In this example of experimental ethnography, the strategies of containment systematically fail to work, and the scientific desire of the ethnographic gaze is distinctly eroticized.

Kubelka's desire to produce strong emotions in this film is realized through a discourse of excess, a refusal to "contain" the power of the spectacle. In the complete absence of voice-over or any other form of explanation, the imagery is radically decontextualized. The African people, most of whom have nothing to do with the safari, are in themselves excessive. That they are frequently naked or semidressed, moreover, links their supplementality to erotic forms of representation. The bodies of the Africans are consistently aestheticized, fetishized, and exoticized, while those of the whites are ugly, banal, and immobile.

Kubelka's highly rhetorical montage situates the eroticized and exoticized Other within a circuit of excess, linking a woman's nipple to the eye of a dead elephant. Shots of killing inscribe a discourse of penetration linked metaphorically to the overdetermined apparatus of vision. An image of a giraffe's hindquarters, extracted from a sequence of butchering and intercut with a woman working, further eroticizes the gaze. Brief shots of hunters mounted on horses and camels, framed squarely from behind, may be ironic, as so much of the film is, but they complete a kind of circle in which eye, gun, ass, and target are caught up in what Deleuze and Guattari have named "a desiring machine."[24]

Indeed, the film exemplifies the "cutting into" and the breaking down that characterizes the desiring machine. Pornography and ethnography share a concern with empirical realism invested in the display of technique and detail, but this film's montage guarantees that no detailed display of specific practices or techniques will unfold. We get so many glimpses of the practices associated with big game hunting, but always incomplete, always interrupted and fragmented. Likewise, with the Africans' activities of working and traveling, none are developed fully enough to constitute knowledge about them. Regional differences are completely obfuscated by mixing shots of Egypt randomly with footage shot in the Sudan.

Despite the consistent transgression of the codes of empirical realism, *Unsere Afrikareise* is nevertheless grounded in an indexical form of representation. Its realism is guaranteed by the representation of death. The animals that are killed in the film constitute the film's most "mechanical" appeal to the emotions. Vivian Sobchack has claimed that death in documentary constitutes an ethical space where the viewer's humanist gaze is necessarily inscribed.[25] If such a view is produced by this film, it is complicated by the spectacularization of the animal deaths. Indexicality here is inexorably drawn into sacrifice, violence, and transgression, as the gaze is never innocent, but totally implicated in the machinery of desire. The eyes of dead animals mark the total breakdown of the machine that nevertheless continues to "mechanically reproduce" its horrible imagery.

The scopophilic desire inscribed in *Unsere Afrikareise* locates its guilt in a historical, rather than a transcendental, subject. It is fed by death as the sign of history, the performative sign of irreversible transformation. History is also signified by the musical selections on the soundtrack, which includes British dance hall music, fragments of the score from *Around the World in Eighty Days,* Egyptian tango, and sixties radio pop music. Many of the Africans are dressed in the colonial uniform of the safari suit, complicit in their own oppression, but all of these representations are drawn into a machine of history, an irreversible trajectory propelled by the punctuating gunshots. It is an obscene history insofar as the viewer is a witness to death;[26] it becomes the motor of the desire of the film.

Consecutive images from *Unsere Afrikareise*
(Peter Kubelka, 1966).

Unsere Afrikareise expels the expository and narrative realism on
which ethnography and pornography depend. In eliminating such devices of containment and control altogether, the film produces a desire
for the subject position that it leaves empty. It denies the colonialist
subject of perception but cannot differentiate between desire for the
Other's gaze and desire for the Other. The desire for some kind of mastery of vision is evoked by the parodic fragments of narrativity, for example, by cutting from a shot of a white man shaking an African's hand
to a zebra's foreleg shaking while being butchered. All representational
codification is stripped down to its linguistic base; shots, sequences, and

sounds become language units, arranged in strategic configurations of repetition, juxtaposition, and contiguity.

The irony of the film is that it is not at all governed by formal patterns of montage, but by its "content," which speaks nothing if not the cinematic language of melodrama. Each image is highly coded, culturally and stylistically. Numerous shots of interactions between the Europeans and the Africans, such as those of boys supporting white men's rifles on their shoulders, are symbolically loaded. As a comparative ethnography of Europe and Africa, it depicts an economy of repression, but one that equally implies a utopian transcendence of colonialism through pastoral primitivism.

Despite its evacuation of subjectivity, *Unsere Afrikareise* is exemplary in many ways of modernist anthropology. The Africans' premodernity serves as a ground for the figuration of the degeneracy of Western so-called civilization. A trope familiar from Conrad and Lévi-Strauss, here it is further informed by a later-twentieth-century image of the return of the repressed African. And yet this repression and its pastoral redemption remain locked into the desiring machine of visual pleasure in which the primitive "pure" African is feminized, and the assimilated "fallen" African is masculinized. The film evokes *Heart of Darkness* with the hunter-tourists found repeatedly traveling on a boat up a river, but Africans and whites are all overexposed, seen clearly and distinctly in relations of empowerment and subjugation.

Kubelka draws the ethnographic body—the exotic/erotic body of otherness—into the "frenzy of the visible," on ontological premises.[27] In a *Film Culture* interview, he describes his desire for spectacle in what he calls his most "naturalistic" film: "I want a big screen for it so you can see the blood and the elephants and the women and the Negro flesh and all the landscapes."[28] Within his ontology of the cinema, these are the signs of visibility, images that are pre-aesthetic. In *Unsere Afrikareise,* African people are the signifiers of ethnographic film, of another film that exists only on the margins, or the cutting room floor of the avant-garde film. Metonymically linked to the spectacle of nature, they are allegories for the purity of form to which the modernist avant-garde aspired.

The film is ultimately a body without organs, rendered wholly unproductive, antiproductive in terms of both ethnographic knowledge and erotic pleasure. The flow of the film, stimulated by the emotional mechanisms, produces only the detritus of desire: the traces of guilt without a legible morality. The last two images of the film juxtapose the woman and the phallus, white and black, Europe and Africa, without naming their relation. A long shot of a peasant woman walking in a wintry northern landscape is crosscut with a close-up of a naked African man walking through dense vegetation. The sequence states a sudden reversal of the feminized African and masculinized European, and the reversal suddenly makes the relation of gender and race completely arbitrary. Over these images, a male voice says in accented English, "I would like to go to your country, if I get chance." However, the bleakness of the West ironically turns the desire of the African against itself, and back to the pastoral allegory of the primitive.

Kubelka has suggested that all film is really only a series of stills, meaning frames, and that film is not movement at all. "It's between frames that cinema speaks."[29] And yet *Unsere Afrikareise* contains a great deal of motion in front of the camera, and of the camera. Equally important to the impact of the film is the soundtrack, which functions chiefly ironically, matching clips of music, fragments of German dialogue, and laughter disynchronously with the image track. The "synch events" are moments of shock, in which the gunshot or the fragment of music is suddenly matched with the image, cutting through time and making it stop. When the eyes of dead animals stare back from the image, Benjamin's words about the barbarism of history ring true. If "a historical materialist cannot do without the notion of a present which is not a transition, but in which time stands still and has come to a stop," *Unsere Afrikareise* is a film that "brushes history against the grain"[30] and turns its documentary practice into a document of barbarism precisely by breaking down representation to its most deadly techniques. The death of the animals is turned back at the panopticonic gaze as a challenge to an apparatus of representation that has the power to redeem, and the power to kill.

Kubelka claims that in Africa he found the ecstatic potential of synch events reproduced in ritual practices. The coordination of drumbeats with the sunset and dancing bodies was an experience he sought to capture in cinema, but not as image, or as re-presentation. "The cinematographic ecstasy" was for him a formal possibility of the cinema, a means of achieving an Other experience, another reality beyond "the laws of nature."[31] No possession rituals are included in *Unsere Afrikareise;* he hoped that the audiovisual montage itself would produce an experience for the viewer that would convey the ultimate synch event of the native ritual. That the effect is deeply disturbing rather than transcendent is testimony to the different subject effects available to the European cameraman and the African dancer. As Benjamin predicted, with the cinema, the shock effect of technology displaces ritual,[32] and Kubelka graphically reproduces the emotional charge of cultural collision, not as "loss" but as a materialist praxis. The film thus embodies and exemplifies the contradictory conflation of modernist anthropology and aesthetics that is at the heart of experimental ethnography.

The title "Our Trip to Africa" may provide two final clues to the effect and significance of this anomalous film. In the first place, it is a travel film, and Kubelka may be understood as a belated traveler, through whose discourse the transformation of Orientalist knowledge might be traced. Ali Behdad has analyzed the discourses of belated travelers of the nineteenth century—Flaubert, Nerval, Eberhardt, and others—who came after the authentic Orient had been subsumed by colonialism. The Orient for them is no longer an object to be dominated, but one to be desired.[33]

With the traveling *cinematographe* of the Lumière brothers, this conflicted desire is fully technologized. The dispersed subjectivity of *Unsere Afrikareise*—one that is only approximately aligned with the techniques of vision, desire, and violence—is that of the traveler who tries to find himself in the Other, identifying at once with marginality and with the colonial gaze. To position Kubelka's film within the monolith of Orientalism[34] is not to discredit the masterpiece of film art that it is but to recognize its language as one not only of film but of postcolonial representation.

The trip to Africa is, finally, denoted as "ours." The ethnographer, hunter, pornographer, traveler, filmmaker, and Orientalist is designated as white and as male. The viewer struggles within and against this position, and it is in this slippage of subjectivity, which is only an either-or alternative, that the desiring machine enacts its power and its impotence. In attempting to reduce "content" to what he believed were its essential features of naturalness and emotion, Kubelka's concern with film language remains a function of his own ethnographic (white, European, male) specificity.

The film encounters the Other within a postcolonial landscape in which the cinema is completely implicated. Kubelka's belatedness is registered most significantly in his inability to shoot a film. He could not make the film he was commissioned to make, and editing his footage and sound recordings over and over again for six years only took him closer to the guilty secret of the cinema's optical unconscious. The film does not simply offer up that secret, though. It historicizes it within a postcolonial discourse in which the African body is seductive, but also mortal. Inscribing a resistance within the formalist project, the ethnographic Other—in her primitivist mode, and also in his mode of assimilation—belongs to a discourse of history.

Reading against the grain of Kubelka's text, reading its other, post-colonial language, the African body and the African gaze are freed of the disciplinary restraints of ethnography. By bringing pornography and ethnography into dangerous alignment, the limits of the visible are brought into relief. This film was made at the same time as European intellectual thought was turning to the elaboration of structures of language, representation, and power. In the early 1960s, both sexual liberation and anthropological humanism were also emergent as modern discourses of representation. *Unsere Afrikareise* accesses their repressed content, but only ironically, suggesting that it is too late to free otherness from its inscription in film language. The colonization of the cinema's optical unconscious is signified by the woman's body, caught in the frame. Her gaze, however, signifies an elsewhere, an alternative regime to that of the visible.

Microcultural Incidents at Ten Zoos: The Master Viewer

Ray Birdwhistell's 1969 film is by no means an "avant-garde" text, but neither is it a conventional ethnographic film; Birdwhistell himself describes it as an experimental film.[35] If we look at it from outside its original context of behavioral psychology (kinesics), if we look at it *as film, Microcultural Incidents* throws the gaze into relief. Seen as a commentary on the gaze, the film demonstrates the proximity of the ethnographic and zoological looks. A hidden camera watches people watch animals in zoos. The film was shot silently, and the soundtrack consists of Birdwhistell's lecture delivered in an auditorium while the film is running on an analytical projector (the type used in film studies classes for detailed shot analyses). The soundtrack thus includes directions to the projectionist to slow down, rewind, and freeze-frame,[36] along with directions to the student-audience to "look at" various aspects of the image. Birdwhistell also occasionally tells us what he thinks people in the film might be saying (anticipating the crude comedy of *America's Funniest Home Videos*).

The supplementary status of the soundtrack as lecture recalls Buñuel, and indeed there is a strong surrealist flavor to the film, but in this case, the ironies are supplied entirely by the film viewer who does not identify with Birdwhistell's students and refuses their submissive interpellation. Such a resistant viewing position is not hard to take up. For film students, the film tends to evoke a combination of hilarity and outrage as the difficulty of using people's images in a scientific experiment is made evident. Birdwhistell's strategies are not only transparent; they are cruelly insensitive, and his choice of the zoo as a site to study family dynamics as they differ across cultures only works against him. It is more, in other words, than a "bad film"; it forces some fundamental problems of ethnographic representation into view.

Birdwhistell's voice-over is enthusiastic, reveling in the discovery of a wonderful new tool for social research. Echoing the nineteenth-century experiments in scientific observation, he even calls his technique of watching loops and freeze-frames a "perceptiscope." His footage is very similar to that of the avant-garde of 1969: the low-grade production values, the reflexivity, the home-movie aesthetic, the play with the projection process, and interference with the image itself are all familiar techniques used by experimental filmmakers.[37] His faith in filmic realism as an epistemology is, however, closer to the instructional and educational films of the 1950s and 1960s.

The zoo is intended to function in *Microcultural Incidents* as a control situation, the idea being that Birdwhistell can observe the behavior of individuals in family groups in ten different cultures, with the zoo serving as a constant reference point. In India, both systems of passive zoo-going observation and nuclear family patterns appear to break down. Birdwhistell says, "This whole India thing has to be looked at in a different way than I'm capable of," and moves on quickly to the next country. His comment abruptly betrays the limitations of his behaviorist method and his ignorance of the cultural contexts of his "microcultural incidents."

Despite the initial conceit of anticipated cultural differences in zoo going, one theme emerges by the end of the twenty-minute film: that most people aren't really all that interested in the animals. They are apparently distracted and preoccupied, often with their families. Birdwhistell describes many instances of "non-directed vision" as being like "watching TV." In the United States, he notes people yawning and looking away; in India and the United States, people just walk past without

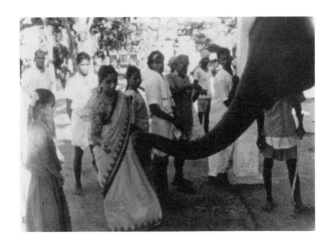

Stills from *Microcultural Incidents at Ten Zoos* (Ray Bird-whistell, 1969): India (*top*) and Italy (*bottom*).

stopping to look at the animals; and yet part of the problem in India, he notes, is the difficulty in analyzing eye contact. This may well be because the elephants are not in cages, and all he has to work with is a crowd. He does find a tourist in India who does look at something off-frame, which provides Birdwhistell with an image of the gaze that he cannot otherwise locate.

Although the study is ostensibly about bodies and body language, it is in fact an embodied gaze that we are asked to look at. Not surprisingly, the body becomes sexualized in Birdwhistell's voyeuristic

Zoology, Pornography, Ethnography **137**

discourse. Two particular scenes in *Microcultural Incidents* betray the nature of Birdwhistell's fascination. In Rome, first of all, we are told to watch how everyone feeds themselves along with the animals; and then, in Birdwhistell's stream of consciousness monologue, he stops at a woman who, for once, is *not* necessarily a mother but may be a nurse-maid (presumably because she is younger and better dressed than the other women in the film). She feeds the elephant by making it catch her peanuts, an interaction with the animals that, we are told, "only happens in Italy." When one of the kids does the same thing, Birdwhistell rewinds to show "the beautiful pelvic thrust" with which the woman rewards the boy. The audience laughs, and Birdwhistell asks the projectionist to go back "to pick up one more pelvic thrust."

In the last scene, taken at the Philadelphia Zoo, a little girl leans against her father's chest to get his attention. Birdwhistell rewinds and freeze-frames on this image of intimacy, but the point he makes to his audience is not an analysis of the behavior, which he says is self-evident, but that with one such loop of film, it is possible to fill an entire day's classroom time. Like the Italian "pelvic thrust," this scene is repeated several times, and the two instances emerge as privileged spectacles in the film. Their vaguely sexual implications remain unaddressed as behavior and are transformed into decontextualized images removed from their referents, a surprising manifestation of a cinema of attractions.

Birdwhistell's commentary on the people's behavior is descriptive and strangely (for a "scientific" film) subjective. He remarks on "the very great beauty" of the scene of the Italian woman, which is why he "kept it in." Unlike the reflexivity of filmmakers such as David and Judith McDougall, Birdwhistell draws attention to the filmmaking process and apparatus, not to temper or qualify his realistic representation of reality, but to amplify his own authority as the master viewer. Like *Las Hurdes,* the distance between image and narration in *Microcultural Incidents* reveals an enormous cultural divide — between the intellectual and "the people," the man and "the family," filmmaker and referent, self and other. The implicit analogy between the camera's frame and the zoo animal's cages renders this divide particularly disturbing. Because they are never directly gazed at by the camera, but are always mediated by the gaze of the multicultural families, the animals function as a kind of endpoint in a chain of looks, setting up an order of difference inscribed in the gaze itself, separating man from beast, and consciousness (the scientist) from body (the people filmed).

Families from different cultures are represented as virtual species in Birdwhistell's traveling zoo; individuals are subjected to the casual gaze of the onlooker like zoo animals—unable to hide and unable to challenge their imprisonment. The discourse of kinesics (body language) is especially invasive, as Birdwhistell attempts to deduce psychological states from outward movements. Such a critique is, arguably, a result of the film's decontextualization, but even as an example of kinesics, Birdwhistell has already ventured into the disciplinary field of anthropology. The experimental gaze becomes undisciplined in this film, which is not to say that it is "wild," or even that it is "unethical" (which it is), but that the look at the Other is stripped down to the naked stare of a technology.

The disinterested gaze of so many of the zoo goers and the different patterns of behavior that Birdwhistell observes in Asia undermine the dominant role of the gaze in the film, which is to observe. When the Japanese family have their photo taken in front of the elephant cage, we are clearly in another domain of visual culture, and it disturbs Birdwhistell again: "The scene was almost too stereotypical to keep it in." Typicality apparently breaks down when it becomes cliché. And in India, there are very few behavior patterns that he can "see," so the scenes that he includes—of a family mounting an elephant, for example—are simply images of families that fit into Birdwhistell's larger pattern of international zoo going.

Microcultural Incidents points to the ways in which ethnography is in constant danger of making individual social actors mere examples of larger social patterns.[38] Birdwhistell's casual indifference to the people in his film circumvents the humanist strategies that had informed ethnography since *Nanook* and reduces people to objects under a microscope. As an "experimental film" (but not an avant-garde film), *Microcultural Incidents* demonstrates the parallels between the disciplinary gaze of the cinema and that of zoology. The zoological gaze exercises a form of epistemological control in which the Other can be observed in an unthreatening "experimental" situation. Birdwhistell's analysis of the image constitutes a frenzied attempt to penetrate the visual scene for the "truths" of subjectivities that he himself admits to being unprepared to know anything about.

The year 1969 is also when Desmond Morris's book *The Human Zoo* was published. Morris's argument is that human nature needs to be studied along the model of caged animals because modern, urban, industrial society has brought about many "unnatural" forms of behavior. Many of our basic animal instincts have become dangerous to us, primary among them the sexual instinct, which Morris describes as having mutated into a plethora of supersexual functions that he describes in some detail. He advocates a return to the " 'village-community' feeling of social identity" as a means of escaping the monkey house.[39] Throughout his book, which became a popular best-seller, along with his previous book *The Naked Ape*, Morris deploys phrases suggesting a global overview of humanity: as seen by a Martian, or seen from the air, or seen as a map. Although what he criticizes as the cages of modern urban culture is precisely the "disciplinary society" analyzed by Foucault, Morris's own technique is fully implicated in the disciplinary technology of panopticonic vision. Like *Multicultural Incidents,* Morris's book ventures into ethnographic paradigms, in this case, the pastoral structure of "primitive society" as a pure society. *The Human Zoo* is another example of how social science in the 1960s turned to the zoo as an experimental model in which the gaze is a fundamental structural component, founding visual knowledge on the construction of otherness.

Simba: Exploitation Cinema

Martin and Osa Johnson's safari film of 1928 might stand in for the film that Peter Kubelka could not or would not make. Produced on the threshold of talking films, a few years earlier than the release of *Las Hurdes, Simba* is one of the last of the adventure films of the silent period.[40] In these popular "factual films," heroic filmmakers penetrate the wildernesses of the world, collecting footage of exotic sights of peoples, landscapes, and animals. The Johnsons were among the most prolific traveling filmmakers of the silent period, having started out on the vaudeville lecture circuit in 1910. Martin had traveled with Jack London, and they had made their name with film footage of so-called cannibals in the South Seas.[41] By the late 1920s, they were popular Americans, closely associated with the sensational adventure-travel genre, which was one of the remaining manifestations of the cinema of attractions of an earlier period. The genre did not survive the transition to sound.[42]

In the 1930s, the travel-adventure premise was integrated with fantasy narratives in films such as *King Kong* (1933) and *She* (1935).

The full title, *Simba, The King of Beasts, A Saga of the African Veldt*, announces the travel-adventure combination of documentary material and heroic narrative drama. The Johnsons' exploitation-entertainment context was even more explicit than Curtis's or Flaherty's, and they claimed no scientific authority whatsoever. The opening titles of *Simba* make the filmmakers' objectives very clear:

The ensuing picture "Simba" is the high mark of attainment in the cinematographic recording of adventures in Africa — the classic land of mystery, thrills and darksome savage drama through all the days of history.

The pages of African annals are bright with the names of Livingstone, Stanley, DuChaillu, Akeley, Roosevelt and Rainey, and now Martin and Osa Johnson by this film record unfold a triumph that is both a sequel and a climax.

This dramatic record of sheer reality comes to you as a presentation of the true Africa, largely without the invading presence of the white man, made at a cost of tireless patience, endless courage, privation and perils, thirst and fevers on 15,000 miles of wild safaris.

You will see thrills without end . . .

As a film about filmmaking, *Simba* displays a reflexivity that serves to champion the camera as a device of penetration, ethnography, aestheticization, and industrialization. Cinematography is poised as the climax of an era, and the triumph of a realist aesthetic. The Johnsons' film announces the advent of modernity in the African jungle and the beginning of the end of a history of savagery. Teasing apart the various levels of representation in *Simba* and its discourses of colonialism, gender, hunting, and the gaze is to get at some of the contradictions that informed the adventure-travel genre.

Simba was produced under the auspices of the American Museum of Natural History. Carl Akeley, the taxidermist-cum-scientist, initiator of the Great African Hall and its spectacular dioramas, had experimented with cinema himself, and he had the museum set up a private corporation to fund the Johnsons' African travels. As Donna Haraway puts it: "The 'naked eye' science advocated by the American Museum perfectly suited the camera, ultimately superior to the gun for the possession, production, preservation, consumption, surveillance, appreciation, and control of nature."[43] The inclusion of Africans with animals as another form of wildlife—a feature of the Johnsons' films and of the museum's dioramas—was fully consistent with the eugenics theories that were held by the museum's president A. P. Osborne. The theoretical superiority of the white race, designed to protect class interests in a rapidly changing North America, insisted on a proximity of blacks to animals. The Johnsons are quoted as having planned a film on "African babies" showing "elephant babies, zebra babies, giraffe babies, and black babies." [44] Thus, *Simba*, a film ostensibly about lions, incorporates the crudest form of American racism, which it awkwardly maps onto "ethnographic" footage.

Osa and Martin Johnson shot the material for *Simba* from 1924 to 1927 in Kenya and Tanzania and released sound and silent versions in 1928. The sound version had a prologue of Martin and Osa "in formal evening wear standing in an elegant living room," [45] an image straight out of a 1920s Hollywood dramatic picture. This synchronized passage and one other—of Frank Munn singing "Song of Safari"—were followed by the silent footage accompanied by a musical score. [46] Although *Simba* has never had a voice-over commentary, the title cards written by Terry Ramsaye and illustrated with painted scenes supply an ideologically loaded "voice" to the film. In 1992 Milestone released a version on video without the Hollywood prologue, and with a soundtrack of African music composed by James Makubuya. Like the soundtrack of *In the Land of the War Canoes,* the African music, including some singing and chanting, is a means of reappropriation that counters the overt colonialism of the image track. It begins the work of prying apart the film's discursive contradictions and reveals the deep fissures of the text.

Although *Simba* was the first film for which Osa Johnson shared credit with her husband as codirector, she is in front of the camera far more often than he is. She is seen hunting with the Africans, waving from a car as it is ferried (by Africans) across a river, training an African cameraman, and posing in her field-camp tent. In addition to these "everyday activities" of life on safari, Osa figures prominently in each of three spectacular animal charges. As Martin films, Osa stands ready with rifle in hand and appears to kill an elephant, a rhino, and a lion before they attack the film crew. In fact, the shots of Osa and those of the charging animals are edited together in suspenseful crosscutting, and Osa and the animals are rarely pictured together in one shot. Her close-ups are fleeting, but her image is the real support for the dramatic effect of the film. Although the intertitles are written mainly in the plural "we"

Still from *Simba, The King of Beasts* (Martin and Osa Johnson, 1928). Osa with George Eastman and an African assistant.

Video image of still from *Simba, The King of Beasts* (Martin and Osa Johnson, 1928). An intertitle before this image says, "Just a little black flapper."

(except for one that says "Osa screamed"), they seem to represent her voice because of her greater screen presence. In contrast with the Hollywood dramatic conventions of endangerment and rescue, in *Simba* the woman appears repeatedly to save herself and her husband.

Osa, who looks a little like the contemporary movie star Clara Bow, is indeed the image of the "modern woman," wearing pants, living a rough life, and appearing on-screen and off as an equal partner with her husband. The last shot of *Simba*, however, defeats this image and redomesticates Osa. After she has apparently killed the last rampaging lion, she is seen surrounded by Lumbwa warriors laughing and chatting about the successful hunt. And then an abrupt cut finds her making pie outside her tent surrounded by African women. It is an awkward but powerful form of narrative closure, curtailing the threat of the independent white woman among "the savages" and recasting her as the American housewife, colonial figure of civilizing goodness.

Osa among the Africans situates their blackness and her femininity as "overvisible," exemplifying the way that both bodies function in the language of silent film as a naturalized opposition of gender and race. As Mary Ann Doane says of *Birth of a Nation*, the white woman "is simply there, undisguised, *naturally* symbolic of all that the white man struggles to safeguard—white purity, white culture, whiteness itself." [47] To maintain the symbolic system, Osa cannot be a great white hunter; it is her body, not her eye, that is technologized in this system. Back in the kitchen making apple pie, her role is that of the great domesticator, even as she herself is domesticated.

Doane argues that the polarization in colonial culture of race and gender entails an invisibility of the black woman. "She has no other." [48] In *Simba*, when the Johnsons visit a Lumbwa village, a group of figures appear covered in heavy leather veils over their entire heads and bodies, with tiny eyeholes poked in them. Title cards explain that this group is "a consignment of wives" for the king, and they are covered "to conceal their fatal beauty." In addition to this very literal invisibility, other African women in the film are the butts of crude racist jokes inscribed on Ramsaye's title cards, most of which betray contemporary American anxieties about modern women. Titles about young girls posing in native costume include: "Just a little black flapper," and "the short skirt movement has gone about as far as possible." An elderly woman smoking a pipe is described as having worn her hair short for years, but "has recently taken up smoking." These sight gags adapted from Hollywood comedy and vaudeville incorporate the women's bodies into a familiar language, thereby containing their threatening visibility. Lacking a discourse of anthropological knowledge and control, the language of popular culture serves the filmmakers' purpose. Osa's maid is even seen applying white powder to her face in an attempt to "cover up" her visibility.

In her analysis of the American Museum of Natural History's collection project of the 1920s, Donna Haraway points out that the study of natural science was closely tied into public education and public health. "Decadence was the threat against which exhibition, conservation, and eugenics were all directed as prophylaxis for an endangered body politic." [49] Thus, in *Simba,* the black woman is denaturalized and rendered a cultural object — to be traded, packaged, laughed at, and scorned — while the black man is a token of "Man's" organic connection with the natural world. The African women become the sign of a decadent and dangerous sexuality, of the disorder that the film and its sponsors needed to contain. Osa herself veers toward such a danger, and the African women serve to displace any anxiety provoked by her role.

The threats posed by the rapidly changing modern world were met by the museum's Great White Men with a rhetoric of natural order. The safaris into the heart of Africa, of which *Simba* was the most fully developed narrative representation, not only were encounters with wild beasts but "proved" the racial superiority of the hunters over "primitives." The role of Africans in *Simba* is instrumental to the cultural project that the film was intended to fill.

The Africans are positioned within a Darwinian hierarchy with the intertitle "Here was the age-old story of Man emerging from savagery." The Africans *are* history, representatives of the childhood of (white) man's history. Sharing a watering hole with the animals, they are positioned as a halfway point between men and animals, providing an organic link that motivates the "camera-hunters" to shoot pictures rather than bullets. In the end, pictures just aren't enough, though. The mandate of conservation meant that the killing of animals needed to be justified, and so a narrative premise of saving a local village from marauding lions is devised to uphold the camera-gun paradigm. It also casts the whites as "protectors" of the Africans, a necessary part of the logic of colonial imperialism. The transition from taxidermy to cinematography still evidently needed corpses as the final guarantee of realism.

The film camera functions in *Simba* not simply as a recorder but also as a means of provoking the scene of wildness. To get the "greatest animal photography ever seen," Martin and Osa appear to get "too close" to the animals, which is why Osa has to defend Martin as he madly cranks away at the camera. The camera is thus a simulacrum of the gun (in fact, the Akeley camera that the Johnsons used was designed with a panoramic device modeled on the machine gun). As a representation of reality, the cinema replaced taxidermy, a practice that Haraway describes as "a craft of remembering."[50] Cinematic realism is, in contrast, immediate and eternal, eradicating the sense of loss that informed the conservationist project. In *Simba* the cinematic image is punctuated by painted pictures on illustrated title cards that evoke pastoral African scenes. Each segment has its own little scenic marker, including pictures of Africans, the different animals, and an African village. The painted images refer to scenes that existed *prior* to the representation. The organic (premodern) medium of painting sits awkwardly with the film footage, but it indicates that in 1928 the transition from gun to camera marked not only a loss of a way of life but the loss of the sense of loss that naturalized that way of life.

One sequence in particular indicates the way that the modernity of *Simba* is pitched against a very different order of representation. Early in the film, a title says that "we set a trap camera with flash lamps to register the lions which prowled about camp at night." A shot of the camera is followed by the illustrated title card that accompanies this sequence—a painted picture of a movie camera on a tripod in tall grass. An intertitle saying, "With a zebra as bait we secured a beautiful lioness" is followed by black leader, a white flash, and a still photo of a lion looking at the camera standing over a zebra's body. Two more shots of the lion, alternating with the title cards, complete this sequence.[51]

Martin Johnson's photos of the lion and the zebra are in fact stunning images, capturing the shock of the moment in which the zoo has traveled to the wilderness. The zebra's body is fixed, dead, as image while the lion's impenetrable gaze registers the unknowability of the Other, her wildness still intact, but barely. In contrast with these photographs, the illustration of the camera in the field, like the other painted scenes in the film, is of an entirely different order of representation. The gaze is absent. The images are oblique, romantic, and stylized, pointing to an idea of Africa that vanishes under the camera's gaze.

Linking the flash of the camera-trap with the pastoral image of Africa, the cinema announces a great leap from natural culture to image cul-

Photograph by Martin Johnson, reproduced in *Simba, The King of Beasts* (Martin and Osa Johnson, 1928). *Courtesy of Martin and Osa Johnson Safari Museum.*

ture. In image culture, the Other cannot be so easily fixed historically, as part of a "great story," of which the present is always the end. The camera's gaze represents that end, that terminus, as a single fleeting moment, and there is the Other looking back in that same moment, that same present. Benjamin's notion of historical materialism as a blasting open of the "once upon a time" of historicism is embedded in the "lightning flash" of the dialectical image.[52] Through photography, the inevitable "progress" of teleological modernity might be interrupted. In *Simba* we can glimpse the tensions between two competing historiographies: the narrative of human evolution, and the temporal fragmentation of discrete moments in time.

The producers of *Simba* may have been interested, simply, in bringing the best images of Africa to the American public. Their motives were a combination of economic and educational enterprises. Their sexism and racism may have been built on the foundations of their class, but in the many contradictions and discursive collisions of the film, those

Zoology, Pornography, Ethnography **147**

foundations can be seen to be crumbling. It is not enough, simply, to show moving pictures of animals. The contextualization of those images within a gendered colonial culture and a mix of representational media demonstrate the full scope of the ideological project. The safari becomes an apparatus and a technology in *Simba,* and it becomes so because of the film camera, which has not yet mastered the tricks of invisibility or humility. Seen again, to the tune of African drumming and singing, the film becomes a documentary not about animals but about the representational system of colonialism that makes itself legible as a sign of its own demise.

Hide and Seek: Looking for Lesbians

The last film that I want to discuss in the context of the various disciplines of the gaze takes up themes of sexuality, zoology, and education from the perspective the 1990s avant-garde and "queer cinema."[53] Gay and lesbian filmmaking, by people such as Marlon Riggs, Pratibha Parmar, Richard Fung, Sadie Benning, and others, is often preoccupied with the representation and organization of the gaze. To think of queer filmmaking as ethnographic is to recognize the problem of representation as one of self-representation, in which the self is socially as well as sexually configured. Gay and lesbian filmmaking is frequently about "culture": gay, straight, or more narrowly defined by a specific ethnic or cultural scene. The marginality of gay culture is perceived ethnographically, but from the inside, and thus provides a model of indigenous ethnography. The look at the Other is necessarily inverted as "the other's look" to become part of the film's aesthetic and epistemology.

American experimental filmmaker Su Friedrich's film *Hide and Seek* might be described as an experimental documentary about adolescent lesbian identity. It combines three different orders of representation that are woven into a one-hour black-and-white film: a dramatic, scripted narrative about a twelve-year-old girl named Lu who struggles with her sexual identity in the context of her female classmates; interviews with adult lesbians, mainly about their childhood memories; and a range of found footage and still photographs, including clips from *Simba* and 1960s sex-education films.

Like much of Friedrich's work, *Hide and Seek* privileges "content" far more than is common in American experimental filmmaking. She works from the idea of the personal film, through autobiography, to articulate "identity" as a cultural construction that is nevertheless embedded in experience. Experimental techniques are deployed as means of personal expression, but equally as means of questioning issues of representation. The representation of lesbians and the articulation of a lesbian look is often downplayed in Friedrich's work, and unlike most filmmakers identified with queer cinema, it is often incidental and even overlooked by many critics.[54] In *Hide and Seek,* she appropriates the disciplinary gaze for her own purposes to explore the various ways of seeing lesbians *and* to represent ways of seeing as a lesbian.

The only hint of an autobiographical aspect to this film is a message scratched onto the film itself in Friedrich's signature style, a technique that she adapted from Stan Brakhage and uses most extensively in *Gently down the Stream* (1981): when Lu hears that her teacher is getting married, the inserted message "I'm never getting married" doubles as the character's and the filmmaker's thoughts as Lu goes to the blackboard. This is not the only inscription of a subjective, psychological space in the film, but it does jump out, especially in contrast to the exercise that Lu proceeds to complete in the classroom: diagramming the grammar structure of sentences. It is significant that Friedrich inscribes herself in this way, in the collapse of the image and the representational apparatus. Unlike Kubelka (or Bill Viola), it is not *her* look that is in question in this film, but a look, a way of looking at, and with, lesbians.

In her use of the *Simba* footage and instructional documentaries, Friedrich adopts a series of different gazes to evoke the experience of an ethnographic subject. Early in the film, several interviewees discuss the "nature-nurture" question, or the "gene theory" of homosexuality. Although most of the women respond that it makes little difference to them, and that they no longer need an explanation for their sexual orientation, it is significant to the film's negotiation of "scientific" and experiential modes of representation. Friedrich inserts a few shots of monkeys and chimps, along with shots of young girls, into this discussion, indicating the way that the nature-nurture discussion places lesbians in the role of monkeys to be studied.

Instead of a scientific explanation, Friedrich inscribes a discourse of desire as a representation of lesbian identity, the causes of which remain a mystery. One of the last confessional voices that is heard in the film, as a voice-over while Lu and her friends visit the zoo, says, "I went through a period of time to try to find the lesbian bits and then realized that that wasn't a narrative I could really impose on those years, 'cause

Still from *The Ape and the Child,* by G. Stoelting, as used in *Hide and Seek* (Su Friedrich, 1996).

Still from *Hide and Seek* (Su Friedrich, 1996). The girls watch a film called *Social Sex Attitudes in Adolescence.*

those years were more about . . . well, especially when I was twelve to eighteen, just holding it together. Or realizing . . . that I was moving through this whole world that I wasn't a part of." The imposition of a narrative is indeed a form of explanation, one that is frequently used in ethnography. This interviewee points out that experience doesn't work that way. It is more contingent, and more about survival. *Hide and Seek* takes up these themes of science and experience (and marginalization) as modes of visual representation and visual culture.

While the interviews, such as the one quoted in the foregoing paragraph, belong to a documentary aesthetic of realism and confessional discourse, Friedrich (like Moffatt and Gaitan) resorts to a fictional mode to dramatize the experience of adolescent lesbianism. The correspondences between the interviews and the dramatic material cast the latter as a form of illustration. When Lu and her friends watch a sex-ed film in class, the relation between Friedrich's footage and the found instructional material becomes clear. Friedrich's adolescent actors are endearing but "stiff," like those in the films they watch; their scenes are likewise written bluntly, almost as if Friedrich is appropriating the style of the educational documentary for her own aesthetic. Moreover, a receding effect of cultural positioning is created through a *mise en abyme* of spectatorship. In a classroom scene, for example, Lu and her friends hear the familiar male voice-over explain, "At about twelve and a half Mary reached puberty. At around this time her friends wanted to talk about sex."

The struggle of understanding one's sexual identity is one of social construction, or of seeing oneself in the "big picture," a struggle that is cast in this film as one of spectatorship and documentary address. *Hide and Seek* borrows its voice-over narration, in fragments, from educational films, and also from the lesbian interviewees. In one hilarious sequence, Friedrich substitutes one form of voice-over for the other. An educational film about "emotional behavior" (shades of Birdwhistell) begins with a man and a woman sitting facing the camera. The set is sparse and lablike. The male voice-over says, "You will see these two people react to stories that they have been prepared to accept as real happenings," and a title announces the first sample story involving Pain. As one of Friedrich's interviewees starts talking about the "bull dykes" at her school as a child, the two people on-screen begin to grimace in disgust. In this sight gag, Friedrich laughs at the epistemological naïveté of the educational film while highlighting the incongruity of gay culture and "straight" culture.

This brief critique of the aesthetics of visual knowledge helps to establish Friedrich's own use of fictional narrative as a viable documentary form. The dramatic footage illustrates many of the experiences recalled by the women: crushes on gym teachers, the ambiguities of friendships, tomboy looks and behavior, learning about sex, learning about one's own body. Although Lu is the "main character" of the narrative, her psychological profile is developed within what might be described as "girl's culture." Slumber parties and party games, little fortune-telling games, pop songs, tree houses, and jealousies constitute a set of ritualistic behaviors that characterize this culture.

In *Hide and Seek,* adolescence and puberty are privileged not as a loss of innocence but as an acquisition of identity. The lack of identity experienced in childhood, before sex, is inscribed within the film through still photos of young girls. Dozens of portraits and snapshots, which are not necessarily linked to the interviewees, are intercut throughout the film, increasing toward the end. Like home movies, many of these images are heavily coded within the frame of the family. It is not clear who these images are of, or whether they are photos of children who grew up to be gay, although the surrounding discourse suggests that possibility. By leaving the identity of each one open, and unfixed, the photo of the child figures as a blueprint of the adult; but unlike a genetic theory of sexuality, it is not deterministic. Insofar as the still image plays a metaphysical role in film, these photos are in another sense cinematic blueprints. They have a contingent aspect, a sense of possibility that is linked not to death but to fulfillment. Indeed, the adult lesbian interviewees project a strong sense of confidence, self-knowledge, good humor, and integrity, in great contrast to the awkwardness of the girls in the photos and the girls in the narrative.

Between these two poles of childhood and adulthood, the problem of understanding one's body, one's sexuality, and one's desires is depicted as a problem of identity. As one of the interviewees says, "I didn't identify with what I was." Friedrich's inclusion of women and girls of color incorporates a heterogeneous sense of identity, which emerges as a process of self-imaging, rather than one of stereotyping. Identity may be linked to the gaze, but it is much more complex than the Lacanian mirror stage might suggest; that is, it is not simply a formal construction. In *Hide and Seek,* the gaze operates as a form of projection and desire, linking the possibility of being seen to the act of seeing. By way of the look at animals, it is also a means of locating otherness in visual culture and opens up a place for lesbian identity within a specifically cinematic space.

In addition to the shots of monkeys at the beginning of the film, animals appear as a means of signifying Lu's inarticulate desires. She goes to see a movie with her best friend Betsey, pausing at a poster for "My Life with the Lions," which turns out to be *Simba*.[55] Friedrich uses clips of animals running through forests and plains, along with shots of Osa Johnson cranking the camera and holding a rifle. She also incorporates title cards indicating the narrative format of the movie. In the midst of the collage of excerpts is a shot of Lu at home cutting images of animals out of a book and sticking them on her wall. Later in the film, while listening to her older sister argue with her mother about dating, Lu "dreams" of more clips from *Simba,* this time including images of Africans. These images become a kind of fantastic escape for Lu, continuing as daydream images while she is alone in her tree house.

The climactic scene of *Hide and Seek* takes place at the zoo, where Lu and Betsey and another friend named Maureen have gone for the afternoon. Lu is intensely jealous of Betsey's friendship with "prissy" Maureen, and Lu tells Betsey of her hope that the two of them could go to Africa together. Betsey says it is too far away (her dream is to get married and live next door to Lu), and she goes off to the snack bar with Maureen, leaving Lu alone watching a pacing lionness. Lu's fantasy of Africa, linked to the imagery of Osa Johnson, is a scene of lesbian desire that Friedrich designs by situating Lu as a spectator — of *Simba* and of the zoo animals. Lu is also seen as a spectator of sex-ed films, but the zoological gaze is privileged as a more appropriate index of her lesbian subjectivity and identity. Because Friedrich's clips include images of Africans as well as the Johnsons and the animals, Lu can be said to identify not with the image but with the ethnographic/zoological gaze and the inscription of Osa and an African camera operator at its point of origin.

While the inscription of lesbian subjectivity has been discussed and theorized in the context of narrative film, most notably by Teresa de Lauretis,[56] *Hide and Seek* extends that construction into the domain of ethnography. The images of Africans from *Simba* evoke a generic discourse of ethnography that is taken up in the film's examination of lesbian adolescence as a cultural site. De Lauretis's argument against

Still from *Hide and Seek* (Su Friedrich, 1996). *Left to right:*
Kirsten Orial, Apryl Wynter, Ariel Mara, Ashley Ferrante,
Chels Holland (Lu).

"positive images" of lesbians insists on the articulation of the conditions
of visibility in lesbian filmmaking. It is not enough to substitute lesbian
content or images into structures of seeing and desire borrowed from
the mainstream, because lesbian fantasy has a fundamentally different
structure, which de Lauretis describes as a conjunction of autoerotism
and female object-choice.[57] A fantasy figure such as Osa Johnson might
thus appeal to the young Lu as both role model and love object; and for
the spectator of *Hide and Seek,* Lu herself is an object and identity that
is configured differently, but not as the Other.

   In the invocation of cinema as daydream in the context of a film
"about" lesbians, *Hide and Seek* suggests the terms of a different orientation of the ethnographic gaze. The look at animals in *Simba* becomes
the projection of a desire for escape and a symbol of marginality in
Friedrich's appropriation. The trip to the zoo is a reality-check for Lu,
who comes to understand her own social construction as a form of ex-
clusion from the pop world of "dream lovers." And yet the last scene of
the film prolongs an earlier one of the dreamlike utopian aspect of girl's
culture: the girls dance together to pop music at a slumber party, their
bodies much looser than their acting, as if Friedrich could finally see

her actors as girls and watch them through the lens of "the gaze" without it becoming a form of knowledge.

The transparency of this final scene is worked for through a thorough deconstruction of the ethnographic gaze. It is not coincidental that Friedrich takes us through the realms of both sex and animals in her exploration of the terms of visibility. The problems of invisibility, which queer cinema has tackled from any number of different angles, are not unrelated to the "overvisibility" of ethnographic conventions of representation. "Being seen" is unequivocally linked to "subjective vision," as the title of the conference and book *How Do I Look?* (in which de Lauretis's article is included) suggests. Any revision of, or experimentation with, the ethnographic gaze must also come to terms with the tripartite structure of the gaze as a triangulation of looks between spectator, filmmaker, and person filmed. *Hide and Seek* deploys the gaze as both dream and knowledge, thus blurring the desires to see, to know, and to possess.

From Vision to Visibility

Ethnography, like zoology and pornography, tends to assume a particular orientation toward the gaze to establish and maintain a relationship between viewer and viewed. Mixing genres of film practices and disciplines of seeing is a means of upsetting these conventional relationships. In keeping with Foucault's theorization of power as that which "comes from below," the gaze is a structure that produces its own forms of resistances. The panopticon generates a discourse of delinquency just as the sexual confession generates "perversities." Foucault says of the discourse of criminality in the nineteenth-century popular press, "Through all these minute disciplines it is ultimately 'civilization' as a whole that is rejected and 'wildness' that emerges."[58]

The "other look" of the avant-garde takes up the ethnographic gaze but looks beside it as well, enabling a view of the disciplinary gaze of the cinema alongside the "wildness," or excess that evades its frame. The educational film, exemplified by *Microcultural Incidents* and deconstructed by Friedrich in *Hide and Seek,* appropriates the gaze as an instrument of pedagogy and social control. Personal film also assumes a certain relation to the gaze as the terrain of an individual's vision. This convention is equally subverted by the undisciplined gazes of *Hide and Seek* and *Unsere Afrikareise,* and in the structural films of the next chapter. Seeing is not believing but a means of making visible, as the rhetoric of discovery in *Simba* makes evident. If the ethnographic gaze conventionally lies somewhere between the cage of the zoological frame and the peephole of the pornographer's desire, these films pose the question of the viewer. Once the subject of vision is destabilized and fragmented, the gaze is transformed into a new way of knowing. The gaze is both a structure of vision and a condition of visibility, and its disciplinarity is always tenuous.

7 Framing People: Structural Film Revisited

Structural/materialist film has no *place* for the look, ceaselessly displaced, outphased, a problem of *seeing;* it is anti-voyeuristic.

— STEPHEN HEATH, *Questions of Cinema*

The unmotivated (Warholian) camera confronts two pulsating materialities, two bodies; one is the character's cinematic body, the other the body of the spectator.

— IVONE MARGULIES, *Nothing Happens: Chantal Akerman's Hyperrealist Everyday*

In the previous chapters, we have encountered structural cinema in a number of different guises. The affinities of the avant-garde and "primitive cinema" tend to revolve around structural film, as does the articulation of the gaze as a disciplinary technology. While this subgenre of experimental film may be perceived as the most extreme form of avant-gardist minimalism, medium specificity, and art for art's sake, it may also be an important form of experimental ethnography. In this chapter, I want to look at structural film from its margins, to look at its earliest inscription in Warhol's pre-1966 films; at the way it is used by Chantal Akerman, David Rimmer, Joyce Wieland, and James Benning; and its manifestation as video in the work of Bill Viola. Structural film should emerge from these readings as a realist aesthetic that is quite unlike the narrative and documentary realisms that inform most ethnographic cinema.

As the two epigraphs at the head of this chapter indicate, structural film is about looking, and in many cases, about looking at people. Produced within the context of the art world, its tendency toward documentation is antidocumentary, but not nondocumentary. Many structural films operate as experiments in seeing. Sometimes "nothing" is seen (in flicker films, for example); but sometimes the scene is inhabited, and in these instances, the film looks at itself looking at others. My objective is neither to expand the category "structural film" nor to challenge its aesthetic program (even if these things follow from the ensuing analyses). Because "content" is not insignificant in many structural films, they enable an analysis of the cinematic gaze as an embodied technology. On the margins of the structural film canon, the films to be discussed here test the definition and push the limits of the form as it was originally theorized.

The term "structural film" was introduced by P. Adams Sitney in a *Film Culture* article in 1969[1] and institutionalized as a chapter in his seminal book *Visionary Film* in 1974. Sitney used the term to designate a group of films in which "shape is the primal impression of the film. . . . what content it has is minimal and subsidiary to the outline." The filmmakers that he chose to represent this tendency were Michael Snow, George Landow, Hollis Frampton, Paul Sharits, Tony Conrad, Ernie Gehr, and Joyce Wieland, of whom Snow was labeled "the dean." Structural film had four characteristics, not all of which needed to be present for a film to be considered a member of the group. These were "fixed camera position (fixed from the viewer's perspective), the flicker effect, loop printing and rephotography off the screen."[2]

The fixed frame is perhaps most distinctive of this filmmaking practice because it registers the imposition of a form onto reality. A frame that has its own autonomy acquires the integrity of a picture frame limiting the view to a strict economy of inside and outside. Inside, there is composition and detail; outside there is an unknown space that is never filled in. The fixed frame represents the intentionality of phenomenological consciousness, but it equally determines the limits of the visible and the knowable. The fixed frame points to the subject of perception, and also to the four sides of the frame, beyond which is the continuity of the real as defined by the discontinuity of the frame.

The theorization of structural film as a radical mode of film practice was taken up by the British filmmaker-theoreticians Peter Gidal and Malcolm Le Grice in their *Structural Film Anthology* (1976) and *Abstract Film and Beyond* (1977) respectively.[3] Drawing on a Brechtian rhetoric of anti-illusionism and Althusserian Marxism, Gidal and Le Grice cast structural film as both "materialist" and "minimalist." They privileged the real-time aesthetic, in which the time of viewing would be equal to the time of shooting, as a means of subverting illusionist codes of montage. Duration, and the reflexive attention to the materiality of the medium, were understood as anti-idealist techniques, and outside the meaning-production mechanisms of dominant ideology. In foregrounding the technology and the process of film, this mode of practice was essentially a mode of knowledge. For Gidal, the proximity of theory and practice was so close that structural film could be considered "theory" (15).

Structural film developed in the avant-garde as a kind of parallel practice to the structuralism that informed apparatus theory in the 1970s. Most commentators deny any relation between the two, and yet both structuralisms entailed a theorization of cinema as an instrument of bourgeois ideology. Sitney, whose discursive frame remained that of romantic American poetics, understood structural film as an unmediated representation of consciousness, "a cinema actively engaged in generating metaphors for the viewing, or rather the perceiving, experience."[4] Both American and British theorists, like apparatus theorists, assumed an analogy between camera and consciousness. The transcendental ego of philosophical phenomenology became the "I" of the viewer/camera/ideological subject. In structural-materialist film, however, the look was supposedly unsutured by narrative and was therefore outside ideology.

Only one writer has taken the Gidal–Le Grice theorization of structural film to task for its idealist critique of idealism. In 1977 Constance Penley pointed to the parallels between apparatus theory and structural-materialist film, arguing that the latter fetishized the viewing process and effectively recentered the subject as the "pure" subject of vision.[5] Far from freeing the spectator from the technology of the gaze, structural-materialist film, according to Penley, secured an identification of the viewer as transcendental subject. Narrativity and illusionism may be negated, but the desire invested in looking is not.

However, insofar as the gaze is linked to a specifically aesthetic practice, the desiring subject is not necessarily abstract. The metaphoric inscription of a window in many of the films (as frames within the frame, or as the surface plane of the image) marks a divide between two spaces, situating the seeing subject in a material relation to the profilmic. Penley's critique may be pertinent to those structural-materialist films that reduced the visual field to the rhythmic flicker of light — which, as she points out, enacts an oscillating presence-absence of the film itself. But when the image attains the status of content, when it "signifies," the seeing subject may be more appropriately described as an observer. As Paul Arthur has argued, structural film denotes a "trajectory in the American [*sic*] avant-garde canon since the late fifties [that] has been the promotion of a dialogue between optical engagement and redefinition of the viewing experience in terms of object and spectator."[6]

Once structural film is rethought as a technique of observation, it may be distinguished from the camera obscura model of spectatorship. Strategies of duration in Warhol's earliest films were specifically designed to challenge the spectator's passivity. One cannot help but be aware of one's own body in the theater as one watches a man sleeping for six hours (*Sleep*, 1963); to leave the theater during the projection is perhaps the epitome of the embodied viewer. Structural-materialist film may thus be an exemplary instance of the inscription of an embodied point of view: precisely the type of observer who emerged in turn-of-the-century actualities. Jonathan Crary describes the new kind of observer who, he argues, came to replace the camera obscura viewer in the mid–nineteenth century:

The body which had been a neutral or invisible term in vision now was the thickness from which knowledge of vision was derived. This opacity or carnal density of the observer loomed so suddenly into view that its full consequences and effects could not be immediately realized. But it was this ongoing articulation of vision as nonveridical, as lodged in the body, that was a *condition of possibility* both for the artistic experimentation of modernism and for new forms of domination, of what Foucault calls the "technologies of individuals."[7]

The voyeuristic seeing subject did not disappear with the emergence of this new type of observer. It became, in Crary's words, "a myth that vision was incorporeal, veridical, and 'realistic'" (34). Structural film often alludes to this myth but puts it in brackets by extending its materialism to a materiality and corporeality of the observer as artist and spectator. In the work of Warhol, Akerman, and others, the voyeuristic gaze is evoked as a mode of representation, not as a disciplinary technology. The question of who is looking, and why, is placed up front, as the question of the gaze is consistently framed as the making of an image. By rendering the "window on the world" a surface image, an image without depth, the observer — filmmaker and spectator — can always catch him- or herself watching. But this effect is only created when there is something or someone to be seen.

As a film practice in which one watches oneself watching, structural film situated itself outside history, abstracting the act of perception from the act of seeing. For Le Grice, this further entailed an elimination of any index of sexual difference, as the image of woman renders the gaze (according to 1970s feminist theory) carnal.[8] Film as film, film referring only to film, engendered a minimalism that brought it into alignment with Greenbergian modernism; thus structural film became somewhat entrenched as a high point of experimentation in the cinema, bringing film into the realm of a high modernism associated with the plastic arts.[9]

In its most refined forms, both theoretically and filmically, structural film made itself redundant to the society of the spectacle, cultivating a "noninstrumentality" that relegated it to an obscure corner of the art world. David James has pointed out that its political stance was one of noncommodification, intervening in the "language wars" of the 1960s by emptying film language of its capacity to make meaning. In the structural film's "sustained marginality" and "resistance to consumer society," "the only permissible knowledge was the knowledge of its own production."[10] Because this "knowledge" constituted a deconstruction and analysis of the alignment of cinema and consciousness, it is worth returning to now, in the interests of understanding the dynamics of visual culture. If we can strip away the polemics that surrounded its production, and pay more attention to its impurities, structural film may provide some insight into the interface of the avant-garde and ethnographic cinemas. It might be recognized as a realist cinema.

Rather than being circumscribed by its own history, structural film needs to be positioned within a larger history of representation and visual culture. Stephen Heath's interest in the "disunity" and "disjunction" of the spectator is, like Penley's, based in the parallels between structural film and apparatus theory, although for Heath the materialism of structural film deconstructs the latter, by evacuating that central space of the transcendental ego.[11] The fetishization of the apparatus is, in Heath's reading, still based in the mechanics of desire, although they fail to confirm the mastery of reality necessary to narrative illusionism. Clearly, structural film is the site of a very specific form of cinematic realism, a foregrounding of the role of the viewing subject in nonnarrative cinema. It is this aspect that is especially relevant to problems of ethnographic representation.

The images that provide the support for structural filmmaking are often "documentary" images (which is not to say that they are not "fictional").[12] Because the temporality of structural film tended to refer back to itself, as form, it eliminated any sense of narrative space[13] and frequently entailed a temporality determined by the profilmic. In its durational aesthetic, "nothing happens" in the film because "nothing happens" in the quotidian realm of the referent.

In theory, most structural filmmakers were in search of "pure cinema" and attributed a specificity to the cinematic gaze that failed to account for that which was gazed at, the profilmic, which lies outside the system. Neither apparatus theory nor structural filmmakers were prepared to account for documentary representation, despite the clear parallels between the viewing apparatus of the cinema and the phenomenology of scientific observation.[14] And yet signification is not easily repressed. In practice, structural filmmaking varied quite widely, even during its heyday in the early 1970s.[15] The filmmakers discussed in this chapter allow "content" to return, to leak into the field of vision, putting three bodies into play: the body filmed, the embodied viewer/artist/filmmaker, and the body of the film itself.

Revisiting structural film in light of postmodern ethnography is a means of suggesting what the negative dialectics of a very formalist type of modernism might contribute to problems of social representation. In the utopian drive to eliminate representation itself from the cinema, the structuralist-materialist project was precisely that which Stephen Tyler advocates for postmodern ethnography: to make "no break between describing and what is being described."[16] To eliminate perspective in the cinema entails a dissociation of the look and the gaze, which is one of the effects of the fetishization of the apparatus that occurs in structural film. The image in this cinema becomes a dialectical site at which the repressed social content (history, the trace of the real) is negated by the very fetishization of the gaze as an allegory of looking. It thus enacts a critical negation that potentially brings form and social theory into dialogue[17] to produce a new theory of cinematic realism.

Chantal Akerman: The Seer Seen

Chantal Akerman stands out as a filmmaker who has been able to develop a unique style from a number of aesthetic histories, a style that addresses cultural and historical questions of representation through aesthetic and formal means.[18] Structural film is one of many techniques on which she has drawn, and she has incorporated its effects into both fiction and documentary texts. Judith Mayne has argued that Akerman is one of several women filmmakers who invoke "primitive" cinema for purposes of narrative revisionism.[19] The problem of "the subject" is, for Akerman, always the seeing subject, and her primitivism constitutes a transformation of structural film aesthetics into an ethnographic gaze.

The two films most relevant to the present discussion of experimental ethnography are *News from Home* (1976) and *D'Est* (1993). The more recent film, which was shot in Eastern Europe as a "document" of a moment in history, or a geography of social change, is perhaps the closest Akerman has come to an ethnographic project. Her camera, almost consistently mounted on moving vehicles, passes the faces of people waiting for trains, waiting in lines, waiting for the camera to pass by. Akerman lingers on the returned gazes, making her invisible presence felt and marking it as foreign. In both this film and *News from Home*, the spectator understands absolutely that the people who are seen are looking at a strange sight: A woman with a camera? A small crew with a lot of equipment? Because the reverse shot is consistently repressed, the gaze is represented in these films as a space, a distance between one body and another, reproduced as a kind of untraversable void.

Although the returned look is a staple of reflexive film aesthetics, in most ethnographic films, it is a brief and fleeting challenge to the film's transparency. In Akerman's films, the returned look is persistent and inquisitive, putting her on trial even in her invisibility. In fact, it becomes a sign of that invisibility, decentering the film and destabilizing the apparatus of vision. By putting the fixed stare in motion, and evoking the aesthetic of travel, her undisciplined gaze becomes very familiar to anyone who has looked out the window of a moving train or car at bystanders — at people who are suddenly rendered marginal to one's own narrative. This is the space occupied by Akerman's authorial signature, the space of observing, looking out at others from an interiority that is just outside, at the margins of the visual field.

D'Est is extraordinarily slow and darkly lit, extending the structural

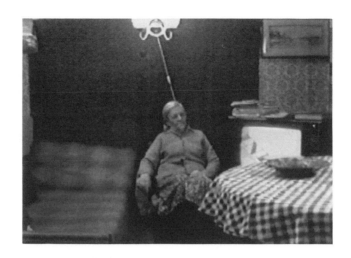

Stills from Chantal Akerman's *D'Est* (1993). *Courtesy of Walker Art Center.*

film aesthetic into a melancholic depiction of people in transit. Their activities of waiting for trains take on a symbolic meaning, as their lack of direction, and the lack of direction of the film itself, is situated very specifically at the point of collapse of the Soviet Union and the open-endedness of Eastern European history. Cultural change is imminent, but not yet evident. The camera moves in slow lateral pans, a fixed movement that registers Akerman's own movement across this landscape, although she betrays no investment in the scene.[20] The consistency of the frame is all that unites the various locations and angles and spaces in the film. Although it is a sound film, Akerman has not added a voice-over and uses only fragments of cello music. The ambient sound of the profilmic is often audible, but the silence of waiting is almost overwhelming. It is a film without any repetitions, moving ever forward, through, and across "the east" simply to see who is there. The occasional forays into apartments are unmotivated and unexplained and retain the fixed-frame format as we watch people sit in their apartments. Akerman frames these interiors like boxes and poses people beside TVs that are turned on but not watched.

The three aspects of structural film that inform the ethnography of *D'Est* are the fixed frame, the durational temporality, and the detail. Akerman's imagery is the essence of the banal, the mundane, and the ordinary, which makes the framing itself an event. People's faces are viewed like landscape. From the slow pans across crowds, portraits emerge and fade away. She offers the viewer glimpses into another world, but the glimpses are fleeting and unconnected. Each shot is a tableau, contained within one long take, a moving picture. In both *D'Est* and *News from Home,* "the public" becomes an object of scrutiny as individuals surface in the crowd, and the crowd itself is part of the specific architectures in which it is seen. The films become historical records by accident rather than by intention.

The voyeuristic gaze is undoubtedly evoked in *D'Est.* Indeed, it is indulged in, although it has been suggested by at least one critic that Akerman elicits a "love and respect" for her subjects similar to that which she gives to Delphine Seyrig as Jeanne Dielmann in the film of that name. Michael Tarantino quotes Akerman on *Jeanne Dielmann:* "The camera was not voyeuristic in the commercial way because you always knew where I was. You know, it wasn't shot through the keyhole."[21] A long, steady 360-degree pan in the middle of a busy train station in *D'Est* points to the filmmaker as the pivot and the center, but

Video image of still from Chantal Akerman's *News from Home* (1976).

is the viewer's position so easily articulated? Is the spectator also at the center of the space? In the end, it is hard to eliminate the keyhole effect of cinematic spectatorship because the viewer in the theater is always absent from the scene, detached from the profilmic, looking in. The closest one can come is to see *beside* the voyeuristic gaze, to see another way of seeing, which is Akerman's, and to be split between identification with the embodied camera as spectacle and with the invisibility of the viewer outside the scene.

One moment in *News from Home* crystallizes the dynamic tension in Akerman's documentary shooting style between passive and active seeing, between the visible and invisible camera, between observation and inquisition. The camera is set up in a New York subway car, facing down the length of the car, symmetrically framed. Some passengers glance quizzically at the camera, but most ignore it as they casually enter and exit the car (and the frame). One man, dressed in yellow, stares intently at the camera, and then, apparently annoyed, turns and walks through to the next car, into the vanishing point of the image and its multiple frames within frames. The film continues to roll, and life goes on for a few more minutes in the subway car before Akerman finally cuts away.

This scene stands out partly because of the passivity of most of the other people whom Akerman stares at in this film. Two images previous to this one linger on individuals simply sitting on chairs on the street, doing absolutely nothing except passing the time. They either don't see the camera because it is hidden, or have been instructed not to "see" it, or—most shockingly—don't care. The man in yellow does care and even seems threatened by the presence of the camera. On the subway, the camera is very literally a trap, and the passengers cannot escape its gaze; and yet it is nothing but an aesthetic trap, a frame waiting to be filled. Its look is benign and passive until it is challenged. Thus Akerman sets up a contest over the gaze and its powers, the stakes of which are not the ethnographic subject, but her own subjectivity as origin of the gaze.

News from Home is a city film, a structural film, and also a kind of "woman's film"—a discursive struggle between a daughter and a mother. On the soundtrack, Akerman reads the letters her mother has sent her from Belgium. She reads them quickly, monotonously, in heavily accented English, rendering her mother's discourse obsessive and slightly pathetic. The "news" consists of local gossip, money problems, medical ailments, and requests for letters. The repressed hysteria of the letters is displaced onto the overloud traffic and subway sounds that occasionally overwhelm the monologue. Akerman "quotes" her mother's small-town old-world speech, turning it into a discursive voice that she resists by appropriating and translating into her own voice. The letters also mark the image track as an attempt on Akerman's part to reposition herself, to literally find herself in New York.

Akerman herself is never seen (although there are a few brief reflections of Babette Mangolte behind the camera), but neither is she a "fly on the wall." The camera angles are almost consistently at 90 degrees to the city, set up in the middle of streets and subway cars, looking perpendicularly at subway platforms and sidewalks, and looking sideways from moving cars. Occasional pans of 45 or 90 degrees, or even 360 degrees, are the only camera movements, and they simply exaggerate the gridlike aspect of the representation of New York. These viewing positions are not familiar or casual but excessively formalized. The color correction makes each image more perfect than an ordinary documentary shot. In every way, Akerman's use of structural film techniques creates the sense of imposing a view onto the city, perhaps that of a newcomer with a map, orienting herself according to intersections.

Ivone Margulies has described Akerman's aesthetics as "hyperrealist," meaning that her realism is always at one remove. In *D'Est* and *News from Home*, this includes an allegorizing of the gaze, largely by means of structural film techniques. "In the passage from untroubled realism to uncanny hyperrealism, a principal device for the filmmaker is extended duration. Hyperreality is attained through a fake impression of depth, the excess of detail resulting from the fixed stare. At the core of the defamiliarizing hyperrealist image, of its simulacrum effect, lies the hesitation between the literal and symbolic registers." [22] The effect of this hyperrealism in the ethnographic terrain of *D'Est* and *News from Home* is to render the "other" oddly theatrical. The frame becomes a proscenium, the subway and train platforms stages. The minimalist aesthetic renders the other not "knowable" but merely referential, a double of the image, prior to the film. Margulies describes this mode of looking as "unmotivated," which is to say unintentional, upsetting the phenomenology of perception by inserting an intermediary stage of the image as a recording technology. Akerman describes *D'Est* as "bordering on fiction":[23] the sign of the border refers to geographical and political borders, the borders of the frame, and the border between indexical and symbolic orders of signification. All these edges become margins in these films, filled out as rich areas of the in-between.

News from Home may also be described as a diary film in which Akerman's images evoke her experience of New York in counterpoint to her mother's expectations. As in the work of Jonas Mekas, another European "finding himself" through film in New York, it is the practice of filmmaking itself that enables Akerman to articulate her subjectivity in transit between two worlds. One of the many things that her mother does not understand about her is the kind of marginal filmmaking in which she is involved. Moreover, as a European newly arrived in America, Akerman's gaze is a revision of the colonial gaze of discovery. African Americans are prominent in the film as the objects of her fixed stare, and yet it is Akerman herself, in her radical absence, who is the real object of the film. The recipient of the loving letters, she disperses her positionality as filmmaker, daughter, and European émigré. She is in New York, but not a New Yorker, and so it is the distance between her and the others, inscribed in the camera's gaze, that the image points to.

In the remarkable final shot of *News from Home,* the camera is set up on the back of a ferry pulling out into New York harbor. As the city slips into the distance, it becomes a fortress, mysterious once again, and the idea of "home" remains problematic. As the shot lingers for almost ten minutes, with only the sounds of engine, water, and gulls, the time passing is a time of forgetting. Throughout the film, long periods of silence between letters create an increasing sense of distance, a distance that is finally visualized in the widening gap between the camera and the receding city. In *D'Est* also, the slowness of the film enacts a time of forgetting, of the impossibility of memory. In the installation version of *D'Est*, Akerman has included references to that other time of transit in Eastern Europe, "old images of evacuation, of people with packages marching in the snow toward an unknown place." [24] If Akerman's privileged public sites are "images of transit," [25] in *News from Home*, it is her own transit that is evoked, and in *D'Est* it is an epic movement of people in history.

News from Home was made almost at the height of the structural film movement, and yet with the supplementary intertext of Akerman's mother's letters, it is an "impure" example of the minimalist style. The content of the letters is the minutiae of everyday life, precisely the stuff of ethnography. As in Akerman's better-known film *Jeanne Dielmann 23 Quai de Commerce, 1080 Bruxelles* (1975), the marginal world of women's household work is narrated. The structural-minimalism consists of an ethnographic gaze that goes both ways, insisting on a slippage between subjects as bodies, embodying the voyeur as a body in space. The image as allegory of reality, as a hyperrealist image, detaches subject and object, viewer and viewed, from any contract with truth, evidence, or authenticity: people perform themselves. Nevertheless, the extended duration of Akerman's shots inscribe a present tense that overrides any sense of ethnographic or mythic time. Nothing is lost in her relentless inscription of the present tense.[26] The uncanniness of these two films is precisely the troubling difficulty of meaningfulness in ethnographic representation—the tension between the literal and the symbolic, the indexical and the abstract, that occurs in the transposition of reality into image.

The Warholian Gaze

Although most critics agree that Warhol lies behind the structural film aesthetic, his own work had become quite different by the late 1960s when Snow, Frampton, and Gehr took up the minimalist form. By 1967 Warhol had begun to lose interest in film and had ceded directorial control to Paul Morrissey, who redirected the Warhol Factory into feature filmmaking. For most of the 1970s, Warhol's earliest films were withheld from circulation by Warhol himself and only became fully available after his death in 1987. Although he may have inaugurated an "ontology of the viewing experience," [27] Warhol's own disinterest qualified the inclusion of his films in the avant-garde canon. His unique approach to his status as artist is not, of course, unrelated to the ethnographic aspect of his structural filmmaking.

From 1963 to 1965, Warhol's films were made by simply letting the camera roll. Without montage, camera movement, or sound, each shot was at first 100 feet long, and then in 1964, with the purchase of an Auricon camera, 400 feet long. Most shots included the reel-end markings, indicating the lack of intervention in the straightforward recording of complete fragments of reality. Films such as *Sleep* (1963), which was six hours, and *Empire* (1964), at eight hours, were infamous for their tedium but in fact misrepresent the erotic content of most of the early work.

Tom Waugh has argued that Warhol's minimalist aesthetic owes as much to the underground gay porn industry as to high modernism.[28] Indeed, in the renewed interest in Warhol's queer aesthetics, he emerges as an ethnographer of a particular subculture — one that was obsessed with exhibitionism, stardom, and theatricality. The structural film aesthetic in Warhol's early films consists of a playful tension between performance and voyeurism. As a realist aesthetic, it is mediated with a high degree of artifice, as Warhol's performers double themselves as movie stars. Among the "essential properties" of the medium as Warhol conceived it is spectatorship; the fixed stare in his cinema often becomes a challenge to the viewer. The gaze becomes a conduit between viewer and viewed in which exhibitionism and voyeurism are diffused in a tedious test of endurance as the sexual spectacle is rendered banal in real time.

I want to pause at two of Warhol's early films, a silent one from 1963 — *Kiss* — and a sound one from 1965 — *Beauty #2* — in order to further explore the realist aesthetic of structural film. Keeping in mind that Warhol made eighteen films from 1963 to 1964, and twenty-six in 1965,[29] these two films are intended as exemplary of this body of work, including its contradictions and its diversity.[30] Their status as experimental ethnography may be fairly oblique, and yet they both demonstrate ways in which the avant-garde ventured into questions of visual knowledge. *Kiss* is a virtual example of a comparative ethnography; *Beauty #2* is an experiment with representation as encounter and interrogation.

Kiss was the first of Warhol's films to be publicly screened, and it was originally shown as a serial. Each segment, featuring a long, drawn-out kiss, was shown at Filmmaker's Co-op to open the evening's screen-

Still from Andy Warhol's *Kiss* (1963). *Copyright 1989*
The Estate and Foundation of Andy Warhol.

ing of avant-garde films. Subsequently edited together, the film runs
fifty minutes. From the most "primitive" period of Warhol's film career,
Kiss was modeled on the Edison film *Kiss of May Irvin and John C.
Rice* (1896), which scandalized audiences and announced the potential
of cinema to corrupt public morals. Warhol's return to the cinema of
attractions may have been motivated by economics and facility ("the
easiest way to make a film"), but his choice of subject matter demonstrates some insight into the dynamics of the gaze in this stripped-down
form of cinema.

Each of the twelve couples in *Kiss* perform a slight variation on the
theme of kissing, from their actual physical technique, to their position,
to their various levels of intensity and passion. Two of the couples are
gay men, two are interracial, and several of the kissers reappear kissing other partners. Most are shot in tight close-up, but in one case, the
camera moves out in a zoom from a gay male couple to reveal their
writhing bodies on a sofa. With the exception of this shot, the kissing
remains very tame, kept mainly in close-up, in an endless prelude of
repetitive anticipation. At about three minutes per shot/scene, the performers sometimes struggle to fill the real time, marking the limits of
documentary authenticity with signs of the theatrical.[31]

Kiss is exemplary of Warhol's ability to extract the theatrical from
the real. Like Akerman's use of the structural aesthetic, in *Kiss* docu-

mentary and fiction merge in the same frame, and any means of distinguishing between the two is eradicated. Fiction becomes documentary, and documentary becomes fiction. For both filmmakers, the Other is trapped in the frame, but if for Akerman that frame is a picture frame, for Warhol it is the studio and the film factory that contain his subjects and transform them into images. As a play with the representation of the couple, *Kiss* reveals the artifice of sexuality while indulging in and prolonging the Hollywood climax free of its narrative props. At the same time, the film becomes a documentary of a promiscuous culture, naturalizing bisexuality, homosexuality, and interracial sexuality within the conventions of the cinematic kiss. If it were not for the absence of a lesbian couple, the film would even adhere to contemporary principles of inclusivity.

One composition that is repeated in several different shots features a woman with her head thrown back and a man leaning over her. The film thus betrays a residue of cultural codification from the mainstream. Despite his attempt to neutralize the gaze, and deauthorize the subject of vision, Warhol's gaze is a gendered gaze. The return to early cinema, or "cinema degree zero," enables Warhol to rethink representation as a form of observation that can never be "pure." Even if the gaze itself could be rendered completely neutral, the framing and the long takes alone constitute a form of desire.

Sexual titillation, the excitement of the spectacle, is rendered empty and boring in its extended duration; and yet, as in many of Warhol's "primitive" films (e.g., *Blow Job* [1963] and *Eat* [1963]), the carnality and orality of the image emphasizes its distance from the spectator. The desire to see becomes fused with tactile pleasures unavailable to the spectator. Paul Arthur argues that the detached stare works as a "relay in the hyperawareness of our own corporality, as if in compensation for what is withheld. . . . By simultaneously reducing, fragmenting, and attenuating the field of action — the body in space — Warhol enforces our active recognition of sensory absence as he relentlessly exploits its representation. Deprived of a comforting charade of fictional involvement, the appeal to certain bodily sensations becomes almost pornographically direct."[32]

The gender codes that inform *Kiss* are foregrounded in *Beauty #2*, a film that situates Warhol within the cinema of cruelty by means, precisely, of a carnal gaze. By 1965, when Warhol made *Beauty #2*, he was working with 1,200-foot rolls of film and sync sound. The film consists of two thirty-five-minute shots, each from the same static camera setup featuring Edie Sedgwick and Gino Piserchio on a big double bed. Chuck Wein, who is credited as writer and assistant director, can be heard speaking to Edie from just outside the right side of the frame. Edie, in her underwear, is spotlit in the middle of the bed with Gino mainly behind her, so that she is centered within a network of three gazes: Gino, her would-be lover; Wein, who demands her attention constantly; and the camera, for which she primps and poses.

As Edie and Gino play with the various props of lovemaking — sipping drinks, lighting and smoking cigarettes — they gradually begin kissing and petting. Meanwhile Wein and Edie maintain a strained yet playful dialogue that includes a certain amount of reflexive commentary on the film itself: "What is a voyeur?" "What is real?" and a pun on the word "board/bored." The camera and anyone behind it (probably Gerard Malanga) [33] are ignored, except for Edie's care to be always in the best light. She seems to play the dumb blonde Marilyn Monroe type, partly in response to Wein's line of questioning. He assumes the position of the analyst, probing the naive starlet for some depth of personality, which she flirtatiously denies or protects. The camera certainly abets her narcissism, as does Gino's desiring on-screen gaze. For both Edie and Wein, Gino is just a body, as neither pay much attention to what he says. A dog named Horse wanders into the frame occasionally, alluding to the drugs that may or may not also be at work in the scene.

A number of tensions and contradictions are put into play in this film. Edie seems to be taken advantage of, and yet she also exhibits a certain control over the image by virtue of the spectacle of her body. The situation has clearly been scripted, and yet there is a great deal of improvisation: Gino and Edie's behavior seems to be exactly in keeping with the amount of alcohol they consume, thus grounding the real-time aesthetic in the profilmic event. The fixed stare of the camera determines the boundaries of on-screen and off-screen space, controlling what is to be seen (and not seen); and yet it is extremely passive, uninvolved in the scene itself.

Where is Warhol in this film? In abnegating the place of the author, Warhol renders the concept of audience equally general and abstract.[34] The network of gazes tends to undercut or subvert the voyeuristic structure of the film by dividing the look. Spectatorship is diffused and distributed across the three looks within the filmic space. The long take likewise deflates the narrative of expectation (will they actually make love?), rendering the exotic banal. While the spectator has no choice but to look at a single image for seventy minutes, there is no guaranteed reward for the exercise, except for the beauty of the photography itself. Both *Kiss* and *Beauty #2* are shot in high-contrast black and white, often with stylized lighting; the set in the second film is lit to emphasize its depth and slightly antiquey furniture. The image in Warhol's films is far from a documentary image but is consistently rendered as spectacle, as an aesthetic attraction. The spectator is thus invited to look (and arguably in both films, to look as a man would look), and to look with desire, along with a disembodied camera—a desiring machine.

Beauty #2 could be described as a form of portraiture, as could many of Warhol's films of this period. Edie, like many of the Factory denizens, plays herself playing a movie star, and Warhol indulges in the spectacle of her body and the construction of character from documentary detail. Paul Arthur describes Edie Sedgwick in *Beauty #2* as "a warped paradigm of the types of characters 'laid bare' in *cinéma vérité* documentary or Italian neorealism."[35] Gino, who was allegedly found "downstairs on the street," looks like a figure out of a Pasolini film, a member of the sexual subproletariat of New York hustlers. The individuals who populate Warhol's cinema are "found" people, filling the Duchampian frame of the camera-as-pedestal.

Warhol's experiment with ethnographic representation consists of a shifting of "aura" in the cinema to the bodies of the people filmed. Behavior is abstracted from both narrative and documentary premises and tends to refer mainly to the act of being filmed. Warhol's radical abnegation of the role of expressive artist, along with the subject of perception and knowledge, leaves the gaze open, free of any claims to veracity. The authenticity of the event becomes linked to the time of the profilmic in a one-to-one structure of duration. As the performer struggles with the gaze, creating the spectacle of being filmed, the time of the once-only is articulated for the spectator watching it at some other time. In this sense, Warhol's films do bear the mark of death, of time passing irretrievably. The strict division of space in *Beauty #2* between on-screen and off-screen leaves Edie and Gino alone in the visual field, as bodies in time.

The early films produced at Warhol's Factory have been described as having an ironic or allegorical relation to metaphysical film theory. Tyler, for example, argues that "the living, organic world we see in *Sleep, Eat, Haircut* and *Kiss* has a visually implosive force whose burden we must bear or else heave off." [36] This reality is not redeemed but consumed by the real time of the filming. Arthur has described Warhol as "the illegitimate son of Bazin," [37] insofar as a film such as *Beauty #2* can be considered a humanist work. Warhol's realism is in fact closely linked to his performers. The tension between structure and sexuality, minimalist art and promiscuity, turns on the bodies of Edie Sedgwick and others, and in this sense it is an ethnographic cinema. Warhol himself is a showman not unlike Edward Curtis, bringing an "unseen" world to light, making marginal films about marginal people — gays, junkies, hustlers, and so forth. His redemptive gesture is limited to the mortal bodies of his stars, and not to "reality" in any more universal sense.

It is definitely a gendered gaze that is enacted in both *Kiss* and *Beauty #2,* and if Warhol's definition of experimental film is that he didn't know what he was doing,[38] he leaves himself open to cultural critique. The gaze is not innocent, even if it is not "motivated." Its cruelty is registered not simply in the legendary fate of Edie Sedgwick, who emerged retrospectively as a victim of Warhol's art, but precisely in the "inhumane" nature of the setup with which Warhol experimented. The act of being filmed constitutes a radical transformation of reality in which authenticity recedes behind the image of authenticity. The gaze of Warhol's structural film aesthetic is not quite disembodied, and here it differs from the technologized camera movements of Michael Snow's films *Wavelength* (1967) and *La Region Centrale* (1971). To the extent that Warhol's gaze is fixed on the eroticized body, it is a desiring gaze.

Akerman and Warhol may be very different filmmakers, but in both of their uses of structural film, the image becomes the site of a contest over the gaze. It bears the trace of an encounter between the viewer and the viewed. In this sense, it can be understood as a dialectical image, one that registers the time of the encounter, a long, drawn-out present tense; and at the same time, it dramatizes the conversion of experience into image, cut off by the rigorous framing, from the "real" from which it is extracted. Both filmmakers have cultivated the art of staring, but they stare very differently, a difference that constitutes very specific inscriptions of the subjectivity of the gaze. Both viewers may be invisible, but whereas Warhol attempts to vacate himself absolutely, Akerman alludes to her "self" as a viewing position that escapes other codifications.

Still from David Rimmer's *Real Italian Pizza* (1971). *Courtesy of Canadian Filmmakers Distribution Center.*

The Inhabited View: Landscape and Ethnography

Landscape is the first order of image content to be admitted to the purist structural project.[39] Mute and empty, landscape answers and rewards the "address of the eye." Although it is often an empty stage, landscape also frames the entry of the human figure into the visual field of structural film. In *News from Home*, for example, people pass in front of the camera setup, so that the view seems to precede the action. When the camera is either completely immobile or restricted to a very controlled panning movement (as in *D'Est*), the framing imposes a form onto reality, transforming it into a "scene." The inclusion of people within imagery that appears to be composed along principles of landscape composition constitutes an ethnography in which "form" intervenes and qualifies the realism. Despite the panoptic effect of the static camera, an aesthetic formalism mediates the representation of the Other. This does not necessarily reduce the human figure to "a component in a formal pattern"[40] but may be an incursion of ethnography into the pictorial field.

In many of David Rimmer's films, landscape tends to be as desolate as Michael Snow's *La Region Central,* and yet in one of Rimmer's films, *Real Italian Pizza,* the structural aesthetic is turned onto a street scene in New York City. *Real Italian Pizza* was shot in New York from September 1970 to May 1971. This is one of Rimmer's most overtly ethnographic films, and because of the setting, it serves as a foil or counterpoint to Snow's *Wavelength.* Outside the loft window, Rimmer finds the life of the street that Snow so radically excludes. Turning the camera onto the patrons of an Italian pizza and sandwich shop, their rhythms of coming and going and just hanging out on the sidewalk, Rimmer assumes the position of the spy. From his elevated angle, across the street, the New Yorkers, many of them African American, look like ants or bees revolving around a buzzing hive. The pizza-makers/shop-owners remain invisible inside the shop. They come out to shovel snow off the sidewalk, but for the most part, their invisibility and centrality on the other side of the scenario mirrors and complements that of the camera.[41]

Each of the three overlapping camera positions in the film has the effect of framing the scene like a stage onto which people exit and enter. Collapsing nine months into thirteen minutes, Rimmer's editing exaggerates the rhythms and patterns of the routines of daily life, lingering on the people who loiter outside the shop during the summer months, pixilating rapid activity. When the police drag someone out of the shop, Rimmer dramatically cuts into the scene to see the apprehended man stuffed into a patrol car. This brief shot is the proverbial exception that proves the rule of the otherwise statically framed film. In comparison to many of Rimmer's films, the "real" documentary image is more or less sustained in its integrity.

Despite the intervention into the image by way of montage and the addition of a jazz soundtrack, Rimmer's camera is extremely passive. Again, this should be contrasted to Snow's zoom inside the loft. The voyeurism of the film's premise is met by the exhibitionism of some of the shop's patrons, who, on a couple of occasions, dance on the sidewalk. Although their steps are almost synced to the film's soundtrack, the silencing of their own transistor music retains the distanciation of the spectacle. The scene of the sidewalk is a public space that is specific to New York and is therefore an ethnographic "sight." Likewise, the people on the street may be "villagers" (inhabitants of a neighborhood), but they are also there "to be seen."[42]

Real Italian Pizza is idiosyncratically suspended between two very different film practices—structural film and *cinéma verité.* The soundtrack of jazz music and traffic sounds helps to accentuate a rhythm of life that is both daily and seasonal. As in any ethnographic text, the film imposes a form and a structure on cultural Others in the very process of transposing them into representation. And yet the fixed camera of structural film has the effect of "framing" that process and quite literally inscribing its limits. Twenty years later, the Afros, the bell-bottoms, and the dance steps are documents of a historically specific culture that occupied a certain public space. Racial difference is embraced within ethnographic difference, which is in turn represented as a spatial difference inscribed within a technology of perception. The form of the film transforms the scene into a theatrical space, just as the twenty intervening years make us now into historical voyeurs, looking but not touching, outside the scene looking in, inside the window looking out.

The framing of history made possible by the structural film's attention to detail is exploited even more explicitly in Joyce Wieland's film *Pierre Vallières* (1972), one of the most "impure" of structural films. Ostensibly an interview with, or documentary on, Pierre Vallières, a militant member of the Front de Libération du Québec, author of *White Niggers of America,* Wieland's camera frames only his mouth. Throughout the thirty-two-minute film, Vallières speaks continuously, espousing his politics in French, as if he were giving a speech. English subtitles appear in the upper part of the frame, inscribing the linguistic difference with which Vallières is preoccupied onto the image in a very literal way. Shot in three rolls of film that include signs of the reel ends but never venture away from the extreme close-up of Vallières's teeth, lips, and mustache, the film ends with a pan out the window onto a snowy landscape.

In keeping with Wieland's painting and quilt work, the image of Vallières's mouth bears a strong resemblance to a vagina, and several critics have commented on the ways that she has imposed a feminist perspective onto Vallières's discourse.[43] In his vastly inclusive politics, women are counted among the ranks of the oppressed — alongside French Canadians, the working class, American blacks, and North American Indians. Quebec liberation is intended by Vallières to be a revolutionary movement that would free all of these groups from their various forms of oppression. Wieland has given Vallières a "platform" and enabled him to have his say, but she also inscribes a subtle critique of his discourse, simply by imposing a minimalist format onto the documentary material.

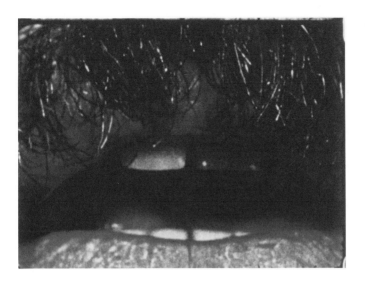

Still from Joyce Wieland's *Pierre Vallières* (1972). *Courtesy of Canadian Filmmakers Distribution Center.*

The intimate close-up reveals details of the body that ordinarily remain outside political language. Vallières's tobacco-stained teeth and untrimmed mustache may indicate his working-class status, but they also supply a sensuous and almost erotic dimension to the film. His language is split into three levels of discourse: the English translation, the sound of the Quebecois French, and the movement of his lips and tongue. If the written English invokes the act of repression, the embodied language evokes that which has been colonized and struggles to break free. However, as Vallières's monologue continues, his voice becomes in turn a colonizing discourse, oppressive in its own totalizing way.

When the camera finally cuts away from the claustrophobic image of Vallières's huge mouth, the relief of the landscape is a visual form of the liberation about which he has spoken at such length. Structural film foregrounds the surface of the image, and in Wieland's films, the use of text often serves this function. Here, the English titles superimposed on Vallières's mouth contrast the flatness of the screen with the depth of the open mouth. The landscape image, over which the camera pans slowly from right to left and back again, is very grainy, shot through a plate glass window, and the grain may in fact be snow. Very little can actually be seen outside the window, and the shot has the effect of registering a sense of alterity that may be "liberating" but is still a function of language.

Wieland's subversive framing of Vallières gives a certain power to the cinematic apparatus, a power of misrepresentation. For Wieland, structural film is an important means of inscribing the language of film onto documentary subjects. Her gaze in *Pierre Vallières* is definitely a gendered gaze and is intended as a means of subversion, or as her slogan puts it, of making "a corrective film" (which is something quite different than a correct image). The formal structure of the image is ethnographic in its registration of detail and its insistence on the body as signifier. A series of tensions and contradictions are put into play that make it difficult for the spectator to "read" either the image or the speech. Vallières's subject is actually colonialism, but his self-identification as victim is rendered inauthentic. His political discourse runs aground on the film's appropriation of the powers of ethnographic representation. The faithfulness of recording becomes an empty form, the fixed frame ultimately analogous to the fixed frame of Vallières's politics of oppression and liberation.

The most profound tension or contradiction within *Pierre Vallières* is the difference between Vallières's militant revolutionary politics and Wieland's politics of representation. Structural film may border on documentary, but it is radically anti-interventionist, as signified by the completeness of film fragments marked by reel ends, a technique Wieland shares with Warhol. The formalism of structural film may be described as a negative dialectics, or as a postmodern tendency to access reality only through the mediating forms of representation and language. *Pierre Vallières* pits this formalism against a political language, producing a new form of cultural critique that is grounded in an audiovisual language. Wieland's treatment of Vallières is extremely subversive. It enables his voice to be heard, but it is free-floating, detached from his body and from the urgency of history. The detail of ethnography provides a specific image, a temporary banality, an afternoon in Quebec.

In the work of James Benning, social consciousness is not "expressed" but developed within slow meditations on viewing and storytelling. *Landscape Suicide* (1986), Benning's feature-length film about two American murderers, anticipates the reality-TV programming of the 1990s. Although Benning is associated with the "new narrative" trajectory of experimental film in the 1980s, this film owes far more to documentary conventions than narrative.[44] The film is divided into two halves. The first is about Bernadette Protti, a teenager from Orinda County, California, who killed a school friend in 1984; the second is about Ed Gein, from rural Wisconsin, who murdered and cannibalized a number of people in the 1950s. Benning's approach to this material is antisensationalist, mainly comprising shots of the landscape of the two locales intercut with actors reading the two murderers' testimony in tight static long-take medium shots.

It is a "fake documentary" insofar as the 1950s scenes have been set up with old cars, and the actors are more or less acting (reading) their parts. Photos of the actual murderers upset any illusionism, as does the inclusion of a few more obviously acted scenes (also shot in single long static shots). Benning describes his aesthetics as hyperreal: "I don't re-create reality. I create a metaphor that suggests reality."[45] His photography of landscape conveys this sense in its excessive formalism. The details of pictorial composition render the space so perfect that one can sense the disruptive criminal activities behind the surface of these communities, as if there were a horror film lurking behind the film that Benning has made (in fact, Gein was supposedly the inspiration for Norman Bates in Hitchcock's *Psycho*).[46] If criminals are frequently perceived within the panoptic structures of a disciplinary society—if indeed they are the support of that structure—in this film they are situated outside it; the structure itself, the disciplinary gaze of power, is represented as an empty form.

The two criminals, who we never actually see, and whose crimes we are only told about, become ethnographic subjects by virtue of their cinematic contexts. Instead of psychological investigation, *Landscape Suicide* offers only cultural clues to the incidents. The two victims are alluded to in two set pieces, long still shots accompanying two songs: "Memories" for the 1980s, and "The Tennessee Waltz" for the 1950s. In addition to a Christian radio broadcast heard over a drive in the rain, there is something extraordinarily banal about the contexts of the two crimes, and something oddly ordinary about the murderers. In fragments of voice-over (spoken by a woman), Benning explains that he traveled to Orinda County and to Wisconsin because of a curiosity about the murderers, but what he discovers are images.

Benning's framing in *Landscape Suicide* points to the limits of visual knowledge. Without attempting to represent the murders directly, the film is about surfaces—a storefront, a school, suburban homes, a Wis-

Still from James Benning's *Landscape Suicide* (1986). *Courtesy of Canadian Filmmakers Distribution Center.*

consin house in the snow, the outsides of prisons and courthouses. Each functions like an establishing shot that leads nowhere. The reading of the testimonies lacks emotion; responding to the questions of an off-screen lawyer, the two actors/murderers are very matter-of-fact, except that both have trouble remembering the crucial events for which they are being tried. As a comparative ethnography, similarities and differences between the two crimes become apparent but remain unaddressed. The way each crime unfolds in minute detail, each seems intimately related to the daily life of the place in which it occurred, sudden unexplained eruptions in the smooth surfaces of two very different communities. The disturbances themselves are deeply buried in the amnesiac murderers and remain outside the sphere of representation.

Like Wieland's film, *Landscape Suicide* is about representation, about looking and about the language of film. While the use of the *fait divers* or newspaper story is a fairly common technique in narrative filmmaking, its treatment here is one of de-dramatization. The imposition of form onto the landscape through Benning's rigorous framing and slow pacing has the effect, again, of showing how reality is transformed into images. At the end of the film, the hyperrealism finally, but gradually, gives way to a scene of two hunters butchering a deer in the Wisconsin forest. The excess that has been so repressed by the film's pacing and quiet control is, in this bloody image, drawn directly from the profilmic, in a gruesome indexicality that has haunted the preceding landscape photography.

Structural film aesthetics may have originated within a medium specificity paradigm of high modernism, but these films by Rimmer, Wieland, and Benning engage closely with photography and painting, as well as audio intertexts. Cinema shares its apparatus of vision and techniques of representation with many other media, and the "structure" of structural film extends far beyond cinema. As a form of experimental ethnography, its phenomenological premises are conjoined with a documentary realism within a specifically aesthetic sphere of representation. When people appear within the "frame" of landscape, they enter the sphere of visual representation through the back door, through the pictorial properties of the medium, and so they can be seen differently, not as exoticized "Others" but as functions or extensions of their environment.

Bill Viola: The Electronic Gaze

As artist-in-residence at the Santiago Zoo in the 1980s, Bill Viola explored the zoological gaze more fully and deliberately as a technology than perhaps any other film- or videomaker. His ninety-minute videotape *I Do Not Know What It Is I Am Like* has become a canonical example of video art, drawing on documentary and ethnographic methods of observation as well as the structural experiments of avant-garde film. As I have already suggested, Viola forces the question of subjectivity into the foreground of documentary representation through an exploration of the undisciplined gaze.

For Viola, the video camera is not like the physical human eye, but more like "the mind's eye," an "instrument for the articulation of mental space."[47] While his tapes consistently invoke metaphysical, utopian, and transcendental experiences and perceptions, they are built up from documentary images and tend to retain something of the materialist aesthetic of structural film. In a tape such as *Hatsu Yume (First Dream)* (1981), a fluidity of light and image constitutes yet another dimension of the hyperrealist possibilities of structural film. In *Hatsu Yume*, which was shot at Kamakura Temple and in a Japanese fishing village, the sense of place and ethnographic experience persists through the special effects that Viola has used to represent light as fluid. Using only static long shots and controlled lateral pans, Viola's camera, once again, imposes a frame onto that which is filmed. People walk into, and out of, the frame, or it moves past them without stopping. In one seven-minute shot, Japanese tourists approach and circle and retreat from a huge rock centered in Viola's frame. A play with perspective endows the rock with a kind of power of presence, a power that seems greater than the gaze itself. Viola's ethnography is a kind of poetics in which the desire to see is neither epistemological nor carnal but is endowed with a spiritual power that is often linked in his work to Asian cultures.

In adapting the aesthetics of structural film to the video medium, Viola augments the fixed gaze of the camera with ambient sound and a heightened sense of presence. If the camera-as-consciousness model of structural film was a disembodied gaze, Viola makes it an index of subjectivity. His gaze becomes an encounter with the world in all its forms; consciousness is no longer abstract and universal but is seated in the artist and in the Other. Within Viola's postcolonial milieu, the apparatus of vision is no longer innocent, and it is this knowledge with which the tape struggles to come to terms. The video signal, furthermore, extends the metaphor of consciousness onto a more material plane, which gives his work its strong documentary impulse. Viola's camera renders the means of perception, the form of vision, as a natural process that mimics the natural flow of nature to circumvent representation allegorically. Along with the audible sound of flies — on a buffalo carcass, or on a decaying fish — the nature of electricity refers back to the technology of representation and the perceiving "self" (Viola) who desires to find himself in the sight of landscape, birds, fish, animals, and other people.

I Do Not Know has five segments, which Viola says correspond to "different consciousness[es] representing the world." Or, more specifically, different models of "inner and outer consciousness, observer and observed."[48] In an introductory passage, the camera plunges into a lake and descends to underwater coral structures, dripping in a dark silence, that look almost like the inside of the human body. In the first section, "Il Corpo Scuro" (The Dark Body), buffalo graze slowly, lazily, peeing and dying in a perfect pastoral landscape. In "The Language of the Birds," birds and fish are observed in close-ups that allow us to study their remarkable features. In "The Night of Sense," Viola himself works in his study (or a studio representation thereof). A German shepherd attacks the camera to initiate the short fourth section, "Stunned by the Drum," a rapidly edited sequence of flash-frame imagery. "The Living Flame," the fifth and final section, consists of fragments of a fire-walking ritual performed in Fiji and to some extent constitutes the narrative climax of the tape, suddenly turning to ethnographic imagery in pursuit of Viola's self-knowledge. (This section of the tape will be discussed further in chapter 8.) Answering the opening imagery, the tape concludes with the camera rising out of the lake, "flying" over a mountain landscape, and descending into the woods to settle finally on the slow sight of decomposing fish until the grain of the video image itself dissolves to darkness.[49]

Throughout most of the tape, Viola employs a static camera and very long takes that draw attention to their occasional movements and zooms, techniques of getting a better look. In Fiji, however, the camera is *in medias res,* picking out and following individual participants in the ritual, pulling back for longer shots and cutting into close-ups with fairly invisible editing. In contrast, the images of animals, birds, and fish are studied images, aestheticized within the conventions of landscape and portraiture. These images, however, pose a problem of subjectivity. John Berger has pointed out that "nowhere in a zoo can a stranger encounter the look of an animal. At most, the animal's gaze flickers and passes on. They look sideways. They look blindly beyond. They scan mechanically. They have been immunized to encounter, because nothing can any more occupy a *central* place in their attention."[50] A buffalo may catch sight of the camera, but it pisses lazily while looking. This disinterested decenteredness extends to the Hindu fire walkers, and to the landscape; they reflect the gaze without seeing, without knowing. Similarly, Viola offers himself up to the viewer's gaze in his study, as another animal in a zoo, but his body seems to be in excess, a supplement or appendage to the workings of consciousness.

I Do Not Know addresses the physical presence of the experimental artist at the source of the documentary gaze. The gaze is at once human —attached to a body in the world—and dehumanized, becoming an appendage of technology. Video may extend the operator's body into the world seen, but it is also an instrument of surveillance. The transcendental gesture of the tape, the desire to overcome the division of representation, can only be accomplished through a critique of its own power relations.

Sean Cubitt has argued that *I Do Not Know* exemplifies what he calls "the final stage of colonialism," that of withdrawal.[51] He points out that "Viola's eye is still that of the ethnographer. Yet much of the work involves a self-scrutiny, under the eye of the bird, which is specifically in the realm of the visible" (73). The most explicit self-scrutiny takes place in the "Night of Sense" segment, which is highly ironic and self-deprecating. In his sterile environment, Viola performs the discourse of reason in all its scientific, colonial, and religious forms. It is a discourse with which Viola clearly identifies, by virtue of his education and ethnicity, but struggles against. Viola's study contains a model pirate ship and a book opened to a page on which a male figure crouching over a fire is labeled "stimulus and response."

On Viola's desk in "The Night of Sense" is a small monitor in which images of birds from the preceding section are juxtaposed with imagery from the forthcoming Fijian section. Viola works on this material, which is rendered exotic and small in his study. At the same time, the body of the artist becomes in its turn material, mortal, and strange. He eats a fish and drinks wine in a ritualistic meal that is so closely miked that the sounds of chewing, swallowing, and the clinking of silverware are excessively amplified. The Christian myth of transubstantiation may be literalized, but the sequence also has a distinct sense of magic as the wealth and power of privilege are transformed into material processes.

Viola wants to circumvent the disciplines of the gaze and pose the question of the alienation of humans from nature anew. If the cinema has been a crucial instrument in the institutionalization of the colonial gaze, video offers an opportunity to rearticulate that look and frame the Other differently. In this videotape, the otherness of animals, along with the otherness of a mystical, spiritual consciousness, serves to place the identity of the viewer in question. "Man" is effectively reduced to the clumsy individual in the red sweater (Viola). Viola's existentialism and his medium-specificity, in odd conjunction with his high-tech medium, make him in many ways "the last modernist." He is also the last man to claim to be "Man," and lurking within the tape's anxiety of identity is a waning of that capital *M*, a withdrawal from its sovereignty.

Viola's technologized gaze enables him to rejoin the natural world in the form of electricity, after the fall from humanism. In the transcendent finale of *I Do Not Know*, video itself becomes magically superhuman and supernatural, flying through the sky (mounted on a crane), over the spectacular scenery of northwest Canada. A fish is mounted across the bottom of the frame, creating a two-tiered perspective of close-up and long shot. The camera then drops down through the pines to the forest floor, where in a series of dissolves, the fish disintegrates. Visited by birds and animals, the decaying fish acts as a kind of bait, or visual

Still from Bill Viola's video *I Do Not Know What It Is I Am Like* (1986).
Photo by Kira Perov.

trap. When it finally disappears, the frame of the image becomes redundant, and the forest becomes an empty stage. The drumming from the ritual in the previous segment continues over the magnificent 360-degree pans but fades out when the fish comes down to earth. The sound of flies buzzing while the fish decays takes over the soundtrack, eventually fading out to silence.

The artist finally "finds himself" fused with technology, identified with representation. In the withdrawal from colonialism (which is emphatically not a critique of colonialism), new forms of subjectivity need to be recognized and reconfigured within the institutions of representation, including both the art gallery and the documentary film. Viola's conceit of placing his own identity in question is in fact a narrative strategy of neutralizing technology. The power of nature is not only mystified, but in the spectacle of landscape, the eyes of animals, and the spirituality of Fijian Hindus, that power becomes an empowerment of the Other in representation.

The visual economy of *I Do Not Know* is reduced to its purist voyeuristic structure within the context of a crisis of subjectivity. For Viola, violence is implicit in the technologized gaze, but its redemptive power rests in the splitting of subjectivities, for which he uses the metaphor of lightning.[52] The image of lightning recalls Benjamin's insistence on the flash and the shock that binds photography to history. The crystallization of the moment as a dialectical revelation of historical time is actually performed in the "Stunned by the Drum" section of the tape, in which a stroboscopic pulse flashes through a rapid-fire sequence of imagery that begins with a photo shoot of a zebra. Viola's use of video technology is situated very deliberately on the threshold of a new "age" of representation. As the "mechanical" gives way to the "electronic," Viola attempts to rediscover auratic experience through a transcendental gesture of naturalizing technology. His redemption of the gaze via Eastern philosophy repositions it as an element of a life cycle in which consciousness is no longer outside bodily experience but is part of a continuum between bodies. Lightning, electricity, pulsating light and noise, become the means by which video absorbs the shock of modernity and dissolves representation into experience.

Passive Realism as a Political Aesthetic

One may be put off by Viola's mysticism, and indeed this question will be investigated further in the next chapter. His tapes, however, indicate an important direction that the structural film aesthetic has taken. All of the filmmakers discussed in this chapter can be described as realists. But in each case, reality is given a frame, transformed into an image that is always slightly removed from documentary veracity. The minimal use of editing allows these pictures to unfold in time, to become theatrical, or to become paintings. Sound is frequently an important indicator of what escapes the gaze, and a crucial element of the formalism. If structural film was originally described as a priority of "shape" over content, for these filmmakers — for whom content is not negligible or accidental — "shape" refers to the temporal priority of the filmic frame. Once the view, and by extension the viewer, is rendered as preceding the people or person filmed, otherness is configured quite differently.

The mystical connotations of *I Do Not Know* are indicative of the dangers of this film practice as a form of ethnography. Radical decontextualization can produce a pictorialism that can be essentialist and exotic; structural ethnography works best when the gaze is doubled or allegorized as in the foregoing examples. Aestheticization is a practice that always tends toward dematerialization, as Benjamin pointed out in his strident epilogue to the "The Work of Art" essay. The aestheticization of politics was the fascist correlative of Benjamin's project in the 1930s.[53] In the late twentieth century, we have to make a similar distinction between an aestheticization of otherness and a politics of representation, even if the stakes do not seem so high, and the distinction is often hard to make in postmodern culture.

Several ethnographic films have been made that might seem to share the structural film aesthetic, but in important ways, they lack the formalism that distinguishes this mode of film practice. Ken Feingold's videotape *India Time* (1987) and Robert Gardner's *Forest of Bliss* (1985), both shot in India, use long real-time sequences to capture something of the temporality of everyday life. Neither employs voice-over commentary or any other anthropological contextualizing device. Both use pictorial compositions that tend to adhere to conventions of Western painting and photography, drawing attention to the act of framing. They both tend toward an "ethnopoetics," and yet they remain texts of "capture," of containing the Other in the visual field.

In both these works, one has the distinct impression of looking in at another world from outside, but without the window frame marking that separation. In *India Time,* each short sequence focuses on an individual or a group of Indians working—at either a craft, a domestic chore, farming, or light industry. The camera occasionally moves, following the laborers, but it is mainly static, staring, watching these everyday activities. Each shot, however, is determined by the profilmic; it holds our interest and fascinates, and the gaze is subservient to the action. Although only a few shots are at a high angle to the people working, the voyeuristic gaze predominates and is not qualified by any sense of the viewer's presence. Like Akerman in *D'Est,* Feingold does not belong there, but he does not pass by.

The activities taped in *India Time* do not have any history. Without beginnings or ends, they are situated in that eternal present tense that structural film fragments and renders temporary. In structural film, the idea of a window frame persists, either literally or metaphorically alluded to in some way by the framing; moreover, one often has the sense that the frame precedes the other body filmed and shares a sense of presentness with it. The ethnographic Other is seen but not "captured," and the gaze can thus be described as "undisciplined," linked to an observer whose desire is strictly for an image, not for possession. Structural film is thus a passive realism and it is that passivity which is missing from *India Time*.

Forest of Bliss falls into a similar trap of negating history and rendering the Other timeless. Despite its extensive use of real time, Gardner's film, like his previous film *Dead Birds* (1963), relies heavily on continuity editing techniques. Sequences of shots follow "characters" through the elaborate Benares architecture, betraying a complex "other time" of shooting.[54] Again, the film is dictated by the prior existence of the Other, whose space we are privileged to look into. *Forest of Bliss* has undoubtedly shaken the crude voice-over structure of Gardner's earlier film, but in becoming an art film, it renders the Other mythic in a romantic aesthetic motivated by the humanist theme of death and rebirth.

The difference of structural film is the transformation of space and time into an autonomous image sphere that may be grounded in a preexisting reality, but is also independent of it. As we have seen in the foregoing very different examples, the Other comes into view in this cinema as a body in space. Structural film is thus able to situate the Other in a present tense that inscribes a mortality into the image itself, not metaphorically, but as a function of representation. The structural film image is dialectical in Benjamin's sense: it allegorizes the real into the now and the past, the time of watching and the different time of experience.

Structural film aesthetics are not necessarily the "answer" or the solution to questions of ethnographic representation. They are clearly not even reducible to a simple formula or coherent set of techniques. Each of these very different examples of "impure" structural film conveys a means of representing "the gaze" or the look at the Other as a constitutive element of the audiovisual text. Structural film is an exemplary incorporation of a theory of looking into ethnographic representation. Going beyond reflexive modernism, the gaze in these films is clearly undisciplined in its naked stare, and yet it also conveys a utopian openness of the empty space. The void cleared by the picture frame enables the ethnographic body to perform itself in an image of space and time.

IV

OTHER REALITIES

Still from *Les Maîtres fous*, by Jean Rouch (1954).

8 Ecstatic Ethnography: Filming Possession Rituals

We are watching a mental alchemy which makes a gesture of a state of mind—the dry, naked, linear gesture all our acts could have if they sought the absolute.

—ANTONIN ARTAUD, *The Theatre and Its Double*

They "ethno-show" and "ethno-talk," and at best, they "ethno-think," or better yet, they have "ethno-rituals." . . . Knowledge is no longer a stolen secret, later to be consumed in the Western temples of knowledge.

—JEAN ROUCH, "Vicissitudes of the Self"

The filming of possession rituals was a fundamental aspect of Jean Rouch's practice of "shared anthropology." Through the magical properties of cinema, he felt that he could join in the ritual as an equal participant and thus bridge the gap between himself and the culture he filmed. The utopian, transcendental aspect of his writing on possession rituals is inspired by the ecstatic character of the rituals themselves, in which individuals are transported out of everyday reality and become others, doubles of the gods and spirits who take control of their bodies. Although Rouch's ethnography may not in fact be as "shared" and "participatory" as he desired, the dissolution of boundaries between self and other is intrinsic to the imagination of possession.

Rouch is not alone in his attraction to possession rituals as a cinematic subject. Absorption into the pulsating rhythm of the dance may be a threat to ethnographic distance and objectivity,[1] and yet this is precisely what attracts filmmakers in search of a subjective entry into the ethnographic scene. The Western fascination with possession is bound up with the fundamental ambivalence of primitivism in the modernist imagination. It produces a fantasy of another, more pure, state of being from which modernity has alienated the Western subject. If the body of the ethnographic other is particularly "primitivized" or exoticized in the filming of possession rituals, it is also a fantastic body, produced in and through representation. The performance of the exotic body is given with a rare uninhibited exhibitionism that invites the gaze, at the same time as it challenges the will to knowledge invested in the ethnographic look. The ritual elements of dance, theater, music, and the language of bodies become a writing that presupposes a doubleness of representation.

The desire to film possession may be motivated by the idea of subjectivity "on display," given theatrical form, and yet it is also a scene of excess, producing something that inevitably escapes representation. The actual experience of possession remains outside the limits of visual knowledge and constitutes a subtle form of ethnographic resistance: films of possession cannot, in the end, represent the "other reality" of the other's subjectivity. Possession is itself a form of representation to which the filmmaker might aspire, but it is also a *mise en abyme* of representation, with its final signified content always beyond reach. I would like to argue that that end point of the possession semiosis is the subjectivity of the Other, which thus resists cinematic representation along with its ideology of visibility.

The conjunction of documentary realism and trance poses a host of contradictions concerning visual evidence, authenticity, and ethnographic subjectivity. The possession ritual is only complete by being witnessed, because the performance constitutes a proof of the existence of gods or spirits. As a spectacle, it challenges conventional forms of spectatorship and passive observation, as spectators are often drawn into the trance. While this is part of the attraction of such rituals to filmmakers, films of possession do not necessarily retain the same structure of spectatorship. The difference between possession rituals and the filming of possession rituals is precisely the inscription of technology. The spectacle of ecstasy stands in for the experience of possession.

The filming of possession is an exemplary intersection of modern aesthetics and anthropology. The sublime transcendence of the indigenous spirit-possessed gives a documentary form to a whole range of Western desires for transcendental experience, from drugs, to dance, to creative trance. For both Antonin Artaud and Jean Rouch, the possession ritual offered an ethnographic instance of a "found surrealism." Artaud's enthusiasm for Balinese theater was informed by an Orientalism that resonates in the films of possession. It represented everything that was missing from the Western theater; it expressed something essentially Oriental; and his enthusiasm was entirely motivated by the use he could make of it in his reform of European theater. Possession provided Artaud with a valuable model for a performance mode that transcended spoken language and relied solely on "a new physical language." Apparently he saw dancers even on the Parisian stage go into trance, which he described as "deep metaphysical anguish." The dancers' gestures appeared to be directly linked to their souls without any mediation, so that the actors became doubles of themselves. In their mechanical and rigid movements, he saw a strategy of exorcism "to make our demons FLOW."[2] Despite the spiritual and mystical orientation of the performance, Artaud also saw it as a novel form of realism: "For though we are familiar with the realistic aspect of matter, it is here developed to the 'n'th power and definitely stylized."[3]

The conflicting modern desires to emulate the Other and represent the Other are manifest in the filming of possession rituals as a subjective realism, an impossible, contradictory form of representation. A tension between psychological and mystical forms of subjectivity informs the conjunction of cinema and ritual as filmmakers attempt to extend the realm of the visible to capture the subjective state of trance. The four examples in this chapter demonstrate how possession rituals have inspired innovations in filmmaking that blur boundaries between ethnographic and experimental modes of practice. They suggest the ways in which, by way of cinema, the possession ritual becomes an exemplary modernist phenomenon.

Margaret Mead and Gregory Bateson's *Trance and Dance in Bali,* which was shot in 1937 and 1939 and released in 1952, is part of a much larger film-and-photo project that was the first systematic use of film in anthropological fieldwork. In 1947 Maya Deren interrupted her career as an experimental filmmaker and went to Haiti. She shot nearly four hours of film footage of possession rituals, although she was not able to edit this material before her death in 1961. Jean Rouch's film *Les Maîtres fous* (1954–1955) is one of the best-known films of possession. It is notorious for its influence on subsequent European theater (via Jean Genet and Peter Brook), and for the opposition expressed by Africans and anthropologists to the representation of "savagery" and "primitiv-ism," which was felt to be a step backward in cross-cultural representa-tion in the 1950s.[4] The climactic segment of Bill Viola's videotape *I Do Not Know What It Is I Am Like* (1986), consisting of footage of Fijian firewalkers, uses the video medium to foreground the representation of subjectivity and the limits of visual knowledge, situating possession within a new context of aesthetic practice.

These four texts represent different phases of the modernist project, and different historical, aesthetic, and theoretical points of intersec-tion between anthropology and the avant-garde. Vincent Crapanzano's definition of spirit possession is "any altered state of consciousness in-digenously interpreted in terms of the influence of an alien spirit."[5] Often described as trance, possession bears both a visual and socio-logical resemblance to hypnotism; in the 1950s, when three of these films were made, interpretation thus tended toward the psychoanalytic rather than the "alien." By the 1980s, the experiential aspect of trance possession had become a feature of North American dance music, and the fusion of world beat music with synthesizers gives rise to a very different representation of possession, evident in Viola's tape.[6] Before moving to the four texts in question, I would like to introduce three themes that locate the possession ritual within the sphere of modern culture and aesthetics: the crowd, the nature of visual evidence, and the melodramatic structure of the return of the repressed.

Although, as we shall see, different cultural "idioms" produce a va-riety of forms of the possession ritual, a common theme is that of the collective, the community and the crowd. Individuals are seen to be possessed by gods and spirits, but the context is often that of the group that shares in the event as witnesses, if not as actual "hosts" for the spirits. Insofar as the spirit-possessed individual "loses himself" in the midst of a mass of people, it constitutes a form of depersonalization. The attraction to Western modernists is indicated by Benjamin's de-scription of the crowd as the central urban scene in the work of Baude-laire and Poe. For the latter, it is a "figure that fascinates" and "lures" the observer "outside into the whirl of the crowd."[7] The Baudelairean *flâneur* invents himself in the midst of the Parisian throng in the ar-cades; he is an ambivalent figure who gently resists the pull of the crowd, but who is nevertheless in its midst. To be in the crowd is to be "out of place."[8]

The filmmaker at the scene of a possession ritual is likewise drawn into it as a sight that fascinates but is at the same time radically outside by virtue of his or her equipment and cultural identity. The attraction of the crowd and the fascination of possession is the loss and/or rearticulation of identity, a reconfiguration of the tenets of ego psychology. Describing Marcel Mauss's fascination with possession rituals at the turn of the century, Crapanzano writes: "There are no longer any individuals but just pieces in a machine, spokes in a wheel, the magical round, danced and sung, being its primitive, ideal image. . . . Here the laws of collective psychology violate, desecrate, transgress, rape, the laws of individual psychology." [9]

Mauss and Durkheim were both interested in *mana* or magic as "an unconscious category of understanding whose origin as a category is, needless to say, social." [10] At the same time as Freud was mapping the individual unconscious, these anthropologists were studying the power of social rituals and *mana* in the collective unconscious. The two lines of inquiry inevitably converged in "a new science of the crowd and collective behavior" that fed directly into the Italian avant-garde and fascist ideology in both Germany and Italy. [11] Like so much of the modernist imbrication of aesthetics and politics, the fascination with the crowd lends itself to both dangerous and progressive social practices. The crowd as a mobilized body politic is at once a savage and eminently modern figure in which psychological structures and social formations obtain dramatic and theatrical form.

The possession rituals performed by native peoples in the expanding horizons of Western knowledge seemed to represent a transcendent, utopian experience of community. In the films of these rituals, however, ecstatic experience is exoticized and fused with the aestheticized, grotesque body of the primitive other. Possession poses a challenge to the ideology of realism, confounding the principles of visual evidence. The spectacle of the writhing body, upturned eyes, and frothing mouth is visual "proof" of the existence of gods or spirits that have entered the body of the performer. The body becomes the signifier of that which has no referent. In resisting referentiality, it marks the limit of visual language and rational thought. It blurs the distinction between signifier and signified, or as Mauss put it, "there is no interval between the wish and its realization." [12] For the uninitiated, those who have not learned to be possessed, the spectacle of the spirit-possessed is in many ways illegible. Moreover, there is no way of knowing the authenticity of the trance. It thus poses a real challenge to anthropological epistemology, providing an ethnographic spectacle that is ultimately unintelligible.

In the Western fascination with the image of possession, the doubleness of the possessed body tends to become a metaphor for other forms of transcendental experience, including sexual ecstasy, political resistance, liberation and escape from the restrictions of reality.[13] Possession rituals clearly lend themselves to a theorization of the return of the repressed, breaking through both colonial repression and sexual oppression. The image of the possessed, like that of the hysteric, might thus be read as a melodramatic structure of expression. Possession, like melodrama, is a structure of representation, in which the body itself becomes a form of writing. In Peter Brooks's theorization of melodrama, it is a modernist aesthetic of excess in which signification itself becomes a struggle. "There is a constant effort to overcome the gap, which gives a straining, a distortion, a gesticulation of the vehicles of representation in order to deliver signification. This is the mode of excess: the postulation of a signified in excess of the possibilities of the signifier, which in turn produces an excessive signifier, making large but unsubstantial claims on meaning."[14] The "moral occult," which Brooks identifies as "the center of interest and the scene of the drama," is, in the possession ritual, a properly metaphysical system. Only when it is filmed and transformed into a new level of language does the moral occult become "the repository of the fragmentary and desacralized remnants of sacred myth"—the moral occult of bourgeois melodrama.

This is not to say that possession rituals are melodramatic, but that they share with melodrama a structure of representation that helps to explain the Western fascination with possession. Once the possessed body is filmed, it becomes a signifier in a language that we know as melodrama. The image of the possessed becomes, in the language of modernist cinema, a hysterical, ecstatic body in which truth functions not as "evidence" but as the return of the repressed. Melodrama also provides the analytical tools to read this discourse of excess as an inscription of the Other's resistance in, and of, representation.

Possession rituals figure as a discourse of veracity in ethnographic representation, pointing to a truth-value greater, or more profound, than that of the image. Possession is thus a delirious language, a form of "reason in action" that is more truthful (more authentic) than the realism of photography. It offers a new regime of veracity to cinematic representation, an alternative realism, that filmmakers have harnessed for different ethnographic and aesthetic ends. The truth of madness for Foucault is bound to the *image* produced by the discourse of madness in which imagination and reality are unified. The possession ritual is in many ways such a discourse of madness, which "begins only in the act which gives the value of truth to the image."[15] Filmmakers such as Deren, Rouch, and Viola are drawn to the scene of possession because it replicates the utopian drive of the cinema: to produce a total hallucination, a complete illusion of reality. Participants in the rituals enter another reality, another body, but the spectator of the film of possession sees only a document of a hallucination, a *mise en abyme* of realities in which the filmic reality is wanting, lacking the ecstatic potential of the ritual. Thus the filming of possession tends to be marked by contradiction and compromise.

Trance and Dance in Bali: Schizoanalysis in Action

In 1953 Gregory Bateson and Margaret Mead's film *Trance and Dance in Bali* was broadcast on CBS in a program moderated by Douglas Edwards. Mead and Edwards stand in front of a fake Balinese temple and look screen right where the film is supposedly being projected. Mead's lecture starts as a conversation with Edwards and continues as the voice-over of the film, and Edwards throws in the occasional layman's question and comment. When one of the dancers falls to the ground and shakes with convulsions, Edwards says, "It looks like shock treatment . . . it's like syncopated psychiatry." Although Mead has said twice that these are "real trances" with "nothing corny about them," Edwards is still skeptical. He asks again at the end of the film: "Are they really in trance?" Given the phony setup of the broadcast, his question seems entirely reasonable: if visual representation is untrustworthy, why should we believe in possession?

Although the TV context may trivialize Mead and Bateson's scientific aspirations, their study of Balinese culture was in fact framed by a concern for the American national character. *Trance and Dance in Bali* is only one element of an extensive collection of data that they assembled from 1936 to 1939: 7,200 boxes of notes, 45,000 feet of film, and 36,000 photographs.[16] The most detailed explanation and analysis of this material is the book and photo-essay *Balinese Character* (1942), which is intended to demonstrate, on the basis of visual evidence, that the Bali-

Still from *Trance and Dance in Bali*, by Margaret Mead and Gregory Bateson (1952). *Courtesy of the Library of Congress and the Institute for Cultural Studies.*

nese culture is one "in which the ordinary adjustment of the individual approximates in form the sort of adjustment which, in our own cultural setting, we call schizoid."[17] Understanding how the Balinese cope with this condition, through rituals such as trance dancing, was supposed to lead to methods of child rearing in America that would reduce the incidence of schizophrenia and thus build a stronger individualist culture.[18]

Trance and Dance in Bali was sponsored by the Committee for Research in Dementia Praecox, as schizophrenia was once known.[19] By schizophrenia, Mead and Bateson meant "a character curiously cut off from interpersonal relationships," with little outward display of emotion, and lacking in "climactic consummations" of emotional release.[20] The proclivity to trance is interpreted as a function of a characteristic egolessness and weakened sense of self caused by particular child-rearing methods. In the trance state, various activities and emotions are acted out that the individuals could not ordinarily express because of their inability to communicate effectively. For those watching trance rituals, the spectacle has a cathartic effect, dramatizing climactic intensities that are absent from everyday life.

Bateson and Mead's research methods and conclusions regarding the

Balinese character have been subject to a rigorous critique [21] and are of much more interest now as a historical convergence of psychology (influenced by psychoanalysis), cultural anthropology, and visual representation than as convincing documents of social science. Mead's faith in visual ethnography was bolstered by two basic assumptions. One was that photographic realism could capture the "ethos" of a culture — those "intangible aspects" not easily translated into a written language. [22] The second was that by preserving cultural forms in the empirical form of photography and film, they would be available for future reanalysis, given the anticipated development of social science methods. If anthropological "progress" has meant a discrediting of her entire Balinese project, it has also produced new ways of conceptualizing schizophrenia as a form of cultural analysis.

Ironically enough, Mead and Bateson's photo-analysis of Balinese culture anticipates Deleuze and Guattari's theory of schizoanalysis as a counter model to Oedipus. As a social machine that enables a free flow of forces and desires, schizoanalysis is a desiring machine with utopian aspirations. Deleuze and Guattari equate Oedipus with colonization and turn to ethnology for the discovery of alternative forms of social functioning and reproduction — alternative desiring machines. Their version of the primitivist salvage paradigm is summarized as follows: "Our definition of schizoanalysis focused on two aspects: the destruction of the expressive pseudo forms of the unconscious, and the discovery of desire's unconscious investments of the social field. It is from this point of view that we must consider many primitive cures; they are schizoanalysis in action." [23] Supernatural powers "move desire in the direction of more intense and more adequate investments of the social field, in its organization as well as its disorganizations" (170).

Most importantly, Deleuze and Guattari argue that it is through Oedipus that the ethnographic Other speaks. Oedipus "is another way of coding the uncodable, of codifying what eludes the codes, or of displacing desire and its objects, a way of entrapping them" (173). Mead and Bateson's representation of Balinese trance dancing demonstrates this process of entrapping and encoding through psychoanalytic paradigms; at the same time, their schizoanalysis points to an organization of desire within a social machine that the anthropologists already implicitly recognized as a mechanism of capitalism. The culture had to be documented, because it would inevitably disappear into the powerful machine of capitalism, but it was thus already part of that machine. The loss of the ego that is displayed in the trance, and that they claim to be endemic to the culture itself, enables an abstraction of desire as a flow and a force. Their study was intended as a contribution to an unnamed "integrated" culture[24] that is much like Deleuze and Guattari's version of capitalism: "The more it breaks down, the more it schizophrenizes, the better it works, the American way."[25]

Mead and Bateson went to Bali looking for schizophrenic-like behavior, and they found it.[26] Another explanation for their findings is a Balinese feeling called *lek,* defined as the "embarrassment or stage fright experienced when faced with a person of higher status."[27] Mead and Bateson's presence in the remote village of Bayung Gede, where they carried out most of their research, no doubt provoked an exaggerated degree of *lek* among their subjects. It has been suggested that Mead herself looked to the Balinese very much like Rangda, the evil witch that is central to the theatrical ritual of the trance performance.[28] While camera shyness is apparent in many of the photographs in *Balinese Character,* the trance dance offered the anthropologists a rare opportunity to film the Balinese free of *lek.*

Trance and Dance in Bali consists of footage shot at two performances and condenses the several hours that the ritual normally takes into twenty minutes.[29] The performances themselves were commissioned by the anthropologists, who even asked that two different plays be combined so that they could shoot both men and women dancers.[30] In 1936 the Balinese had already modified the plays to please American tourists, and the change requested by Mead and Bateson was established as yet another version of the ritual.[31] Clearly the authenticity of the larger structure of the ritual was less important to the novice filmmakers than the authenticity of detailed gestures and movements of individual dancers, which are the focus of the film.

The film begins with titles explaining the story that the theatrical ritual dramatizes.[32] As in the TV broadcast of the film, Mead's voice-over is continuous on the film's soundtrack, explaining not only the narrative events being dramatized but the costumes, characters, and gestures in each shot. Often her descriptions are redundant, excessively reduplicating the information in the image. Shot silently, in very short, quick takes, the performance is fragmented and disjunctive, and there is no sense of the rhythmic or environmental context of the performance. While the main characters of Witch and Dragon are enveloped in elaborate costumes with masks, the dancers impersonating the dis-

Still from *Trance and Dance in Bali,* by Margaret Mead and
Gregory Bateson (1952). *Courtesy of the Library of Congress and the
Institute for Cultural Studies.*

ciples are all young men and women in sarongs. The performance has
a strong narrative trajectory, climaxing in the final scene in which the
men and women threaten to stab themselves with *krisses,* ceremonial
daggers. This part of the ritual constitutes the bulk of the film, followed
by shots of the dancers lying in one another's arms slowly coming out
of trance with the supportive assistance of priests and older women.

Like most possession rituals, the Balinese performance is set in a compound surrounded by spectators and not on a stage. The edited film
lacks any sense of spatial orientation as the camera is constantly moving
to get good shots of entranced dancers. It is in the resulting disorientation (produced by a handheld camera that anticipates the *cinéma vérité*
style) and the difficulty of spectator positioning that films of possession rituals tend toward a formal aesthetic of experimentation. Because
Mead and Bateson were mainly concerned with the individual body,
they cut from one performer to another with little continuity other than
Mead's explanatory voice-over. As Bateson's hand-wound Movikon allowed only short takes,[33] the fragmentation was due in part to available
technology, but the resulting film conveys a strong sense of being *in
medias res,* disoriented by a lack of distance from the spectacle.

The compound in which the Rangda-Barong play/ritual is performed is surrounded by villagers, who can be glimpsed in the background of many of the shots. At one point, an older woman goes into trance, and Mead explains that the woman had not wanted to but could not resist. This seems to be a common feature of the Balinese performance and underlines the different form of spectatorship provoked by possession rituals. The possessed state of the dancers is like a contagion that spreads to the audience witnessing the presence of spirits. And yet there is no chance of the contagion spreading to the spectator of the film, distanced in time and space. Mead's voice-over makes meaning out of every gesture, preventing the erotic stimulation of the performance from leaking out. Except for one shot at the beginning of the film, the musicians are not seen, and the soundtrack of gamelan music is turned down to a low atmospheric background noise.

Throughout the film, the viewer relies on Mead's authority as to who is in trance and when. She apparently relied on native informants to whom she showed the footage to tell her when a trance state had been obtained,[34] although there is no trace of doubt in her discursive authority. The dancers begin with very specific movements, with a slightly mechanical or automaton aspect to them, but the point at which the dance has provoked a full possession is not obvious to the untrained eye. In fact, the real event of the dramatic possession ritual is invisible, which is what makes it such an ironic document of visual anthropology. When the dancers appear to be trying to stab themselves, Mead assures us that "if anyone is actually hurt, the trance is not real." The performance of suicide, in other words, can be proven false, but there is no evidence of authenticity.

Margaret Mead's methodology for her experiments in visual anthropology in Bali was influenced by the surveillance techniques designed by the psychologist Arnold Gessell, whose theory of "cinemanalysis" was supposed to analyze a child's intellectual development on the basis of observed behavior.[35] She thus assumed from the outset that the unconscious, or interiority, could be "read" in the writing of the body. The phenomenon of trance enabled her to authenticate her interpretation of Balinese behavior as a transparent reading. However, *Trance and Dance in Bali* relies heavily on cinematic technique to provide a legible document.

Although Mead herself was skeptical of any "artistic" use of photography in the field, Bateson, who did most of the camera work for *Trance and Dance,* abandoned the tripod for a more "relevant" document. In a 1977 discussion about the Balinese footage, the two of them argue about one of the central dilemmas facing a scientific use of visual anthropology. Mead says, "It's rich, because they're long sequences, and that's what you need . . . long enough to analyze." Bateson replies, "There are no long sequences." He points out that the film works as a "document" because he kept moving the camera to get better views. "Of the things that happen, the camera is only going to record one percent anyway. I want the one percent on the whole to tell." [36]

The film also includes slow-motion footage shot by Jane Belo,[37] which might be what Mead is referring to. While slow motion certainly lends itself to analysis, and is almost always used in films about possession rituals, it also mimics the effect of trance, the "otherworldliness" of the spectacle. The fragmented nature of Bateson's footage, combined with the slow motion, suggests that the imperative of accurate documentation extends to capturing the "feel" of trance. If this cannot be imparted to the spectator of the film, how can the event be known? Thus, the fundamental tension in *Trance and Dance in Bali* lies between sound and image tracks, between two different orders of epistemology as the team attempted to document the "ethos" of the culture.

Mead and Bateson were clearly struck by the sexual energy flowing through and from the performance, and in attempting to represent it as "ethos," they fell back on the classic Western narrative that links sexuality to hysteria. Their diagnosis of schizophrenia implicitly recognized the different organization of desire in Balinese culture. And yet in the theatrical ritual of possessed trance dancers, they read a therapeutic narrative designed to restore Oedipus and the male ego to its familiar place.

In their attempt to interpret what they saw in Balinese trance, Mead and Bateson turned to the scientism of psychoanalysis to anchor ethnographic spectatorship. It provided an interpretive model for reading the eruptions of the unconscious in visible behavior. Although no explanation is offered in the film itself, in *Balinese Character,* the dramatic performance of threatened suicide is interpreted as the "absent climax" of Balinese life. For Mead, the drama expresses a male fear of female sexuality. The young girls in the play are transformed from sexy beauties to dangerous witches, thus replicating (in Mead's view) their transformation into mothers after marriage. As the mother in Mead's theory is the cause of the Balinese character disorder of withdrawal and weak ego, she is a figure of great fear. The play thus dramatizes the male fear of marrying a witch-mother.[38]

Although *Trance and Dance in Bali* was made with little aesthetic theory behind it, the film anticipates the discourse of therapy within subsequent *cinéma vérité* filmmaking. The psychological substratum of the possession ritual constitutes a veracity of experience that Jean Rouch would subsequently develop as a realist aesthetic. *Trance and Dance* may not have been the first film of possession rituals, but it was the first to locate the spectacle within a discourse of modernist represen-tation. The anthropologists recognized "the unconscious" on display but failed to read it as the subjectivity of the Other, preferring to "con-tain" it within a psychopathological diagnosis. The excess produced by the signifying body is read not as an interiority, or as a discourse of the occult, but as a transparent document. The film concludes with a slogan of universal humanism, canceling out the difference of Balinese culture altogether: "And so the Balinese reenact the struggle between death on the one hand and life protecting ritual on the other."

Maya Deren: The Artist as Anthropologist

Maya Deren's interest in Haitian possession rituals preceded her first film, *Meshes of the Afternoon,* and eventually outlasted her filmmaking activities. Although she was inspired by Mead and Bateson's Balinese film, Deren understood the phenomenon of possession as a metaphysi-cal, creative, and religious practice. It is Deren who, along with Artaud, has articulated most clearly the modernist fascination with possession. For her, the trance was a hallucinatory realism in which reality and subjectivity were indistinguishable. The ethnographic context served to ground the trance in bodies and lived experience, which attracted her as an ideal cinematic spectacle but proved finally to exceed the limits of visual representation.

Deren's first trip to Haiti was in 1947 on a Guggenheim grant, and by 1951, she had made four trips. Various explanations have been offered for her inability to edit the film footage and sound recordings that she collected there. Although she had traveled to Haiti to make a film "as an artist," she ended up writing a book, "recording, as humbly and accu-rately as I can, the logics of a reality which had forced me to recognize its integrity, and to abandon my manipulations."[39] Moreover, a film could show only the "surface" of the rituals, not their underlying principles and mythology.[40] Nevertheless, the existence of the footage, and the story of her unsuccessful attempt to make a film, offer some insight into the shared territory of experimental and ethnographic film practices.

Within the history of avant-garde filmmaking, Deren is a key figure linking the French surrealists of the 1920s and 1930s to the postwar American avant-garde. P. Adams Sitney describes Deren's films and those that she inspired as "trance films." Unlike those of her surrealist precursors, Deren's psychodramatic films explore an interiority of consciousness. "She encounters objects and sights as if they were capable of revealing the erotic mystery of the self."[41] Sitney contrasts this to the "mad voyeurism" of the surrealists. *Meshes of the Afternoon* (1943), *At Land* (1944), and *Ritual in Transfigured Time* (1945) all engage with dream states and hallucinatory imagery in keeping with Deren's theory of cinema as the meeting of reality and creative imagination — "the creative use of reality."[42]

Deren's status as one of the first stars of the American avant-garde cinema, one of the first and most visible exponents of personal cinema, provides an ironic contrast to the theme of "depersonalization" in her filmmaking. Maria Pramaggiore has argued that "Deren's promotional efforts helped create an image of the modernist artist-auteur (inflected by contemporary discourses of gender), whereas her multiplied and fragmented film protagonists refuse to 'guarantee' textual meaning through persona."[43] In addition to the splitting and replication of her own image in *Meshes of the Afternoon,* Deren's experimental filmmaking used body movement as a narrational technique, often in conjunction with montage, to create hallucinatory, surreal effects of the body in space. Separating body movement from subjective forms of "character" was not intended to destroy the individual, but through ritual, "it enlarges him [sic] beyond the personal dimension, and frees him from the specializations and confines of 'personality.' "[44] In Pramaggiore's reading of the experimental work, Deren creates "the sense of bodies subsumed by forces different from and larger than the individual will"[45] — precisely the subject effect of possession rituals.

"Depersonalization" is the term that Deren uses to denote her interest in ritual as a cinematic category,[46] and there is no question that her quest for forms of depersonalization is what took her to Haiti. And yet I would argue that the category of the individual subject is not actually challenged by Deren's experimental practice but is masked by a romantic notion of the community and the crowd as an expression of identity.[47] The representation of fragmented subjects in Deren's experimental films is ultimately subsumed by the creative force of the artist, through whose vision they can be reassembled into conceptual wholes. She herself learned how to enter trance and became famous in certain New York social circles for her ability to disrupt everyday reality by being suddenly possessed.[48] Haitian possession becomes one more component of the radicalized identity of the avant-garde artist.

By treating possession as a cultural and aesthetic form, Deren manages to dismiss the historical context of Haitian voodoo, along with the revolutionary potential of "depersonalization." Deren was not really interested in the role of voodoo in Haitian revolutionary movements of the early nineteenth century, or in the underground African unity discourse that it preserved within slave culture.[49] These are mentioned in passing in her writings, only as an explanation for the power invested in, and derived from, the *loas*—the gods who mount the possessed dancers.[50] Nor is she interested in the conditions of everyday life of the participants in the rituals—what they do when they are not dancing. Deren's ethnographic method, like her aesthetics, is a romantic one that seeks a transcendent form of experience. What distinguishes her project from similar programs and manifestos on transcendent forms of art—such as those of Artaud and Brakhage—is the role of the body in her texts. Her fascination with the actual movements by which Haitian dancers invite the gods to possess them is what took her to Haiti. Deren pursues the conjunction of art and anthropology much further than her contemporaries, and she articulates, however crudely, the fundamental attraction of the avant-garde to native cultures that has persisted since the surrealists.

Before going to Haiti, Deren viewed Mead and Bateson's Balinese footage of trance. Deren was so inspired by this material that she planned to include sections of it in her own film, exploring with Bateson the possibilities and problems of a "cross-cultural fugue" that would also include children's games filmed in New York—a juxtaposition of different ritual performances.[51] In diary notes on the Balinese footage, she takes issue with Bateson's theory of the frustrated climax and suggests instead that the Balinese trance performance constitutes an extended climax. Energy in trance is channeled into "a tension plateau which serves the continuity both of personal and communal relations."[52] She notes that in the Balinese film, "when clothes fall off they have to be adjusted for theatrical, not personal reasons," and thus "Freud wouldn't do so well in Bali. Hooray for the Balinese."

Deren effectively rejects Mead and Bateson's implied theory of therapy. Not only does Balinese trance performance not have a pathological explanation, but Deren finds that it lacks a cathartic form of spectatorship. She points out that there is a complete indifference between spectators and performers in the film, a lack of identification that challenges the conventional spectator-exhibitionist structure of theatrical performance. The term "exhibitionism," she says, simply does not apply to the Balinese footage.[53] The lack of star performers, along with the lack of a stage with its strict delineation of the space of performance, suggests to Deren a form of ego-less theatricality. In Haiti she hoped to find a similar spectacle that would place new demands on filmmaker and audience alike.

Stan Brakhage claims that Deren struggled with her Haitian footage for ten years.[54] Regardless of whether this struggle took place in the editing room or in Deren's creative imagination, her project highlights a vivid tension between personal filmmaking and the observational mode of ethnography as it is played out around the phenomenon of possession. The Haitian material may have grown out of Deren's prior filmmaking practice, but it also challenged many of the assumptions within her aesthetic theory, most explicitly the romantic individualism underscoring her quest for "depersonalization." The rituals that she found in Haiti were an expression of a complex cosmology of highly individualized deities; and the expression itself, the performing bodies, was charged with an eroticism otherwise absent from Deren's oeuvre. Haitian possession consisted of two very different discourses, the invisible knowledge of the gods, and the visible evidence of the possessed body. Her failure to make a film is, ultimately, a failure to reconcile these two forms of representation.

Deren eventually wrote a book that supplanted the film as the more adequate representation of Haitian voodoo. *Divine Horsemen* is written from the perspective of the initiate, and its slogan is "When the anthropologist arrives, the gods depart." In her introduction, Deren establishes her credentials to write about possession on the basis of her status as an artist. Since her métier was to deal on the level of subjective communication, she claims to have had an insight into the rituals unavailable to the anthropologist. She also claims an affinity with the marginal status of native peoples vis-à-vis modern industrial culture.

Artists, she says, are an "ethnic group," subject to the full "native" treatment—exhibited, denounced, feasted, forgotten, misrepresented, and exploited by a society on which they are dependent.[55] The difficulties she had completing the film need to be read back into that precarious alignment of artist and "native" that she herself sets up.

In 1942, five years before she went to Haiti, Deren published an article on the anthropology of dance, in which she develops a theory of possession as a psychological and creative practice. Recognizing a parallelism between hysteria and possession, Deren makes two important points that make a real break with the analytic framework developed by Mead and Bateson. One is that "in our culture hysteria is an antisocial phenomenon; in Haitian and African culture, possession is not at all antagonistic to its social environment but rather a part of it."[56] Secondly, the communal context of possession constitutes an active and validating form of spectatorship: "For when the objective surrounding, or community, confirms the subjective impression of the individual, the concept upon which those two forces are in agreement constitutes, within that particular frame of reference, a reality."[57] Deren insisted that despite the parallels between possession and psychopathological states, possession was neither "delusional" nor abnormal in Haiti. Both hysteria and possession occur in social contexts, she argues, but possession is culturally determined whereas hysteria is privately determined. She hoped that the social confirmation of a hallucinatory reality could in some way be achieved in modern American dance.[58] Although she arguably outgrew the Orientalism of this article, she remained guided by the theory of hysteria as a key to possession phenomena.

After viewing the Balinese material, Deren went back to her earlier article and found that despite her critique of Mead and Bateson's use of psychoanalysis, her own theory of possession as "an hysterical release of a subconscious system of ideas" still held.[59] Throughout her writing on ritual performance there is the sense of it as a return of the repressed: "Psychosomaticism is the re-creation in immediate terms of unrecollected memory."[60] For Deren, "primitive" forms of spirituality differ from modern ones only in their degrees of intensity,[61] and thus the experience of possession in Haiti is not completely alien to the psychology and physiology of ecstasy in other more "modern" cultures.

In uniting the spectacle of the body with a dream state that tended toward the somnambulistic, possession seemed to share basic metaphysical properties with the cinema. Given the parallels between her experimental films and her writing on possession, what Deren hoped to find in Haiti was a means of making the mind visible. From her background in dance and her interest in psychoanalysis,[62] she viewed the bodies of the possessed dancers as manifestations of the mind, as images of the unconscious. To really understand possession, it had to be experienced subjectively — by an artist like herself.[63]

Divine Horsemen reads more like a religious tract than an anthropological study. The detail is extraordinary, but it is concerned solely with beliefs and ritual practices. Each of the *loas,* who have distinct and dramatic personalities, and each of their ceremonies are described, along with the hierarchies of the priesthood, the metaphysics of the religion, and the music, costumes, symbols, and accoutrements. Deren's writing is inflected with the passion of bringing the gods to life and culminates in the final chapter in which she describes her own possession by the *loa* Erzulie:

To be precise, I must say what, even to me, is pure recollection, but not otherwise conceivable: I must call it a white darkness, its whiteness a glory and its darkness terror. It is the terror which has the greater force, and with a supreme effort I wrench the leg loose — I must keep moving! must keep moving! — and pick up the dancing rhythm of the drums as something to grasp at, something to keep my feet from resting upon the dangerous earth. No sooner do I settle into the succour of this support than my sense of self doubles again, as in a mirror, separates to both sides of an invisible threshold, except that now the vision of the one who watches flickers, the lids flutter, the gaps between moments of sight growing greater, wider. I see the dancing one here, and next in a different place, facing another direction, and whatever lay between these moments is lost, utterly lost.[64]

As this passage suggests, *Divine Horsemen* is clearly much more than reportage. The impressions of doubling and split vision are evocative of *Meshes.* Moreover, her language is stylized, expressive, and subjective. In this passage, metaphors of vision, along with imagery of light and darkness, inscribe the spectacle of race that lies hidden within her project. Writing, no less than filming, is only a means of representing possession, which is itself a form of representation. She found film to be an inadequate means of penetrating the layers of signification set up by ritual performance, and so she wrote the book as an interpretation of the performances she witnessed. The characters of the *loas* are not perceptible on film because those who are seen are not those who are present. The *loas* remain invisible to the film spectator, and since the purpose of the rituals is to prove the existence of the *loas,* the film fails as a document of reality.

The film that was released in 1985 as *Divine Horsemen,* edited by Cheryl Ito, is an attempt to bring Deren's writing, film footage, and sound recordings together. Unfortunately, it resorts to a format of ethnographic filmmaking that runs counter to Deren's perspective on anthropology. The explanatory male voice-over is greatly removed from the act of filming. The voice, and the text itself, is of an entirely different order of language — impersonal, objective, authoritative, and oblique. As a narration, Deren's extremely literary writing is heavy and overwrought. A woman's voice-over is used for one passage, but the softer, less expository tone that may have been an attempt to capture Deren's experiential attitude is simply a clichéd feminization.

The disjunction of sound and image in *Divine Horsemen* is more than a function of the production history of the film. A profound ambiguity lies at the heart of the voodoo ritual itself, creating a real problem for documentary representation. When individuals are "mounted" or possessed by a *loa,* they take on that personality and are no longer "themselves," but visually, they are still themselves acting differently. When, for example, a man is seen giving out money and people appear to be bumping into him, the narrator says: "The spirit of Ghede is mounting the body of the priest. He is known as a trickster and delights in playing games to confuse people. . . . Clown though he may be, he is also history — the experience from which the living learn — and in this role is as deeply responsible and trustworthy as he is bizarre in his other aspects. . . . Ghede is also a god of fertility. The women bump against him to ensure healthy children." [65] In the cinematic configuration of sound and image, "he" is the man on-screen acting as the *loa* Ghede, impersonating him. The image of the eroticized body is a much more direct and legible signifier than the descriptive language superimposed on it. The Haitian possession rituals that Deren filmed challenge the cinematic construction of performance by exhibiting an unintelligible theatricality.

The Ito version of the film includes a soundtrack composed of Deren's own recordings, but it is overwhelmed by the voice-over and functions more like background music than as an integral part of the ceremonies. Each segment is introduced with a graphic design or painting associated with one of the *loas,* thus incorporating yet another level of meta-discourse into the film. The editing is fairly quick, moving between different dancers, settings, activities, and practices, even within segments. As a result, the montage of people dancing, ritual animal sacrifices, parades, and so on is reduced to the status of images that illustrate a preconceived commentary. As an ethnographic film, it is a voyeuristic structure that runs contrary to Deren's insistence on the holistic, psychological, emotional, and experiential quality of her approach to Haiti.

Deren's own silent footage assembled by Anthology Film Archives runs three and three-quarters hours. There is a great deal of in-camera editing and an assembly of rolls of film complete with flares indicating reel-ends. Although the film is nominally "unedited," a curious repetition in which the same trio of three people dancing in a clearing recurs after cutting away to quite different scenes, suggesting that some kind of reordering of scenes may have been done. However, the lack of intention behind the montage enables us to describe this footage as "raw." Deren's failure to edit it, to manipulate it or subject it to secondary revision, leaves us with a document that is not "a film" — but neither is it an observational record shot by a nonintrusive surveillance camera. It is an extremely moving and emotional depiction of possession, even though it may not be "evidence" of the presence and activities of the *loas*.

Deren's shots are long, with constant movement, including handheld photography, swish-pans, and zooms. Close-ups and medium shots predominate over long and establishing shots. The few images of landscape tend not to be integrated into possession scenes. Every new scene begins from the inside, paying close attention to the movements of feet and bodies, often cutting or panning to the drummers. The rhythm of the ceremonies becomes visible, and each new set of dancers is given film time to develop, so that the transition from dance to possession is often apparent, without anyone pointing it out. Details such as the way dancers lose their balance as they are "mounted," their stunned look as they come out of trance, the spitting of liquor and the incorporation of Euro-American dance steps such as a jig, a jive, or waltz, are clear as visual signs. Without a voice-over, the image is legible on its own — as a different order of knowledge. Without a soundtrack, the image is a qualified realism, at a distance from the viewer, and the presence of the musicians inscribes a silence and an attendant awareness of limits.

Many sequences are shot in slow motion, perhaps to follow the com-

Stills from *Divine Horsemen*, by Maya Deren (1947–1985).

plex dance steps and body movements. In contrast with the voice-over version, the dancers perform in their own time with their own knowledge intact. It is an other time, although not a vaguely other ahistorical setting. It is not a shared time between spectator and profilmic; it is historical time marked by once-only events, particularly the deaths of animals. At least seven sacrifices take place, including chickens, goats, and a bull, each of which is carried out somewhat differently. A convention of ethnographic film, bloodletting practices often contribute to the negative stereotype of the primitive, and they can often challenge the norms of Western spectatorship. This is implied even in Artaud's theater of cruelty, but here the cruelty is only in the eyes of the non-Haitian spectator. As Deren says in her book, in the context of Haitian voodoo, sacrifice is not "morbid" but a practice of renewal and rejuvenation by which the *loa* is infused with life and vigor.[66] As a cinematic spectacle, animal sacrifice constitutes an indexical inscription of the otherness of time and history as the spectator becomes a witness to that which has occurred only once: it is thus redemptive. In Deren's footage, the frequency of animal sacrifices and their ceremonial integration normalizes the practice and challenges the spectator.

As with most possession dances, the Haitian rituals are set in a circular compound, sometimes with a shed roof over it, but without a stage or proscenium structure. Spectators surround the dancers, and Deren's camera moves around, to and from different points in the circle. (The footage also includes a number of setups in which people are clearly performing for the camera, especially in the carnival sequences.) Despite the discontinuity of her editing and the lack of a stable spectator position, the bodies of the dancers tend to anchor the view. Their erotic, sensual, and fluid movements function as an attraction to the *loas* who eventually possess the most spectacular dancers — but also to the spectator. Deren emphasizes the role of the community and its virtual eroticization by the possession ritual, a scene from which the film spectator, in silence, is excluded. One can watch other spectators become affected by the contagion of possession, but it does not spread beyond the frame.

Despite the dynamic character of Deren's footage, which culminates in a carnival parade, the different form of knowledge implicit in possession is ultimately unavailable to the film spectator. Haitian voodoo dances involve many explicit expressions of sexuality — flirting, couple dancing, and eroticized body movements. They also frequently involve gender confusion and ambivalence, but this is not apparent to the film spectator. In one sequence, on the level of the visual alone we see a woman dancing seductively with the drummers. We may know from Deren's book that women are often possessed (or mounted) by male *loas* and take on their characters, but we cannot see that the woman is "not herself." As visible evidence, it remains the image of a woman dancing seductively. Sexuality in Haitian possession is indeed a fluid and communal form of expression, and eroticism is not simply carnal but a transcendent form of being. Ghede, says Deren, "is amused by the eternal persistence of the erotic and by man's eternally persistent pretense that it is something else." [67] Ecstatic ethnography is entirely bound up with this pretense that eroticism is a function of the material, visible, sensuous body.

That Ghede likes to wear sunglasses further suggests that the discourse of desire in Haitian possession is invested in the eye as well as the body. Possession, for Deren, is about witnessing, about the communal recognition of a reality confirmed by the spectacle of the body. [68] And yet she found that film was inadequate; in fact, it renders the *loas* invisible and absent. Her own observations on Mead and Bateson's footage, that there is no identification between dancers and audience, ultimately come back to haunt her; she can only know the loas through her own performance. If it was only by writing that she could bring the *loas* to life, it was because she could write herself into the scene of possession more easily in words than in images.

Missing from her footage is the spectacle of Deren herself dancing among the Haitians. How could she have filmed this without looking like Osa Johnson among the Africans, or Marlene Dietrich in a gorilla suit, or Leni Riefenstahl among the Nuba? [69] Positioning herself behind the camera, Deren eliminates her whiteness, and its attendant discourse of race. But at the same time, she eliminates the level of experience that she claimed to be necessary for an understanding of possession. Her subjectivity is reduced to a strictly phenomenological inscription of viewing, a status that irrevocably separates her from the Haitians. Photography is a different form of witnessing than that called for by possession. Through writing, she could overcome the visible difference of race and the phenomenological separation of mechanical reproduction; but only through dance could the mediation of witnessing be removed.

Deren's unfinished film constitutes an experiment with ethnographic language, a document of the limits of cinematic representation. Whereas her written document constitutes a translation of Haitian voodoo into another language—English literary/academic prose—the film footage is an attempt to represent experience directly without mediation. The result situates the auratic truth of the image out of reach, along with the subjective reality that the ritual ostensibly documents. The ethnographic spectacle is not "evidence" of the *loas,* which will always escape the attempt to inscribe them in documentary form. The means by which the Haitians are able to become Others through the language of the body might be an instance of what Walter Benjamin describes as the "mimetic faculty" that is in decay in modernity:

We must suppose that the gift of producing similarities—for example, in dances, whose oldest function this was—and therefore also the gift of recognizing them, have changed with historical development. . . . For clearly the observable world of modern man contains only minimal residues of the magical correspondences and analogies that were familiar to ancient peoples. The question is whether we are concerned with the decay of this faculty or with its transformation.[70]

The cinema was for Benjamin an inscription of this transformation, in which a language of similarity and analogy is allegorized in mechanical reproduction. For Deren, the auratic potential of cinema was its ability to make the facts of the mind visible. While it was possible in her experimental films to give her own mind, her own subjectivity, imagistic representation, in Haiti the gap between experience and cinematic representation became unbridgeable, and the aura disintegrates.

The fascination with possession is bound up with the different order of knowledge and language that it embodies. Its occult and mystical properties ultimately proved more powerful than Deren's faith in cinematic "magic," and yet in its unfinished form, her footage provides a rare document of possession. For Artaud, the utopian possibilities of the cinema were invested in the freedom from language and the promise of a direct visceral experience in and through representation. "Raw cinema, taken as it is, in the abstract, exudes a little of this trance-like atmosphere, eminently favorable for certain revelations."[71] Although Deren's "unedited" record of possession can be considered "raw film," it cannot divine the "secrets of the depths of consciousness" that Artaud hopes for. In turning away from her own subjectivity, and exploring the mind of the Other, Deren's ethnographic imagery can register only the trace of the occult, which becomes in its absence the aura of the subjectivity of the Other—something lost in the translation to film.

Deren's failure to represent the Other's subjectivity is bound up with the primitivist paradigm that aligns native subjectivity only with occult phenomena. Its failure is not unrelated to Deren's profound neglect of the socioeconomic and political history of voodoo. Her purely metaphysical interest in Haitian possession that enabled her to identify with "the natives" also wrote history out of the picture. Thus, the spirit of Carnival and the discourse of race are rendered ineffective as resistant discourses. Depersonalization in the Haitian context is deeply embedded in political resistance. Perhaps the gap between experience and film, between aura and language, might be overcome if voodoo were understood as a political language of ethnic resistance. Within Deren's modernist aesthetics, possession remains a metaphor of language, a utopian ideal of a form of knowledge inaccessible to the fallen consciousness of industrialized subjectivity.

Jean Rouch: *Ciné-transe*

The figure of Jean Rouch looms in this history of experimental ethnography as the dominant figure in postwar methods of visual anthropology. His ethnography consistently stressed the role of the subject of vision, and his innovative techniques were shared by the burgeoning auteurist cinema of the French New Wave. More than that of any other filmmaker, Rouch's filmmaking spanned anthropology and the avant-garde systematically over an extended period of time, influencing the directions of both modern cinema and modern anthropology in important ways. His vision may have been utopian, and his ethnography was truly experimental, and yet his work remains limited within certain cultural paradigms, most particularly that of gender.

Possession rituals played a central role in Rouch's anthropology and in his filmmaking of the 1950s and 1960s. In 1978 he claimed to have attended several hundred possession ceremonies and to have filmed about twenty, almost all of them performed by the Songhay of West Africa.[72] His extensive fieldwork in the culture[73] gave him unprecedented access, and he privileged the filming of possession rituals as an instance of shared, or participatory, ethnography. Moreover, the scene of possession became the catalyst in Rouch's development of *cinéma vérité*, as it offered a particular profilmic support for the development of a new form of realism, a different order of truth.

In a series of articles and interviews about his filming of possession rituals, Rouch developed a theory of *ciné-transe* that linked a cinematic ontology with the phenomenon of trance. He argued that the act of filming lifted the filmmaker onto a plane of magic and out-of-body experience akin to that of the spirit-possessed. Or, more precisely, he felt that the filmmaker would appear so to those he filmed:

I now believe that for the people who are filmed, the "self" of the filmmaker changes in front of their eyes during the shooting. He no longer speaks, except to yell out incomprehensible orders ("Roll!" "Cut!"). He now only looks at them through the intermediary of a strange appendage and only hears them through the intermediary of a shotgun microphone. . . . For the Songhay-Zarma, who are now quite accustomed to film, my "self" is altered in front of their eyes in the same way as is the "self" of the possession dancers: it is the "film trance" *(ciné-transe)* of the one filming the "real trance" of the other.[74]

Rouch has also said that "because I made films, I have never been possessed,"[75] indicating an eradicable difference between his trance and those possessed by spirits. *Ciné-transe* refers to the creative euphoria of filmmaking, of losing oneself at one's work — behind the camera, at the editing table, and writing and recording narration. It will always entail some distance from the experience of possession that is filmed and comes to function as a means of legitimizing Rouch's ethnographic practice. When he is modified by equipment, he claims to gain the confidence of the African, who enters into an "ethno-dialogue" with him.[76]

In claiming that the magical and transformative properties of cinema approximate the fantastic aspects of possession, Rouch anticipates Michael Taussig's observations on the new forms of vision enabled by technology. Via Benjamin, Taussig says that "the scientific quotient of the eyeful opened up by the revelations of the optical unconscious is also an artistic and hallucinatory eye, a roller-coastering of the senses dissolving both science and art into a new mode of truth-seeking and reality-testing."[77] For Rouch, the incorporation of "fiction" into ethnography is a metaphor for subjectivity, desire, fantasy, and imagination that might be fused with the empirical, indexical documentary image. Beyond mere truth, *cinéma vérité* could potentially produce a new reality, a science fiction blending objective science and subjective art.[78]

Both Rouch and Taussig refer back to Dziga Vertov as the model of truth that informs this new technologized way of seeing. The term *cinéma vérité* is derived from Vertov's *kinopravda*,[79] although it is unlikely that Vertov would have approved of Rouch's new application of the "new organ of perception," the *ciné*-eye: "It is the camera that allows me to see the gods."[80] The *ciné-transe* produced a filmic truth that could be distinguished from "pure truth" or mere empiricism: it produced a special veracity available only to cinema. Thus *cinéma vérité* emerges as a new form of knowledge in which film technology is united with the mimeticism of "primitive" religion. Like the spirit-possessed who leave "themselves" and become their doubles in the spirit world, the filmmaker in a *ciné-transe* leaves "himself" and becomes one with the equipment strapped to his body.

The film that most perfectly demonstrates the *ciné-transe* as ethnographic technique is *Tourou et Bitti: Les Tambours d'Avant* (1971),[81] a ten-minute film shot in one long take. Rouch's voice-over reiterates the claim made in all the synopses of the film: that after four days of waiting for the members of a certain village to go into trance, he took up his camera to film the musicians and actually provoked the possession ritual into happening. Walking around the village compound with the camera to his eye, not turning it off until the magazine was empty, Rouch may well have been a curious sight. His claim to have been possessed by the film is, however, offset by the voice-over that was recorded later, in which he intones the voices of the spirits themselves. Here, as elsewhere, Rouch's claim to have crossed over into the consciousness of the Other is really a claim about himself, his subjectivity, and his presence, which dominates the soundtracks of so many of his films.

In the development of "direct cinema" in Canada, the United States, and France from 1958 to 1962, Rouch's contribution was perhaps the most auteurist and the most provocative, *Chronique d'un été* (1960), which he codirected with Edgar Morin, being one of the central texts of this movement. As Mike Eaton has pointed out, Rouch's method of provocation and acceleration, by which the camera would be a causal agent in the *production* of reality, allowed him to pose as "a shaman, the master of ceremonies at a cinematic ritual."[82] The new authenticity of *cinéma vérité* was due to two key innovations. One was the inscription of the filmmaker into the diegetic space of the film. This ostensibly produced a new "honesty" of representation and an integrity of presence that did not jeopardize the objective veracity of the profilmic. The other innovation was the use of synchronized sound, by which the people filmed could express themselves in their own voices.[83] The *ciné-*

transe was Rouch's theorization of these techniques as motivated by the content of ethnographic reality itself. *Cinéma vérité* aspired to the subjective realism of possession, but at the same time, it shifted the focus of the film from the profilmic event to the act and event of filming.

Rouch's interest in possession rituals was equally inspired by surrealism, and many of the contradictions and ironies surrounding his notion of *ciné-transe* might be traced to the odd pairing of *cinéma vérité* and surrealism. The two aesthetics do not sit easily together, and yet the possession ritual marks a curious point of intersection as it is filmed and discussed by Rouch. He is unequivocal about the ways that the ethnographic surrealism of Paris in the 1930s shaped his formation as an anthropologist and stimulated his fascination with possession. The first rituals he saw reminded him of experiments by Breton and Eluard, and from the very beginning, he said, "There's only one way to study that, it's to make a film." [84]

Like automatic writing or hypnotism, *ciné-transe* and spirit possession are potential means of making the unconscious visible, of breaking through conscious, bourgeois (and possibly colonial) layers of rationality and repression. And yet in all of Rouch's writing—and in the many celebratory articles and interviews written about this tendency in his work—one has to ask, whose unconscious is being revealed? Rouch's desire to transcend the limits of reality in the utopian thrust of the *ciné-transe,* his desire to "write with the body," is all about *his* body with its appendages of motion picture equipment. Surrealism offers Rouch the inheritance of the avant-garde and a valuable point of entry onto the ethnographic scene, but by the 1950s, surrealism may not have been the most appropriate means of approaching an Africa on the verge of independence.

Les Maîtres fous polarized its first audience in 1954 at the private screening at the Musée de l'Homme. The film is about the Hauka cult in the Gold Coast (which gained its independence and became Ghana in 1957) who are possessed by spirits that take the form of figures of colonial authority. African intellectuals, as well as French anthropologists, including Rouch's mentor Marcel Griaule, were scandalized by the film and demanded that it be destroyed.[85] Rouch's perseverance and commitment to the film demonstrated his adherence to the surrealist aesthetics of transgression and guaranteed its mythology of broken taboos. For Paul Stoller, the film demands a "decolonization of thought" from its spectator. The challenge of the grotesque, along with the epistemological problem of possession (seeing the unknowable), constitutes a rupture great enough to "transform its audience psychologically and physically."[86]

On the other side of the debate, Teshome Gabriel has reiterated the African opposition to the film, describing it as a racist treatment of African people as "scientific specimens, laboratory subjects and insects."[87] Legend has it that when the Senegalese director Blaise Senghor saw the film in a Paris theater, the spectators said to each other, "Here's another one who is going to eat dog!"[88] On one level, Les Maîtres fous is indeed a film about the survival of primitive rituals within modern Africa. Political resistance and traditional mysticism are reduced, together, to an exotic spectacle of otherness. The power of the film is invested in the shock effect of its images, which seem to have halted any attempts to actually look at the film as a text.

Contrary to the aesthetics of cinéma vérité, Les Maîtres fous contains neither long takes nor synchronized sound. It was shot with a handheld camera and edited mainly in the camera with a shooting ratio of only eight to ten.[89] The average shot length is about five seconds. Although Rouch is clear in his voice-over that the event takes an entire day, his editing is so smooth and his narration so fluid that the ritual is collapsed into twenty minutes with nothing apparently missing. Framing the Hauka ceremony are a prologue and an epilogue of scenes shot in Accra in which the "everyday lives" of the participants are illustrated. Les Maîtres fous thus has a very tight narrative structure, motivated by the possession ritual and its own internal structure of entering and leaving trance. The film takes "us" out of Accra (with shots on the road) to a rural compound, climaxes with the eating of dog meat, and is completed with the "smiling faces" of the Hauka cult members happily digging ditches in front of a mental hospital.

The epilogue serves to reestablish the "normality" of the members of the cult, but it has the effect of reducing the ritual to a therapeutic process. Rouch suggests on the soundtrack that the men, who are employed in fairly menial jobs ("The general is just a private"), have found a way of dealing with the stress of modern life. Their "panacea against mental disorders" saves them from the mental hospital, even if their behavior while possessed suggests that that is where they belong. Echoing Mead and Bateson's analysis of Balinese trance, Rouch applies a Freudian paradigm as a means of rationalizing what has been demonstrated as being completely irrational, or at least unknowable.

Still from *Les Maîtres fous,* by Jean Rouch (1954).

Although he has since rejected this ending as a mistake,[90] its inclusion is testimony to the confluence of psychoanalysis and ethnography in the Western representation of possession in the middle decades of the century. The closing shots of the film show the Africans as fully cooperative "working" members of colonial society, and they are indeed seen "like insects" in a colony, cogs in a machine.

The opening titles of *Les Maîtres fous* very briefly introduce the Hauka cult as originating in 1927, but the contextualization is extremely scanty. Paul Stoller has filled in some of the details of the cult in his book on Rouch, pointing out that the Hauka spirits are "outlaws" even within Songhay culture. They challenged not only the colonial administration but also the "order represented by the chieftaincy."[91] Originating in Niger, the movement migrated to the Gold Coast in the 1920s, where the Hauka spirits came to take the form of British colonial figures. In the possession ritual in *Les Maîtres fous,* the cult members are mounted by the governor, the corporal of the guard, a captain, a doctor's wife, a lieutenant, a train engineer, and Madam Salma, the wife of a captain. As an elaborate form of parody, the Hauka ritual combines the mysticism of Songhay religion — in which possession is a frequent occurrence and many different kinds of possession cults exist — and a theater of the absurd.

The theatricality of this ritual is underlined by the fact that Rouch was invited to film it. In the opening titles, he states that the high priests of the Hauka requested that the ritual be filmed, although Rouch never actually showed the finished film to the participants.[92] Participatory ethnography begins with the possession ritual because "when the moment comes that the observer becomes a simple spectator among other spectators . . . he participates just like his neighbors."[93] In his *ciné-transe,* Rouch may have been accommodated in the Hauka compound, but the ritual itself is once again unintelligible without commentary. Rouch tells us everything—who is being possessed by whom, what they are doing, what they are saying, where they are going, and what their movements mean—in such detail that it does become a piece of theater, but only as seen with an interpreter. The ritual achieves a rare coherence, but the film spectator shares very little, in the end, with the original spectators, who linger in the background of the shots, at the periphery of the compound.

Although Jeannette De Bouzek claims that Rouch's narration in *Les Maîtres fous* was recorded "spontaneously," without a written script,[94] this is difficult to accept. Given the pace of the editing and the necessity of the voice-over to make sense of the imagery, it is too tight to have been improvised. Although sound recorded at the ritual is used on the soundtrack, it is mixed at a much lower volume than the voice-over and merely functions as ambient background noise. Rouch's commentary, moreover, tends toward the rhetorical. Twice he poses questions: "They are waiting for a dog. Why a dog? Because it is a strict taboo and if the Hauka slaughter and eat a dog they will prove they are not men but Hauka." At another point, as a possessed man breaks an egg over the statue of the governor, Rouch says, "Why an egg? To imitate the plume worn by the British governor on his helmet."

These questions, phrased to draw the viewer into the film on an intellectual level, are of a very different order of knowledge than the *ciné-transe* would suggest. The question about the egg, moreover, leads into one of the film's most striking montage sequences—the interjection of a scene from colonial Africa. The voice-over continues: "Here is the real governor at the trooping of the colors at the opening of the assembly at Accra." Over high-angle shots of the formal ceremony, Rouch suggests that there are Hauka dancers in the crowd looking for their model. Cutting back to the chaotic scene of possessed men strutting and foaming at the mouth, he says, "If the order is different here from there, the protocol remains the same." This sequence is an unusual instance of Eisensteinian montage in an ethnographic film.[95] Rouch has juxtaposed disparate imagery to make a point of comparison, not only between the Hauka and the British colonial administration, but between the Hauka and modernist representation. The egg is "like a plume" only in the most abstract sense, and the implied debasement of authority aligns it with nothing so much as surrealism.

Surrealism does not influence Rouch's aesthetics or method of representation but functions more as a parallel politics to the Hauka ritual. The latter is valorized by way of comparison. Rouch's method, meanwhile, is extraordinarily "intellectual." In the final juxtaposition of flashback images of possessed men with their "everyday" selves in Accra, he imposes a logic of closure onto the film. Repeating images from the preceding film is a device that seals a narrative, creating a sense of return and completion, leaving no sense of anything remaining unsaid or unaccounted for.[96] Indeed, the status of Les Maîtres fous in Rouch's oeuvre and in ethnographic cinema is precisely its narrativity.[97] The possession ritual for Rouch is most importantly a found narrative, a "raw" dramatic production, that lends itself to cinematic language as a language of structure, ordering, and storytelling.

As a narrative text, Les Maîtres fous is structured around a specific mode of address, which may be described as "cruel," given the grotesque nature of the imagery. It may also be described as auteurist, given Rouch's "possession" of the film in his distinctive mode of narration. I would like to suggest that it is also specifically male. With one exception, all the participants in the Hauka ritual are men. They are introduced in the film's prologue as migrants from the North. Attracted to "the great adventure of African cities," in Accra they have become "cattle boys, bottle boys, timber boys, gutter boys, gold mine boys." Two groups of women are seen parading, one a group of prostitutes protesting lower wages (?!), the other "daughters of Jesus singing their faith." Rouch thus sets up a division between men as individual laborers and adventurers and women as guardians of the community (a distinction that also informs his 1967 film Jaguar).

Within the film there are several hints that the possession ritual has a sexual significance, that its cathartic character refers in some way to sexual roles and behavior. One man confesses before being possessed that he has been having sex with a friend's wife, but now he is impotent; the ritual cures him and makes his girlfriend happy. Another man is possessed by a female Hauka, and in the epilogue, Rouch describes him as an "effeminate man with a lot of vaseline in his hair, but a good shop clerk nevertheless." The only woman in the ritual is described as the "Queen of the Prostitutes," and she is possessed by a "she-demon," Madam Salma, but nothing is said of her in the film's conclusion. She is never returned to "everyday life." In the ritual as Rouch represents it, gender confusion, sexual excess, and sexual transgression figure as traces of desires that are resolved for the men through performance.

These various unconnected references inscribe a discourse of male sexuality that is more directly represented in the swaggering body movements of the possessed dancers. If the object of parody, ridicule, and mimicry in the Hauka ritual is a military exercise, the performance is an exaggerated form of machismo. The participants need to eat dog, put their hands in boiling water, and touch burning brands to prove that they are stronger than "men." Visually, however, they are not their doubles but themselves. Given the limited information on the sound-track, for the spectator of the film, they are men engaged in bizarre means of proving their own strength (the Queen of the Prostitutes is not seen engaged in these activities). That the film was commissioned as an exhibition or performance only adds to the discourse of swaggering bravado as its mode of address.

The violence and aggression of the Hauka possession ritual can also be read as exemplary of an Artaudian "theater of cruelty." An analysis such as Stoller's praises the film's grotesquery, which as a form of uto-pian modernism tends to supplant a politics of representation.[98] The kind of theater proposed by Artaud was informed by both a surrealist desire for shock and a primitivist fantasy of alterity: "It is in order to at-tack the spectator's sensibility on all sides that we advocate a revolting spectacle."[99] The cruelty of the spectacle is precisely the language of ex-cess that he felt would renew theater as a social practice, but it is also a formalism that turns to ethnographic forms for a discourse of alterity, not for their "content" — the creative imagination of the Other.

Cinema itself was, for Artaud, a potentially "innocuous and direct poison, a subcutaneous injection of morphine."[100] It may be that Rouch saw something of this in cinema himself, which is why he believed it to be the most appropriate medium to represent possession. Indeed, his analysis of the process of doubling by which Songhay possession occurs is curiously parallel to Artaud's theory of the Double as the essence of theater. In both instances, reality and fantasy are so closely intermingled that one cannot read them as separable. There is no "acting" in either Artaud's theater or Songhay possession — merely being. In the theater, a "virtual reality" develops as an illusory world;[101] in possession, "each man has a *bia* or 'double,' who lives in a parallel world, that is a 'world of doubles.' "[102]

The image of possession inscribes a splitting of body and consciousness in a language of performance. The possessed can thus be read as an uncanny figure of the doubling of the self and its other, a splitting or fragmentation of the ego, or a structure of mimicry harboring a fundamental ambivalence concerning identity. While this process of doubling points to the role of possession in the modernist imagination, it also suggests how it produces a resistance in the field of the Other. Cinema replicates the possession phenomenon in its strict separation of image and subjective experience, reproducing the radical ambiguity of the colonized subject. Homi Bhabha's theorization of "the mimic man" as a figure of colonial discourse refers to the colonial subject of assimilation — "in which to be Anglicized is *emphatically* not to be English."[103] As a figure of ambivalence in colonial culture, the mimic man performs his identity. If the possession ritual represents the most "savage" and "crazed" figure of the Other, it also represents a subjectivity that remains uncolonized.

The Hauka cult may be an exemplary instance of spirit possession taking such an explicit form of anticolonialist drama, using mimicry as a structure of appropriation. The doubling that takes place in this ritual identifies colonial figures (the "Governor," the "Conductor") with gods and spirits, the ritual participants being the vehicles that make this identification possible. The effect is to render colonial history an imaginary parallel world, separated from the everyday "mortal" world of the African subjects. If the cult members who go into trance are each identified with a particular colonial figure (transformed into a deity), they are also performing their difference, the utter impossibility of them identifying with those colonial figures. The great gap between the Africans and the white men is as great as that between humans and gods. Only in the liminal space of the possession ritual can that gap be overcome.

However, Rouch's expressive use of spoken language, on top of his strategic structuring of film language, interferes with the direct performative language of the spirit-possessed. He cannot go beyond the spectacle of the body. In *Les Maîtres fous,* the aura of a performance of mimicry is discernible, but only in fragmentary form, as the memory of an experience that is already broken down into flashbacks. The authenticity of the ritual may not be in question, but its cruelty is coded as a male rite, an exhibition of cruelty. In Benjamin's famous formulation from the "Work of Art" essay, cult value can be seen already transformed into exhibition value.[104] And as Benjamin predicted, this transformation is also a shift from a ritual function to a political function; what Rouch privileges in the Hauka performance is the drama of anticolonialism, not the magic of spirit possession.

In the end, the ritual is portrayed as a highly discursive form of political resistance, one that is finally contained and curtailed by another discourse of therapy and catharsis that renders the cruelty a mere fantasy of empowerment. The utopian thrust of filming possession rituals is to see the unseeable, to penetrate the mind of the Other. Most of the commentary on Rouch tends to echo Rouch's own utopian vision, without noticing his blind spots. His debt to the surrealists gave him the inheritance of the avant-garde, and indeed he should be recognized as having embraced the fantastic within ethnography and given it narrative form. At the same time, we need to understand the implications of Rouch's own body language as it is inscribed into the Hauka possession ritual. Through the myth of the *ciné-transe,* Rouch enters the ritual with film as his spiritual guide. It gives him the power to join in, and it also gives him the power to possess the film through all the techniques of shooting, editing, and narrating.

To isolate a discourse of gender in *Les Maîtres fous* is not to claim that the film is "sexist" but to point to the effects of textualization, the "work of the text." *Les Maîtres fous* is not a ritual but a film. To read it as a text of swaggering bravado and machismo is to cut through the mythology of primitivism and *ciné-transe* and to understand "possession" as one discourse among many that inform the film. Rouch's goal of "participatory ethnography" entails his own identification with the Africans, whom he perhaps had to perceive as male. *The Mark of Zorro,* a movie poster that he finds tacked up in the Hauka compound, is a sign of cinema that is already part of the ritual and enables him to cast it as a masculine rite (Zorro is a legendary masked swashbuckler).[105] The macho persona is the figure that Rouch, as the explorer-adventurer-filmmaker, could assume as his double in the Hauka compound.

The critique of the film as "racist" is equally inappropriate because it implies that Rouch's intentions were insidious, when in fact they were quite progressive for the early 1950s. He suggests that the film is about a "knowledge not yet known to us," even if he does not relate this back to the inadequacy of visual representation. We have to understand that the participants in the ritual are "acting" as savages, but if they are acting, they are not truly possessed. This is the impossible contradiction of the *ciné-transe*. The Hauka may be able to appropriate cinema and accommodate it into their ritual, but the cinema cannot penetrate the world of doubles.

Rouch understood possession rituals as a site of radical practice, a schizophrenic model for collective opposition to colonialism.[106] Through surrealism, he also understood possession as a site of unconscious expression; but in representing it as a political form of the unconscious, the ontology of trance is subsumed by mechanical reproduction. In *Les Maîtres fous*, it is perhaps most clear how the experience of possession becomes a language of modernity. As a film, it is more successful than the efforts of either Mead and Bateson or Maya Deren. Rouch is able to transcend the scientistic empiricism of the former and to theorize the affinities between film and trance that Deren failed to reconcile. And yet, despite the film's utopian and surrealist ambition, the African unconscious remains unknown and invisible, as the trace of experience within mechanical reproduction.

Bill Viola: Existentialism, Technology, and the Other

The last segment of Bill Viola's tape *I Do Not Know What It Is I Am Like* is called "The Living Flame." Although Viola's approach to possession is from the art world, he does not figure as a "participant" in the ethnographic encounter. He represents himself as another Other. Like Rouch and Deren, he sees possession as a site where the difference between self and other can potentially be broken down, but his strategy, through the medium of video, is to transform culture into an effect of representation. Rather than trying to penetrate to the subjective reality of the trance, he explores it as a form of realism, a new kind of signifier, a surface of subjective experience.

The imagery of men in trance flagellating themselves and walking on hot coals is a sudden turn to ethnography in the context of the tape's pursuit of self-knowledge. Followed by an epilogue set in the Canadian Rockies, and preceded by a stroboscopic flash-frame sequence of rapid-fire found imagery, the sixteen-minute sequence filmed in Fiji is distinguished stylistically from the rest of the tape's imagery of landscape and animals. Although Viola deploys structural film techniques in all of the other sections of the tape, in Fiji he assumes more of a *cinéma vérité* style of camera work. Both sound and image are slowed down to accentuate the rhythm of the performers, producing a slightly distorted representation, an unfaithful form of realism. Despite the shift in style in Fiji, Viola and the viewer of the tape in the art gallery are, of course, still staring.

In being completely divorced from its sociopolitical context, the ritual in *I Do Not Know* is essentialized, but at the same time, some of the mystery that is so often violated in films of possession is restored. Viola offers no indication of the cultural specifics of the ritual, except for a location reference in the final credits.[107] Although the scenes shot in Fiji might be described as "ethnographic" in their cultural detail, epistemological inquiry is entirely absent from the tape. Viola's project is preoccupied with "Man," not in its humanist manifestation, but as a species of technology that strives to find itself in the world of nature. The firewalkers thus figure as both spectacle and subjective phenomenon in Viola's metaphysics.

The camera lingers on the faces of men punctured by skewers. They do not wince in their trancelike state or respond emotionally to the whipping and piercing, and yet the pain is tangible. *I Do Not Know* also elicits a cruelty against the spectator, and the transformative effect is perhaps closer to Artaud's original conception of cruelty than Rouch's or Stoller's account of Rouch. Artaud writes, "Cruelty is above all lucid, a kind of rigid control and submission to necessity. There is no cruelty without consciousness and without the application of consciousness."[108] "Consciousness" in *I Do Not Know* always refers back to Viola's consciousness, the artist's gaze, that the spectator may or may not identify with. In Fiji he encounters another consciousness that is visible but impenetrable. In the phenomenology of the video gaze, the grotesque image functions as a challenge to the viewer: you must see this, you must imagine this experience of pain. Cruelty becomes an important means of embodying the gaze, of giving it a physical extension in the disparate realities of Fiji and the viewer's own body. In the "other realism" of possession, pain is not pain but a means of transcending the limits of the real.

Viola's fusion of technology and spirituality veers toward another form of humanism, and we need to recognize how he flirts with what can only be described as a "New Age" aesthetic of holistic spirituality that transcends cultural differences. The representation of nature and the theme of decay, death, and rebirth suggest an existential concep-

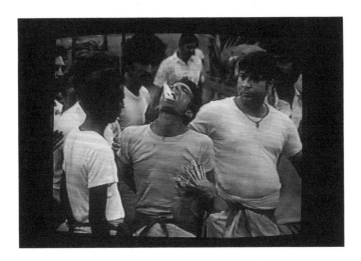

Still from Bill Viola's video *I Do Not Know What It Is I Am Like*
(1986). *Photo by Kira Perov.*

tion of "mankind" bound up, through contemplation and beauty, in
a grand aesthetic gesture. In comparison to the surrealists, Viola does
not challenge the category of art but remakes it in a new technology.
It is significant that this is accomplished by way of a detour through
documentary, because where Viola's work departs from "ethnopoetics"
(the New Age version of universal humanism) [109] is through the implied
commentary on the gaze.

The firewalking sequence emerges from the flashing lights and images
in a series of unfocused dissolves, anticipated by the soundtrack that
pulses electronically, almost like a dance club beat. Gradually fused into
the drumming of the Hindu ritual, its rhythm is transformed into the
seductive beat of the trance. The firewalkers never return the gaze of the
camera. They are completely involved with their own activity; their attention is turned entirely inward, not only to themselves as individuals
but to each other as a community. If we can agree that Viola's depiction
of "consciousness" is also a discourse of power, a contest over the gaze,
the men in Fiji resist the inquisition with a refusal to be known.

The public context of the ritual further deflects the penetration of
secrecy, as the firewalkers literally perform their interiority. As the ceremony is observed by tourists on bleachers, the "authenticity" of the
ritual is placed in question. The firewalkers have urban haircuts, pot-
bellies, and familiar Western clothing mixed with their saffron-colored

robes. In this tape, "possession" is proven by the ability to walk on fire, eat fire, and sustain flagellation and skin piercing, but they are feats available only as images, not as experience. Viola tests the limits of the visible by filming people who are not only other than, and other to, the filmmaker, but whose consciousness transcends the knowable, as well as the discourse of reason that gives rise to the desire to know.

Demystification of the ritual may contravene Viola's anti-epistemological aesthetics, but it is instructive to compare his version with the anthropologist's. Carolyn Henning Brown has offered some intriguing insights into this ceremony, in particular that this *puja,* performed by Hindu descendants of the Southern Indian indentured laborers brought to Fiji by the British in the 1870s, is a demonstration of a disenfranchised ethnic minority. Although few British remain in Fiji, people of Indian descent now comprise about 50 percent of the Fiji population, but they are marginalized economically and culturally by the indigenous nationals. Firewalking is a major tourist attraction and, since the 1930s, has become an important means of preserving South Indian identity.[110]

Within the diasporic Fijian context, where Indians are economically marginalized, firewalking is a display of spiritual empowerment. The devotees are not Brahmin or religious professionals but working men who want to commune with the goddess in gratitude for some gift of providence, or simply to accumulate good karma.[111] Firewalking is only the climax of a complex series of ordeals that the men undergo in one afternoon, including the flagellation and skin piercing that are depicted in Viola's tape.[112] The resistance to fire and pain, the supernatural ability to withstand heat, is proof of the participants' faith and proof of the goddess's (Maariama) presence in their bodies.[113]

The firewalking attracts not only tourists but large numbers of local Indian and Fijian residents, most of whom watch the ceremony from outside the temple compound, behind a chain-link fence on the surrounding hills.[114] (Both ranks of spectators can be seen in the background of some of Viola's footage.) Brown argues that the tourists validate the firewalking ritual by representing the gaze of the world outside the islands. They are "simply used by their hosts in the only game that matters, the game of interethnic competition."[115] It may be that Viola is "being used" in the same way, except that he quite radically decontextualizes the interethnic contest. The new framework for the firewalking strips the participants of their historical identities and isolates the spiritual essence of the ritual within a strictly audiovisual economy. We do not know what the anthropologist knows.

The authenticity of the ritual is never doubted by Brown, although she does suggest, rather obliquely, that the coals might not be as hot as one might think.[116] If "the idea of danger must be protected" by the community, Viola eliminates any sense of danger from his depiction. The facial expressions and body movements of the participants convey only intense concentration. Although the mediated version has even more potential for duplicity, we cannot doubt our perception because we don't know what to doubt. With no terms of reference, the behavior is mystified rather than psychologized, perhaps even more so than in the circus-type arena in which it was originally performed.

In the rest of *I Do Not Know*, the frame signifies the gaze; but in Fiji, the frame disappears, and the viewer has neither an explanation for the ritual nor a point of view. The sequence moves from the dark temple interior, to the ocean-side procession outside the temple grounds, to the fire pit without warning. This refusal to contain, to orient or offer a point of view, is reminiscent of Deren's footage, and also Mead and Bateson's. Viola uses sound, rather than visual space, to draw the viewer into the scene as the continuous hypnotic drum beat is fused with the electronic signal of the medium. The other culture in *I Do Not Know* becomes, in a sense, a fantasy, a collusion of illusion and reality enhanced by Viola's technology. In a video trance, as the cultural landscape is superseded by a purely audiovisual landscape, objective reality is merely a clue to a subjective reality that cannot itself be known or experienced.

It is at this point that Viola makes the most significant break with traditional anthropology and ethnography. Under the auspices of the human sciences, these practices assume an ontological bond between cultures that it is their ambition to resurrect. Similarities between observed and observing cultures form the ideological support for a discourse of differences, a communality that "participatory cinema" attempts to recover in essence. The Fijian Hindus, however, performing for huge crowds, appear to be oblivious of any reality beyond the most spiritual and subvert any premise of humanism. As Deren noted of the Balinese possession ritual, there is no exhibitionism, and without exhibitionism, there is no identification, no link between spectators and performers other than the beat of the drum, which is not psychological but physiological. Moreover, it is precisely when Viola's camera is turned on to the human "other" in *I Do Not Know* that it becomes both inquisitive and invisible, inscribing a certain voyeurism and desire for knowledge and vision that is only frustrated by the inaccessibility of the subjectivity of the other. He shares nothing with these men except a desire to transcend the limits of embodied reality.

The conjunction of video and ritual performance in *I Do Not Know* produces a discourse on history that is the inverse of nostalgia. The ethnographic other, represented as a subjective presence in a visual economy, does not belong to a lost past but enters into a utopian discourse of intercultural knowledge. By bringing his high-tech electronic apparatus, the state of the art in imaging technology, into the ethnographic relation, the balance of power may be tipped toward the observer, but in Fiji Viola finally encounters a power equal to his own.

In *I Do Not Know What It Is I Am Like*, the psychoanalytic framework is finally dismantled, as Viola does not hope to penetrate the unconscious of the other by filming possession. Viola's firewalkers represent community as something other than, and other to, the singular structure of perception, as something that evades representation and its reference to ego. The unconscious does not erupt in *I Do Not Know* but is seen from a distance. This does not mean that Viola has finally found a "correct" way to film possession. Indeed, the spectacle refers back more than ever to the subject of perception, the man behind the camera who is still lost within a primitivist fantasy of alterity. The firewalkers in Viola's tape become not others but the Other in the most mythic sense as Viola enacts an Orientalism of the electronic age.

Viola's use of video is informed by an existentialist theory of medium specificity. His treatment of possession is thus ontological and in many ways a more successful version of the *ciné-transe* imagined by Rouch. At the same time, the documentary veracity of the indexical image is heightened as a form of mystery, as if the magic of the image was rediscovered in electronic form. Indeed, the ritual is finally interrupted by the spectacular sequence of a fish being raised from underwater, fixed in the camera frame, and lifted high above a northern landscape — a virtuoso display of special effects and high-tech imagery over which the Fijian drumming continues. Viola banishes hysteria from the possession ritual and in doing so achieves a sense of melancholia that pertains more to his own perception than to the Fijian experience. He may be able to blur reality and fantasy through technology as surely as those who are possessed by gods, but the price to be paid is the knowledge of eradicable difference and cultural isolation.

Possession as an alternate form of reality has many theoretical links with cinema, especially the cinema of consciousness that came to dominate the American avant-garde, and the aesthetics of *cinéma vérité*. Somnambulism, trance, and hypnotic states are familiar tropes of modernist cinema and surrealist art. They provide a kind of middle ground between cinema and dream, embodying the fascination and lure of cinema, but maintaining a sense of the body and physicality that is absent from a more pure dream state. As a trope of cinema specificity, the trance incorporates the real act of spectating into the unreal status of the image.[117] Possession offers the dissolution of distance between spectator and text, and between ethnographer and native, because it offers another order of representation, one in which the self is split and fragmentary, almost fluid. This is its utopian promise, its fantasy of another apparatus of spectating and performing.

Indigenous possession rituals are, however, informed by quite different concepts of subjectivity that vary from one culture to another. The filming of these rituals necessarily involves a transformation or translation into images, into the language of cinema. Thus despite the apparent ontological parallels between cinema and spirit possession, possession rituals cannot be fully represented on film, resisting the epistemological equation of visibility and realism. In fact, the alternate reality of possession escapes representation and defines the limits of mechanical reproduction. Possession is an uncanny discourse that destabilizes subjectivity, but it is ultimately the Other's subjectivity that remains unknown and unknowable.

One recurring feature of the four texts discussed here is a tendency on the part of each filmmaker to cut into the possession ritual with in-camera editing. Handheld cameras and fairly short shots, together with a relative lack of spatial orientation, are the means by which each seems to emulate the chaotic scene on the level of film technique. Possession rituals are community events and are intended to be witnessed, but they are not addressed to a spectator. The lack of secure visual positioning is inconsistent with those theories of *ciné-transe* and hypnotic states of cinema that imply a sort of automatic or fixed point of view.

Schizophrenia would seem to be the more appropriate psychoanalytic model that emerges from these attempts to document possession. In the filming of possession rituals, people are reduced to their images, which are detached from the experience of possession. However, the "unreality" in these cases is an excess of reality, a subjective "surreality" that is not lost, but produced outside the realm of the visible. It is lost to film, but not to "reality." In this sense, possession constitutes the flip side of Jameson's postmodernism, a return of the real.[118] Its schizophrenia is closer to that of Deleuze and Guattari—a political model of social functioning based in "desiring-production" or "group fantasy."[119]

The possession ritual is an important point of contact between artistic praxis and anthropology, which is perhaps why it has become a plum of ethnographic cinema. However, the attempts to film possession tend to circumscribe the potential transcendence of representational and social realities. Explanatory voice-over may be the point where anthropology and the avant-garde will always part company, and the films discussed here are no exception. Only Deren's raw footage and Viola's video allow the performances to make their own meaning, and they thereby distance the spectator, for whom the drama is incomprehensible. In both instances, the scene of possession takes on other, aesthetic effects, enhanced by both Deren's and Viola's use of slow motion. As another means of replicating the "feel" of the ritual on film, slow motion produces the effect of gaps in the real, or an alternate reality that transcends the film.

Of the four examples of possession discussed here, only *Trance and Dance in Bali* situates the Other culture in a mythic prehistoric past cut off from the modern world. In the other films, the participants in the rituals are dressed in twentieth-century clothing, and their activities are contextualized by a modernity that is not negated by possession but modified by it. For Deren it is modern dance, for Rouch anticolonialism and surrealism, and for Viola an existentialist metaphysics. And while these are interests and values brought from the avant-garde to bear on the indigenous cultures, the possession ritual gives back to the avant-garde a discourse of the occult as subjective realism. Possession infects the real with a truth-value that is neither objective nor empirical, but transcendent and sublime.

If possession can tell us anything about another realism that might be described as postcolonial, it is simply that such a realism is not "lost" in the age of mechanical reproduction. It places new demands on visual culture, and it may yet emerge with new forms of subjectivity. Possession challenges cinematic representation because it produces a form of reality that will always be supplemental to, or in excess of, the image.

If possession rituals are so often linked to forms of cultural resistance, it is because they keep indigenous subjectivity safe from the forces of colonial oppression. Possession rituals are often linked to underground cults outside the mainstream of colonized cultures,[120] precisely because of the political power of ambivalence embedded in doubling and mimicry. The spectacular visibility of the body challenges the conventions of filmic performance at the same time as it feeds the insatiable appetite of the society of the spectacle. The Other thus enters modernity via films of possession as a simulacrum, a fluidity, a deterritorialized "flow" of desire.

The uncanny theatricality of possession, its ambivalence about identity, and its transcendence of empiricism, are important means by which the utopian impulse of primitivism can be recovered in postmodern, postcolonial culture. The films and video discussed here suggest how possession has been filmed as an experimental form of realism, and how it challenges modernist forms of subjectivity and epistemology. Possession rituals constitute a form of representation that is grounded in a culturally specific body, but they point to a reality that exceeds the image of the body. They thus have the potential to subvert all the codes and conventions of cinematic inquiry, pointing to other forms of knowledge and representation.

9 Archival Apocalypse:
Found Footage as Ethnography

It takes imagination and courage to picture what would happen to the West (and to anthropology) if its temporal fortress were suddenly invaded by the Time of its Other.

— JOHANNES FABIAN, *Time and the Other*

Found-footage filmmaking, otherwise known as collage, montage, or archival film practice, is an aesthetic of ruins. Its intertextuality is always also an allegory of history, a montage of memory traces, by which the filmmaker engages with the past through recall, retrieval, and recycling. The complex relation to the real that unfolds in found-footage filmmaking lies somewhere between documentary and fictional modes of representation, opening up a very different means of representing culture. Found footage is a technique that produces "the ethnographic" as a discourse of representation. It denies the transparency of culture. The found image always points, however obliquely, to an original production context, a culturally inscribed niche in the society of the spectacle, be it Hollywood, home movies, advertising, or educational films.[1] Because the filmmaker works with images that are already filmed ("ready-mades"), she can distance herself from the body filmed. In the intertextuality, fragmentation, and discursivity of found-footage filmmaking, the body has a very different status than it does in conventional ethnography. It is no longer representative of culture, but an element of culture, a signifier of itself. The body of the "social actor" takes on what Roland Barthes calls an obtuse meaning, a supplementality that exceeds its role in the production of meaning. This is the potential of the form, but it is only realized on the cusp of an eclipse of "the real" in representation.

My purpose here is not to define a category of found-footage filmmaking but to explore its relation to ethnography as it is produced in a selected group of texts, including Leslie Thornton's *Peggy and Fred in Hell* (1981–1994), Bruce Conner's *A Movie* (1958), the archival project of *Atomic Café* (1982), Craig Baldwin's *Tribulation 99* (1991), and Black Audio Film Collective's *Handsworth Songs* (1985). These films are not necessarily representative of the vast spectrum of film and video that incorporates found footage, but they are suggestive of the ethnographic potential of the practice and indicative of the ambivalence with which it is underscored. In these films, the implicit challenge of found footage to aesthetic conventions of individual authorship, memory, and vision is exploited as a problem of subjectivity, authority, and, most importantly, history.

Andreas Huyssen argued in 1986 that the historical avant-garde is a thing of the past, and "it is useless to try to revive it." Technologized mass culture, he argued, has taken over the techniques on which the avant-garde was built, although it has also preserved the avant-garde's utopian aspiration in distorted form.[2] In a more recent book, *Twilight Memories,* Huyssen has shifted his position slightly, saying that the task of the avant-garde in postmodernity is a creative act of forgetting. To reconstruct memory in the face of historical amnesia is to interrupt the eternal present of simulation culture.[3] Memory as a form of radical time is a means by which the avant-garde can productively engage with cultural history and revitalize its aspirations of social transformation. In the cinema, found-footage filmmaking is one practice that might point the way of a postmodern avant-garde, not simply because it is based on an appropriation of technologized mass culture, but because it is a discourse of memory and history. In this chapter, I want to argue that it also constitutes a specific type of ethnographic temporality.

The great variety of found-footage filmmaking falls under a number of rubrics, including collage film, compilation film, and archival film. William Wees has distinguished between compilation as a documentary aesthetic grounded in the realist aspect of the found image, collage as the modernist avant-garde variant, and appropriation as the postmodern treatment of the archive as simulacrum.[4] His examples of these three types include Emile de Antonio's *Point of Order* (1964) as a compilation film, *A Movie* as a modernist collage film, and a Michael Jackson music video as an instance of postmodern "appropriation."[5] Wees's typology is useful for mapping the different roles of found footage, but in fact they cannot always be distinguished from each other. The deep ironies of this mode of filmmaking derive from the overlapping and coextensive aesthetics of realism, modernism, and postmodern simulation, a combination that might most adequately be subsumed within the theory of allegory.

The movement within dialectical images, their status as allegories of history, is an interruption of narrativity as a symbolic system. In the process of being appropriated, the original image gives over its meaning to the new text and is manipulated by the new filmmaker on the level of the signifier. Craig Owens describes allegory as "the epitome of counter-narrative, for it arrests narrative in place, substituting a principle of syntagmatic disjunction for one of diegetic combination."[6] Allegory implies a certain randomness, a seriality without necessity, rendering the logic of narrative necessity null and void. "If the symbol is a motivated sign, then allegory, conceived as its antithesis, will be identified as the domain of the arbitrary, the conventional, the unmotivated."[7]

The dialectical potential of found-footage filmmaking is inseparable from the role of archival imagery in documentary practices as an unquestioned realism. All too often, the archive serves as visual evidence of history, with the role of found footage reduced to the textual authority of the documentary fact. At the other end of the scale, "scratch video" has become a filmmaking technique available to anyone with two VCRs. The compilation of found imagery is a form of collecting culture, domesticating the exotic, and producing profoundly "inauthentic art."[8] Archival images may always bear the sign of history, but some found-footage films go further, to interrogate the allegory of historiography that archival practices mobilize. They foreground the role of intertextuality in history and force the question of cultural representation into a posthumanist field in which discursivity explodes narrativity. There is no recipe for this effect, and an exhaustive list of all the works that do this would be inevitably incomplete,[9] although key works in addition to the ones discussed here would include Guy Debord's "situationist" films. The theoretical terminology of *détournement*, coined by Debord in the 1960s, designates precisely the allegorical sense of the dialectical image that will be developed in this chapter. His extensive practices of appropriation were intended as an analysis of "the function of the spectacle" in modern society.[10]

The work of filmmakers who have experimented with the documentary status of the archival image evokes alternative, invasive, and dialectical forms of temporality and history. Recycling found images implies a profound sense of the already-seen, the already-happened, creating a spectator position that is necessarily historical. For many filmmakers, found footage constitutes a means of recycling the excess waste of consumer culture. Not only is it a cheaper way to make films, but it often violates copyright law and becomes a form of media piracy and a challenge to commercial cinema. As an assembly of cultural detritus, found-footage filmmaking is an investigation of the margins of the media in which outtakes, trailers, B movies, and TV commercials are re-viewed as "documents" not unlike those retrieved by the surrealists in the 1930s. Boundaries between art and everyday life are thoroughly blurred.

Often including apocalyptic scenarios of crisis and destruction, found-footage filmmaking tends toward an "end of history." The techniques of appropriation, recycling, and re-presentation place the status of the past, the history of the referent, in question. As the aura of the filmmaker's "having been there" is eclipsed, the media-scape of found-footage filmmaking renders history itself as "lost." But what kind of history is it that is lost if found-footage filmmaking is also about a re-invention of memory as cultural representation and imagination? The appropriated image points back to the profilmic past as if it were a parallel universe of science fiction: a "science fictional space that exists parallel to the normal space of the diegesis — a rhetorically heightened 'other realm.' "[11] There is no diegesis of a found-footage film, no represented noncontradictory world, only the traces of a reality (or multiple realities) outside the film, beyond representation.[12]

Collage forms of filmmaking date back to the 1920s, but it is not until the 1950s that the use of television and film archives become apocalyptic. Apparently unlimited access to the discontinuous fragments of image culture has the effect of representing culture as a tapestry of documents, a simulacral sphere of representation. It is the collage style of the age of television that renders history and memory unstable and fragmentary. Found-footage filmmaking evolved in the 1960s and early 1970s, often in conjunction with structural film techniques of rephotography. With Craig Baldwin, Leslie Thornton, and Abigail Child in the

1980s, the form enjoyed a revival as filmmakers realized its potential as fragments of a cultural dreamworld. Child describes it as "the landscape of our brains, shaped by the social. I access that landscape, ethnography of the seen."[13] Within this history, this landscape, the 1950s remains a key cultural site and privileged archive for collage filmmakers, constituting a "primitive" site of mediated childhood memory.

That found footage came into its own in the 1950s, and that the imagery of that decade is so prevalent in the genre as it developed, is not coincidental. In fact, the key years are perhaps more correctly pegged as the period between 1955 and 1965. As David James has argued, this period embraced two competing and contradictory themes: a utopian optimism in scientific authority on the one hand, and a critique of the mass media on the other.[14] The ubiquitous authoritative voice-over of industrial, training, and educational films was accompanied by a growing understanding of the fabrication of visual evidence as a tool in ideological warfare. During the Cold War, "America" was constructed in the media as a culturally specific domain of family values, democracy, and free enterprise with the small town and suburban nuclear family as its focal point. The paraphernalia of consumer capitalism, in the form of household appliances and prepared foods, constituted the ethnological detail that circulated around the American housewife as consumer queen.

The discursive landscape of postwar America is exemplary of what Dana Polan has described as a dialectic of power and paranoia. Against, and in response to, the emergence of nuclear weapons, Americanized psychoanalysis, social science, and consumer capitalism there developed parallel discourses of hysteria, paranoia, delinquency, sexual excess, and anxiety.[15] The symbiotic structure of containment and excess becomes legible in the image bank of this period, as television and film were deeply implicated in the network of new technologies and fears. In fragmented archival form, the imagery from this period—including home movies made by the newly available eight-millimeter Kodak camera—constitutes a fictional document, or an allegory of history.

What Sharon Sandusky has called the "toxic film artifact" is the means by which refilming a film fragment exposes the dangerous engineering and manipulation that it might have had in its original context.[16] Sandusky conflates archaeological and psychological metaphors to describe the archival art film as "the unearthing of a film *trauma*." While the metaphors are apt, her reference to the successful work of art as the "cure" to the dangers of the past is unfortunate. I would prefer to say that archival filmmaking promotes a schizophrenic dispersal of discourses of mastery, authenticity, and authority through fragmentation, cutting up, and interruption. The work of art is thus thoroughly bound up with a cultural schizophrenia that limits "vision" to endless revision.

In the 1950s, the toxicity of the media was particularly high, as was the fear of its power as a form of social engineering. Thus, although the materials of archival filmmaking date from the entire history of film, TV, and photography, postwar America serves as an exemplary site of the allegorical nature of found footage. Its ethnographic discourse emerges as the uncanny reality of an apocalyptic culture of amnesia. Anxieties of domesticity, media, and Cold War ideology served as the new "content" of collage, catapulting the surrealist, modernist aesthetic into a new form of representation. In the discontinuous fragments of image culture, the mechanics of representation can be most clearly perceived, and signifiers and signifieds can be pried apart to produce the indexical referent as an afterthought and a point of excess. It is this supplementary discourse of singularities, of bodies dislocated in cultural histories, that I want to develop as a discourse of ethnography.

The relationship between ethnography and found footage has been addressed most directly by Leslie Thornton in her film-and-video epic *Peggy and Fred in Hell*. Produced as a series of installments from 1981 to 1994, *Peggy and Fred* combines archival images and sounds with live-action footage of two children who perform "themselves" in an apocalyptic, ruined landscape. The archival imagery is an extension of the clutter and debris of the postindustrial setting in which the two children subsist. If in their performances the children appropriate the language of adults and the discourses of popular culture, the framework of found footage likewise functions as a sphere of traces and voices that are detached from their origins. In the assemblage of a cultural landscape, the children's bodies are "found" as interruptions in a fictional space, as points of reference in an otherwise random, unordered series of images and events.

In Thornton's own writing on the *Peggy and Fred* series, she evokes ethnography as a practice of storytelling, a means of creating "true fictions" to make culture intelligible. As an epic tale of the "exfoliations" of twentieth-century American culture, *Peggy and Fred* is a "warped science-fictionalized catalogue of its images, technologies, frustrations and desires." Children, she says, "are not quite us and not quite other.

Janice Reading in Leslie Thornton's *Peggy and Fred in Hell*
(1981–1994).

They are our others. They are becoming us. Or they are becoming other.
They are at a dangerous point."[17] Peggy and Fred are primitives cast
adrift in a world that has imploded under the weight of technology, and
they are the locus of a new, yet-to-be-defined form of subjectivity. "And
since the only other people they ever see are on TV, they don't know
they're not as well. They figure that people are watching, and learning from and ignoring them as well. This constitutes their idea of the
social."[18]

Thornton's combination of archival imagery with original footage
tends to blur the edges between the two orders of representation, mainly
because she has shot the scenes with the children in an off-centered, disinterested way, evoking the sense that is often created by found footage,
of a lack of purpose.[19] The question "Why would anyone have filmed
this?" points to another order of the image, a randomness that is its
greatest challenge to narrativity and especially to narratives of history.
Ethnography functions in her work as a conjunction of cultural representation and the documentation of the historical body. The children
grow older over the thirteen years of the series, but their environment
seems to regress deeper into the recesses of the archive. *Peggy and Fred*
deploys a wealth of biblical imagery to evoke the apocalypse at the
same time as it experiments with nonteleological forms of memory and
imagination.

The imagery within which Peggy and Fred find themselves consists primarily of landscape, industrial apparatuses, and birds and animals. It is largely unpopulated, setting the children off as historical protagonists. The 1950s and 1960s are obliquely evoked by the style of much of the found footage, the domestic set with its proliferation of appliances, and the space program, although references to Michael Jackson and Jack Nicholson point to later years. The footage is marked by a profound temporal disorder, thereby suggesting that the ethnographic aspect of found footage is not simply a question of cultural or human representation but one of historical temporality.

Peggy and Fred underscores the key discourses of historical time that is inscribed in found-footage film. As a radical practice of historical inversion, interruption, and memory, it poses one of the fundamental problems of experimental ethnography, that of the body in the machine, "the machine" here being the image bank of the archive. The radical juxtaposition of disparate imagery in found-footage filmmaking is often a texture of discontinuity and shocking collisions. It is Walter Benjamin to whom we must turn for the intrinsic connection between the modernist aesthetic of montage and an ethnographic theory.

The *flâneur* and his attitude of allegorical representation is produced by and in the crowded city streets of Paris. His practice of looking at others and briefly meeting their passing gaze induces a crisis not only of subjectivity but also of time. Benjamin is most interested in the defense mechanism by which the shocks of urban stimuli are parried by the poet. If the real threat of shock is manifest in war trauma, the protection against stimuli—described by Benjamin as Freud's theory of consciousness—is equally threatening to experience. To be prepared against stimuli is to prevent impressions from entering experience; they become simply remembrances. Benjamin's conception of the *mémoire involontaire,* on the other hand, is destructive and is produced by the inefficient shock mechanism of a poet such as Baudelaire. The limits and gaps of consciousness leave memory traces that are incompatible with the system of consciousness. They become the repressed data of the unconscious.[20]

Returning to the same question of the stimuli of early-twentieth-century culture, Mary Anne Doane argues that the invention of cinema at the turn of the century constituted an anxiety of "total representation." She describes "the effect of time" in the cinema as a challenge to auratic memory. Freud's theory of the unconscious was developed in part as a "shield against the stimuli of modernity"—from World War

I shell shock, to mass transportation, to "the flood of photographic images" — that rendered time discontinuous. For Freud, Doane argues, "Time is that which leaves behind no record — it emerges from the failure of representation. This scenario produces the unconscious as the dream of a memory uncorrupted by time." [21]

Ethnographic time developed in colonial anthropology as the fulfillment of that dream of a memory of human civilization. The cinema, however, "could not dissociate itself from the realm of the contingent or the material." [22] Ethnographic film has thus always been something of a system of contradictions, leaning toward modernist representation at the same time as empirical documentation. As Benjamin recognized, cinema was an instrument of the "shock of modernity," a sign of the transience of the present as one in a series of discontinuous moments. Doane suggests that Freud (and Etienne-Jules Marey) resisted the cinema because of its threat of "overpresence, of excessive coverage" that challenged the limits of memory and its link to consciousness as the means of retrieval. Especially in its dissemination of information, the cinema offered "too much." Narrativity, as a representation of time, displaced the actualities of early cinema, according to this argument, as a protection against the threat of cinematic contingency. Found-footage filmmaking is precisely a realization of the threatened "blizzard of images" that renders memory an inadequate means of organizing time, reinventing the shock experience as a form of cultural representation. Memory traces of collective history attain a material form of experience that is not subsumed as empirical knowledge or developmental history because it originates in the present, as memory, and not in the past as origin. In the age of electronic reproduction, the memory trace takes on an even greater historical burden as a point of access to the real, to a materiality of experience. The return of the real constitutes a traumatic historiography, an interruption of the fabricated reality of image culture by a radical form of memory.

Atomic Ethnography

By all accounts, Bruce Conner is the prime mover of found-footage filmmaking. In twelve films made between 1958 and 1982, he assembled fragments of stock footage bought in bulk. His first film, *A Movie*, made in 1958, was influenced by the new television medium, Hollywood trailers, experimental filmmaking, and the "dream sequences" of Hollywood films.[23] The predominance in his work of images of atomic explosions and images of consumer products speaks to an American dreamworld of empty desires, of utopia turned dangerous and apocalyptic. In 1976 Conner made a film called *Crossroads*, which consists entirely of military footage of the atomic tests at Bikini Island, and in 1967 he made *Report*, a recycling of images of John F. Kennedy's assassination mixed with other TV and film footage. Both films explore the "cult value" of media images as a catastrophic form of repetition; they locate violence and sacrifice at the apex of the society of the spectacle.

The first sequence of *A Movie* links together galloping horses from a Western, charging elephants, speeding trains, race cars, and tanks, all on the basis of matching and opposing screen directions. The sequence climaxes with the crashing and flipping of race cars and a vintage car falling off a cliff, followed by a title announcing The End. Speed, spectacle, authorship, and narrative time are all put into play as filmic codes that are completely arbitrary and unfixed. In the second, middle section of the film, shots of marine disasters, waterskiing accidents, odd bicycles, motorcycles wallowing in mud, tightrope walkers over a big-city intersection, a plane crash, and an atomic explosion are combined with one of the film's most famous sequences of a submarine periscope cut with a primping pinup model (a sequence that explicitly addresses the scopophilia of the cinematic spectacle). The sense of disaster and failed progress is built on a rhythm of verticals and horizontals, a rising and falling grid that plays balance and emplotment against the movement of history. The grid also registers the surface of the image as detached from its referential origins.[24] Within this spatiotemporal grid, the mushroom cloud becomes the emblem of dangerous technology as a spectacular freezing of time.

The final section of *A Movie* emerges from black leader and low music. The symphonic soundtrack (found movie music) gradually rises in pitch and volume, structuring the emotional appeal of the imagery according to narrative conventions of suspense, climax, and release. The end of the twelve-minute film consists of a series of climaxes corresponding to its most horrifying imagery: bodies hanging upside down in a city square,[25] piles of corpses, a dead elephant, starving Africans. A burning blimp falling from the sky and a suspension bridge swaying above a huge chasm are images that recur in different sections of the film, as spectacular sights of failed transportation technology. The film ends with a scuba diver descending to a sunken wreck and swimming down into the dark hole of a submerged hatch.

Among the themes that *A Movie* introduces to found-footage filmmaking is an epic sense of historical time. Conner's perspective is one of a warning or prophecy at the advent of television, of a media-saturated world, and in many ways the film anticipates the theoretical debates of postmodernism. Apocalypse is linked to the instability of representation, which Conner aestheticizes as a kind of melancholy elegy for a lost depth of representation, betraying his modernist orientation. Even so, the film introduces the key thematic of "the real" as an endangered sphere of representation in the accelerated pace of modernity.

The reduction of history to data bank entails a failure of historical progress, and yet the depiction of catastrophe contains the trace of history as the forgotten real. The memory trace that is produced within the catastrophe has been theorized by Mary Ann Doane, who argues that television as a medium blurs the difference between an endless flow of information and "the punctuated discontinuity of catastrophe."[26] Televisual catastrophe comes to represent discontinuity and death in the form of accidental interruption. But this form of death provides access to the real only in the form of contingent accidental access, such as the eyewitness or the "liveness" of the reporter in the field. "The real" is produced or constructed through television as a residue or remainder in excess of the discursive system of representation. Perpetually deferred, reality as referentiality is the promise of catastrophe, and it is always linked to bodies and death as the trace of the real.[27]

While one can certainly read this situation as dystopic, as the amnesia of a culture losing its hold on the historical real, one might also conceive of it as the form of a new kind of knowledge. According to Doane, catastrophe theory is "a theory about singularities. When applied to scientific problems, therefore, it deals with the properties of discontinuities directly, without reference to any specific underlying mechanism."[28] If catastrophe is about sudden interruptions of a continuous system, it is at once produced by a system such as televisual flow and perpetuates it as a nonnarrative temporality. Unlike crisis, catastrophe is about instantaneousness and shares with "information" an urgency and forgettability. If television obscures the distinction between crisis and catastrophe, found-footage filmmaking is a technique of retrieving the temporality of catastrophe.

Stills from Bruce Conner's *A Movie* (1958).

Still from Bruce Conner's *A Movie* (1958).

To explore the significance of this "new kind of knowledge" to ethnography, I want to return to the few images that signify the ethnographic in *A Movie,* images of native peoples that tend to break into the
perpetual catastrophe of modernity, interrupting its breakneck speed
with the traces of another time. In addition to the image of starving
Africans, there are two consecutive pastoral scenes of Asians farming
and flute playing inserted in the middle section of the film, one brief
shot of bare-breasted women of color carrying tall stacks of fruit on
their heads followed by a man and an image of African hunters surrounding a fallen elephant, brandishing machetes.[29] We need to ask,
first of all, what are these people of color, these Others, doing in this
movie? What is the role of the Other in Conner's catastrophic view of
history?

Especially in the case of the shivering, naked African child, the ethnographic encompasses a cliché of Western guilt, global inequities, and
the spectacle of poverty. As a critique of "progress," its meaning is self-
evident, but at the same time, in the context of *A Movie,* it is an image
of an image, a quotation of the ideology of guilt, of which the African child is a signifier. The pastoral imagery, possibly taken from an
Indian fiction film, is likewise another ethnographic cliché of the uncorrupted, premodern world of the Other. Thus the people in these shots
are always already subsumed as language in a textual play that leaves
out the referent. They exceed their status as mere images by posing

questions of who, what, and where that will never be answered. They thus foreground the radical ambiguity of the collage form. In the absence of names of cultures, countries, or activities, the images are fragments of incomplete information in which the referent is rendered as a singularity, an eruption of the real within a system of ethnographic representation. That system becomes not a science but a practice of stolen imagery that Conner simply steals once again.

Juxtaposed with Conner's avalanche of imagery, the people in these ethnographic fragments seem to own their images in a way that those who are more complicit with the society of the spectacle do not. The scene of the women walking with huge stacks of fruit on their heads is perhaps the most complex of the film's quotations of ethnographic representation. Whereas most of the rest of the film's images are events, scenes of action and occurrence, this one stands out as an extraordinary scene of daily life. Unlike the white pinup women posing to be seen, these women are caught in the gaze. The composition of the shot, with its vertical towers and horizontal movement, "fits" with the film's visual theme of the grid, but it introduces a historical grid in which cultural difference intersects with, and cuts across, the teleological historiography of "progress." It is the latter that produces the Other as primitive.

The ethnographic in *A Movie* constitutes an interruption of the perpetual catastrophe of failed progress. In the collapse of technology, the Other represents the memory of the body in the machine of modernity. While this is certainly another variation of the myth of primitivism, it also points to the way that "the ethnographic" will become discursive and allegorical in postmodernity. The ethnographic imagery signifies another order of time, outside apocalyptic, atomic history. The Other may be a victim of modernity in being transposed into the realm of images, but at the same time, she is free from referentiality. The scientific paradigms of empirical representation fall apart in the ruins of Conner's collage, which acts as a process of radical decontextualization, leaving the referents of stolen images to signify another order of knowledge in another, parallel universe that we might call the profilmic. Although these images in *A Movie* are extremely brief, lasting only a second or two before being shuffled off into the blizzard of Conner's montage, they constitute a return of the repressed within the film.

If the salvage paradigm denotes the recovery of lost cultures, here it is allegorized and inverted as a form of what Andreas Huyssen calls a radical forgetting.[30] Once it is rendered allegorical, ethnography as a system of representation is recognized as part of the society of the spectacle, while its referents, the bodies of Others, cannot be contained by its codes. In their supplementary, excessive status, these bodies are linked to death. Thus one finds so many corpses in found-footage film-making, as the emblematic fusion of excess and indexicality, the "cost" of the teleological historiography of modernity. Within the apocalyptic sphere of the image bank, the body of the Other signifies a return of historical imagination in another, dialectical form.

The "end of history" that is inscribed in *A Movie* is only the end of a progressive form of history that hierarchizes past, present, and future. In its place, the repressed memories of the archive posit a different history, one in which reality is under perpetual construction and reconstruction. The potential of found-footage filmmaking lies in its status as an allegorical form of the salvage paradigm, and its capacity to resist ethnography's implicit theory of history. In traditional ethnography, the anthropological Other was conventionally linked to the past, and otherness was constructed within a teleological, progressivist historiography. Johannes Fabian has argued that a truly revised, postcolonial ethnography needs to imagine an invasion by "the time of the Other," a historiography that does not hierarchize the present over a less-developed past, and, I would add, one that can conceptualize otherness within a history of the future. The collage nature of found-footage filmmaking creates a discontinuity that is not only spatial but temporal and produces a historical effect that might be described as, precisely, this time of the Other. It does so by eclipsing referentiality as the link to originary otherness.

Appropriation, as an aesthetic practice, is a discourse of the uncanny, producing a figure of lack doubled by a masking of that lack. The found image doubles the historical real as both truth and fiction, at once document of history and unreliable evidence of history. Within this slippage of representation, the ethnographic body emerges as a sphere of repressed referentiality. Its indexical claim to the real belongs to a contingent order of time that resists the narrative of history implied by the salvage paradigm, and it is this counternarrative of the memory trace that is produced in found-footage filmmaking. The appropriated image may, in fact, be the exemplary dialectical image. Indexicality does not make an image more real or more accurate but inscribes a difference within it that Walter Benjamin understood as the fundamental allegory of the photographic image.

Dialectical images create a "now" that is always transitory and momentary. The reference to the past in the form of an image produces the present as a moment in a historical continuum that is in perpetual change. The imagination of the future is thus grounded in the imagery of a past that cannot be salvaged but only allegorically recalled. Benjamin's conception of dialectical images was in fact developed in the context of surrealist collage and German photomontage and is thus particularly appropriate to archival and compilation film practices. Montage was Benjamin's own critical method that aimed to break with "historical naturalism." It was a technique that replaced theory by a "construction of facts," an art of "citing without citation marks." As the aesthetic of modernity, montage brought technology and nature together in an *in*organic "new nature."

If the ethnographic discourse within *A Movie* evokes the primitive as a premodern subject, it does so without appealing to a nostalgic narrative of origins. Inorganic history is allegorical history, one that produces what Paul de Man calls "a temporal void, in which nostalgia is renounced."[31] If nostalgia is the signature of modernity's ambivalent embrace of technology, its renunciation constitutes a postmodern view of history as a discontinuous, nonnarrative temporality. By means of montage (a technique that is neither strictly modern nor postmodern in this reading), the past is transformed from a fixed space of forgetting to a dynamic time of historical imagination. The past is the allegorical form of the future, especially when it is perceived as already embedded in technology, as it is in found-footage filmmaking.

Images in Conner's collage films become commodities that circulate independently of their original sources. For Benjamin, commodities constituted the new form of allegory in the nineteenth century insofar as they embodied a form of novelty completely detached from their use value. They harbored a secret dialectic for him, of "the phantasmagoria of 'cultural history' in which the bourgeoisie enjoyed its false consciousness to the full," an infinite sameness that conjured up death as a failure of the modern.[32] Conner's found footage constitutes a detachment of signifiers from signifieds and the production of free-floating images that are only tangentially related to their original role in the production of meaning. These images embody a dialectic of the illusions of the mass media, doubled with an aesthetic of mortality—the emblematic and omnipresent image of the mushroom cloud. Once history has become a data bank, instantly retrievable from storage, Benjamin's dialectical images suggest how the commodity form of the image harbors a historical dialectic.

Benjamin's materialism challenged modernist theories of utopia that were grounded in opposition to reality, as a transcendence of it.[33] In postmodernity, "reality" is placed in question, and utopia becomes a search for the real, not a transcendence of it (which may be why so much contemporary theory has found its way back to Benjamin). Thus the role of the avant-garde shifts from a desire to sublimate art into life, to a desire for a temporality that is best achieved through the creative art of memory. Huyssen summarizes the Baudrillardian notion of postmodern simulation culture thus: "What is lost according to this account of a society saturated with images and discourses is not utopia but reality. At stake is the agony of the real, the fading of the senses. . . . Utopia is no longer needed, or so it is claimed, because all utopias have already fulfilled themselves, and that fulfillment is fatal and catastrophic."[34] For Huyssen, reality and memory are intimately bound, not as a function of truth, but as a function of historical temporality. The most progressive aspect of the avant-garde at the end of the century is thus the search for the real within the fictional, a refiguring of memory as a form of representation. Moreover, the desire for temporality is also a desire for a kind of mooring within a fragmented social sphere. According to this theory, the "real" can be understood as the indexical trace of the past that subsists in historical memory.

In Arthur Lipsett's seven-minute film *Very Nice Very Nice* (1961), produced within the institutional framework of the Canadian NFB, still images predominate. Lipsett's critique of the mass media and its fomented amnesia is very close to Conner's in *A Movie,* although the ethnographic register is far more explicit. Images of "ordinary people" circulate within the discursive cataclysm of an overwhelmingly Americanized commercial culture. The crowd—the people on the street—are however broken down to a discrete selection of static glimpses that operate a little differently from the moving images collected in *A Movie.* The stasis of the people is contrasted to the movement of rockets, planes, and mushroom clouds—suggesting that they are victims of techno-culture, their victimization rendered poignant by their appropriated status in Lipsett's film. Like Conner, Lipsett finds in the archive both the symptoms of historical crisis and, ironically, a method of addressing its deleterious effects.

Atomic Café is a 1982 production of the Archives Project, consisting of Kevin Rafferty, Jayne Loader, and Pierce Rafferty. Composed entirely of archival material, the film examines 1950s American atomic culture using film clips that are longer and somewhat more complete than Conner's fleeting images. At ninety-two minutes, *Atomic Café* fits more easily than *A Movie* into mainstream circulation and enjoyed a fairly wide theatrical release. Wees describes it as a "compilation film" that "does not continually question the representational nature of the images it uses," [35] and yet one of the most striking things about the film is its extensive use of military training films and government-produced propaganda designed to alleviate fears about atomic weapons. Many of these are extremely crude films with terrible acting and transparent ideological motives that force the question of representation into the foreground precisely by means of their use of "fiction."

As documents of historical fiction, many of these clips are at once shocking and sad: the Bikini Islanders who happily turn over their island to bomb testing, the GIs who are exposed to high levels of radiation on desert test sites, the schoolchildren who "duck and cover" to be safe from an atomic blast under their desks. The historical gap between us and them enables us to see these actors as victims of history, playing roles in a fantasy America that produced a simulated version of itself to offset the fear of death. *Atomic Café* could only have been a found-footage film, and it points to the fundamental relationship between image culture and atomic culture, as systematic and mutual means of extinguishing historical memory. The annihilation of people in apocalyptic image culture is registered most emphatically by the aerial shots of Hiroshima after the bomb; the barrenness of the city is echoed in subsequent shots of modern, treeless American suburbs.

The discourse of ethnography in *Atomic Café* is a narrativity that functions as an eclipse of the real. For example, in one segment, a small town in America is apparently infested with communists, but it turns out to have been a dramatic experiment in which the whole town participated to demonstrate the evils of the Red menace. False representation is thus used as a form of education. As a species of allegory, found footage enables us to separate fiction from what escapes its narrative control. There are no people in this film, only images of people,

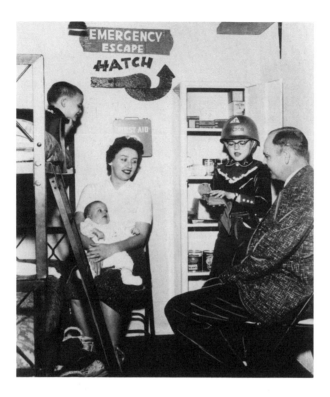

Still from *Atomic Café*, by the Archives Project (1982):
Official Civil Defense Photo. *Courtesy of the Museum
of Modern Art.*

and in their absence, the film points to their annihilation within atomic
culture as it displaces reality with a simulated version.

In lieu of a documentary voice-over, the makers of *Atomic Café* have
used many of the soundtracks of the original footage, authoritative
voices of science that compare the risks of atomic annihilation to slip-
ping on a bar of soap. The last vignette of the film assigns this voice
to a father protecting two small children, which is indeed the film's
dominant paradigm. Real people are like the children who submit to
the system of MAD (mutual assured destruction).[36] Thus we have the
"ordinary citizens" who are caught up in the propaganda machine:
the Girl Scouts who solemnly demonstrate the contents of a survival
kit (canned mashed potatoes, canned peaches, napkins). Men who ex-
pound Dr. Strangelove scenarios likewise devise narrative strategies for
coping with the incomprehensible catastrophe of nuclear war.

Still from *Atomic Café,* by the Archives Project (1982): Official
Civil Defense Photo. *Courtesy of the Museum of Modern Art.*

Andreas Huyssen neatly sums up the affinities of the *Atomic Café* footage with the Fluxus avant-garde movement of the 1950s: "The insidious
dialectic of mere accident and total rational control is perhaps nowhere
as evident as in the ultimate Fluxus event of the 1950s, one performed
millions of times over, but never by a Fluxus artist: schoolchildren line
up, arms covering their heads, in nuclear war drills. Nuclear war was,
after all, the trauma of the 1950s generation." [37] Huyssen implies that
the image taken from *Atomic Café* is of real children, performing a real
drill. And yet the film footage is necessarily a propaganda document,
and thus a performance of a drill. *Atomic Café* could only be a found-
footage film because it is about the representation of rational control,
which falls apart precisely on its fabricated status, its void of referentiality. The children in this image are performing their fear of nuclear
holocaust, but it is only a paranoid symptom of the apparatus of power
that has created the image, to circulate as a perpetuation of the paranoia, to augment its power, and so on.

Atomic Café may not be an avant-garde film, and yet the events that
it documents are absurd, surreal, and ironic. As a found-footage film,
it poses the question of the real outside this fabricated fantasy world of
the controlled catastrophe. Only in the opening sequence of the bodies

of Japanese corpses, the Hiroshima and Nagasaki footage repressed for so long by the U.S. government, do history and the real briefly coincide. Even here, though, an American investigator is seen drawing an outline of a vaporized body in chalk on the pavement. The Japanese victims become ghosts within the film's compilation of fake scenarios and constructed alibis. If we can think of the fictions of *Atomic Café* as fragments of a fabricated ethnography, the bodies of the men, women, and children become doubled as actors. Beside their fictional roles, they are also the others who remain outside the narrative facade of U.S. army information. A single color shot of a Japanese man looking up at a blue sky (possibly from a Godzilla film) is a fictional insert that opens a space for other stories, other fictions about nuclear holocaust.

The atomic age is represented in both *A Movie* and *Atomic Café* as a new era of representation. The mobilization of images to cover the threat of mutual assured destruction in the 1950s culminates in the spectacle of the mushroom cloud itself. Found-footage filmmaking picks up the pieces of the media facade and reconfigures the fragments as visible evidence of the fiction of history produced in that era. One of the effects of this dream analysis is to find the repressed bodies within the image bank, to salvage them as traces of other histories and other temporalities. In both films, to be sure, the ethnographic body is infantilized: poor people of color in *A Movie,* children in *Atomic Café.* In the systems of representation that the filmmakers deconstruct, the Other becomes a fiction, a discourse of images of victims necessary to the logic of authority and control.

In *A Movie* and *Atomic Café,* the ethnographic Other also becomes a floating signifier. Detached from referentiality, the fundamental link to the past is broken, and as a fiction, the ethnographic enters a different temporal schema, one based on metonymic combination rather than metaphor, symbolism, and narrativity. If metaphor implies a depth of meaning, metonymy takes place on the surface, constructing a language of appearances and signifiers.[38] Whether the sources of images are "documentary" or "fictional" texts, found images are always documents of the profilmic, historical bodies. Decontextualization is the means by which the archive offers up history as a nonnarrative series of bodies and events. As film aspires to the condition of photography in found-footage practices, the indexical trace of the photographic image is produced as a supplement in excess of the fictions of time, history, and representation. The traces of another historical narrative challenging the ideology of capitalist progress are grounded in bodies in time, and ethnography is produced within the allegorical nature of found footage, in its dialectics of history.

The circulation of ghosts in found-footage filmmaking is even more explicit in Alain Resnais's *Night and Fog* (1955), a film that combines film and photo imagery of the Holocaust with contemporary shots of overgrown, decaying concentration camps. Huyssen notes that as the documentary footage from the Nazi period began to circulate in Europe in the 1950s, it had "a paralyzing effect on the visual imagination of a whole generation."[39] As a classic example of experimental documentary, *Night and Fog* represents the archive as an unfixed, problematic document of history. The past cannot easily be retrieved but challenges the present as its linear descendant. Alan Sekula has described the conventional use of the archive as a means by which "the spectator comes to identify with the technical apparatus, with the authoritative institution of photography."[40] What is most shocking is that the atrocities in *Night and Fog* were filmed at all. Offered the sight of historical trauma, such as emaciated naked bodies, or the ruins of Hiroshima, the viewer becomes deeply implicated in a cruelty of which the camera is an agent. The image thus becomes dialectical, bringing past and present together in what Benjamin calls a "monad of history." *Night and Fog* evokes a surrealist aesthetic of absurd juxtaposition with the accumulated piles of glasses and hair gathered from Holocaust victims. And yet the shock is much greater than an aesthetic of defamiliarization because it contains the trace of the real, an index of the historical trauma. The ghostly referents of *Night and Fog* speak to a problem of memory and the need for a new theory of historical time, one that can redeem the past. To this extent, the film contributes to a form of experimental ethnography based in the archive as a locus of nonlinear historical memory. As Sekula argues: "The archive has to be read from below, from a position of solidarity with those displaced, deformed, silenced, or made invisible by the machineries of profit and progress."[41]

If the terror of *Night and Fog* lies in the implication of an original viewer of the atrocities documented, thirty-five years later, this horror has been tempered by a cynical postmodernism and an annihilation of the subject of vision and responsibility. Television images are the products of a dispersed, corporate subject. In Craig Baldwin's *Tribulation 99,* the ethnographic referent is recast as a threat to representation and history. However, in his depiction of a perpetual catastrophe of im-

Still from *Tribulation 99*, by Craig Baldwin (1991).

pending apocalypse, the horror of a lack of horror keeps the repressed referent of history from asserting itself. Drawing on the image bank of American information films and newsreels, Hollywood science fiction, thriller, and adventure movies, and TV programs, Baldwin constructs a scenario of conspiracy and paranoia. Layering the imagery with written intertitles and a whispered voice-over, *Tribulation 99* is a palimpsest of floating signifiers that subsume history in an impossible network of metonymic relations.

The premise of *Tribulation 99* is that U.S. security, with its vast arsenal of mass media, military, and government institutions, is mobilized against the threat of alien invaders from outer space. Moving through Guatemala to Cuba, Chile, Granada, Nicaragua, and Panama, the history of U.S. intervention in Central and South America is depicted as a science fiction thriller. Interspersed with the footage of flying saucers, monsters, mad scientists, Latin American actors, diagrams, maps, and American politicians are scenes of Latin American laborers, religious processions, and newsreel footage of street violence in Chile and Nicaragua. The verbal and written texts describe a complex conspiracy of anticommunist personnel organized through the CIA, the United Fruit Company, and the Warren Commission, which is battling a supernatural conspiracy of the Bermuda Triangle, Haitian voodoo, and a Mayan-alien alliance. In the apocalyptic finale, the Panama Canal is flooded by secret dumping of American atomic waste, "the Atlantic and Pacific merge . . . the world comes to an end, for which we are grateful." The Chosen Ones flee to Mars via stealth mother ships and damn those left behind.

The accelerated pace of Baldwin's montage and the elliptical character of his narration constitute a barrage of information that thoroughly mixes truth and fiction, fact and fantasy. *Tribulation 99* is the epitome of what Bill Nichols has described as "the paranoid style" of documentary representation that circulates around and emanates from the JFK assassination and American conspiracy culture of the 1950s and 1960s. The collage form is emblematic of the partial knowledge and decenteredness of a lack of mastery over reality.[42] Baldwin pushes this paranoid style to a point of excess so that history becomes a product of the fertile imagination of anticommunist propaganda. U.S. intervention in Latin America appears to be motivated by the media imagery of monstrous invasion that generates a counterconspiracy thoroughly duped by its own fictions.

In *Tribulation 99,* the crisis of representation is most clearly also a crisis of historical time and colonial power. The "end of history" is apparent not only in the spectacle of failed technology but equally in the neocolonial exploitation of Third World peoples whose challenge to the military-industrial complex lies in their escape from representation. Allegorized as invaders from another planet, as monsters and supernatural phenomena, "the alien" has no referent but exists as pure representation. From the ideological construction of the alien in American culture, Baldwin produces signifiers that are not grounded in any history but transcend referentiality altogether. Fiction and myth are constructed as arbitrary linkages of images in which the oppressed and the colonized are produced as threats to both American security and realist representation.

In the conjunction of science fiction and anthropological history, the dialectical images of *Tribulation 99* constitute a revision of the notion of the repressed. While the paranoid style evokes the repressed, here, in the form of dialectical images, the repressed becomes detached from memory. Baldwin's collage is drawn from an image bank so vast that it suggests the wholesale obliteration of linear memory. Images are recalled instead by arbitrary links to storage in this postmodern variant of the found-footage film.

Mobilizing these images as cultural documents, *Tribulation 99* functions as a kind of random-access memory of American Cold War cul-

Still from *Tribulation 99,* by Craig Baldwin (1991).

ture. The discontinuity of catastrophe is once again symptomatic of apocalypse culture and its crisis of representation. Among the images of disaster are an earthquake in Nicaragua (possibly filmed in miniature) and the same swaying suspension bridge seen in *A Movie,*[43] plus a slew of plane crashes and explosions. As a postmodern variant of *A Movie,* Baldwin's film inscribes a discourse of political activism in which the ethnographic is not a mute signifier of historiographic memory but a sign of historical trauma. In the void created by the onslaught of images, the possibility of historical resistance to the military-industrial complex is eclipsed. This is the real crisis of the film, its traumatic undercurrent. Baldwin can address neocolonialism only as a problem of representation, not of history; the film has no access to the "truth" of U.S. intervention in Central and South America, as the media "cover-up" has become a totalizing form of coverage.

Whereas most of the imagery of Latin American people is heavily coded as tourist or industrial footage, some of the newsreel footage of street demonstrations jumps out of the film as another order of representation. Civilians dodging sniper bullets and being assaulted by police in Chile and Nicaragua document a historical struggle that cannot be subsumed by any narrative temporality. These scenes are shot in a realist style that is otherwise absent from the film, and while they do not *necessarily* have a greater claim on the real than any other shots, they tend to point to another level of representation, one in which the referent finally breaks through the fiction of the signifier. Only in its most traumatic form does the ethnographic correspond with the historical real.[44]

In Baldwin's allegory of invasion, the aliens infest the interior of the earth and threaten those above, a structure that quickly becomes fused with the American-Mexican border: "Earth's creatures flee in terror," announces a graphic title while the narrator says, "Their activities drive huge armies of soldier ants and killer bees past the Rio Grande . . . our southern border ditches as permeable as paper towels." In the few newsreel images in the film, this threat from below is also a threat of referentiality, a challenge posed to the "surface" of representation that is the fabric of Baldwin's collage, the network of images through which U.S. policy in Central and South America justifies and perpetuates itself.

Tribulation 99 is an extremely ambivalent film, symptomatic of its own paranoid strategies that ultimately curtail the possibility of historical agency in the inaccessibility of a "real" outside the onslaught of images. And yet it points to the discursive potential of found footage to produce the ethnographic as a radical form of memory. The retrieval of the singular, the accidental, and the contingent by means of Benjamin's *mémoire involontaire* runs counter to the effect of abstraction by which the social actor loses his or her identity and becomes a representative of his or her culture. The inscription of a historical specificity outside of linear time challenges the aura of essentialism that plagues colonial paradigms of anthropological knowledge. Found-footage filmmaking is a means of accessing history in the form of an unordered archive populated by historical subjects that pressure representation "from below," from their status as referents. Retrieved into new textual forms, they are salvaged as image, as allegories of a historical real that is not itself retrievable but stands in dialectical relation to a temporary and impermanent present.

The apocalyptic narrativity of *Tribulation 99* is generated through the accumulated conflicting narratives of which each image is a mere fragment. Although the fabrication of memory is emblematic of the simulated history of postmodern culture, Baldwin's film does not foment a historical amnesia. It is not a film about forgetting. Both the verbal narration and the visual montage recall a tremendous amount of information. The problem is of assembling a coherent history, but by deliberately rendering the history incoherent, Baldwin invokes the inadequacy of narrative representation to historical struggle. That struggle becomes, instead, a contest in and of representation, even if in this particular film it is one that is ultimately lost to a narrative closure of Christian redemption and satanic damnation.

How would the "time of the other" differ from the hierarchization of time that informs colonialist anthropology? In his rhetoric of "invasion" in the quoted epigraph to this chapter, Fabian offers a clue to how the found-footage film might function as a counternarrative to the denial of coevalness. By means of juxtaposition, fragmentation, and interruption, the archival film brings past, present, and future into a new nonlinear temporality. Found footage literalizes the salvage paradigm, making each rescued image into an allegorical form of representation, a ruin, in Benjamin's words, of another time. It is important that the answer to "the denial of coevalness" is not simply a lapse into a perpetual present that might obliterate the traces of cultural memory. This is the danger with which *Tribulation 99* flirts, and to which it ultimately succumbs.

If one of the major thrusts of the contemporary critique of anthropology is its implicit theory of history, dialectical images and archival film practices offer a means of interrupting and disrupting the salvage paradigm. The filmic image always contains a dual temporality: the time of filming is a coeval time, but the time of viewing an edited film will necessarily be later, rendering the image as past tense. It is in this sense that the cinema has contributed to the denial of coevalness by which anthropology has constructed its object, the Other.[45] While narrative and documentary codes tend to cover up this difference, found-footage filmmaking feeds on it.

Handsworth Songs: The Trauma of History

As a found-footage film, *Handsworth Songs* mobilizes the archive quite differently than the films discussed in the previous section. In its commitment to historical struggle and its exploration of identity politics, this film seeks to re-present the imagery of the past in the interest of a transformed future. Lacking the cynicism of *Atomic Café* and *Tribulation 99,* and without the total melancholia of *A Movie* or *Night and Fog,* this is an attempt to construct a text of cultural memory. In its fragmentary and multilayered form, it responds to the difficult, complex, and violent construction of diasporic Black subjectivities in Thatcher's England.[46] Its ethnographic aspect is thus deeply grounded in questions of representing race, nationhood, and community. The historical referents of the found footage are described as "ghosts" who haunt the present, as the film's most evocative slogan implies: "There are no stories in the riots, only the ghosts of other stories."

The riots in question are those of Handsworth and Broadwater Farm, suburbs of Birmingham, in 1985, with echoes of those that took place in Brixton in 1981. The apocalypticism of this film belongs to a specific historical moment of a specific social formation. Black Audio Film Collective, who produced *Handsworth Songs* in 1985, is a workshop that was formed in 1983. The group came together to produce films for and about the Black community in Britain, and its members—John Akomfrah, Reece Auguste, Eddie George, Lina Gopaul, Avril Johnson, and Trevor Mathison—are all graduates of sociology and communication theory programs. Well versed in the cultural studies theory of Stuart Hall, Paul Gilroy, and Homi Bhabha, these filmmakers sought to challenge the conventions of representing Blacks in the British media.[47] Particularly concerned about the prevailing image of dangerous and violent Black youth that emerged from the riots of the 1980s, they felt the need not to "correct" the representation of Blacks but to excavate the imagery of Blacks in Britain and interrupt its historical trajectory.

Among the fragmented imagery of *Handsworth Songs* is original footage shot by the collective, and also TV newsreel footage of the riots. Juxtaposed with film clips of Caribbean immigrants arriving in England in the 1950s, the events of the early 1980s also become history. A historical narrative of failed promise and thwarted ambition is obliquely implied, but not as a simple, linear story. Moving back and forth between historical periods, most of which are undated and uncredited but speak through their various production values and media aesthetics, the collage is deliberately poetic and romantic. The technique of "poeticizing every image"—through selection, juxtaposition, and music—was a means of countering the truth-values of the authoritative discourses of British TV newsreels from which much of the footage is borrowed. At the same time, despite the title that promises a kind of elegiac aesthetic, the film's romanticism is deeply fissured and fractured. The film's director, John Akomfrah, says of this strategy: "The triumphalist vision of race and community operates on the assumption that there is essentially a core of affect that is structured around oratory, around song—giving it an irreducible unity—which wasn't present in the film. It played with it, at some stages discards it, it takes it on board, then it says it's probably not possible, . . . but the film doesn't fix its sentiments around it." [48]

Along with several other films by Black Audio and Sankofa (another Black filmmaking collective formed in the 1980s), *Handsworth Songs* generated a debate about the role of avant-garde techniques in Black filmmaking. The fragmentary decentered aesthetic was felt by many to be inappropriate to the filmmakers' responsibility to produce "positive images" of the community.[49] Black Audio's articulate defense of their choice of aesthetics excludes any claim to a heritage within the avant-garde. Instead, they point to television culture, with its fast-paced editing, nonnarrative structures, and radical juxtapositions, as an important source of experiments with cinematic realism.[50] Moreover, the question of identity within the diasporic Black community is one of radical dislocation. The multiplicity of cultural histories from which diasporic identity is constructed, or positioned, is strongly evoked by the collage form of *Handsworth Songs.*

The archival imagery includes both newsreel footage and more informal shots that have a home-movie aesthetic. Immigrants arriving on boats and planes, social dancing, schoolchildren, families and wedding photos, all depict "community" as a network of images that are lost to the past. In several instances, still photos are posted in a studio setting, and the camera moves past and around them, graphically depicting the distance and difference between then and now. The museological frame renders these photos as monuments to a past beyond reach. In this respect, *Handsworth Songs* exemplifies Andreas Huyssen's argument that the museum has been transformed in postmodernity as "a space for creative forgetting." If the museum once stood in opposition to an avant-garde that demanded a complete break with a fossilized past, the museum is now fully part of the society of the spectacle, offering "an alternative to channel flicking that is grounded in the materiality of the exhibited objects and in their temporal aura." [51] "In relation to the increasing capacity of data banks, which can be seen as the contemporary version of the American ideology of 'more is better,' the museum would be rediscovered as a space for creative forgetting. The idea of the comprehensive data bank and the information superhighway is just as incompatible with memory as the television image is with material reality" (34).

Unlike most found-footage filmmaking, *Handsworth Songs* evokes the "museal gaze" to enhance the "auratic effect" of archival photography. Remembering the Caribbean immigrants and factory workers who came to Britain in the 1950s and 1960s is depicted as a difficult but strategic task in the construction of the diasporic subject looking back from the distance of the present. The film footage of factory workers and children is dominated by close-ups of faces, individuating those who populated the past, permanently caught within an ethnographic gaze. In the context of the violence of the 1980s, that gaze is decentered and inscribed as a discourse of race. One black-and-white sequence in which a woman finally turns and swings her handbag at a camera that has been following her underlines the contest over the gaze implied in so much of the archival footage. Another sequence of a fully assimilated black man who has accepted his subservient role in British society as a uniformed guard is offered as a site of subjectivity and identification that is highly ambiguous. His faith in the icons of British industrialism and national culture is depicted in the film fragment as highly fictional and staged—which is not to say that it is not a true story.

Intercut with this rich archival material are interviews with Margaret Thatcher and other politicians, as well as footage that is best described as marginal to the mainstream news media. Disrespectful of the conventions of the TV interview, angry members of the Black community challenge politicians on the street or speak their minds directly to the camera. Interviews with formally seated members of the Black and Asian communities imply a social formation quite separate from that of official British politics. Instead of a televised public forum, we get only the elaborate preparations for a TV show that will clearly make any real dialogue impossible. The explanations for the riots are multiple, conflicting, and incomplete. The riots themselves are represented mainly by a massive police presence, burning cars, and a shot of a boy with dreadlocks being chased and tackled by policemen. This particular shot of street violence is precisely the kind of image that has contested political meanings and significance; repeated in slow motion, in the collage context, it becomes a signifier available to different mobilizations with no original, essential meaning.[52] As a documentary of the Handsworth riots, the film forces the question of representation into the foreground. For example, Cynthia Jarrett's daughter describes how her mother died after being accosted by police, but neither the speaker nor the incident is shown. Instead, as she speaks, we see the outside of a dull gray apartment building with a crew of disappointed photographers gazing at it.

TV images reproduced in *Handsworth Songs*, by Black Audio Film Collective (1985).

One of the themes that links the heterogeneous fragments of *Handsworth Songs* is the role of industry in the construction of the British subject, and its importance for the problematic alignment of race and class in late-twentieth-century Britain. The Anglican hymn "Jerusalem," which was written in the nineteenth century with lyrics by William Blake, is about the utopian memory of a preindustrial England. It is heard twice in *Handsworth Songs*, the first time in a sampled reggae version by Mark Stewart and the Mafia, over news headlines describing Handsworth as "the bleeding heart of England." (In this and other points in the film, Black Audio suggest an allegiance with the sampling techniques of Afro-Caribbean popular music.) When "Jerusalem" is played again toward the end of the film, the hymn is played in a more churchlike spirit over shots of an industrial wasteland, workers' row housing, and various arched railroad tunnels. Black Audio's appropriation of this particular song is a means of posing the question of the redemption of the black working class in Britain, and they map another memory onto its redemptive strains — the pastoral scene of the Caribbean homeland. The film is completed by a series of images of fire, street demonstrations, a repetition of the boy being captured by police, and, finally, old footage of Black and Asian immigrants arriving full of hope. In the final shot, a woman walks away from the camera into a street walled by red bricks.

Despite the lyricism of *Handsworth Songs*, the film still has something of the apocalyptic sense of other found-footage films. However, in this case, it is linked to a redemptive aesthetic. There is a salvage paradigm at work here, which is best described as a redemption of history within a culture of simulation and amnesia. As a history of fiction, images, and disjunctive stories, it is an allegorical form of history in which the real remains outside, in the form of ghosts. The use of archival and newsreel footage constitutes a mediascape from which Black British subjectivity might be constructed. Outside the essentialism of nationhood, cultural identity depends on retelling, not reproducing, the past. The distinction is critical. As Stuart Hall explains, "Cultural identities come from somewhere, have histories. But, like everything which is historical, they undergo constant trans-formation. Far from being eternally fixed in some essentialized past, they are subject to the continuous 'play' of history, culture and power." [53] In the retelling of the past, it is important that it does not slip into a simulacral, fabricated image sphere cut off from the historical real. (This is the lesson of *Tribulation 99*.) Thus the invocation of the museal gaze, along with romantic lyricism, works within the fissures of the image bank to render the phantasmagoria allegorical.

Handsworth Songs suggests how found-footage filmmaking can function as a form of experimental ethnography that challenges the modernist temporality of "progress" in which ethnography and cinematic representation are conventionally bound. We have seen how the collage style of filmmaking tends toward an apocalyptic "end of history." With the amnesiac erasure of historical referentiality, an aesthetic of simulation entails a collapse of historical time as a theory of priority, teleology, and hierarchy. When there is nothing to remember, there is nothing to overcome; when there is no depth to representation, there is nothing lost and nothing to redeem. This postmodern condition, however, reconstructs the real outside representation, as an other order of temporality and history. In cutting the present off from the past, amnesiac culture is also allegorical, producing the possibility of dialectical images in which past and present might correspond in new, nonlinear ways. Once the postmodern image bank is recognized as a cultural data bank, its materials might be reformed, through appropriation, for new forms of memory. *Handsworth Songs* demonstrates the potential role of nonlinear memory for the positioning of postcolonial subjectivities and diasporic culture.

Between Photography and Television

Taken together, the films discussed in this chapter delineate an ethnographic discourse that is founded on traumatic histories of exploitation, colonization, and appropriation. From the excesses of the society of the spectacle, the fabric of "coverage" is ripped apart to produce a historiography of radical memory in which the indexicality of the image resists the symbolization of progressive, "natural" historicism. This is what I have described as the inscription of the time of the Other. Whereas the breakdown of the defense mechanism of "coverage" constitutes a melancholia of loss in the 1950s, in the 1980s "the power of remembrance" is challenged by the other time of randomly accessed memory traces. It is significant in this respect that films such as *Tribulation 99*, Baldwin's *RocketKitKongoKit* (1986), *Handsworth Songs,* and many other films and videos of the last fifteen years address issues of colonial culture by means of archival imagery. The crisis of representation may have become associated with the "end of history," but it may also be an important means of challenging the teleological historiography of progress with a discourse of singularities, contingencies, and dispersed histories.

After all, the shocks of modernity must include the multiculturalism of the global crowd. If colonialism is a closed, linear system in which the discourses of power, cultural imperialism, and racial hierarchies have cohered as a defense mechanism against the threat of the Other, Benjamin's theory of memory, time, and allegorical representation might be the point at which the time of the Other interrupts the system. As the visual evidence of progress, ethnography operated as a salvage paradigm within a system of remembrance. But within the context of failed progress and unreliable representation, the ethnographic takes on a new role as a historical counterpoint to the linear historiography of colonial time.

The Other haunts found-footage filmmaking in the form of ghosts, lingering just "below" or outside the images of people drawn from long-forgotten narratives. In the radical decontextualization of montage, the ethnographic subject is cast out of narrative and takes up a position outside the teleological thrust of historical "progress." The apocalyptic tenor of found-footage films points back to the singular status of the body in the archive,[54] and a fragmented social history that resists the linear unfolding of filmic time. Once the retrieval and recycling of images has transformed the imaginary space of memory into a randomly accessed data bank, images may be properly dialectical, inscribed with forgetting as a radical form of the Other.

It is tempting to think of archival practices as a kind of archaeology, and yet what is immediately evident in these films is that found footage is a discourse of surfaces. Origins and sources are effaced, producing an image sphere with a highly ambivalent relation to history. *Atomic Café* and *Tribulation 99* both embrace the kitsch aesthetic of a lack of depth,[55] but it is precisely that surface quality that renders found footage particularly ethnographic. The limits of visual evidence render the profilmic as a cultural space outside representation. All images become documentary images once their original contexts are stripped away; in being repositioned within another serial organization of images, they document an Other time and place.

Film seems to aspire to the condition of photography in these texts, and yet the breakdown of cinematic temporality also invokes the multiplicity and redundancy of television. The cinema in found-footage filmmaking falls between the memorial function of photography and the amnesia of TV culture. Filmmakers such as Thornton, Conner, Baldwin, and the Black Audio Film Collective have found ways of mobilizing this ambivalence for their different experimental ethnographic practices. Once cinematic space and time are broken down into the terms of the Other mediums of photography and television, those practices can then be appropriated as techniques of memory construction. Wrenched from the individual, memory becomes a kind of forgetting that is insistently social and historical, and it becomes a form of allegorical representation.

The techniques that produce the radical ambiguity of found-footage filmmaking are those of juxtaposition and irony. Through allegory, archival cinema enacts a dialectic of "original" and "copy" in which the body belongs to the parallel universe of the original footage, cut off from—indeed annihilated from—the appropriated image and its machine of modernity. As a form of recovery, found footage renders culture not as a lost property but as an image sphere in which the real is found in a new form. Once the salvage paradigm is allegorized and rendered uncanny, the Other is relocated in a history that is not vanishing but exceeds and transcends representation, resisting its processes of reification.

V

CONCLUSION

Sadie Benning in *A Place Called Lovely* (1991).

10 Autoethnography: Journeys of the Self

In those early years I got to know the "town" only as the theater of
purchases, on which occasions it first became apparent how my father's
money could cut a path for us between the shop counters and assistants and.
mirrors, and the appraising eyes of our mother, whose muff lay on the
counter.

—WALTER BENJAMIN, "A Berlin Chronicle"

In Benjamin's chronicle of his Berlin childhood, he places the problem
of memory centrally. "For autobiography has to do with time, with sequence and what makes up the continuous flow of life."[1] The fragmentary recollections that he offers are rich in detail and, like the passage
quoted in the epigraph, situate him as a child within a complex network
of social relations. A class analysis is projected onto fleeting memories,
along with a recognition of gender roles, and even an analysis of the
gaze. The materialism of Benjamin's autobiographical account of Berlin is made even more explicit in his Moscow diary, which he described
as a text in which "factuality is already theory."[2]

Throughout his various autobiographical writings, a sense of the self
emerges that is thoroughly grounded in experience and observation.
Walter Benjamin develops as a socially constructed identity, one who
finds himself in a shifting series of others, in the topography of city
streets, and in the detail of daily life. Theory, philosophy, and intellectual life were inseparable from his own experience of modernity, and
his identity as a German Jew pervades his writing in the form of experience, rather than essence. Susan Buck-Morss suggests that "Benjamin
perceived his own life emblematically, as an allegory for social reality,

and sensed keenly that no individual could live a resolved or affirmative existence in a social world that was neither."[3]

As literary genres, autobiography and ethnography share "a commitment to the actual," and Michael Fischer has argued that "ethnic autobiography" should be recognized as a model of postmodern ethnography.[4] Autobiography is a technique of self-representation that is not a fixed form but is in constant flux. He describes "contemporary autobiography" as an exploration of the fragmented and dispersed identities of late-twentieth-century pluralist society. In this context, ethnic autobiography is an "art of memory" that serves as protection against the homogenizing tendencies of modern industrial culture. Moreover, autobiography has become a powerful tool of cultural criticism, paralleling postmodern theories of textuality and knowledge. Fischer describes the "writing tactics" of autoethnography thus: "Contemporary ethnic autobiographies partake of the mood of metadiscourse, of drawing attention to their linguistic and fictive nature, of using the narrator as an inscribed figure within the text whose manipulation calls attention to authority structures" (232).

This ethnographic mode of self-representation is pervasive in what has become widely recognized as a "new autobiography" in film and video.[5] Autobiography becomes ethnographic at the point where the film- or videomaker understands his or her personal history to be implicated in larger social formations and historical processes. Identity is no longer a transcendental or essential self that is revealed, but a "staging of subjectivity" — a representation of the self as a performance. In the politicization of the personal, identities are frequently played out among several cultural discourses, be they ethnic, national, sexual, racial, and/or class based. The subject "in history" is rendered destabilized and incoherent, a site of discursive pressures and articulations.

The fragmented and hybrid identities produced in the multitude of "personal" films and videos have been celebrated by critics and theorists as forms of "embodied knowledge" and "politics of location."[6] Their tactics are similar to those of the literary form described by Fisher, and yet they also destabilize the very notion of ethnicity. One's body and one's historical moment may be the joint site of experience and identity, and yet they don't necessarily add up to ethnicity as an anthropological category. Autoethnography is a vehicle and a strategy for challenging imposed forms of identity and exploring the discursive possibilities of inauthentic subjectivities.

Mary Louise Pratt introduced the term "autoethnography" as an oppositional term: "If ethnographic texts are a means by which Europeans represent to themselves their (usually subjugated) others, autoethnographic texts are those the others construct in response to or in dialogue with those metropolitan representations."[7] Although she denies that autoethnographic texts are "authentic" texts, her attribution of this genre to marginalized subjects is characteristic of writing on autoethnography. My inclusion of Chris Marker's *Sans Soleil* (1982) in this chapter is an attempt to expand and modify a concept that, in Pratt's usage, reaffirms the duality of center and margin. Autoethnography can also be a form of what James Clifford calls "self-fashioning," in which the ethnographer comes to represent himself as a fiction, inscribing a doubleness within the ethnographic text: "Though it [ethnography] portrays other selves as culturally constituted, it also fashions an identity authorized to represent, to interpret, even to believe—but always with some irony—the truths of discrepant worlds."[8] Once ethnography is reframed as a self-representation in which any and all subjects are able to enter discourse in textual form, the distinctions between textual authority and profilmic reality begin to break down. The imperial eye looking back on itself is also a subject in history.

The oxymoronic label "autoethnography" announces a total breakdown of the colonialist precepts of ethnography, and indeed the critical enthusiasm for its various forms situates it as a kind of ideal form of antidocumentary. Diary filmmaking, autobiographical filmmaking, and personal videos can all be subsumed within what Michael Renov has described as the "essayistic" impulse in recent film and video. The essay is a useful category because it incorporates the "I" of the writer into a commentary on the world that makes no grand scientific or totalizing claims but is uncertain, tentative and speculative.[9]

A common feature of autoethnography is the first-person voice-over that is intently and unambiguously subjective. This is, however, only one of three levels on which a film- or videomaker can inscribe themselves, the other two being at the origin of the gaze, and as body image. The multiple possible permutations of these three "voices" — speaker, seer, and seen — are what generate the richness and diversity of autobiographical filmmaking. In addition to the discursive possibilities of these three voices is another form of identity, which is that of the avant-garde filmmaker as collagist and editor. This is perhaps the surrealist heritage of the form, the role of juxtaposition, irony, and *rétrouvé*, through which the film- or videomaker "writes" an identity in temporal structures. By inscribing themselves on the level of "metadiscourse," film- and videomakers also identify with their technologies of representation, with a culture of independent filmmaking, alongside their other discursive identities.

Much of the new autobiography emanates from queer culture, from film- and videomakers whose personal histories unfold within a specifically public sphere.[10] It is also produced by many for whom ethnicity or race casts their own history as an allegory for a community or culture that cannot be essentialized. Themes of displacement, immigration, exile, and transnationality are prominent in this mode of filmmaking.[11] Some of the film- and videomakers associated with the "new autobiography" include Richard Fung, Marlon Riggs, Su Friedrich, Rea Tajiri, Deborah Hoffman, Vanylyn Green, Margaret Stratton, Lynn Hershmann, Mark Massi, Hara Kazuo, Tony Buba, Mona Hatoum, and many others. Marilu Mallet's *Journal Inachévé* (1986), Hara Kazuo's *Extremely Personal Eros* (1974), Akerman's *News from Home* (1976), and Michel Citron's *Daughter Rite* (1978) are all important examples of the form as it developed in the 1970s. Family histories and political histories unfold as difficult processes of remembering and struggle. Specific, resonant images echo across distances of time and space. Documentary truth is freely mixed with storytelling and performances. The many film- and videomakers who have made and continue to make autoethnographies find "themselves" in diverse image cultures, images, and discourses. Many are concerned with transforming image culture through the production of new voices and new subjectivities.

A prominent theme in contemporary personal cinema is the staging of an encounter with the filmmaker's parent(s) or grandparent(s) who embody a particular cultural history of displacement or tradition — for example, Richard Fung's *The Way to My Father's Village* (1988) and *My Mother's Place* (1990), *History and Memory* (Rea Tajiri, 1991), *Measures of Distance* (Mona Hatoum, 1988), *The Ties That Bind* (Su Friedrich 1984). The difference between generations is written across the filmmaker's own inscription in technology, and thus it is precisely an ethnographic distance between the modern and the premodern that is dramatized in the encounter — through interview or archival memory or both. One often gets the sense that the filmmaker has no memory and is salvaging his or her own past through the recording of family memory.

The testimonial, confessional character of autoethnography often assumes a site of authenticity and veracity, originating in the filmmaker's experience. And yet fake diaries and autobiographies by Orson Welles (*F Is for Fake*, 1975), Michele Citron (*Daughter Rite,* 1979), Jim McBride (*David Holzman's Diary,* 1968), and Joe Gibbons and Tony Oursler (*Onourown,* 1990) demonstrate the unreliability of the form. The confessional mode is a testimonial discourse with no necessary validity beyond the viewer's faith in the text's authority. Autobiographical film and video tends to be couched within a testimonial mode, as the authorial subjects offer themselves up for inspection, as anthropological specimens. But they do so ironically, mediating their own image and identifying obliquely with the technologies of representation, identifying themselves as film- and videomakers. Because autoethnography invokes an imbrication of history and memory, the authenticity of experience functions as a receding horizon of truth in which memory and testimony are articulated as modes of salvage.

The film- and videomakers who I will discuss in this chapter are Jonas Mekas, George Kuchar, Sadie Benning, Kidlat Tahimik, and Chris Marker, artists whose films and videos foreground many of the contradictions and tendencies of the diary film. As a genre of "personal cinema," the diary film can in many cases be cast as a form of experimental ethnography, and these examples are suggestive of the role of the diary film and video in the rethinking of ethnographic knowledge. The role of identity in these films and tapes demands an expanded notion of "ethnicity" as a cultural formation of the subject. Indeed, what unites these diverse texts is the articulation of identities that are split, insecure, and plural. Memory and travel are means of exploring fragmented selves and placing ethnicity at one remove, as something to remember, to see, but not quite to experience.

The journeys undertaken by these filmmakers are both temporal and geographic, sometimes tending toward epic proportions. The diary form involves a journey between the times of shooting and editing; traveling becomes a form of temporal experience through which the film- or videomaker confronts himself or herself as tourist, ethnographer, exile, or immigrant. These film- and videomakers may not be representative of the extraordinary diversity of personal, autoethnographic film forms, but they do cover a range of techniques and strategies that merge self-representation with cultural critique. They suggest that the subjective form of ethnography distinguishes itself above all from the passive scientism of conventional ethnographic forms by destabilizing "ethnicity" and its constraints on subjectivity.

When P. Adams Sitney first discussed autobiography as an avant-garde film form, he concluded that "it is the autobiographical cinema *per se* that confronts fully the rupture between the time of cinema and the time of experience and invents forms to contain what it finds there."[12] Subjectivity cannot be denoted as simply in film as with the written "I" but finds itself split in time. The image of the filmmaker, when it appears in a diary film, refers to another cameraperson, or to a tripod that denotes an empty, technologized gaze. As Janine Marchessault points out, "The image of someone behind the camera encompasses its own impossibility as a representation unable to access its origin, to invert its own process."[13] Subjectivity is split again between the seeing and the filmed body. While Sitney argues that the "self" of autobiographical filmmaking is united in the notion of authorship, I want to suggest that an ethnographic subjectivity, a self that understands itself as culturally constituted, is fundamentally split in the autobiographical mode. Even when the subject in history is constructed as a point of origin for memories, geographic and spacial distance comes to evoke a distance in time that separates different moments of the self.

The autoethnographic subject blurs the distinction between ethnographer and Other by traveling, becoming a stranger in a strange land, even if that land is a fictional space existing only in representation. As a diary of a journey, the travelogue produces an otherness in the interstices of the fragmented "I" of the filmic, textual self. As the memory of the trip becomes enmeshed with historical processes and cultural differences, the filmic image becomes the site of a complex relationship between "I was there" and "this is how it is." Travel films are collections of images made for other spectators in distant cultures and therefore constitute a kind of traffic in images with the traveler-filmmaker as their unreliable referent and point of origin. Needless to say, the utopian impulse of autoethnography relies on a certain mobility of the filmmaker and remains in many ways couched in modernist, imperialist, and romantic discourses.

If filmic autobiography exploits the temporal lag between filming and editing, video diaries tend to have a slightly different temporal effect. One of the things I want to suggest in this concluding chapter is how the history of autoethnography intersects with the slow fade in independent filmmaking from film to video. If autobiography is about time and history, as Benjamin suggests, these two mediums produce very different effects of temporality that has some bearing on the historical subjectivities and identities produced within their technological spheres. Video offers an economics of "coverage" that is impossible to match with sixteen-millimeter film production costs, and so the diaristic mode is in many ways being renewed as filmmakers take advantage of the economies of the new medium. (This is not to say that avant-garde film is "dead," just that it is becoming increasingly difficult to finance.) Autoethnography in film and video is always mediated by technology, and so unlike its written forms, identity will be an effect not only of history and culture but also of the history and culture of technologies of representation.

Trinh Minh-ha has written about the Inappropriate Other as the subject whose intervention "is necessarily that of both a deceptive insider and a deceptive outsider."[14] She implies that such a figure actually lurks within every "I," and if one of the goals of a postcolonial ethnography is to become aware of how subjectivity is implicated in the production of meaning, the Inappropriate Other is the figure to be developed. By exploring autoethnography as an intercultural, cross-cultural method, I hope to suggest how the Inappropriate Other functions as a time traveler who journeys in memory and history.

Jonas Mekas and the Loss of Experience

Jonas Mekas's diary films are perhaps the prototypical autoethnographies, at the same time as they mark a kind of penultimate romanticism that has long been eclipsed in postmodernism. Although a great deal has been written about his project,[15] it needs to be situated within an ethnographic frame to appreciate fully the way that the film medium mediates between individual and social histories, and between memory and historical time. Mekas's role in the development of the American avant-garde involved the promotion of both personal filmmaking and a film culture that would form itself around the "truth" and "freedom" of a noncommercial, independent cinema. His diary project, which comprises about thirteen hours of edited footage,[16] is testimony to his commitment to these twin goals.

Memorialization and loss are the defining characteristics of Mekas's diary films, and he renders them as features of the medium itself, enhanced by his poetic, melancholy narration. The temporal gap between the collection of images and the editing of them into films many years later renders every image a memory, a trace or fragment of a time in a trajectory that reaches back to what David James has described as "the absent center of the entire project, the footage of his childhood in Lithuania." James points out that not only was this footage never shot, but "it is historically and logically inconceivable," because the lost past is a preindustrial, pastoral ideal.[17] James also suggests that Mekas "lived modernism's master narrative, the history of the displacement of the organic and the rural by the industrial and the urban" (146).

Mekas was very explicitly attempting to "salvage an identity" from his practice of filming. At the same time, that identity is precisely that of a displaced person. If homelessness is Mekas's self-image, it is also his filmic technique, his refusal to stop on any image, to synchronize any sound and image, or to narrate any image. Mekas's diary films assume a structure similar to that of found-footage filmmaking: the image track is highly fragmented and belongs to the past, while the sound track provides a narrational continuity that belongs to the present. It is as if, editing his own material, Mekas "finds" the images and retrieves them, reenacting the structure of memory in found-footage filmmaking, the difference being the inherently subjective status of the found images. It is a highly redemptive project insofar as he brings together the fragments of his memory and integrates them in an avant-garde film, which immediately assumes all the trappings of a "work of art" in the cultural politics of Mekas's milieu.

Mekas's project has been described as an exemplary instance of "secondary revision," the process by which, in psychoanalysis, the patient recounts the dream, revising it and substituting a verbal narration for what was originally "experienced" as dream.[18] As Renov explains, "We are all of us lost in the chasm between our desire to recapture the past and the impossibility of a pristine return, no one more than Mekas himself."[19] In the revisionary process, Mekas casts himself as both anthropologist and native informant. When, near the beginning of *Lost Lost Lost*, Mekas says, "and I was there with my camera," he reveals his mission as the self-appointed documentarian of the Lithuanian community in New York.

Over shots of a man in a dark kitchen, Mekas says, "You never know what a DP [displaced person] feels like in the evening, in New York," indicating the epistemological limits of his silent film footage. And yet the wholesale melancholia of his narration ascribes feelings to many of the people in his films. His extensive use of classical music and folk songs provides the films with an emotional register that is lacking from the relatively neutral image track. Although the poetics of the soundtrack make the diary Mekas's own, the central, unresolved contradiction of his films is that they are of other people. The people he films—the Lithuanian community in exile in New York, his friends in the world of avant-garde film, his family in Lithuania, and the many people he films on the streets of New York—become the bystanders of his life.

Mekas's diary films provide a heuristic model for all subsequent autobiographical filmmaking because they illustrate how the conceit of displacement masks a control over images. In the split between sound and image tracks, Mekas inscribes himself as a journey, as a survivor of his own past. Having spent time in a German labor camp, he has earned the right to such an identity, one that he then maps onto a specific set of social spheres and communities. *Reminiscences of a Journey to Lithuania,* made in 1972 from footage shot in 1971 and the 1950s, is the film in which Mekas confronts himself as ethnographer. It is a role that he refuses to assume, and he takes refuge in the avant-garde community where the weight of history and identity can be transcended through art.

Mekas's voice-over begins the American section of the film by designating a moment "when I forgot about my home." He is walking in autumn woods with friends but edits in some snow scenes as he says this, so that the "moment" cannot be pinned down. If his voice-over constitutes a form of secondary revision, it is consistently inadequate. The forgetting is as pervasive as the remembering, and the voice-over seems to follow its own trajectory through the film, registering a present tense that is inspired by the re-viewing of images of the past but is extremely distanced from it. From the 1950s in the United States, the film moves to "100 Glimpses of Lithuania" and a final section shot in Vienna, both sections filmed during a trip in 1971.

The Lithuanian footage in *Reminiscences* is far more brightly lit than any other imagery in the film, and it is virtually all shot outside, in fields, on roads, by rivers and forests, and in front of homes. Mekas takes full advantage of the Bolex camera's light weight and shutter control. The camera is in constant motion, cutting up and cutting into the field of vision. Faces last only marginally longer than other body parts, as Mekas breaks down everything he sees into partial views. Each of the

Still from *Reminiscences of a Journey to Lithuania,* by Jonas
Mekas (1972).

one hundred glimpses seems to be edited in-camera, including pixi-
lated sequences as well as some longer takes of landscape. Many of the
people are seen only in long shot, and it is not easy to identify the members of Mekas's large family, despite occasional intertitles introducing
them. Mekas himself appears fairly often in family groups, and he seems
to fit right in. In fact, many people besides Jonas wield cameras in this
film, as the whole family appears intent on the celebratory memorialization of Mekas's project. The fragmentary nature of these glimpses
seems destined to eradicate a present tense and to see everything as if it
were already memory.

Lithuania in 1971 may not be the Edenic return to childhood for
which he longs, but it is a preindustrial rural culture that his family
represents. In a catalog entry, Mekas describes the film: "You don't see
how Lithuania is today; you see it only through the memories of a
displaced person back home for the first time in twenty-five years."[20]
Maureen Turim has pointed out how Mekas's mother in the Lithuanian section of *Reminiscences* constitutes "the *fantasy* of a center"; the
memories, like the mother, cannot be possessed.[21] She also comments
on Mekas's failure to refer to contemporary Lithuanian politics, returning again and again to the history of his own anti-Nazi activities that
led to his exile.[22] Time appears to stand still in Lithuania, and Mekas

tries hard to make it represent his past: "Those were beautiful days." He wonders where all his childhood friends have gone to, listing the various horrors of wartime Europe: graveyards, torture rooms, prisons, and labor camps. "Your faces remain the same in my memory. They have not changed. It is me who is getting older." We see people entering a barn, doing farm chores, as he says this, standing in for those lost friends.

Mekas introduces his friends Peter Kubelka and Annette Michelson as "saints." He worships their ability to be "at home" in culture, and this is in fact the way that Mekas finds his "home" in the New York avant-garde. As Jeffrey Ruoff has described, Mekas's films constitute the "home movies" of the avant-garde, at once assuming and creating a network of familiarity with the various members of his community.[23] But Mekas's place in the art world he documents is still behind the camera, still split between the two selves filming and speaking, still displaced, at home only when he is not at home.

The longing for the past that Mekas expresses constructs memory as a means of splitting oneself across a number of different axes: child and adult, old world and new, pastoral and metropolitan, natural and cultural. Filmmaking is inscribed in a film such as *Reminiscences* as the means of transcending this splitting. Represented as a process and a practice, filmmaking is a craft that is not necessarily antithetical to the preindustrial ideal of Mekas's Lithuanian childhood. The idea of a film diary, according to Mekas, "is to react (with your camera) immediately, now, this instant." [24] Like the *vérité* filmmakers, Mekas's film practice was motivated by a notion of phenomenological and emotional truth. The authenticity of the footage is completely bound up in the honesty and humility of the filmmaker. And yet the diary film, as a product, overlays this raw experience with a complex textuality of sound and image.[25]

Unlike home movies, Mekas's films betray a deeply poetic sensibility that is alienated not only from the past but from the very immediacy of experience that informs the diary imagery. The ethnographic discourse of Mekas's films is at once a lost innocence and a pursuit of "freedom" modeled on his escape from European tyranny. Many scenes shot in Lithuania, and in Austria with Kubelka, feature people "playing" like children, running about, hands held high. In a sense, Mekas performs his childhood, constructing a complex world on a fantasy of loss. Childhood was a privileged theme in the avant-garde of the 1960s as the site of a spontaneity and uncorrupted vision that was sought as an ideal of visionary cinema.[26] For Mekas, the spontaneity of direct cinema, like childhood, is always located in an inaccessible past.

If autobiographical cinema constitutes a journey of the self, Jonas Mekas mapped that dislocation onto the historical and geographical dislocation with which so many contemporary filmmakers have become preoccupied. Mekas tells us that there is something inherent within cinematic representation that dislocates the self. The fantasy of identity is produced by the techniques of film practice, and if his diaries indulge this fantasy, they also reveal its limits as ethnography. Mekas's films are all ultimately about himself, and by subsuming history within his own memory, the Others become fictional products of his memory, their own histories evacuated by the melancholia of his loss. Superimposing himself, his desires, his memories, his ego, onto everyone and everything, Mekas's romanticism is a form of possession. For example, in *Reminiscences,* to some children playing, he says, "Run children, run. I hope you never have to run for your lives."

Mekas is perhaps the exemplary figure of modernist exile, adapting to film what Caren Kaplan has described as a literary genre that tends to generate "aesthetic categories and ahistorical values" by recoding issues of "political conflict, commerce, labor, nationalist realignments, imperialist expansion, structures of gender and sexuality." Mekas's nostalgia and melancholia are indicative of the way that displacement functions as a modernist value: "The formation of modernist exile seems to have best served those who would voluntarily experience estrangement and separation in order to produce the experimental cultures of modernism."[27] Mekas's alienation is ultimately registered as an unbridgeable gap between himself and others, those whose images he possesses as memories of moments that he imagines to be harmonious social encounters, forgetting that he was, even then, behind the camera.

Video Diaries

George Kuchar's video diaries are extensive, voluminous, sometimes tedious, always cynical, and often amusing. He creates the impression that he carries a camera with him everywhere, and that it mediates his relation with the world at large. His use of the video medium creates a sense of infinite "coverage," potentially breaking down the difference between experience and representation. Like Mekas, Kuchar documents a community of artists and filmmakers, with whom he is "at home." For

Kuchar, this world is centered at the San Francisco Art Institute, where he teaches filmmaking. In his diaries, he often includes glimpses of class projects which are always schlock horror films in the style of Kuchar's own films of the 1960s. Kuchar identifies himself sexually, rather than ethnically, but his sexuality is bound up with a host of insecurities that his video practice seems only to aggravate. More so than any other videomaker, Kuchar uses the camera as a tool of social interaction.[28]

From 1986 to 1990, Kuchar released forty-five tapes that fall into two main series: weather diaries and video diaries. The first document his annual trips to "Tornado Alley," in the central and southern United States, where he goes to view tornadoes. The second include trips to visit friends in different states as well as diaries made of his activities closer to home; these tapes feature his friends, colleagues, and students. A constant overlap between the diaries, and an internal referentiality, link them as an ongoing record of Kuchar's life. At the end of *Weather Diary 3,* for example, he says, "*Weather Diary 4* will take place in Milwaukee, so see you then," borrowing the conventions and ephemerality of a television series.

Where this diary project differs most profoundly from Mekas's is in Kuchar's use of video without a process of secondary revision. He always shoots with synchronized sound and offers an ongoing commentary on what he is seeing, often talking to people in front of the camera. Most of his music, including snippets of "movie music" indicating suspense, is recorded from live sources, and the soundtrack is full of ambient noise, including dogs and cats, traffic, weather, TV, and radio. He also claims that the tapes are entirely edited in-camera, including sequences that are taped over previous ones, enabling him to construct nonchronological editing patterns. The effect is one of randomness and improvisation, enhanced by his off-the-cuff synch-sound narration.[29] Whether this is true or not[30] is less important than the effect of immediacy it creates, the way in which experience is rendered textual, without historical depth or distance.

Kuchar often intercuts close-ups of himself, employing principles of continuity editing to inscribe his point of view into the tapes. This narrative technique endows the texts with a certain hermeticism, accentuating the sense of infinite coverage by creating a seamless diegesis despite the ad hoc, improvised style of narration and shooting. Kuchar invokes memory only through the proffering of still photos to the video gaze, and not as a structure of loss and salvage. Compared to Mekas's

George Kuchar in *Weather Diary 3* (1988).

Still from George Kuchar's *Weather Diary 3* (1988).
George spies on some boys through a crack in a fence.

tragic sadness, Kuchar's video and weather diaries are ironically cynical, and his self-analysis is often self-deprecating. Although Kuchar also "finds" himself through the practice of filming, his project is not a redemption.

Kuchar represents his life as a tedious banality emblematized in the annual tornado-viewing trip. The catastrophe of the storms themselves is dispersed into the monotony of waiting in motel rooms, where the tornadoes are finally viewed on television. In the weather diaries, he is most explicitly identified as a tourist, traveling to different parts of the country, staying in motels ostensibly to document weather phenomena, but inevitably finding people in the process. He never travels outside of the United States, and yet his mode of production has the effect of inscribing a threatening "otherness" in everything and everyone he shoots. A discourse of horror is extracted from the banality of rural America.

Weather Diary 1, Kuchar's pilgrimage to rural Oklahoma in the height of its tornado season, is most basically an extended analogy between severe storms and gastric distress. In *Weather Diary 3,* he returns to the Reno Motel, and this time he obsesses about his unfulfilled sex life. He tapes some boys at the motel pool through a crack in a fence and lustily boils hotdogs in his room. Kuchar's scatological humor is at times juvenile, but whereas many avant-garde filmmakers have masturbated for the camera, when George does it, he understands the pathetic irony of the act. He forces the viewer to watch him as we would a horror movie. In *Weather Diary 3,* Kuchar meets another storm chaser, who he takes out on dates to the local shopping mall. "Mike" goes along with the constant videotaping, performing "himself" with restrained good humor. The fact that he is probably straight and possibly oblivious to Kuchar's desire adds a dimension of sexual tension that the viewer shares with George at Mike's expense. After he leaves, Kuchar consoles himself with physique magazines, comparing his own shirtless pose to those of the models.

By privileging his own bodily processes, desires, and appearance, Kuchar crucially subverts the valorization of consciousness in avant-garde film. Compared to Mekas, Kuchar's suffering is biological, not existential. The camera is explicitly situated as an extension of his vision, but also of his body. In close-ups of food or of himself, the proximity of the profilmic to the lens is defined by the length of his reach. His practice of speaking while filming inscribes a highly personalized, and therefore possessive, voice-over commentary onto the imagery. As in all of Kuchar's videos, a profound sense of solitude is established, not only through his self-deprecating humor, but through the restricted field of vision and the mediated relation to the world. One effect of his physical identification with the camera is that every shot of another person becomes an encounter.

In almost all of his video diaries, Kuchar spies on people, whispering to the spectator as he points his camera at strangers outside his window. Within the tape's larger structure of comparative internal and external natural phenomena, the people in Oklahoma are aligned with the weather as "outside." In representing himself as a body rather than a subject, Kuchar's encounters with others, and with the larger cultural and physical environment, are consistently physical. His fellow Americans all become different than himself, but it is above all a difference of space and distance, relationships defined by motel architecture. Sometimes those differences are perceived as ideological, and when he decides his neighbors are Christians or hippies, Kuchar retreats further into the privatized space of the motel room.

Kuchar's journeys to rural American towns are modeled on ethnographic fieldwork, but he casually violates all the conventions of humanist anthropology. The Other becomes exotic and often threatening, but Kuchar himself becomes equally strange in the eyes of the Other. Kuchar's documentary subjects are his own first audience, as he makes himself, both on- and off-frame, a spectacle of equal magnitude. A circuit of looks, in which the viewer takes on the role of voyeur, is thereby completed. Like the hyperreality of the televised tornado, Kuchar's encounters with others are always exaggerated. His friendships are also presentations of those people to future audiences. It is by way of his own body and subjectivity that Kuchar presents one culture (rural Oklahoman) to another (urban artists and intellectuals). A couple of mainstream documentaries, *Sherman's March* (McElwee, 1987) and *Roger and Me* (Michael Moore, 1989), involve similar conceits of self-representation, but Kuchar's tapes differ in their spontaneity and banality. The extremely low production values of these diaries exaggerate their experiential quality while thoroughly mediating it.

Comparing Kuchar's aesthetics to Mekas's, the video is ugly, with garish colors that emphasize the tackiness of everyday America. Kuchar's use of video does not aestheticize, which enables us to compare Mekas's project as a process of redemption. Mekas transcends the alienating loss of experience by transforming the experienced world into images; Kuchar inhabits a world of images, with no indication of a referential reality outside that sphere. He represents himself as an alien in his own country, someone who is always alone in a crowd. However, this alienation is inseparable from the fact that he always has a camera between himself and others. There is nothing "prior" to the making of the tape. As a postmodern form of autoethnography, it renders society as an image, or a televisual discourse, and poses the problem of identity through a location of "self" within image culture.

Another filmmaker who has used video to inscribe herself within a world of images is Sadie Benning. In the late 1980s, Fisher Price put a children's video camera on the market that produced such a low-definition image that it came to be known as pixelvision. Except for extreme close-ups, the pixels of the digital image are readily visible, providing a highly mediated form of representation. The black-and-white image is framed by a thick black border when it is transferred onto half-inch videotape. Because pixelvision is restricted to a level of close-up detail, it is an inherently reflexive medium and is especially appropriate to experimental ethnography. The "big picture" is always out of reach, as the filmmaker is necessarily drawn to the specificity of everyday life. (A number of film- and videomakers have used pixelvision, most notably Peggy Ahwesh and Margie Strosser in their 1993 tape *Strange Weather,* a "documentary" about crack-addicted teenagers in Florida.)[31]

Benning's tapes suggest once again that identity is inscribed not only in history but in technologies of representation. Benning shoots most of her tapes in her bedroom, incorporating found footage, newspaper and magazine fragments, and written notes that pass in front of the camera like secret messages to the viewer. Each tape is scored by a selection of pop music, contextualizing the very personal stories within a cultural sphere. As a young lesbian, Benning's persona is constructed against the trappings of youth culture, media culture, and feminism. She performs herself by dressing up, wearing different wigs and makeup, and offering lingering close-ups of different parts of her face and body. Her first-person voice-over narration is confessional and poetic, rhetorical and playful, occasionally synchronized with her moving lips.

Benning uses pixelvision as the language of youth, of a small voice. *A Place Called Lovely* (1991), the tape that is most explicitly about childhood, opens with some children's drawings, suggesting that pixelvision is the technological equivalent of a primitivist style of representation. The tape was made when she was eighteen, and Benning assumes the voice of childhood, identifying with American children in general. She tells us about a seven-year-old classmate who grabbed her hair and chased her into an alley. She fights back at him, taking shots at the camera, but a scrawled note says she was still scared, and she cuts to a clip from *Psycho*. This memory is brought into close proximity with the present, collapsing the distance of the past. She tells a story about a man who tried to abduct her, and she offers photos of schoolchildren over the sound of a music box. Then she talks about twenty-seven children who were found murdered in southwest Atlanta in 1979, showing pictures of black children, and concluding that "when these children died, every child died a little." While we should be somewhat skeptical of a white girl playing with a children's video camera in her bedroom "identifying" with these victims, Benning's perspective is a hybrid construction of innocence and cultural critique.

Benning's own image is in constant flux, appearing at times with her hair long and at others with it short and cropped. In the tape's longest sequence, she stands in front of an American flag while "America" plays, and she mimics the emotional trajectory of the music with her face and hands, forcing a smile throughout the song. She follows this performance with a message saying, "that scared me too." If in other tapes she works with the contradictions of growing up gay, in this one she confronts the contradictions of being an American child. Benning is too media savvy, and her imagery is too highly developed aesthetically,[32] for her naïveté to be believable, and so she creates a kind of constructed primitivism. Her confessional first-person narration may or may not refer to "the truth," but she nevertheless uses autobiography as a domain of referentiality that works with and against the signs of American culture.

Benning's construction of her lesbian identity intersects with her youthfulness in an ongoing "coming out" diary that links the various videotapes.[33] *It Wasn't Love* is a tape dedicated to "bad girls everywhere." She poses with a girlfriend for the camera, dresses up like a boy, and tells a story about meeting a woman in Beverly Hills. Benning says, "We didn't need Hollywood. We were Hollywood," and indeed the tape is very much about playing adult games, "putting on" a sexuality that is insinuated in pop music and blues songs. As autoethnography, Benning's tapes produce a subjectivity that evades authenticity. In this

Sadie Benning and a friend in her pixel-vision tape *It Wasn't Love* (1991).

she shares something with a videomaker such as Richard Fung, about whom José Muñoz writes: "To perform queerness is to constantly dis-identify; to constantly find oneself thriving on sites where meaning does not properly 'line up.' This is equally true of hybridity, another modality where meaning or identifications do not properly line up. The postcolonial hybrid is a subject who occupies a space between the West and the rest."[34] Benning's position between childhood and adulthood shifts easily into a queer discourse that Laura Kipnis has described as a "license." "It's a tape that refuses victimhood, sees desire as having its own integrity, and uses sex to carve out a sphere of freedom."[35] Benning's "party on the margins" uses collage in conjunction with the diary format to construct a hybrid identity that refuses to be pinned down. It is, moreover, flaunted as something she dreams up in her bedroom, drawn from the minimal resources of her body, her camera, and her collection of props, images, and music.

The notion of hybridity is key to the diary film and video because it suggests how the multiple subject effects of voice, vision, and body can produce new forms of subjectivity. Through hybridity, postcolonial subjects as well as other identities can potentially escape the limits of nation and gender. This implies a very different notion of "freedom" than the aesthetic of spontaneity advocated by Jonas Mekas and the *vérité* diarists. In 1968 Jim McBride made a *vérité* diary film that was also mainly shot in a bedroom, but *David Holzman's Diary* was a fake documentary, satirizing many of the tropes of *cinéma vérité*'s discourses of honesty, confession, and truth. The film circulated around a character/filmmaker named David Holzman, whose self-indulgence was in fact a nonidentity. His voyeurism masked a void of referentiality and a receding discourse of desires to know, possess, and see — the underlying aesthetic of the *vérité* project that refers back to a seeing subject.

If diary filmmaking can no longer take the identity of the filmmaker for granted, identity becomes a site of contestation and negotiation. For a videomaker such as Sadie Benning, the diary mode becomes a space of cultural transgression and critique, a site where she can become anyone she wants and is thus able to transcend any assigned roles of gender or age. Both Benning and Kuchar embrace video as a medium of consumer culture, working within the codes of home video as well as those of the avant-garde. Through an appropriation of television as a discourse of the quotidian, their diaries are means of constructing identities from the techniques of image culture.[36]

The journeys undertaken by Sadie Benning in her bedroom-studio-laboratory are through the fragmentary discourses of popular culture. Her use of found footage refers back only to herself as an ethnographic referent, a body whose sexuality, youth, and appearance are not fixed, but in transit among a plethora of intertexts. By fragmenting her body into the image sphere of pixelvision, she becomes completely textual, a constellation of effects that are quite removed from the verbally narrated "I," and from the name of the videomaker. In this way, she cannot be figured, herself, as a representative lesbian or a representative child. Although few other people appear in Benning's tapes, images of people — in magazines, in her stories, in her dressing up, and in photographs — abound. As in Kuchar's tapes, people are perceived only through the mediating effects of the medium. For neither Kuchar nor Benning is the video camera an instrument or metaphor for consciousness; it denotes a public sphere in which they represent themselves as effects of discourse.

Homi Bhabha has theorized postcolonial identity as a process of doubling, a "spatialization of the subject" in place of "the symbolic consciousness" of Barthes, and, I would add, "Visionary Cinema."[37] In their video diaries, Kuchar and Benning represent themselves as bodies in space. The camera as an instrument of vision serves as a means of making them visible, a vehicle for the performance of their identities. Bhabha argues that it is through this splitting of the self that the Other is understood as a part of oneself: "That disturbance of your voyeuristic look enacts the complexity and contradictions of your desire to see, to fix cultural difference in a containable, *visible* object. The desire for the Other is doubled by the desire in language, which *splits the difference* between Self and Other so that both positions are partial; neither is sufficient unto itself." [38] He goes on to suggest that "by understanding the ambivalence and the antagonism of the other," by deconstructing the homogenization of the Other, "a celebratory, oppositional politics of the margins" will be possible.[39] I would argue that this is true not only of postcolonial identities but also of queer and hybrid subjectivities that seek to represent themselves through an articulation of the gaze. Video provides a degree of proximity and intimacy that enables this spatialization of the body. Instead of a transcendental subject of vision, these videos enact the details of a particularized, partialized subjectivity.

Kidlat Tahimik: Diary of a Third World Filmmaker

Kidlat Tahimik is the filmmaker who has developed the diary film most extensively within a discourse of postcolonial cultural critique. His distinctive filmmaking technique pries apart the various levels of self-representation so that the primitive, the native, and the premodern are ironically constructed within a discursive bricolage centered around his own subjectivity. Although all his filmmaking, including his best-known film *Perfumed Nightmare* (1977), is autobiographical, the three-hour diary project *Why Is Yellow the Middle of the Rainbow?* (1981–1993) is most explicitly so. The history in which the diary evolves is at once that of the Philippines, Tahimik's own family, and global processes of colonialism and neocolonialism. Incorporating found footage, newspaper headlines and TV broadcasts, home movies, travel footage, and documentation of public events and political demonstrations, the film is extraordinarily far-flung—to Germany and Monument Valley, to Magellan and Ferdinand Marcos—while consistently localized in Baguio, Tahimik's hometown in the Philippines.

The episodic structure of *Why Is Yellow* is much like that of *Perfumed Nightmare*, which Fredric Jameson has described as a co-optation of "travelogue language." Tahimik's films are made for the Western film festival market, but he is very conscious of his role as native informant, playing with it so as to foreground "the inauthenticity of the Western spectator." [40] Documentary footage is mixed with scripted performances, and he continually reverses expectations of First and Third

Production still of Kidlat
Tahimik in *Why Is Yellow the
Middle of the Rainbow?* (1993).
*Courtesy of the Yamagata
International Film Festival.*

World cultural scenes. His movement between cultures casts him as an
exemplary Inappropriate Other.

As we have seen in the previous instances of diary filmmaking, the
format tends to have three levels of self-representation, and Tahimik exploits each somewhat differently. His voice-over is written as a dialogue
with his son Kidlat, who actually opens the work with a first-person account of accompanying his father to Germany and America at the age
of about eight. Although Tahimik himself takes over most of the narration, this conceit allows Tahimik to frame his voice-over as words of
wisdom to the next generation. The text delivers an unambiguous message about the spiritual superiority of native peoples, the dangers of
industrialized modernity, and the economics of cultural imperialism.[41]
Tahimik's verbal message is, however, qualified by his vocation as an
independent filmmaker and intellectual, married to a German woman
and father of three children, two of whom are blond. His speech, in
other words, originates in a body that is fully part of industrialized
modernity. His politicization of everyday life in what he refers to as the
Third World is anything but a primitivist fantasy of identity, even while
he champions the cause of native peoples.

Tahimik also inscribes himself on a second level, at the source of
the documentary gaze, although his is always a fleeting look. He rarely

looks very long at anyone, except his own children, at which point he assumes the role of the father in a domesticated mode of film production. The kaleidoscope of imagery also includes the work of other Filipino artists, his own installation works, performance pieces, and indigenous music. Because he cuts back and forth in time, incorporating so many fragments, and because he never shoots in sync, the film, like so many diary projects, is made in the editing room. Shots of him at the steenbeck are often used to link sections of the film so that the phenomenology of seeing is sublimated in an aesthetic of collecting.

Filmmaking, for Tahimik, is above all a craft, through which he can be aligned with preindustrial modes of production. In his video *Takadera mon amour* (1989), he constructs a bamboo camera, and in *Why Is Yellow* he and his son build a "Third World projector" out of rusted junk scavenged in Monument Valley. Its blurry, unstable image introduced at the opening of the diary film is the one that Tahimik embraces as his own vision, significantly aligned not with the subjective eye of the camera but with the public one of the projector.

Artistic process is represented very explicitly in *Why Is Yellow* as a Third World model of recycling, low-tech bricolage. Tahimik carries out, perhaps more than any other filmmaker, Benjamin's theorization of the artist as producer, adopting the very techniques of the medium to a politicized content.[42] This extends even to his role as a performer, the third level of self-inscription: "The only way I can explain things is through my personal experiences, I'm confessing my own contradictions, so I have to throw myself in. It's also because I'm the only person available and willing to be filmed this way! The actor who is always on call! And cheap too!"[43] *Why Is Yellow* includes a clip of Tahimik's first film experience, playing the "last savage Indian specimen" in Werner Herzog's *Kaspar Hauser,* as well as clips from Tahimik's ongoing work-in-progress, about Magellan's slave. By playing the role of the slave, Tahimik is able to offset his own postmodern mobility with a discourse of forcible travel and historical displacement, even if it is one that he manages to romanticize as a fiction of revenge and return.[44]

Tahimik's performances throughout the diary place the authenticity of his experience in question, although his body remains a site of historical indexicality. Over the thirteen years that the diary covers, Tahimik's physical appearance gradually changes from the pixieish naïf of *Perfumed Nightmare* to a longhaired bohemian. As his image becomes doubled as both father and slave, its aging is intimately bound to the deepening understanding of this doubleness and its epistemological possibilities.

In Jameson's analysis, Tahimik's critique of Western progress produces "something like cultural nationalism,"[45] and yet Tahimik's "Third World energy" is not limited to the Philippines. Moreover, the story of Philippine political history that is told over the course of the film is not a solution to the problem of cultural imperialism. The euphoria of Cory Aquino's victory in 1986 gives way to the subsequent struggle for democracy in the post-Marcos years and the ongoing role of American mass culture in Tahimik's children's lives. Far from a "nationalism," though, he situates himself within the circuits of global capitalism through which First and Third Worlds are inextricably linked.[46]

John Ford's Point in Monument Valley is a site to which Tahimik frequently returns in Why Is Yellow. The footage he shot on his first trip in 1983 with his son becomes a memory, over which his return trips constitute layers of gradual degradation. In 1988 he finds his Navajo friends posing for tourists and keeping a generator in their hogan to watch Westerns on TV. The desert is littered with junk, which Tahimik recycles as props. "John Ford's point," says Tahimik over a hollow TV set in the desert, "is that the only good Indian is a dead Indian." His role as the redeemer of native peoples is overtly romantic, and yet it is assumed as a search for something within postmodernity, not as a practice of salvage. Linking the Igorots in the Philippines with the Navajo is perhaps an essentialist ploy, and yet it is also a function of his assumed identity as Magellan's slave. His own name, Kidlat Tahimik, is an Igorot name that he originally gave to his character in Perfumed Nightmare but later assumed for himself instead of his given Spanish name.[47]

At one point in Why Is Yellow, Tahimik visits a native community in the interior of the Philippine Cordillera, providing the film's most "ethnographic" footage of men building a dam by hand. His segue into this scene from political demonstrations in Manila is an explanation to young Kidlat: "Native peoples join us in our call for justice for Ninoy [Aquino] but they are more concerned with the loss of their ancestral lands, just like the Native Americans. Kidlat, we have a lot to learn from our Igorot brothers." In the film's only talking-head interview, Lopes Na-uyac explains that because the government in Manila treats them only as tourist attractions, the Igorot have to build bridges without government engineering. Bridges made out of vines and scrap metal

Coke signs are supplemented by dams to provide water deep enough for saving lives. This passage is indicative of Tahimik's admiration for native ingenuity and efficient management of resources. In his transformation of the salvage paradigm, ethnography remains linked to memory, but not to vanishing cultures. It is his own memory that structures his ethnography as his family grows up and he can edit his own experiences in the form of flashbacks. Memory in this diary is not a discourse of loss but of a layering of cultural forms.

The colonization of the Philippines, first by the Spanish, and then by the Americans, situates Igorot culture as a repressed identity that Tahimik attempts to recover, not as an authentic indigenous culture, but as a constituency in postmodernism. The eruption of Mt. Pinatubo becomes a metaphor for the cultural layering and smothering that the film documents, and an earthquake in Baguio finally isolates the filmmaker from his son, who is now away in university. Toward the end of the diary, young Kidlat is behind the video camera, so if the film spends an inordinate amount of time with Tahimik's children, it also finally allows the son to make the transition from ethnographic subject to ethnographer. The primitivism of children is thus a temporary condition, subject, like native peoples, to the transience of history.

Tahimik's collage is above all an aesthetics of ruins, recycling the surplus waste of commodity culture. The discourse of ethnography in his filmmaking is a form of memory that encompasses the "radical forgetting" of found footage but also embodies it as a form of experience. The autoethnographic self is a performance of the primitive, through which Tahimik mobilizes the avant-garde as a mode of allegorical ethnography. One technique that Tahimik shares with Sadie Benning and several other American avant-garde filmmakers such as Su Friedrich and Peggy Ahwesh is the use of toys and models. The little cars and trucks that Tahimik borrows from his kids serve as another form of "acting out" and "playing primitive."

Children's toys are in some respects the emblematic waste of consumer culture, made of nonbiodegradable materials for temporary use. Recycling toys as props in films is a means of recalling childhood in a strictly allegorical form, a form in which the signifier itself has a material history. Tahimik's use of toys is like his use of found images and headlines. They are allegorical in their doubleness, to which he gives an economic rationale: don't let anything go to waste. The excess of the First World is the condition of life in the Third, and he aims for a Third

World aesthetic that would recast the ethnographic as an allegory of the subject. He produces a subjectivity that is consistently double, inappropriate, and hybrid, signified by the body of the Other, a body that is inauthentic, textual, ironic, transnational. Appropriation is an economics, an aesthetic, and an identity.

Echoing Mekas's role in New York, Tahimik is very active in the art world of the Philippines, having established a film collective in Baguio, and his identity as a filmmaker is as important as his ethnicity. If this is a subtext of the diary film in general, Tahimik transforms it into a global, intercultural identity. On the way to Monument Valley in 1983, he meets Dennis Hopper and goes to a film conference run by Francis Ford Coppola where *Perfumed Nightmare* is playing. Cinema, for Tahimik, is not a means of freedom from cultural imperialism but provides a language in which he can inscribe himself as a dispersed and multiple subject. Instead of Mekas's nostalgia, Tahimik's cinema represents history as a text in which his own experience is one discourse among many. Neither history nor identity is a fixed entity; they are under continual revision. About his Magellan project, unfinished for lack of a galleon in which to shoot it, he says, "History is not the monopoly of cultures who have books and computers, who can store it in their archives. So I imagine a lot of the material from the slave's point of view."[48] Like Magellan's Igorot slave, the "first man to circumnavigate the globe," Tahimik is himself a construct of multiple languages, cultures, memories, and desires made possible by the techniques of cinematic bricolage.

In the 1993 Yamagita Film Festival catalog, Tahimik lists subsequent installments of the diary up to the year 2001. However, in 1994, he said the film would stop at the earthquake because "I got insecure about my wife's criticism of the film as my ego-trip,"[49] a statement that says much about the family dynamics behind Tahimik's home-movie practice. The contradictions of a globe-trotting father are implicit in Katrin de Guia's relative absence from the film. Her performance at the end of *Perfumed Nightmare* of giving birth in the back of a jeepney (a Philippine taxi made out of recycled U.S. army vehicles) to the "first Kidlat born on the other side of the planet" (Germany) suggests the limits of Tahimik's global perspective. His historical passages from slave to master and from father to son remain inscribed within a gendered discourse that writes women out of the picture. Within Tahimik's postmodern, postcolonial voyage lurk many remnants of a modernist exilic discourse, and yet he does not yearn for a lost authenticity, or a vanishing reality. He constructs a subjectivity within a material history of colonial history. As a collage of identities "embodied" in the Filipino filmmaker, ethnicity is thoroughly deconstructed into a plethora of fantasies, memories, and histories.

Sans Soleil: The Infirmities of Time

I've chosen to end this book with Chris Marker's monumental film *Sans Soleil* (1982) because it is a film that recapitulates so many of the themes of experimental ethnography. As an autoethnographic text, it is distinctly silent about the identity of its maker, who hides himself within an intricate pattern of first-person pronouns. The voice-over narration, read by a woman, is written in the form of her retelling the contents of letters she has received from a man who travels around the world filming people, places, and animals, a man who is named in the end credits as Sandor Krasna. Footage shot in Japan, Guinea-Bissau, Iceland, the Cape Verde Islands, Hong Kong, San Francisco, Isle de France, and Okinawa is edited together as a global travelogue, linked only by the eye of a fictional filmmaker.

Despite his heroic effort of decentering himself, Marker's invisibility, omniscience, ubiquity, and mobility situate him as yet another belated traveler. His preoccupation with gender and the Other is not masked but foregrounded as a fascination with images. While the literary text of the narration mediates on the nature of images as memories, as traces of history, the image track constitutes a new form of voyeurism, one in which the naked stare is reframed as a desperate effort to find something to hold onto in a world where one no longer possesses images. The identity of the filmmaker is unambiguously a Western male (what else do Krasna and Marker share?), but in the attempt to disavow his own gaze, Marker finds himself cut off from history.

Most critics of *Sans Soleil* have praised its textuality, its rare use of *écriture* in an ethnographic context, and its decentered transience that seems to move fluidly between disparate times and places.[50] It is indeed a masterpiece of editing, of literature, and of *cinéma vérité* shooting, an exemplary instance of the meeting of the avant-garde with anthropology. It remains in many ways a modernist text, anchored in a melancholia of loss, and this loss is understood as a production of cinematic representation itself. Cultural otherness — "Africa" and "Japan" — come to represent a premodernity subsisting within postmodern technolo-

Still from Chris Marker's *Sans Soleil* (1982). This image is one of the computer-manipulated images produced by Hayao Yamaneko in the film. *Courtesy of the Museum of Modern Art.*

gies and politics. While Marker can be accused of essentializing these cultures, which become meaningful only in relation to the absent presence of Euro-American modernity, he also maps out the scale of the task of inverting the salvage paradigm and representing the coevalness of disparate cultures in the cinema. He addresses the impossibility of his own perspective.

Sans Soleil is a film that washes over the viewer, mesmerizing with its complex mode of address as he, the filmmaker, offers images to be seen while she, the receiver of letters, reads a text that is infinitely removed from the places and people filmed. The correspondences between voice and image appear casual, magical, and unmotivated. The rhetorical strategies of the narration place the images at a distance that takes on the aspect of memory: words and image often do coincide, but the description of the depicted scene is doubly or triply mediated. Sandor Krasna's letters are written in the form of memories, dispatched "from another world, a world of appearances." One of the effects of this strategy is that Marker can describe a method of filmmaking that the viewer might accept as the method of the film. In fact, the film has a very different method that remains unaddressed in the narration.

To undo some of the contradictions of *Sans Soleil* is to return to the critical potential of experimental ethnography, the imbrication of cultural critique with aesthetic formalism. Marker's melancholia is in many ways directed at the loss of a militant avant-garde, the disintegration of a guerrilla cinema of the 1960s when the camera could be considered a weapon in revolutionary independence movements.[51] The discursive structures of experimental ethnography, so evidently displayed in *Sans Soleil,* lend themselves to a different interventionist role that operates on the level of a politics of representation. In many ways, this film wears its "incorrectness" on its sleeve, referring to the Japanese at one point as "these yellow men" and to the Cape Verde Islanders as a "people of nothing," words that point back to a subject of enunciation that cannot be trusted. The duplicity and rhetorical strategies of *Sans Soleil* are ultimately means of questioning the "origins" of ethnographic images, in the field of the Other and at the source of the gaze.

Most of Marker's description of method comes in the first ten minutes of the film. Over images of people on a pier in Cape Verde, the narrator says, "Frankly, have you ever heard of anything stupider than to say to people, as they do in film schools, not to look at the camera?" Although the people in this particular sequence do return the gaze, few other people in the film look back. Actually, Marker's footage is for the most part extremely oblique, catching people sleeping, praying, reading, playing video games, and performing rituals. A more accurate version of the film's method is suggested by way of images of Takanoko dancers in a Tokyo park, whom the narrator describes as "baby martians" and goes on to say, "They want people to look at them, but they don't seem to notice when people do. They live in a parallel time sphere; a kind of invisible aquarium wall separates them from the crowd they attract." This description of filming trance designates the opposite pole from the returned gaze, and it comes much closer to describing the technique of *Sans Soleil.* For the spectator of this film, and most ethnography, the spectacle of the Other is safely contained within a "fishbowl realism," behind an invisible wall.[52]

Marker's key ethnographic model is said by the narrator to be Sei Shonagon's *Pillow Book.* This diary of a lady-in-waiting in the emperor's court in tenth-century Kyoto is composed of incidents of daily life, and lists of "things," such as "Presumptuous Things," "Squalid Things" (this category includes "a rather unattractive woman who looks after a large brood of children"), and the list that Marker likes best: "Things That Quicken the Heart."[53] Marker sets aside Shonagon's aristocratic notes on proper behavior and adopts her poetic sensibility as a model of random notation. He forgets, perhaps, that Shonagon's world was a static one, in which her movements were extremely restricted by social protocol, and historical time was circumscribed by the genealogy of the imperial family.[54]

The arbitrariness of Shonagon's diary form suggests a model of image collecting that Marker further links to the lack of modifiers in Japanese poetry. Just to name things, to list them, is sufficient. But the disparate images that he has collected and edited together in *Sans Soleil* do not work quite that way. His montage is quick, with dynamic juxtapositions, interruptions, and repetitions. The voice-over may be detached, but it is nevertheless richly descriptive. Few of the images are formalized, aestheticized, or contemplative; all are in transit, with movement or action, or they bear signs of temporal processes such as decay or sunsets. The extremely subjective narration, as the meandering thoughts of a fictional character, prevents the images from becoming, simply, a list of "things."

Marker cannot just let things be, allowing their meanings to appear self-evident, and the ongoing commentary has the further effect of silencing the image track. For all its reflexivity, *Sans Soleil* fails to understand its own practice of enhancing ethnographic imagery with a soundtrack of electronic music. Ambient sound is heard only occasionally for rituals and ceremonies; other voices are heard only in the form of advertising and public speeches. The long lenses that Marker no doubt used to capture some of the more intimate scenes preclude the use of microphones. In the fragmentation of the gaze, the Other is distanced within a voyeuristic vertigo, silently reduced to images only one step removed from those Marker finds on Japanese TV.

One more description of method that is given early in the film, prefaced by the usual "He used to write to me," is the claim that "my constant comings and goings are not a search for contrasts. They are a journey to the two extreme poles of survival." But what is *Sans Soleil* if not a comparative ethnography? How can Marker compare African time, Asian time, and European time, if not to compare cultures? "Africa" in this film is depicted solely through images of a rural culture, struggling for independence, fighting starvation, fighting itself. "Japan" is depicted solely through images of Tokyo crowds, surviving high technology through the maintenance and adaptation of ritual practices. The third point in the film's cultural triangle is Iceland. A single sequence of three blond children on a road is "grafted" onto the film to signify the other Other of European ethnicity, and it is this image that comes to bear the weight of memory as the scene is subsequently lost to the eruption of a volcano.

The Icelandic scene may be a scene from childhood, but it is not the filmmaker's childhood. Memory, in *Sans Soleil*, is unstable, unreliable, and impersonal. It is described elliptically as "the lining of forgetting"; it is to the world of appearances what history is to reality. "Reality" may not be a term in the film's vocabulary, but it subsists in the images as their "pre-text," a profilmic space that existed prior to the shot, and to the film. After the volcanic eruption, the pre-textual space of the children in Iceland is destroyed, and the image becomes an emblematic memory. Described as an "image of happiness," the pastoral scene is underlit, as if it were twilight or the onset of a storm, and the children are wary of the camera; the footage is treasured for its sense of transience, the moment caught, stolen, and collected. Is it thus insignificant that the children are white and that the landscape setting is stripped of cultural references? Is memory for Marker a formal category that reestablishes Euro-American identity as a nonrace, a nonidentity at the mythical origins of representation? Is the elimination of history a loss of "his" history, his visual authority, the death of the (great white) author?

Sans Soleil demonstrates the impossibility of an absolutely postmodern, decentered ethnographic film. In the labyrinth of reflecting mirrors, the dislocated global perspective ultimately points back to the subject position of the Western avant-garde filmmaker and his complicit audience. (The narrator says that Japanese TV is watching "you," but who is it watching except the Western spectator, the viewer of the film?) Marker does inscribe himself in the film, via a detour through the growth lines of a sequoia tree in *Vertigo*, as the maker of *La Jetée*, another film with such a tree in it. The dialectic of the frozen moment and the irrevocable time of history is focused in *La Jetée* on the identity of a man who remembers his own death. In *Sans Soleil* the dialectic is projected onto the identity of the Other who, caught in the gaze, moves between history and memory, experience and image.

The images are collected and edited together as if they had been "found," but although a few sequences were filmed by other people (credited at the end of the film), most shots originate in the gaze of the absent filmmaker. *Sans Soleil* is a film that constantly turns back on itself, systematically detaching images from their "origins" while lamenting the loss inscribed in this process. One of the most explicit instances of this production of aporias is also, ironically, the one in which Marker announces the gender of his gaze.

After a sequence about the struggle for independence in Bissau and the continued difficulties of a postcolonial economy, the narrator says, "My personal problem is more specific: how to film the ladies of Bissau." Over a close-up of an African woman, the narrator continues, "I see her, she sees me. She knows that I see her. She drops me her glance, but just at an angle where it is still possible to act as though it were not addressed to me. At the end the real glance, straightforward, that lasted a twenty-fourth of a second, the length of a film frame." With the words "the real glance," Marker cuts away to other close-ups of women in the marketplace. This flirtatious dramatization of the returned gaze embraces the failure of film to actually represent the gaze. Who sees whom in this exchange? The filmmaker and the woman are lost in a web of looks that includes the viewer and the female narrator. Moreover, the sequence implies that the "real glance" is so quick that it cannot be captured on film.[55]

My point in stressing the gendered gaze of Sans Soleil is not to psychoanalyse Chris Marker but to suggest how "identity" in this film is coded as the gaze of modern(ist) man. When the narrator says that in Tokyo in January "all you see are the girls," girls are, in fact, all we can see. They are wearing kimono, so they are Other girls, and in superimposing a scopophilic frame onto the ethnographic gaze, Marker stresses the role of desire in the collecting of images. The African woman's look is threatening because it addresses someone behind the camera, but when the still image, the one twenty-fourth of a second, returns later in the film, it is distanced from that origin, cut off from the experience of being filmed. Only then can it be summoned up from memory, as a fetish.

After the fleeting shot of the African woman's returned look, the narrator says, "Women have a grain of indestructibility. It's men's task to make them realize it as late as possible. After a close look at African women, I wouldn't necessarily bet on the men." Women, for Krasna, are clearly objects of the gaze, who can nevertheless resist a penetrating stare and thereby become symbolic of ethnographic otherness, their bodies the terrain on which the battle for equality is fought. They are experience, history, materiality, voice; consciousness and vision belong to men. Although Krasna may not speak for Marker, the discourse on sexual difference is so pervasive in the film, it is clear that the anxiety

Still from Chris Marker's *Sans Soleil* (1982). *Courtesy of the Museum of Modern Art.*

over the gaze that is played out in *Sans Soleil* is produced within the terms of Western patriarchy. The ethnographic principle of visible evidence is here made synonymous with a desire to possess. Despite his recessive articulation of identity, Marker does not relinquish his stakes in possessive vision but hides himself within a voyeuristic vertigo.

When the African woman returns, she is "in the Zone." Along with a series of other images from the film, she reappears in the form of a synthesized video image produced by Hayao Yamaneko, Sandor Krasna's Japanese friend. Marker's images thus become "found" images that not only are appropriated, reassembled, and decontextualized but become digitalized, abstracted, and ghostly in their video form. The futuristic medium of video, which promises total instant recall of all history, has an apocalyptic edge to it in *Sans Soleil,* as if the special properties of film to dialectically produce irrevocable loss and an eternal present tense are in jeopardy. The image summoned back in this form is not the same; it enacts a cut in time, a different, nonlinear memory, which is not "his" but Hayao Yamaneko's.

At one point, Marker takes us to a display of stuffed animals copulating in a Japanese museum-chapel–sex shop complex. The dioramas are lit with a flashlight while the narrator wonders if these scenes represent "a cosmic innocence," an "earthly paradise" before the Fall — before the U.S. occupation—or if they signify the great rift of Japanese society, between men and women, which is to say, between "violent slaughter" and a "discrete melancholy." In this inscription of the gaze, zoology and pornography are brought together to substitute for that which ethnographic representation cannot show: culturally specific desires and sexualities. Japanese sexual practices are here alluded to within a temporal framework in which desire is always a desire for the past. If taxidermy freezes a moment in time, violently interrupting the continuum of history (and the life of an animal), a feminine principle of melancholy activates the gaze as a form of memory.

The project of *Sans Soleil* might be described as an attempt to recognize the autonomy of images separated, finally, from their origins in history. If all images are memories, cut off from experience, and if all memory is photographic, that which is not filmed is lost. Japan is the future in this film, a world of appearances, digital images disconnected from photographic pre-texts, cut off from history. Marker's melancholia is more complex than the "imperialist nostalgia" that Caren Kaplan describes as the lament of the modernist exile. He does not mourn for vanishing cultures. His loss is far more metaphysical and is compounded by his chosen medium of representation, the cinema. In Japan, Marker finds a culture in which an ancient aesthetic of transience, of "the impermanence of things," is fused with rapid modernization. Japan becomes an intermediary zone between First and Third Worlds, retaining the traces of traditional culture within a high-tech environment, and producing something like postmodernism in the process. Marker is by no means alone in this Western view of Japan as being somehow endemically postmodern,[56] although he is also concerned with documenting the traces of religious practices, animism, and rituals that are still pervasive in Japanese daily life.

Japan in *Sans Soleil* designates the uneven development of modernity. The implied comparison with "Africa" is between hyperdevelopment and underdevelopment, both of which refer back to a notion of the "regular development" of the First (Euro-American) World. Michael Walsh has suggested that *Sans Soleil* demonstrates how global capital has created spheres of relative development with their attendant connotations of "progress" and "backwardness."[57] Certainly the film demonstrates the "difficulty of thinking in images of relationships between the world's most developed and destitute regions," but the ensuing vertigo is read back onto aesthetic and ethnographic relationships, not onto economic ones.

If in *Vertigo* Jimmy Stewart/Scottie is finally cured of a fear of heights, the problem in *Sans Soleil* (which is not "cured" but is certainly subject to analysis) is a fear of the Other, or to put it less dramatically, a problem of looking at others: how to travel, to collect the images that might document one's experience of cultural diversity, without commodifying or objectifying, without assigning the Other a place that exists only in memory, without "othering." Geographical distance will always become temporal distance in the travelogue form that privileges the filmmaker's experience and renders the images as memories of the trip. The problem becomes one for the spectator, who has no point of origin with which to identify. The woman reading the letters has not necessarily seen the images that are described in her narration.

In problematizing the point of origin of his images, Marker attempts to establish an aesthetic distance that might restore a coevalness — an equality of time and space — to the imagery of Japan and Africa. But in doing so, he creates another kind of distance, that of the voyeur who hides himself in order to obtain a certain transparency of the spectacle. He casts Sandor Krasna as a "bounty hunter" of images, which is perhaps the film's most accurate description of its own method, and then laments the effect this produces. As the pre-text is cut off in the image, the Other becomes a perpetual memory, the sign of another time that is never the present. Caught in a trap that produces loss at every turn, Marker turns to science fiction for a narrative device that might invert the historical trajectory of ethnographic time. Over shots of various landscapes, in-between and transitory spaces, the narrator introduces a man from the fortieth century, when the human brain is capable of total recall, a man who has "lost forgetting."

In a world he comes from, to call forth a vision, to be moved by a portrait, to tremble at the sound of music, can only be signs of a long and painful prehistory. He wants to understand. He feels these infirmities of time as an injustice, and he reacts to that injustice like Che Guevara, like the youth of the 60s, with indignation. He is a Third Worlder of time. The idea that unhappiness had existed in this planet's past is as unbearable to him as to them is the existence of poverty in their present. Naturally he'll fail. The unhappiness he discovers is as inaccessible to him as the poverty of a poor country is unimaginable to the children of a rich one. He has chosen to give up his privileges, but he can do nothing about the privilege that has allowed him to choose. His only recourse is precisely that which threw him into this absurd quest, a song cycle by Mussorgsky. They are still sung in the 40th century. Their meaning has been lost, but it was then for the first time he perceived the presence of that thing he didn't understand. Which is something to do with unhappiness and memory, and towards which slowly, heavily, he began to walk.

Of course I'll never make that film. Nevertheless I'm collecting the sets, inventing the twists, putting in my favorite creatures. I've even given it a title, the title of those Mussorgsky songs, "Sunless."

This is, arguably, the central monologue of the film, the place where Marker abandons a discourse on method and imagines an ideal film. From the perspective of the future, the inequalities of the present will be difficult to represent because, like thirst or hunger, they are beyond representation. Perhaps what Marker longs for is an ability to transcend a politics of representation, but he understands that this is not even possible in the realm of fiction. The Third World is not, after all, an imaginary space, and his own subjectivity cannot be distanced by two thousand years. By finally stepping back from the vision of the "Third Worlder of time" and designating this film *Sans Soleil* as its inadequate precursor, he inscribes himself as an editor who "puts in" and "invents twists." A shot of an owl with the words "my favorite creatures" further suggests an identity, a "self" behind the film that is not reducible to the generalized identity of a white man.

Earlier in the film, two dogs on a beach are designated as "my dogs," who are said to be restless because it is the Chinese new year and the beginning of the Year of the Dog. While these first-person references remain mired in the reflexive depths of the narrator's nonidentity, they enable Marker to refer to the possessive status of the image. *Sans Soleil* is perhaps a radical attempt to disown images, to dislodge them from a pre-text in which the filmmaker is deeply implicated. And yet he can't quite let go. It is authorship that is at stake in a fully postmodern ethnography, and Marker lingers on the brink of modernity. The gaze is still a contest, one that is engendered and politicized, despite his attempt to separate images from history. He cannot be Sei Shonagon, documenting the things that "quicken the heart," because unlike her, he is part of history and works in a medium that embodies and reproduces historical time, transforming it in the process to a time of memory.

The violence of history, represented in *Sans Soleil* in the form of military aircraft, kamikaze pilots and African independence movements, is also a discourse of images. The horror at the center of *Apocalypse Now* is as crucial to the pre-text of images as is the seductive gaze of the African woman. If Marker's editing patterns reproduce the shock effect of modernity, the traumatic effect is "cushioned" (in Benjamin's words) by the continuity of the narration. The pre-text of the images is precisely the inequities of global capital, but when they are cut off from their historical "origins" and enter the world of appearances, the shock of discontinuity is obliterated by the nostalgic operations of the traveler's memory, unable to detach himself from his having-been-there. The disintegration of aura, in *Sans Soleil,* is linked to the dissolution of the trauma and violence of historical experience. Memory ultimately constitutes an anesthetizing cure to the "infirmities of time"—the coevalness of uneven development. The condition of unhappiness escapes the regime of memory, the regime of images, which is why the only good film is a film without sun, without images.

The Vanishing of Cinema

The epic scope of *Sans Soleil* is inconsistent with the scale of most experimental ethnography. Its nomadic homelessness is by no means representative of a film practice that more often spins out from the delimited sphere of a local, circumscribed epistemology. Its essayistic nature is, however, typical of the kind of films and videos that work across boundaries of documentary, experimental and fiction film practices. As in Akerman's *News from Home,* the epistolary form of narration implies an address, a structure of communication, foregrounding the role of enunciation that all film plays. The question of "who speaks" may be the fundamental one of a politics of representation, and yet the point of enunciation can never really be pinned down with certainty. Film "originates" in a fractured, plural form of identity.

The narrators in each of these autoethnographic texts achieve a rare degree of intimacy with the viewer, who is consistently addressed on an emotional level. Thus, even when the "I" of this discourse is a fiction, as in *Sans Soleil,* the I-you structure provides a discourse of veracity that is subjectively, rather than objectively, based. Marker renders the testimonial form of the letter slightly ironic by refusing to identify his narrator or elaborate on her fictional relationship to either Krasna or himself.

The fundamental relationship (of identity) that is typically established in ethnography between filmmaker and spectator is destabilized and demystified.

These examples of personal filmmaking suggest some of the contradictions implicit in the notion of autoethnography. The subject "in history" will always be a destabilized self, one for whom memory and experience are always separate. Even a diaristic project such as George Kuchar's, in which there is no apparent break between experience and representation, inscribes subjectivity as a form of writing, a performance of the self. The journeys undertaken by these film- and video-makers are very different ones, and not necessarily representative of the great range of filmmaking that might be designated by the term "auto-ethnography." But they do suggest the possible ethnographic effects of placing oneself under scrutiny. Autoethnography produces a subjective space that combines anthropologist and informant, subject and object of the gaze, under the sign of one identity.

Sadie Benning's use of pixelvision and Kidlat Tahimik's epic home movies not only are means by which they perform themselves but constitute visual styles that signal their difference. Moreover, the ironic tone of all the narrators signals a distance from the authenticity of images, and from the authenticity of the self. Jonas Mekas plays out the fundamentally allegorical structure of autoethnography, transforming all images into memories, traces of experience, signs of the past to be salvaged in cinematic form. Through irony, each of the other filmmakers is able to inscribe himself or herself in the future as another moment in time, and to understand the fiction of the past as a "cosmic innocence." These filmmakers come to understand how they themselves can exist in "a world of appearances," falling back on their identities as filmmakers to reach back to a material reality that precedes images, a domain of agency and history.

Autoethnography in film and video exemplifies Fischer's recognition of the autobiographical model of ethnography but also suggests an expanded sense of the term "ethnic." The full scope of identities that are articulated in the new autobiographies includes sexual orientation, class, generation, and nation. As personal cinema becomes the foundation of cultural critique, "ethnicity" becomes something forged from experience and is reconfigured as a vital form of knowledge. And as Fischer argues in the context of literary autoethnography, diary filmmaking serves as an important model of ethnographic representation appropriate to a pluralist social formation. These films and videos suggest how the audiovisual medium of the cinema functions as a means of splitting and fragmenting identity, not only into the parallel tracks of sound and image, but within the status of the image itself. If "ethnicity" refers to an inherited identity, a fixed history of the self, autoethnography in film and video destabilizes and disperses that history across a range of discursive selves.

When autoethnography becomes an archival practice, as it does in these works, memory is fragmented into a nonlinear collage. The pieces that are assembled into the shape of a diary forsake the authenticity of documentary realism for a fiction of forgetting. The filmed memory situates the filmmaker-subject within a culture of mediation in which the past is endemically fictional. To recall that past by way of memory traces is to render it "another culture" in an ever receding palimpsest of overlapping cultures, of which past, present, and future are merely points of perspective. Subjectivity subsists within image culture as an "other reality" — a utopian space where hierarchies of vision, knowledge, and desire are diffused and collapsed. The journey to this parallel universe is linear neither in time nor in space, moving across histories and geographies to produce a dialectics of cultural representation. Benjamin suggested the urgency of such a practice in the early 1930s: "The remembered world breaks up more quickly, the mythic in it surfaces more quickly and crudely, [so] a completely remembered world must be set up even faster to oppose it. That is how the accelerated pace of technology looks in the light of today's pre-history. *Waking*."[58]

The video-film dialogue that informs so much contemporary filmmaking inscribes the "accelerated pace of technology" into the text itself, setting up allegories of cultural conflict, tension, and transition within the sphere of memory and its representation. In the cinema, self-representation always involves a splitting of the self, a production of another self, another body, another camera, another time, another place. Video threatens to collapse the temporal difference of filmic memory, not only because it can eliminate the structure of secondary revision, but because of its "coverage," its capacity as an instrument of surveillance. The economics of videography transform the collecting process into one of recording. Video lacks the death drive of film, unable to exploit the dialectic of still and motion photography. But neither can video "forget" film and its auratic fantasy of transparency, its memory of the (celluloid) body in the machine.

In its immediacy, without that intermediary "liminal" phase of the photographic negative, video threatens the structures of memory on which autobiographical conventions are founded. The video image shifts the terms of realism from lost aura to an eclipse of auratic memory, or at least it holds out the possibility of such a transformation. Self-representation likewise shifts into something much more fluid and open, discursive and intertextual, even fictional and fantastic. Both Tahimik's diary film and Marker's travelogue inscribe video as a futuristic transformation of cinema, one that will alter our conception of memory and history. Everything will be retrievable; nothing will be lost, except the sense of loss. But cinema has been vanishing since its inception, deeply implicated in colonialist practices of salvage ethnography. Its techniques of mummification are, however, merely an effect of its realist mandate.[59] Dismantling the ideology of realism demands that the otherness of the referent be likewise dismantled. This is the achievement of video for film, a domestication of the technology and an inscription of impermanence and temporality, of allegory into the photographic image.

Medium-specific aesthetics will always break down on the variety of applications and forms that a medium produces — its plenitude of "contents" — and this is especially true of video, which draws on so many cultural, aesthetic, institutional, and consumer forms. Experimental ethnography is a critical method that might enable us to think of video as an extension of film. The deployment of video in autoethnography, as in ethnography and the avant-garde more generally, is only the first step in thinking about the diversification of film into a host of digital media. The fear that these media will "replace" film is exemplary of the means by which video has reinvented cinema as a discourse of vanishing, of a particular modernist sensibility that finds itself always on a historical cusp.

Notes

Preface

1 Marc Manganaro, *Modernist Anthropology: From Fieldwork to Text* (Princeton, N.J.: Princeton University Press, 1990).

2 Walter Benjamin, "The Work of Art in the Age of Mechanical Reproduction," in *Illuminations,* trans. Harry Zohn (New York: Schocken Books, 1969), 217–52.

3 See Timothy Corrigan, *A Cinema without Walls: Movies and Culture after Vietnam* (New Brunswick, N.J.: Rutgers University Press, 1991), for a discussion of the effects of video on mainstream cinema.

4 Michael Renov and Erika Suderburg, "Resolving Video," in *Resolutions: Contemporary Video Practices,* ed. Michael Renov and Erika Suderburg (Minneapolis: University of Minnesota Press, 1996), xv.

5 The text that comes closest to this project is Michael Renov, ed., *Theorizing Documentary* (New York: Routledge, 1993).

6 The term "intercultural" is Laura Marks's, in "The Skin of Film: Experimental Cinema and the Intercultural Experience" (Ph.D. diss., University of Rochester, 1995).

1 Another Look

1 George Marcus, "The Modernist Sensibility in Recent Ethnographic Writing and the Cinematic Metaphor of Montage," in *Visualizing Theory: Selected Essays from V.A.R., 1990–1994,* ed. Lucien Taylor (New York: Routledge, 1994), 48.

2 Trinh T. Minh-ha, *When the Moon Waxes Red: Representation, Gender, and Cultural Politics* (New York: Routledge, 1991); Trinh Minh-ha, *Framer Framed* (New York: Routledge, 1992).

3 Trinh, *When the Moon Waxes Red,* 35.

4 For a critique of Trinh Minh-ha's film practice see Jane Desmond, "Ethnog-

raphy, Orientalism, and Avant-Garde Film," *Visual Anthropology* 4 (n.d.): 147–60; Martina Attille and Maureen Blackwood, "Black Women and Representation," in *Films for Women,* ed. Charlotte Brundson (London: British Film Institute, 1986), 202–8.

5 James Clifford, "Beyond the 'Salvage' Paradigm," in *Discussions in Contemporary Culture* 1, ed. Hal Foster (Seattle: Bay Press, 1987), 122.

6 James Clifford, "On Ethnographic Allegory," in *Writing Culture: The Poetics and Politics of Ethnography,* ed. James Clifford and George E. Marcus (Berkeley: University of California Press, 1986), 115.

7 Clifford, "On Ethnographic Allegory," 113.

8 Johannes Fabian, *Time and the Other: How Anthropology Makes Its Object* (New York: Columbia University Press, 1983), 28.

9 Clifford, "On Ethnographic Allegory," 118.

10 Craig Owens, "The Allegorical Impulse: Toward a Theory of Postmodernism," in *Art after Modernism,* ed. Brian Wallis (New York: Museum, 1984), 203.

11 Ibid., 214.

12 Walter Benjamin, "The Work of Art in the Age of Mechanical Reproduction," in *Illuminations,* trans. Harry Zohn, ed. Hannah Arendt (New York: Schocken Books, 1969), 224.

13 Ibid., 233.

14 Ibid., 15.

15 Ibid., 236–37.

16 Ibid., 229.

17 Anne Friedberg, *Window Shopping: Cinema and the Postmodern* (Berkeley: University of California Press, 1993), 3. Time-shifting refers to the taping of television programs that enables viewers at home to interact with broadcast TV schedules.

18 Walter Benjamin, *The Origins of German Tragic Drama,* trans. John Osborne (London: New Left Books, 1977), 178.

19 Histories of ethnographic film include Emilie de Brigarad, "The History of Ethnographic Film," in *Principles of Visual Anthropology,* 2d ed., ed. Paul Hockings (New York: Mouton de Gruyter, 1995), 13–44; Eliot Weinberger, "The Camera People," in *Visualizing Theory: Selected Essays from V.A.R., 1990–1994,* ed. Lucien Taylor (New York: Routledge, 1994), 3–26.

20 Karl Heider has attempted to explain how to make films in which "reality" is represented in a complete and unmanipulated a way as possible, at the same time as that reality is scientifically analyzed. Even he comes up only with axioms—although he does exhibit a striking naïveté regarding the construction of cinematic realism. Karl Heider, *Ethnographic Film* (Austin: University of Texas Press, 1976).

21 Scott Murray, "Tracey Moffatt," *Cinema Papers* 79 (May 1990): 21; Coco Fusco, "Sankofa & Black Audio Film Collective," in *Discourses: Conversations in Postmodern Art and Culture,* ed. Russell Ferguson, William Geander,

and Marcia Tucker (New York: New Museum of Contemporary Art/MIT, 1990), 19.

22 Rachel Moore, "Marketing Alterity," in Taylor, *Visualizing Theory*, 126–39.

23 Faye Ginsberg, "The Parallax Effect: The Impact of Aboriginal Media on Ethnographic Film," *Visual Anthropology Review* 11, no. 2 (fall 1995): 64–76; see also Ginsberg, "Mediating Culture: Indigenous Media, Ethnographic Film, and the Production of Identity," in *Fields of Vision: Essays in Film Studies, Visual Anthropology, and Photography*, ed. Leslie Devereaux and Roger Hillman (Berkeley: University of California Press, 1995), 256–91.

24 David MacDougall, "Beyond Observational Cinema," in Hockings, *Principles of Visual Anthropology*, 115–32.

25 Trinh, *When the Moon Waxes Red*, 35.

26 Fatimah Tobing Rony, *The Third Eye: Race, Cinema, and Ethnographic Spectacle* (Durham, N.C.: Duke University Press, 1996), 91.

27 Trinh, *When the Moon Waxes Red*, 44.

28 Constance Penley and Janet Bergstrom, "The Avant-Garde: History and Theories," *Screen* 19 (autumn 1978).

29 Peter Wollen, "The Two Avant-Gardes," and "Ontology and Materialism in Film," in *Readings and Writings: Semiotic Counter-Strategies* (London: Verso, 1982), originally published in 1976 and 1974 respectively.

30 Paul Arthur, "The Last of the Last Machine? Avant-Garde Film since 1966," *Millennium Film Journal* 16–18 (fall–winter 1986–1987).

31 Paul Arthur, "No More Causes? The International Film Congress," *Independent* 12, no. 8 (October 1989). That issue of the *Independent* also includes an open letter to the Experimental Film Congress from a group of filmmakers challenging its premises, and a response by Bart Testa as a member of the congress executive. See my essay, "Will the Reel Avant-Garde Please Stand Up?" *Fuse* 13, nos. 1–2 (fall 1989): 37–43. See also Mahola Dargis, "The Brood," *Village Voice*, 20 June 1989.

32 Paul Mann, *The Theory-Death of the Avant-Garde* (Bloomington: Indiana University Press, 1991), 14.

33 See David James, *Allegories of Cinema: American Film in the Sixties* (Princeton, N.J.: Princeton University Press, 1989), for chapters on Warhol and Mekas. James's book has been the most successful historical analysis of the 1960s experimental film scene, cutting through some of the reifying discourse that surrounded the movement.

34 Stan Brakhage, *Metaphors on Vision* (New York: Film Culture, 1963). In one of the first texts on avant-garde cinema, Brakhage describes the analogy between the camera and vision as a kind of disembodiment, a purified form of consciousness.

35 Stephen Tyler, "Post-Modern Ethnography: From Document of the Occult to Occult Document," in *Writing Culture: The Poetics and Politics of Ethnography*, ed. James Clifford and George Marcus (Berkeley: University of California Press, 1986), 125.

36 Bill Nichols, *Blurred Boundaries: Questions of Meaning in Contemporary Culture* (Bloomington: Indiana University Press, 1994), 17–42; Lynne Kirby, "Death and the Photographic Body," in *Fugitive Images: From Photography to Video,* ed. Patrice Petro (Bloomington: Indiana University Press, 1995), 72–86.

37 Donna Haraway's theory of cyborg culture offers an important key to a science fiction fantasy of posthumanism. Her critique of the way that nature has been reified and possessed in discourses of science points to the fundamental links between the primitive and the feminine that inform not only ethnography but the whole spectrum of social and natural sciences. Donna Haraway, "The Promises of Monsters: A Regenerative Politics for Inappropriate/d Others," in *Cultural Studies,* ed. Lawrence Grossberg, Cary Nelson, and Paula A. Treichler (New York: Routledge, 1992), 295–337.

38 Tyler, "Post-Modern Ethnography," 140.

39 Ibid., 139.

40 David Thomas, "Manufacturing Vision," in Taylor, *Visualizing Theory,* 281.

41 Steven Webster, "The Historical Materialist Critique of Surrealism and Postmodern Ethnography," in *Modernist Anthropology: From Fieldwork to Text,* ed. Marc Manganaro (Princeton, N.J.: Princeton University Press, 1993), 293.

42 For a fuller account of the relationships between feminism, theory, and the avant-garde, see Patricia Mellencamp, *Indiscretions: Avant-Garde Film, Video, and Feminism* (Bloomington: Indiana University Press, 1990).

43 Ivone Margulies, *Nothing Happens: Chantal Akerman's Hyperrealist Everyday* (Durham, N.C.: Duke University Press, 1996), 1–20.

44 Bill Nichols, *Blurred Boundaries,* 83.

45 Hal Foster, *The Return of the Real: The Avant-Garde at the End of the Century* (Cambridge, Mass.: MIT Press, 1996), 183.

46 Rey Chow, *Primitive Passions: Visuality, Sexuality, Ethnography, and Contemporary Chinese Cinema* (New York: Columbia University Press, 1995), 198. Chow develops a theory of ethnography in this book that is parallel to the one I have sketched. She evokes Benjamin's theory of translation to describe the process by which ethnic cultures are translated into the forms of mass media. Ethnography as a form of translation underscores the role of language in a process in which the concept of "the original" vanishes into the realm of myth.

47 Caren Kaplan, *Questions of Travel: Postmodern Discourses of Displacement* (Durham, N.C.: Duke University Press, 1996), 88.

2 Surrealist Ethnography

1 James Clifford, *The Predicament of Culture: Twentieth Century Ethnography, Literature, and Art* (Cambridge: Harvard University Press, 1988), 120.

2 Dennis Hollier, "The Use-Value of the Impossible," trans. Liesl Ollman, *October* 60 (spring 1992): 21.

3 George Ribemont-Dessaignes, *"Hallelujah,"* trans. Dominic Faccini, *October* 60 (spring 1992): 47–48.

4 Michael Leiris, "Fox Movietone Follies of 1929," trans. Dominic Faccini, *October* 60 (spring 1992): 43–46.

5 James Lastra, "Why Is This Absurd Picture Here? Ethnology/Heterology/Buñuel," unpublished manuscript.

6 Ibid., 10.

7 Francisco Aranda, *Luis Buñuel: A Critical Biography,* trans. David Robinson (London: Secker and Warburg, 1975), 93. Buñuel had thoroughly researched his subject, and the film and his narration are partially inspired by a 1926 study by Maurice Legendre (Aranda, 89), and a 1922 travel essay by Miguel Unamuno. According to Lastra, these two writers attempted to rehabilitate the Hurdanos as Spanish citizens in response to earlier accounts of them as savages (34). Buñuel rejects these writers' romanticization but adopts their self-serving anthropological voice.

8 Ibid., 93.

9 Nicholas Thomas, "Colonial Surrealism: Louis Buñuel's *Land without Bread,*" *Third Text* 26 (spring 1994): 26.

10 E. Rubinstein, "Visit to a Familiar Planet: Buñuel among the Hurdanos," *Cinema Journal* 22, no. 4 (summer 1983): 8.

11 Nichols describes these conventions of ethnography in *Blurred Boundaries: Questions of Meaning in Contemporary Culture* (Bloomington: Indiana University Press, 1994), 67.

12 Rubenstein, "Visit to a Familiar Planet," 9.

13 S. M. Eisenstein, V. I. Pudovkin, and G. V. Alexandrov, "A Statement on the Sound Film," in *Film Form,* ed. and trans. Jay Leyda (New York: Harcourt Brace and World, 1949), 257–60.

14 Vivian Sobchack, "Synthetic Vision: The Dialectical Imperative of Buñuel's *Las Hurdes,*" *Millennium Film Journal* 7–9 (1980–1981): 149–50.

15 Bill Nichols, *Ideology and the Image: Social Representation in the Cinema and Other Media* (Bloomington: Indiana University Press, 1981), 238.

16 Bill Nichols, *Representing Reality: Issues and Concepts in Documentary* (Bloomington: Indiana University Press, 1991), 218.

17 Rubenstein, "Visit to a Familiar Planet," 5.

18 Hollier, "Use-Value of the Impossible," 19.

19 Trinh T. Minh-ha, *When the Moon Waxes Red: Representation, Gender, and Cultural Politics* (New York: Routledge, 1991), 148.

20 Lastra, "Ethnology/Heterology/Buñuel," 18.

21 Roland Barthes, "The Great Family of Man," in *Mythologies,* trans. Annette Lavers (London: Paladin, 1973), 100–102.

22 Georges Bataille, "Architecture," entry in "Critical Dictionary," *Documents* 1, no. 2 (May 1929); reprint, trans. Dominic Faccini, in *October* 60 (spring 1992).

23 The film was banned in Spain, and foreign embassies were instructed to keep it from being shown abroad because authorities felt it was injurious to Spain (Aranda, 90) — indicating a level of guilty identification with the Hurdanos as Spaniards.

24 Tom Conley, "Documentary Surrealism: On *Land without Bread,*" in *Dada and Surrealist Film,* ed. Rudolf E. Kuenzli (New York: Willis Locker and Owens, 1987), 185.

25 It may be that the filmmakers have killed the goat to feed the Hurdanos, but if this is true, it is equally significant that it is not mentioned. Such humanism is relegated outside the limits of the text, which revels instead in its own cruelty.

26 Georges Bataille, *Erotism: Death and Sensuality,* trans. Mary Dalwood (San Francisco: City Lights Books, 1986).

27 Conley, "Documentary Surrealism," 186.

28 André Bazin, "Mort tous les aprés-midi," in *Qu'est-ce que le cinema?* vol. 1, *Ontologie et langage* (Paris: Editions du cerf, 1969).

29 Walter Benjamin, "Theses on the Philosophy of History," in *Illuminations,* ed. Hannah Arendt, trans. Harry Zohn (New York: Schocken Books, 1969), 256.

30 "Surrealism," in *Reflections: Essays, Aphorisms, Autobiographical Writings,* trans. Edmund Jephcott, ed. Peter Demetz (1929; New York: Schocken Books, 1986), 189; see also Susan Buck-Morss, *The Dialectics of Seeing: Walter Benjamin and the Arcades Project* (Cambridge: MIT Press, 1989), 34.

31 Benjamin, "Surrealism," 192.

32 Clifford, *Predicament of Culture,* 117.

33 Tracey Moffatt, interview by Scott Murray, *Cinema Papers* 79 (May 1990): 21.

34 Ibid., 22.

35 Moffatt is also known as a photographer, and she specializes in large-scale cibachrome images.

36 Oshima Nagisa, "Banishing Green," in *Cinema, Censorship, and the State,* trans. Dawn Lawson (Cambridge: MIT Press, 1992), 208–11.

37 For an explanation of the cinematic discourse of melodrama, see Thomas Elsaesser, "Tales of Sound and Fury: Observations on the Family Melodrama," in *Home Is Where the Heart Is: Studies in Melodrama and the Women's Film,* ed. Christine Gledhill (London: British Film Institute, 1987), 43–69.

38 Langton has in fact written on *Night Cries.* She points out that Moffatt's revision of the *Jedda* text is an attempt to "correct . . . the Western fascination with the 'primitive.' " *Well I heard It on the Radio and I Saw It on the Television . . .* (Sydney: Australian Film Commission, 1993), quoted in Patricia Mellencamp, "Haunted History: Tracey Moffatt and Julie Dash," *Discourse* 16, no. 2 (winter 1993–1994): 142.

39 Laleen Jayamanne, "Love Me Tender, Love Me True, Never Let Me Go . . . : A Sri Lankan Reading of Tracey Moffatt's Night Cries," *Framework* 38–39 (1992): 92.

40 Nichols, *Blurred Boundaries,* 100.

41 Ibid., 96–97.

42 Benjamin, "The Work of Art," in *Illuminations,* 233.

43 Stephen A. Tyler, "Post-Modern Ethnography: From Document of the Occult to Occult Document," in *Writing Culture: The Poetics and Politics of Ethnography,* ed. James Clifford and George E. Marcus (Berkeley: University of California Press, 1986), 123.

44 Patricia Mellencamp, "An Empirical Avant-Garde," in *Fugitive Images: From Photography to Video,* ed. Patrice Petro (Bloomington: Indiana University Press, 1995), 175.

45 Hal Foster introduces this term in his discussion of the surrealism of Chirico, Ernst, and Giacometti in *Compulsive Beauty* (Cambridge: MIT Press, 1993), 57.

46 In her interview by Scott Murray, Moffatt says, "I was raised by an older white woman and the script became quite a personal story. The little girl who appears in some of the flashback sequences looks a lot like me. That was quite intentional" (22).

47 Eduardo Cadava, "Words of Light: Theses on the Photography of History," in Petro, *Fugitive Images,* 221–44.

48 Benjamin, "Theses on the Philosophy of History," in *Illuminations,* 255.

49 Hal Foster, "Exquisite Corpses," in *Visualizing Theory: Selected Essays from V.A.R., 1990–1994,* ed. Lucien Taylor (New York: Routledge, 1994), 169.

50 The best example of the condescending aspect of "humane" ethnology is the fundamental similarity between *National Geographic* documentaries about animals and people. See chapter 6 for a further discussion of the relation between animals and people in ethnographic representations.

51 Foster, *Compulsive Beauty,* 98.

52 Benjamin, "Surrealism," 189.

3 The Body as the Main Attraction

1 Tom Gunning, "The Cinema of Attraction: Early Film, Its Spectator, and the Avant-Garde," *Wide Angle* 8, nos. 3–4 (1983): 64. Gunning cites Robert C. Allen, *Vaudeville and Film: 1895–1915* (New York: Arno Press, 1980), 212–13.

2 Tom Gunning, "Tracing the Individual Body: Photography, Detectives, and Early Cinema," in *Cinema and the Invention of Modern Life,* ed. Leo Charney and Vanessa R. Schwartz (Berkeley: University of California Press, 1995), 18.

3 Fatimah Tobing Rony, *The Third Eye: Race, Cinema, and Ethnographic Spectacle* (Durham, N.C.: Duke University Press, 1996), 36–43.

4 Walter Benjamin, "Theses on the Philosophy of History," in *Illuminations,* ed. Hannah Arendt, trans. Harry Zohn (New York: Schocken Books, 1969), 262.

5 Ibid., 263.

6 Noël Burch, "A Primitive Mode of Representation?" in *Early Cinema,* ed. Thomas Elsaesser (London: British Film Institute, 1990), 220–27.

7 *Film before Griffith* is the name of a collection of articles edited by John L. Fell in 1983 (Berkeley: University of California Press) that provided one of the first historical surveys of early cinema. The "end of early cinema" is necessarily vague, as the narrative patterns that eventually came to dominate the industry developed slowly and inconsistently over the first decade of the century.

8 In addition to "The Cinema of Attraction," Gunning has developed his argument in "An Aesthetic of Astonishment: Early Film and the (In)credulous Spectator," *Art and Text* 34 (spring 1989): 31–45.

9 Gunning, "The Cinema of Attraction," 63–64.

10 Gunning, "'Primitive' Cinema: A Frame-Up? Or, The Trick's on Us," in Elsaesser, *Early Cinema,* 97.

11 Miriam Hansen, *From Babel to Babylon: Spectatorship in American Silent Film* (Cambridge: Harvard University Press, 1991), 41.

12 Gunning, "The Cinema of Attraction," 70.

13 Rony, *Third Eye,* 28.

14 Ibid., 38.

15 Fatimah Tobing Rony, "Those Who Squat and Those Who Sit: The Iconography of Race in the 1895 Films of Félix-Louis Regnault," *Camera Obscura* 28 (January 1992): 278.

16 Rony, *Third Eye,* 26.

17 Homi K. Bhabha, *The Location of Culture* (New York: Routledge, 1994), 82.

18 Benjamin, "The Work of Art in the Age of Mechanical Reproduction," in *Illuminations,* 234.

19 Michael Taussig, *Mimesis and Alterity: A Particular History of the Senses* (New York: Routledge, 1993), 20.

20 Taussig, "Physiognomic Aspects of Visual Worlds," *Visualizing Theory: Selected Essays from V.A.R., 1990–1994,* ed. Lucien Taylor (New York: Routledge, 1994), 206.

21 Rony, *Third Eye,* 21.

22 The parallels between the two time machines of cinema and anthropology have been developed by Rony throughout her book. The term originates with George Gellner, in *Thought and Change* (Chicago: University of Chicago Press, 1964) quoted in Fabian, who notes, "Just because one condemns the time-distancing discourse of evolutionism he [*sic*] does not abandon the allochronic understanding of such terms as *primitive*" (39).

23 Scott MacDonald, *Avant-Garde Film: Motion Studies* (New York: Cambridge University Press, 1993), 116. Joel Katz describes Comerio as an "official court cinematographer in the early 1900s and a pioneer of Italian documentary" ("From Archive to Archiveology," in *Cinematograph* 4 [1991]: 100–101).

24 Benjamin, "The Work of Art," 242.

25 Ibid., 241. Benjamin does not give a source for the Marinetti text.

26 Scott MacDonald claims that the film functions as "a sustained critique of the ideology embedded within Comerio's original imagery" (*Avant-Garde Film: Motion Studies* [New York: Cambridge University Press, 1993], 17). This is indicative of avant-garde criticism that strives to see a critique that is not there. One expects it, but MacDonald does not make a convincing case. Joel Katz is a bit more cautious. He suggests that the filmmakers' point is that "sensory experience and political conscience" are "not mutually exclusive" (100).

27 Chris Jenks, "Watching Your Step: the History and Practice of the *Flâneur,*" in *Visual Culture,* ed. Chris Jenks (New York: Routledge, 1995), 155.

28 Here I would disagree with MacDonald, who argues that we both see and see through the Comerio footage (17).

29 Trinh T. Minh-ha, *When the Moon Waxes Red: Representation, Gender, and Cultural Politics* (New York: Routledge, 1991), 99.

30 Structural film is an experimental, minimalist film style that emerged in the late 1960s in the United States and England. See chapter 7 for a fuller description and history of this mode of film practice.

31 Bart Testa has described in detail the "issues of cinematic representation" that were analyzed by experimental filmmakers in their recycling of early cinema. Bart Testa, *Back and Forth: Early Cinema and the Avant-Garde* (Toronto: Art Gallery of Ontario, 1992).

32 Testa, *Back and Forth,* 19. Testa lists other key examples of structural films using early found footage: Ken Jacobs, *Tom, Tom, the Piper's Son* (1969); Hollis Frampton, *Public Domain* (1972), *Gloria!* (1979), and *Cadenza #1* (1977–1980); Ernie Gehr, *Eureka* (1974) and *History* (1974); Al Razutis, *Visual Essays: Origins of Film* (1973–1984); and Malcolm LeGrice, *After Lumière* (1974) (Testa, 36).

33 Testa, *Back and Forth,* 92.

34 See my article, "David Rimmer's Found Footage: Reproduction and Repetition of History," *CineAction!* (spring 1989): 56.

35 Clifford, "On Ethnographic Allegory," in *Writing Culture: The Poetics and Politics of Ethnography,* ed. James Clifford and George E. Marcus (Berkeley: University of California Press, 1986), 113.

36 See my "David Rimmer: Twilight in the Image Bank," in *David Rimmer: Films and Tapes* (Toronto: Art Gallery of Ontario, 1993).

37 Roland Barthes, *Camera Lucida: Reflections on Photography,* trans. Richard Howard (New York: Hill and Wang, 1981), 34.

38 Dai Vaughan, "Let There Be Lumière," in Elsaesser, *Early Cinema,* 65.

39 David James, *Allegories of Cinema: American Film in the Sixties* (Princeton, N.J.: Princeton University Press, 1989), 247.

40 Specific references to Muybridge can be found in *Documentary Footage* (Morgan Fisher, 1968) and *INGENIVM NOBIS IPSA PVELLA FECIT* (Hollis Frampton, 1975). Also see Scott MacDonald's *Avant-Garde Film* for a discussion of the impact of Muybridge's "serial organization" on experimental film (9–11).

41 *The Human Figure in Motion* (New York: Dover Publications, 1955), jacket

copy. See also p. vii for an indication of the influence of Muybridge's photos on painters and sculptors in the 1890s.

42 Rosalind Krauss, "The Originality of the Avant-Garde: A Postmodernist Repetition," in *Art after Modernism: Rethinking Representation,* ed. Brian Wallis (New York: New Museum of Contemporary Art, 1984), 18–19.

43 Testa, *Back and Forth,* 61.

44 Linda Williams, "Film Body: An Implantation of Perversions," *Narrative, Apparatus, Ideology: A Film Theory Reader,* ed. Philip Rosen (New York: Columbia University Press, 1986), 511, 520.

45 In his introduction to the 1955 edition of *The Human Figure in Motion,* Robert Taft says that the models had to be professionals because they performed nude ("An Introduction: Eadweard Muybridge and His Work," x). Williams denounces this as an explanation for the nudity, noting that women are categorically more nude than the men (520–21).

46 Leo Charney, "In a Moment: Film and the Philosophy of Modernity," in Charney and Schwartz, *Cinema and the Invention of Modern Life,* 289.

47 Anne Friedberg has argued convincingly that women's "mobility through urban space" was a major factor in the shifts in visual culture that took place at the turn of the century. *Window Shopping: Cinema and the Postmodern* (Berkeley: University of California Press, 1993), 35.

48 Margaret Cohen, "Panoramic Literature and the Invention of Everyday Genres," in Charney and Schwartz, *Cinema and the Invention of Modern Life,* 231.

49 Noël Burch, *Life to Those Shadows* (Berkeley: University of California Press, 1990), 11.

50 Benjamin, "Some Motifs in Baudelaire," in *Illuminations,* 176.

51 Krauss, "Originality of the Avant-Garde," 22.

52 Katz, "From Archive to Archiveology," 102.

4 Ethnotopias of Early Cinema

1 James Clifford, "Traveling Cultures," in *Cultural Studies,* ed. Lawrence Grossberg, Cary Nelson, and Paula Treichler (New York: Routledge, 1992), 101.

2 Elizabeth A. Williams, "The Science of Man: Anthropological Thought and Institutions in Nineteenth Century France" (Ph.D. diss., Indiana University, 1983), 27, cited by Fatimah Tobing Rony, "Those Who Squat and Those Who Sit: The Iconography of Race in the 1895 Films of Félix Regnault," *Camera Obscura* 28 (January 1992): 271.

3 Bill Nichols, *Representing Reality* (Bloomington: Indiana University Press, 1991), 218.

4 Jeanette DeBouzek, "The 'Ethnographic Surrealism' of Jean Rouch," *Visual Anthropology* 2 (December, 1989): 304. DeBouzek's article is based on an interview with Rouch.

5 Despite the playful contributions of Rouch's collaborators Lam, Damouré, and Illo, the narrative structure of *Jaguar* remains in Rouch's control. The three men from Niger play out a familiar adventure story from Western literature in which they leave their village, travel to the Ghanaian coast, and return as mature, wealthy men, ready to marry the women who have waited for them at home. Although the three men are given some degree of agency by being cast as actors and narrators, instead of merely being "themselves," they are nevertheless infantilized within the decoupage and play the picaresque naïfs while Rouch stays outside the field of vision, supplying only narrational commentary. The film is vulnerable, also, to a critique of its narrative codes of gender, as women are identified with "home" and men (Rouch and the Africans) with adventure and discovery. In the context of 1950s anthropology and the emergent independence movements in Africa, however, when the film was shot, the mix of social observation and dramatic narrative constituted a strong sense of historical desire and historical change. See chapter 8 for a more extensive analysis of Rouch's project in the context of *Les Maîtres fous*.

6 Christopher Pinney, "Future Travel: Anthropology and Cultural Distance in an Age of Virtual Reality or, A Past Seen from a Possible Future," in *Visualizing Theory: Selected Essays from V.A.R., 1990–1994,* ed. Lucien Taylor (New York: Routledge, 1994), 422.

7 Fredric Jameson, "Progress versus Utopia: Or Can We Imagine the Future?" in *Art after Modernism: Rethinking Representation,* ed. Brian Wallis (New York: New Museum of Contemporary Art/David R. Godine, 1984), 247.

8 Fredric Jameson, "Magical Narratives," in *The Political Unconscious: Narrative as a Socially Symbolic Act* (Ithaca: Cornell University Press, 1981).

9 Walter Benjamin, "N [Theoretics of Knowledge; Theory of Progress]," trans. of *Passagen-Werk* by Leigh Hafrey and Richard Sieburth, in *Benjamin: Philosophy, Aesthetics, History,* ed. Gary Smith (Chicago: University of Chicago Press, 1983), 65.

10 Benjamin, "The Storyteller," in *Illuminations,* trans. Harry Zohn, ed. Hannah Arendt (New York: Schocken Books, 1969), 83–110.

11 Margaret Cohen, "Panoramic Literature and the Invention of Everyday Genres," in *Cinema and the Invention of Modern Life,* ed. Leo Charney and Vanessa R. Schwartz (Berkeley: University of California Press, 1995), 240.

12 The British series was probably distributed by Edison in North America, although the catalog lists dozens of films with titles similar to those in the *Living Canada* series (*Tobogganing in Montreal, Skiing in Quebec,* etc.), so it is hard to know if they are in fact the same films or not.

13 *Montreal Daily Star,* 20 May 1903, 7.

14 The CPR films were produced and distributed by Charles Urban's Bioscope Company of Canada. Peter Morris, *Embattled Shadows: A History of Canadian Cinema, 1895–1939* (Montreal: McGill-Queen's University Press, 1992), 34.

15 The *Montreal Daily Star* ran advertisements for, and reviews of, the program

regularly from 12 June 1903 to 23 June. On 20 May, an article on the photographer Joe Rosenthal notes that he had shot footage on Mt. Royal, and in British Columbia, and had recently returned from shooting "views" of the Boer War.

16 Tom Gunning, "Before Documentary: Early Nonfiction Films and the 'View' Aesthetic" (unpublished paper, 1996), 20.

17 Livio Belloï, "Lumière and His View: The Cameraman's Eye in Early Cinema," *Historical Journal of Film, Radio, and Television* 15, no. 4 (1995): 464.

18 Tom Gunning has described early film's tendency to privilege the single viewpoint as a form of continuity. In the trick films, the fixed frame often produced an illusion of continuity based on spatial codes. "Primitive Cinema: A Frame-Up? Or, The Trick's on Us," in *Early Cinema,* ed. Thomas Elsaesser (London: British Film Institute, 1990).

19 See David Clandfield, "From the Picturesque to the Familiar: Films of the French Unit at the NFB (1958–64)," in *Take Two,* ed. Seth Feldman (Toronto: Irwin Publishing, 1984), 112–24.

20 Paul-André Linteau, René Durocher, and Jean-Claude Robert, *Quebec: A History, 1867–1929,* trans. Robert Chodos (Toronto: James Lorimer, 1983), 40, 402.

21 Walter Benjamin, "A Short History of Photography" (1931), trans. Stanley Mitchell, *Screen* (spring 1972): 7.

22 Michael Taussig, *Mimesis and Alterity: A Particular History of the Senses* (New York: Routledge, 1993), 193–211. Taussig's most provocative example of the display of "white man's magic" is Flaherty's use of the phonograph in *Nanook of the North.* The screening of films for natives by Flaherty and other early filmmakers is likewise a display of magical powers potentially matching those of the local culture.

23 Benjamin, "N," 50.

24 Ibid.

25 The French press focuses more on the international scope of the series, hardly mentioning the local views. The biggest hit was the scenes from the life of Jeanne d'Arc, which evoked glorious memories of the Motherland (*La Presse,* 9 December 1903).

26 Tom Gunning, "Before Documentary," 20.

27 Trinh T. Minh-ha, *When the Moon Waxes Red: Representation, Gender, and Cultural Politics* (New York: Routledge, 1991), 49.

28 Miriam Hansen, *From Babel to Babylon: Spectatorship in American Silent Film* (Cambridge: Harvard University Press, 1991).

29 Jameson, "Progress versus Utopia," 243.

30 Linda Williams, "Film Body: An Implantation of Perversions," in *Narrative, Apparatus, Ideology: A Film Theory Reader,* ed. Philip Rosen (New York: Columbia University Press, 1986), 531. See also Lucy Fischer, "The Lady Vanishes: Women, Magic, and the Movies," in *Film before Griffith,* ed. John Fell (Berkeley: University of California Press, 1983), 339–54.

31 Walter Benjamin, *The Origins of German Tragic Drama,* trans. John Osborne (London: New Left Books, 1977), 214.

32 Walter Benjamin, *Passagen-Werk,* Konvolute M2, *Gesammelte Schriften,* vol. 5, pp. 46–47 (1935 exposé), trans. and quoted by Susan Buck-Morss, *The Dialectics of Seeing: Walter Benjamin and the Arcades Project* (Cambridge: MIT Press, 1989), 114. The opening quotation is from Jules Michelet.

33 Gaitan was at one time married to Cinema Novo filmmaker Glauber Rocha.

34 I would like to thank Catherine Benamou for introducing me to this film and clarifying some of the ethnographic and geographic details.

35 A popular music video by Smashing Pumpkins (*Tonight Tonight*) recreated most of Méliès's tableaux, indicating the proximity of his fantastic *mise-en-scène* to postmodern screen space.

36 Benjamin, "N," 60.

37 Deleuze and Guattari, *Nomadology: The War Machine,* trans. Brian Massumi (New York: Semiotext[e], 1986). The nomad also appears in *A Thousand Plateaus,* trans. Brian Massumi (Minneapolis: University of Minnesota Press, 1987).

38 Teshome Gabriel, "Thoughts on Nomadic Aesthetics and Black Independent Cinema: Traces of a Journey," in *Out There: Marginalization and Contemporary Cultures,* ed. Russell Ferguson, Martha Gever, Trinh T. Minh-ha, and Cornel West (New York: New Museum/MIT Press, 1990), 404.

5 Playing Primitive

1 Marc Manganaro, "Textual Play, Power, and Cultural Critique: An Orientation to Modernist Anthropology," in *Modernist Anthropology: From Fieldwork to Text,* ed. Marc Manganaro (Princeton, N.J.: Princeton University Press), 12.

2 Daan Hertogs and Nico de Klerk, eds., *Nonfiction from the Teens: The 1994 Amsterdam Workshop* (Amsterdam and London: Nederlands Filmmuseum and the British Film Institute, 1994), 58–66.

3 Miriam Hansen, discussion at 1994 Amsterdam Workshop, *Nonfiction from the Teens,* 62.

4 In an earlier version of this chapter, published in *Visual Anthropology* 8, nos. 55–77 (1996), I described the 1914 *Headhunters* as a lost film. Since then, Brad Evans has found Curtis's original footage, apparently intact, at Chicago's Field Museum. His comments are published as a response to my article in *Visual Anthropology* 11, no. 3 (1998): 221–41. I have modified my original article somewhat in light of his findings, and my response to his "discovery" can be found in the same issue of *Visual Anthropology.*

5 *Headhunters* opened in New York and Seattle in 1914 and ran in "theaters around the country" until 1915. It was hand tinted and accompanied by full orchestra. Curtis financed the film through his own production company,

the Continental Film Company, which never recovered the production costs. The huge investment was justified by Curtis's expectation that "the Indian Pictures, owing to their historical and ethnological importance, will remain in existence for all time: rather than being junk in six months, they will become of increasing value, paying a dividend on the cost for years to come." Quoted in Bill Holm and George Irving Quimby, *Edward S. Curtis in the Land of the War Canoes: A Pioneer Cinematographer in the Pacific Northwest* (Vancouver: Douglas and McIntyre, 1990), 113.

6 Evans's description of the extant film would seem to contradict this claim by Holm and Quimby, although many of the shots included in their remake are evidently damaged.

7 Brad Evans, "Commentary: Catherine Russell's Recovery of the Head-Hunters," *Visual Anthropology* 11, no. 3 (1998).

8 Ibid., 4.

9 D. W. Griffith alone had made at least eighteen films featuring Indians played by white actors. Although some films pictured Indians as rampaging savages, a good many portrayed individual Indians as sympathetic characters abused by whites, and some romantic melodramas were set entirely in Indian communities with no "white" characters at all. Eileen Bowser, *The Transformation of Cinema, 1907–1915* (Berkeley: University of California Press, 1990), 173–77. The Library of Congress Paper Print Collection offers plot descriptions of many "Indian pictures." In addition to the Griffith films, there are a number of others worth mentioning: *The Indian,* by Klaw and Erlanger (1914), a three-reeler featuring 250 Indian extras; and *The Tourists,* by Mack Sennett (1912), in which Mabel Normand accidentally seduces an Indian chief.

10 One intertitle early in the film reads: "Motana again builds his fire on the heights where he fasts and dances, still seeking spirit power. The sorcerer's daughter resolves to spare him and win his love, but he spurns her, and she returns to her father with Motana's hair and neck-ring."

11 Holm and Quimby, *Edward S. Curtis,* 26.

12 Evans, "Commentary," 6.

13 *The Shadow Catcher: Edward S. Curtis and the North American Indians* (T. C. McLuhan, 1974) includes early *actualité* footage shot by Curtis of both Hopi and Navajo ceremonies.

14 Examples offered by Holm and Quimby include the fact that Motana, the ostensible hero of the film, is seen to hunt both sea lions and a whale as part of a "test." The Kwakiutl have never hunted whales, and killing sea lions was a part of everyday life, not a test of manhood (66). In one of the ceremonial scenes, a huge number of costumed dancers appear, but the various mythological figures represented would never normally appear together. In another instance, a dance is performed in a circle, and the participants remember Curtis drawing a circle on the floor, "apparently to guide the dancers to stay in camera range" (102).

15 Holm and Quimby, *Edward S. Curtis,* 27.

16 Christopher M. Lyman, *The Vanishing Race and Other Illusions: Photographs of Indians by Edward S. Curtis* (Washington, D.C.: Smithsonian Institution Press, 1982).

17 Edward Curtis, *The North American Indian: Being a Series of Volumes Picturing and Describing the Indians of the United States and Alaska,* vol. 1, ed. Frederick Webb Hodge (Cambridge: Harvard University Press, 1907–1930), xiii.

18 Gloria Cranmer Webster, former curator of the U'Mista Cultural Society, the Kwakiutl-run museum that now houses the treasures stolen by the Canadian government, says of the Kwakiutl, "We are the most highly anthropologized group of people in the world" (*Box of Treasures* [Chuck Olin, 1983]).

19 Pierre Stevens of the Canadian National Archives has estimated that "more than 200 films about Northwest Coast natives were made prior to 1940." Like Webster's remark, this of course begs the question of the relation of the Kwakiutl to the many other native groups in the area, a problem that has preoccupied many anthropologists of the Northwest Coast. Rosalind C. Morris, *New Worlds from Fragments: Film, Ethnography, and the Representation of Northwest Coast Cultures* (Boulder: Westview Press, 1994), 13.

20 Jeanne Cannizzo, "George Hunt and the Invention of Kwakiutl Culture," *Canadian Review of Sociology and Anthropology* 20, no. 1 (1983): 45.

21 Holm and Quimby, *Edward S. Curtis,* 57; Cannizzo, "George Hunt," 45.

22 Trinh T. Minh-ha, *When the Moon Waxes Red: Representation, Gender, and Cultural Politics* (New York: Routledge, 1991), 75.

23 James Clifford, "Traveling Cultures," in *Cultural Studies,* ed. Lawrence Grossberg, Cary Nelson, and Paula Treichler (New York: Routledge, 1992), 97.

24 Lyman explains how Curtis's work was appreciated neither in art-photography circles nor in ethnographic circles. His photography, however, was a huge commercial success, at least until about the time of *Headhunters* (*Vanishing Race,* 39–43, 78).

25 James Clifford, *The Predicament of Culture: Twentieth Century Ethnography, Literature, and Art* (Cambridge: Harvard University Press, 1988), 235.

26 Helen Cordere, introduction to *Kwakiutl Ethnography,* by Franz Boas (Chicago: University of Chicago Press, 1966), xv.

27 Ibid., xvii.

28 Morris, *New Worlds,* 43.

29 It is not clear why exactly Boas did not edit his footage. Although he believed it to be lost, it was compiled, posthumously, by Bill Holm in 1973 as *The Kwakiutl of British Columbia* (Morris, *New Worlds,* 43).

30 Holm and Quimby, *Edward S. Curtis,* 42.

31 Ibid., 31.

32 Franz Boas, *Kwakiutl Ethnography* (Chicago: University of Chicago Press, 1966), 172.

33 Homi Bhabha, *The Location of Culture* (London: Routledge, 1994), 241–42.

34 Lang's films in the German context constitute a radical de-Wagnerization of the Teutonic myth. Instead of passion, Sturm und Drang, he offered an

allegory of opera, the characters frozen in gothic, silent tableaux, and he played up the ethnic representation of Aryans and vaguely Semitic "others" to the extent that it became a Nazi favorite. A key image in *Siegfried* is the skull that appears as a kind of vision to Kriemhild in a premonition of her husband's death. In Lang's antirealist mise-en-scène, this "death's head" becomes the emblem of his thoroughly allegorical style. Its symbolism is effectively drained by its heavy-handed use. If Lang's skull, in symbolizing fate, announces the textuality of the film, the skulls in *Headhunters* likewise symbolize "savagery" in such a stylized way that they can be said to free the natives from documentary.

35 Frances Flaherty, quoted in Jay Ruby, " 'The Aggie Will Come First': The Demystification of Robert Flaherty," in *Robert Flaherty, Photographer/Filmmaker: The Inuit, 1910–1922,* exhibition catalog (Vancouver, B.C.: Vancouver Art Gallery, 1980), 456 n.

36 Ibid., 60.

37 See Tom Gunning, *D. W. Griffith and the Origins of American Narrative Film: The Early Years at Biograph* (Urbana: University of Illinois Press, 1991).

38 Ruby, "The Aggie Will Come First," 68.

39 Bowser notes that one of the attractions of the Indian picture was the near naked bodies of white men playing natives. Charles Inslee became most well known for his portrayal of noble savages (*The Transformation of Cinema,* 176).

40 Holm and Quimby, *Edward S. Curtis,* 85.

41 In one of Curtis's earlier *actualités* of a Navajo dance, the dancers reputedly performed the dance backward to secularize it for the film camera. The "mistake" was identified by contemporary Navajo viewers of *Shadowcatchers* (Lyman, *Vanishing Race,* 69).

42 Curtis, quoted in "Filming the Headhunters: How the Vanishing Race Is Being Preserved in Moving Pictures," *Strand Magazine,* American ed., August 1915; (reprinted in Holm and Quimby, *Edward S. Curtis,* 122). Holm and Quimby note the unreliability of this article, and indeed the piece is full of exaggerations and misrepresentations designed to exoticize the production as an anthropological adventure.

43 Holm and Quimby, *Edward S. Curtis,* 59.

44 Dai Vaughan, "The Aesthetics of Ambiguity," in *Film as Ethnography,* ed. Peter Ian Crawford and David Turton (Manchester: Manchester University Press, 1992), 114.

45 Stephen Bush, "*In the Land of the Head Hunters:* Remarkable Motion Picture Produced by Edward S. Curtis, Famous Authority on North American Indians," *Moving Picture World* 22 (1914): 1685.

46 Vachel Lindsay, *The Art of the Moving Picture* (New York: Macmillan, 1915), 114.

47 Judith Mayne, *The Woman at the Keyhole* (Bloomington: Indiana University Press, 1990), 183.

1 J. Hoberman, "The Reflecting Pool: Bill Viola and the Visionary Company," in *Bill Viola,* ed. Barbara London (New York: Museum of Modern Art, 1987), 71.

2 Some of the key texts of apparatus theory are Jean-Louis Baudry, "Ideological Effects of the Basic Cinematic Apparatus" (1970), reprinted in *Narrative, Apparatus, Ideology,* ed. Philip Rosen (New York: Columbia University Press, 1986), 286–98; Jean-Louis Baudry, "The Apparatus: Metapsychological Approaches to the Impression of Reality in Cinema" (1975), in Rosen, 299–318; Stephen Heath, *Questions of Cinema* (Bloomington: Indiana University Press, 1981); Christian Metz, *The Imaginary Signifier: Psychoanalysis and the Cinema,* trans. Celia Britton, Annwyl Williams, Ben Brewster, and Alfred Guzzetti (Bloomington: Indiana University Press, 1982); Laura Mulvey, "Visual Pleasure and Narrative Cinema," *Screen* 16, no. 3 (autumn 1975): 6–18.

3 Linda Williams, introduction to *Viewing Positions: Ways of Seeing Film,* ed. Linda Williams (New Brunswick, N.J.: Rutgers University Press, 1995), 1–22.

4 Teresa de Lauretis, *Alice Doesn't: Feminism, Semiotics, Cinema* (Bloomington: Indiana University Press, 1984), 85.

5 Jean-Louis Baudry, "The Apparatus," in Rosen, 299–318.

6 Michel Foucault, *Discipline and Punish: The Birth of the Prison,* trans. Alan Sheridan (New York: Vintage Books, 1979), 201.

7 Bill Nichols, *Representing Reality: Issues and Concepts in Documentary* (Bloomington: Indiana University Press, 1991), 201–28. The chapter "Pornography, Ethnography, and the Discourses of Power" is actually coauthored with Christian Hansen and Catherine Needham and is a revised version of an article by the same three authors: "Skinflicks: Ethnography/Pornography and the Discourses of Power," *Discourse* 11, no. 2 (spring 1989): 65–79.

8 Foucault, *Discipline and Punish,* 215.

9 Raymond Corbey, "Ethnographic Showcases, 1870–1930," *Cultural Anthropology* 8, no. 3 (1993): 338–69.

10 John Berger, "Why Look at Animals," in *About Looking* (New York: Pantheon Books, 1980), 11.

11 Donna Haraway, *Primate Visions: Gender, Race, and Nature in the World of Modern Science* (New York: Routledge, 1989), 11.

12 Linda Williams, *Hard Core: Power Pleasure and the "Frenzy of the Visible"* (Berkeley: University of California Press, 1989), 34. Foucault uses the term *scientia sexualis* in *The History of Sexuality,* vol. 1, *An Introduction,* trans. Robert Hurley (New York: Pantheon Books, 1978), 51–73.

13 Williams, *Hard Core,* 36.

14 P. Adams Sitney, *Visionary Film: The American Avant-Garde, 1943–1978,* 2d ed. (New York: Oxford University Press, 1979), 369.

15 Peter Kubelka, "The Theory of Metrical Film," in *The Avant-Garde Film: A*

Reader of Theory and Criticism, ed. P. Adams Sitney (New York: New York University Press, 1978), 158. Kubelka's use of the soundtrack was informed by Dziga Vertov as well as the Viennese composers Webern and Schoenberg.

16 P. Adams Sitney, "The Standing Ovation: The Recognition of Peter Kubelka," unpublished paper in Anthology Film Archives documentation library, 10.

17 Elena Pinto Simon also notes, with some surprise, that "there is even a vague invitation to various social statements implied in the content of the frame, which can de-emphasize the filmic event itself." Elena Pinto Simon, "The Films of Peter Kubelka," *Art Forum* 10 (April 1972): 43.

18 Peter Kubelka, interview by Jonas Mekas, *Film Culture* 44 (spring 1967): 43.

19 Rosalind Krauss, *The Optical Unconscious* (Cambridge: MIT Press, 1993).

20 Sitney says that Kubelka was "an Austrian filmmaker and an American theoretician" ("The Standing Ovation," 8). He lived in the United States periodically during the 1960s and 1970s, teaching at New York University, SUNY Binghamton, San Francisco State University, and Middlebury College, and also presented his films and film theory on numerous occasions in New York and elsewhere.

21 Robert Breer, interview with Scott MacDonald, *A Critical Cinema 2: Interviews with Independent Filmmakers* (Berkeley: University of California Press, 1992), 39; Kubelka, interview by Mekas, 44.

22 Nichols, *Representing Reality,* 223.

23 Ibid., 223–24.

24 Gilles Deleuze and Félix Guattari, *Anti-Oedipus: Capitalism and Schizophrenia,* trans. Robert Hurley, Mark Seem, and Helen R. Lane (Minneapolis: University of Minnesota Press, 1992).

25 Vivian Sobchack, "Inscribing Ethical Space: Ten Propositions on Death, Representation, and Documentary," *Quarterly Review of Film Studies* (fall 1984).

26 For André Bazin, documented death in film is obscene. As the mechanical reproduction of the singular event, it challenges the redemptive capacity of cinema. Death is the sign of history that intrudes on the eternal nature of filmic realism. "Mort tous les aprés-midi," *Qu'est-ce que le cinema? 1. Ontologie et langage* (Paris: Éditions du cerf, 1969).

27 The term "frenzy of the visible" is Linda Williams's. She describes the hardcore knowledge-pleasure produced by the *scientia sexualis* of the very conception of cinema with Muybridge as "neither an aberration nor an excess.... The desire to see and know more of the human body . . . underlies the very invention of cinema" (36).

28 Kubelka, interview by Mekas, 45.

29 Kubelka, "Theory of Metrical Film," 140.

30 Walter Benjamin, *Illuminations,* ed. Hannah Arendt, trans. Harry Zohn (New York: Schocken Books, 1969), 256.

31 Kubelka, "Theory of Metrical Film," 158.

32 Benjamin, *Illuminations,* 217–52.

33 Ali Behdad, *Belated Travelers: Orientalism in the Age of Colonial Dissolution* (Durham, N.C.: Duke University Press, 1994).

34 Behdad argues that Orientalist discourse is in a process of continual transformation, constantly recuperating those strategies designed to counter its formation. The slippage and discontinuities produced by the belated traveler's discourse are reinscribed within an economy of "continual variation" (17).

35 *Microcultural Incidents* has two parts. The first presents the edited zoo footage and is about twenty minutes long; in the second, ten-minute section, Birdwhistell describes his technique in more detail. The second part begins with Birdwhistell's talking-head address, in which he describes his technique as a "record of observation," and "an experimental film of experimental filming." This is followed by a scene shot in a Paris café, shot by Birdwhistell's cameraman, Van Flack. Van Flack explains in voice-over that he didn't notice the "pickup" at a newsstand that he shot through the café window, but in slow motion, we can see what Birdwhistell saw, a woman touching a man with whom she then walks off. The footage of Paris looks like a scene straight out of the French New Wave. In Van Flack's monologue, he admits to his inferiority to Birdwhistell, the psychologist and master viewer, in a bizarre revelation of academic hierarchies.

36 The final film is probably an edited version of the original lecture, as no actual rewinding is included.

37 Hollis Frampton describes another Birdwhistell film, *The Age of a Baby,* as an example of the ability of cinematic vision to see more than the naked eye. Birdwhistell analyzes the contradictory signals given by a mother to her baby by analyzing filmed activity on a frame-by-frame basis. "If there is a monster hiding here, it has cunningly concealed itself within time, emerging, in Birdwhistell's film, on four frames . . . that is, for only one-sixth of a second." *Circles of Confusion: Film, Photography, Video Texts, 1968–1980* (Rochester: Visual Workshop Press, 1983), 103.

38 Bill Nichols, *Ideology and the Image: Social Representation in the Cinema and Other Media* (Bloomington: Indiana University Press, 1981), 238.

39 Desmond Morris, *The Human Zoo* (New York: McGraw-Hill, 1969), 246.

40 For a history of the silent adventure-travel film, see Kevin Brownlow, *The War, the West, and the Wilderness* (New York: Alfred A. Knopf, 1979).

41 For a history of the Johnsons, see Pascal James Imperato and Eleanor M. Imperato, *They Married Adventure: The Wandering Lives of Martin and Osa Johnson* (New Brunswick, N.J.: Rutgers University Press, 1992). The title refers to Osa's 1942 publication *I Married Adventure,* written after Martin's death in 1937.

42 One indication of the fate of the adventure-travel genre is provided by the Johnsons' contemporaries Ernest Schoedstack and Merian Cooper, who made *Grass* in 1925, *Chang* in 1927, and *King Kong* in 1933. Whereas *Grass* lacked a narrative framework for its spectacular documentary imagery, *King*

Kong resorted to fantasy entirely, and *Chang* is like *In the Land of the Head-hunters* in its use of native people and locations for a dramatic script.

43 Haraway, *Primate Visions,* 45.

44 Ibid. Haraway's source is the October 1923 prospectus to the AMNH microfilm 1114a.

45 Imperato and Imperato, *They Married Adventure,* 142.

46 The Imperatos note that there are five different versions of *Simba* at the AMNH, varying in length, some tinted and some with musical soundtracks (268).

47 Mary Ann Doane, "Dark Continents: Epistemologies of Racial and Sexual Difference in Psychoanalysis and the Cinema," in *Femmes Fatales: Feminism, Film Theory, Psychoanalysis* (New York: Routledge, 1991), 230.

48 Ibid., 231.

49 Haraway, *Primate Visions,* 55.

50 Ibid., 41.

51 This scene of the zebra being photographed is echoed fifty-eight years later in *I Do Not Know What It Is I Am Like*'s flash-frame sequence of a zebra photo shoot. Zebras also appear in *Unsere Afrikareise* (dead) and in *Sans Soleil* (stuffed and copulating—see chapter 10). The pattern of zebra skin provides spectacular cinematic material; it is a form of "found modernism," graphic abstraction found in the wild.

52 Benjamin, *Illuminations,* 262; "N [Theoretics of Knowledge; Theory of Progress]," translation of *Passagen-Werk* by Leigh Hafrey and Richard Sieburth, *Benjamin: Philosophy, Aesthetics, History,* ed. Gary Smith (Chicago: University of Chicago Press, 1983), 64.

53 I've borrowed the phrase "looking for lesbians" straight from Chris Holmlund's article "Fractured Fairytales and Experimental Identities: Looking for Lesbians in and around the Films of Su Friedrich," *Discourse* 17, no. 1 (fall 1994): 16–46. It was written before *Hide and Seek* was made, anticipating Friedrich's indirect and unique approach to lesbian representation in this film.

54 Ibid., 33.

55 "My Life with the Lions" is a Joy Adamson film, another scenario of a woman among wild animals appealing to young girls.

56 Teresa de Lauretis, "Film and the Visible," in *How Do I Look? Queer Film and Video,* ed. Bad Object Choices (Seattle: Bay Press, 1991), 223–63.

57 Ibid., 237.

58 Foucault, *Discipline and Punish,* 292.

1 P. Adams Sitney, "Structural Film," *Film Culture* 47 (summer 1969): 1–10.

2 P. Adams Sitney, *Visionary Film: The American Avant-Garde, 1943–1978,* 2d ed. (New York: Oxford University Press, 1979), 370.

3 Peter Gidal, ed., *Structural Film Anthology* (London: British Film Institute, 1976); Malcolm Le Grice, *Abstract Film and Beyond* (Cambridge: MIT Press, 1977). Le Grice put a subsequent Derridean twist on his theory of structural film in *Materialist Film* (London: Routledge, 1989).

4 James notes that Sitney endowed structural film "with a quasi-spiritual motivation that enables him to situate it as the logical culmination of the visionary tradition through its capacity, not simply to record, but to induce extraordinary states of consciousness." *Allegories of Cinema: American Film in the Sixties* (Princeton, N.J.: Princeton University Press, 1989), 242 n.

5 Constance Penley, "The Avant-Garde and Its Imaginary," *Camera Obscura* 2 (fall 1977): 3–33. See also Constance Penley and Janet Bergstrom, "The Avant-Garde: History and Theories," *Screen* 19, no. 3 (autumn 1978).

6 Paul Arthur, "Structural Film: Revisions, New Versions, and the Artifact," *Millennium Film Journal* 1–2 (spring 1978): 12.

7 Jonathan Crary, "Modernizing Vision," in *Viewing Positions: Ways of Seeing Film,* ed. Linda Williams (New Brunswick, N.J.: Rutgers University Press, 1995), 34. Crary quotes Foucault from *Discipline and Punish,* 225.

8 Le Grice cites Catherine MacKinnon ("Men have sex with the image of women") to support his prescription for a film form that would make it impossible to construct identities (*Materialist Film,* 134).

9 The "pure cinema" aesthetic was attacked most notably by Peter Wollen, who designated it as a new post-Bazinian filmic ontology. Wollen pointed out that "materialism" is "inseparable from the problem of signification," and that in the negation of reproduction as a photographic property of the cinema, the materiality of the profilmic, of history, structuralist-materialist film ironically abandoned realism in its quest for a radical cinema. Peter Wollen, "Ontology and Materialism in Film," *Readings and Writings: Semiotic Counter-Strategies* (London: Verso, 1982), 204.

10 James, *Allegories of Cinema,* 268, 279.

11 Stephen Heath, "Repetition Time: Notes around 'Structural/Materialist Film,'" in *Questions of Cinema* (Bloomington: Indiana University Press, 1981).

12 The limitations of the terms "documentary" and "fiction" are most particularly related to the false opposition that they presuppose. Structural filmmakers frequently worked with "found fictions" from early cinema.

13 Paul Arthur has pointed out that Sitney's description of structural film varied quite a bit from 1969 to 1977, and that his definition of "shape" was never adequately pinned down. "Structural Film: Revisions, New Versions, and the Artifact. Part Two," *Millennium Film Journal* 4–5 (summer–fall 1979).

14 Annette Michelson's essay on Michael Snow suggested that experimental film might in fact make a contribution to the philosophy of consciousness: "Epistemological inquiry and cinematic experience converge, as it were, in reciprocal mimesis." "Toward Snow," in *The Avant-Garde Film: A Reader of Theory and Criticism,* ed. P. Adams Sitney (New York: New York University Press, 1978), 173.

15 In fact, as Paul Arthur has pointed out, "the unalloyed investigation of film's material substrate exists as a tiny chapter in the history of the American avant-garde and a not much larger episode in Structural Film's moment." "The Last of the Last Machine? Avant-Garde Film since 1966," *Millennium Film Journal* 16–18 (fall–winter 1986–1987): 81. In addition to the films and filmmakers discussed here, one could add Standish Lawder's *Necrology* (1970) and many of Hollis Frampton's films, which consistently investigate the construction of meaning in photographic images, as instances of experimental ethnography.

16 Stephen Tyler, "Post-Modern Ethnography: From Document of the Occult to Occult Document," in *Writing Culture: The Poetics and Politics of Ethnography,* ed. James Clifford and George E. Marcus (Berkeley: University of California Press, 1986), 137.

17 Steven Webster's analysis of postmodern ethnography is developed from the Benjamin-Adorno debate over the status of social content in aesthetic form. Webster's theory of ethnographic representation privileges the integration of textual form with social practice. If we understand the "social practice" of structural film to be on one level its self-imposed marginality and radical noninstrumentality (as James has suggested), and on another, the repressed "content" of the image, it does indeed embody such an integration. Steven Webster, "The Historical Materialist Critique of Surrealism and Postmodernist Ethnography," in *Modernist Anthropology: From Fieldwork to Text,* ed. Marc Manganaro (Princeton, N.J.: Princeton University Press, 1990), 266–99.

18 In the 1970s, Akerman became something of a *cause célèbre* among feminist film theorists for her ability to bridge the "two avant-gardes" described by Peter Wollen. The key article to position Akerman as the "answer" to the problem of avant-garde cinema as it was being canonized by Sitney and others was Constance Penley and Janet Bergstrom, "The Avant-Garde: History and Theories." They saw in *News from Home* the crucial posing of the question of "who speaks" and "a shifting of attention to the entire process of signification, rather than limiting it to the play of the signifier" (125–27).

19 Judith Mayne, *The Woman at the Keyhole: Feminism and Women's Cinema* (Bloomington: Indiana University Press, 1990), 184–222.

20 As a child of Jewish Polish émigrés to Belgium, Akerman certainly has an investment in the scene. Her desire to know is in fact linked to her self-knowledge, although this is not apparent from the film itself. See Ivone Margulies, *Nothing Happens: Chantal Akerman's Hyperrealist Everyday* (Durham, N.C.: Duke University Press, 1996), 202.

21 Michael Tarantino, "The Moving Eye: Notes on the Films of Chantal Akerman," in *Bordering on Fiction: Chantal Akerman's "D'Est"* (Minneapolis: Walker Art Center, 1995).

22 Margulies, *Nothing Happens,* 46.

23 Chantal Akerman, "On *D'Est,*" in *Bordering on Fiction,* 17.

24 Quoted in Catherine David, "*D'Est:* Akerman Variations," in *Bordering on Fiction,* 63. The installation was initially installed at the Walker Art Center in Minneapolis and consisted of three viewing chambers. The first had the full film of *D'Est;* the second, looped segments of the film on a multichannel setup; and the last, Akerman reading a biblical passage in Hebrew as well as her own writing on the film.

25 Margulies, *Nothing Happens,* 224.

26 Margulies makes this point regarding *D'Est* (203). *News from Home* bears the signs of the seventies in its fashions and cars, but it is a lived seventies, not a mythic seventies.

27 Sitney, *Visionary Film,* 373.

28 Thomas Waugh, "Cockteaser," in *Pop Out: Queer Warhol,* ed. Jennifer Doyle, Jonathan Flatley, and José Esteban Muñoz (Durham, N.C.: Duke University Press, 1996), 62.

29 Michael O'Pray, ed., *Andy Warhol: Film Factory* (London: British Film Institute, 1989), 186–88.

30 In his essay on Warhol, Paul Arthur also privileges *Kiss* and *Beauty #2.* They seem to be exemplary texts of the realist aspect of the Warhol oeuvre, serving as the most effective theoretical commentaries on the group of films as a whole.

31 Parker Tyler makes this point about *Kiss:* "The human subjects involuntarily betrayed that a sort of theater was present, a 'show' which felt obliged to sustain the 'interest.' " "Dragtime and Drugtime or Film à la Warhol," in O'Pray, *Andy Warhol: Film Factory,* 101.

32 Paul Arthur, "Flesh of Absence: Resighting the Warhol Catechism," in O'Pray, 150.

33 Gerard Malanga is usually credited with being behind the camera in *Beauty #2* (Arthur, 152), although there are no credits on the film itself.

34 David James, "The Producer as Author," in O'Pray, 144.

35 Arthur, in O'Pray, 152.

36 Tyler, in O'Pray, 98.

37 Arthur, in O'Pray, 152.

38 Gretchen Berg, "Nothing to Lose: An Interview with Andy Warhol," in O'Pray, 58.

39 Arthur, "Structural Film Part Two," 127.

40 Ibid.

41 The tightly structured scenario of the empowered gaze that is reproduced in *Real Italian Pizza* is a variation on that described by Foucault in "Las

Meninas." Michel Foucault, *The Order of Things: The Archeology of the Human Sciences* (New York: Vintage Books, 1973).

42 Rimmer has identified the location as the Upper West Side, around Eighty-fifth Street and Columbus. Rick Hancox claims to have spotted Rimmer himself eating pizza on the other side of the camera, suggesting a further breakdown of the voyeuristic setup. "Short Films," *Cinema Canada,* 2d ser., 14 (June–July 1974): 58–60.

43 Pam Cook, *"Pierre Vallières," Monthly Film Bulletin* (September 83): 256–57; Lauren Rabinowitz, "Radical Cinema," (Ph.D. diss., University of Texas at Austin, 1982), 215.

44 A good example of the development of structural film principles into narrative filmmaking is Jim Jarmusch's *Stranger than Paradise.* For an excellent account of the diversification of structural film, see Paul Arthur, "The Last of the Last Machine?"

45 James Benning, interview with Scott MacDonald, *A Critical Cinema 2: Interviews with Independent Filmmakers* (Berkeley: University of California Press, 1992), 246.

46 Ibid., 244.

47 Viola, "Selected Works and Writings," in *Bill Viola,* ed. Barbara London (New York: Museum of Modern Art, 1987), 39.

48 Michael Nash, "Bill Viola's Re-visions of Mortality," *High Performance* 37 (1987): 63.

49 The five segments of the tape are named only in the end credits and are not actually as distinct as this description might imply. It is not at all obvious, because of the transitional material and diversity of imagery within sections, where Viola's five subtitles might fall. Unlike the first three sections, which are clearly demarcated by fade-outs, the Fijian section is dissolved at both its beginning and its end. I am assuming that the prologue and epilogue, both set in the Canadian Rockies, are untitled.

50 John Berger, "Why Look at Animals," in *About Looking* (New York: Pantheon Books, 1980), 26.

51 Sean Cubitt, "Video Art and Colonialism: An Other and Its Others," *Screen* 30, no. 3 (autumn 1989): 68.

52 Bill Viola, "Selected Works and Writings," in London, *Bill Viola,* 23.

53 Walter Benjamin, *Illuminations,* trans. Harry Zohn, ed. Hannah Arendt (New York: Schocken Books, 1969), 241.

54 Ákos Östör, who coproduced the film with Gardner, uses the term "characters" to describe the three figures who reappear most frequently in the film. In his article *"Forest of Bliss:* Film and Anthropology," *East/West Film Journal* 8, no. 2 (July 1994): 70–104, he explains the "meaning" of the details of the film.

1 Bill Nichols, *Representing Reality: Issues and Concepts in Documentary* (Bloomington: Indiana University Press, 1991), 221.

2 Antonin Artaud, *The Theatre and Its Double,* trans. Mary Caroline Richards (New York: Grove Press, 1958), 60.

3 Ibid., 59.

4 Mick Eaton, "Chronicle," in *Anthropology/Reality/Cinema: The Films of Jean Rouch,* ed. Mick Eaton (London: British Film Institute, 1979), 6.

5 Vincent Crapanzano, introduction to *Case Studies in Spirit Possession,* ed. Vincent Crapanzano and Vivian Garrison (New York: John Wiley and Sons, 1977), 7.

6 In 1989 David Byrne made a video called *Ilê Aiyê* about Candomblé music in Bahia, featuring a possession ritual performed to African American rhythms.

7 Walter Benjamin, "On Some Motifs in Baudelaire," in *Illuminations,* ed. Hannah Arendt, trans. Harry Zohn (New York: Schocken Books, 1969), 173.

8 Ibid., 101.

9 Vincent Crapanzano, "The Moment of Prestidigitation: Magic, Illusion, and Mana in the Thought of Emile Durkheim and Marcel Mauss," in *Prehistories of the Future: The Primitivist Project and the Culture of Modernism,* ed. Elazar Barkan and Ronald Bush (Stanford: Stanford University Press, 1995), 101. The Mauss text to which he refers is *Esquisse d'une théorie général de la magie,* originally published in 1902–1903.

10 Crapanzano, "The Moment of Prestidigitation," 103.

11 Robert Nye, "Savage Crowds, Modernism, and Modern Politics," in Barkan and Bush, *Prehistories of the Future,* 42–55. Freud's "Group Psychology and the Analysis of the Ego," published in 1921, is another example of the convergence of psychology and sociology in the early part of the century. For Freud, the group was basically a mass or a crowd, the behavior of which he believed was a natural continuity of the individual ego and could be analyzed according to similar principles.

12 Crapanzano, "The Moment of Prestidigitation," 103, quoting Mauss from *Esquisse,* 56.

13 The Christian tradition has its own imagery of possession (and indeed its own possession cults), including Bernini's statue of St. Theresa, of which Lacan notes, "And what is her *jouissance,* her *coming* from? It is clear that the essential testimony of the mystics is that they are experiencing it but know nothing about it." The mystical, for Lacan, is not "not political" just because it is sexual; and it is a politics of representation, the articulation of subjectivity as a form of knowledge, that is invested in the image of the possessed. Jacques Lacan, *Feminine Sexuality,* ed. Juliet Mitchell and Jacqueline Rose, trans. Jacqueline Rose (New York: W. W. Norton, 1985), 147.

14 Peter Brooks, *The Melodramatic Imagination: Balzac, Henry James, Melo-*

drama, and the Mode of Excess (New York: Columbia University Press, 1984), 199.

15 Michel Foucault, *Madness and Civilization: A History of Insanity in the Age of Reason,* trans. Richard Howard (New York: Random House, 1965), 94.

16 Patrick Laughney, in a presentation at the opening of the Margaret Mead Film Festival at the Museum of Natural History, 8 November 1996.

17 Margaret Mead and Gregory Bateson, *Balinese Character: A Photographic Analysis* (New York: New York Academy of Sciences, 1942), xvi.

18 Andrew Lakoff, "Freezing Time: Margaret Mead's Diagnostic Photography," *Visual Anthropology Review* 12, no. 1 (spring 1996): 1–18.

19 Lakoff points out that by 1951, "schizophrenia" had replaced "dementia praecox" as a diagnostic label, and the existence of a "dementia praecox" committee in 1951 is a bit strange (1).

20 Mead and Bateson, *Balinese Character,* 47–48.

21 The most thorough critique is Gordon D. Jensen and Luh Ketut Suryani's *The Balinese People: A Reinvestigation of Character* (Singapore: Oxford University Press, 1992). The authors critique Mead and Bateson's analytical methods, as well as their use of psychoanalytic concepts, and correct many of their basic assumptions about the culture; they also offer their own anthropological assessment of some of the phenomena, including trance, that Mead and Bateson cover. See also Tessel Pollman, "Margaret Mead's Balinese," *Indonesia* 49 (April 1990).

22 In the 1930s, Bali had already become a popular destination for bohemians and artists from the West in search of an alternative to industrial capitalism. Mead and Bateson lived and worked within this community, and actually sparked a cultural revival in Bali (Ira Jacknis, "Margaret Mead and Gregory Bateson in Bali: Their Use of Photography and Film," *Cultural Anthropology* 3, no. 2 [May 1988]: 163). Their innovations in visual anthropology are introduced (in *Balinese Character*) as an attempt to translate into science something that is much more easily "caught" by the artist (xi).

23 Gilles Deleuze and Félix Guattari, *Anti-Oedipus: Capitalism and Schizophrenia,* trans. Robert Hurley, Mark Seem, and Helen R. Lane (Minneapolis: University of Minnesota Press, 1983), 167.

24 Mead and Bateson, *Balinese Character,* xvi.

25 Deleuze and Guattari, 151.

26 Lakoff suggests that the availability of funding from the Committee for Research in Dementia Praecox inspired the whole trip to Bali ("Freezing Time," 14 n. 2); see also Mead's *Letters from the Field, 1925–1975* (New York: Harper and Row, 1977), 53.

27 Jensen and Suryani, *The Balinese People,* 61. They cite Clifford Geertz's work on Bali, *Person, Time, and Conduct in Bali: An Essay in Cultural Analyses* (New Haven: Yale Southeast Asia Studies, 1966).

28 Jensen and Suryani, *The Balinese People,* 47.

29 The dances were filmed on 16 December 1937 and 8 February 1939 in the village of Pagoetan (Jacknis, "Margaret Mead," 171).

30 The combination of the two plays—the witch play called *Rangda* or *Tjalonarang* and the dragon play called *Barong*—results in a narrative that Mead and Bateson interpret as a symbolic family drama. The witch is unambiguously a mother, and the dragon is a father (*Balinese Character,* 164). This is a point about which Jensen and Suryani are particularly skeptical, finding no evidence of such an interpretation in Balinese culture. The witch and dragon figures represent the powers of gods who are held in awe, not feared as Mead suggests (80).

31 Jacknis, "Margaret Mead," 168.

32 Mead and Bateson's footage is far more extensive than "the film" labeled *Trance and Dance in Bali.* The version I am referring to is available on video from the Penn State University Audio Visual Department. For the anthropologists, "raw film" constitutes a set of field notes that are as valuable to them as an edited film is to an avant-garde filmmaker. For Mead and Bateson, the many versions of their Balinese footage are merely packages for the film that can still be viewed on "original" reels at the Library of Congress.

33 Jacknis, "Margaret Mead," 164.

34 Margaret Mead, "Visual Anthropology in a Discipline of Words," in *Principles of Visual Anthropology,* 2d ed., ed. Paul Hockings (New York: Mouton de Gruyter, 1995), 8.

35 Lakoff, "Freezing Time," 4–6.

36 "Margaret Mead and Gregory Bateson on the Use of the Camera in Anthropology," *Studies in the Anthropology of Visual Communication* 4, no. 2 (winter 1977).

37 Jacknis, "Margaret Mead," 171.

38 Mead and Bateson, *Balinese Character,* 36.

39 Deren, *Divine Horsemen: The Living Gods of Haiti* (1953; reprint, Kingston, N.Y.: Documentext, 1991), 6.

40 Lucy Fischer, "Maya Deren's Haiti Footage," *Field of Vision* 7 (summer 1979).

41 P. Adams Sitney, *Visionary Film: The American Avant-Garde, 1943–1978,* 2d ed. (New York: Oxford University Press, 1979), 11.

42 Maya Deren, "Cinematography: The Creative Use of Reality," in *The Avant-Garde Film: A Reader of Theory and Criticism,* ed. P. Adams Sitney (New York: New York University Press, 1978).

43 Maria Pramaggiore, "Performance and Persona in the U.S. Avant-Garde: The Case of Maya Deren," *Cinema Journal* 36, no. 2 (winter 1997): 19.

44 Maya Deren, "Notes on Ritual and Ordeal," *Film Culture,* no. 39 (winter 1965): 10, quoted in Pramaggiore, "Performance and Persona," 27.

45 Pramaggiore, "Performance and Persona," 27.

46 Ibid.

47 "The crowd" is represented in *Ritual in Transfigured Time* as a claustropho-

bic, superficial cocktail party in which a couple meet and dance into an open space; the collective and the crowd are symbols and metaphors of psychic states in Deren's poetics.

48 Stan Brakhage, *Film at Wit's End: Eight Avant-Garde Filmmakers* (New York, McPherson, 1989), 104–5, 108.

49 Deren mentions the political context of voodoo briefly in "Religious Possession in Dancing" (485). For an account of this history, see David Nicholls, *From Dessalines to Duvalier: Race, Color, and National Independence in Haiti* (Cambridge: Cambridge University Press, 1979), 31, 170.

50 Deren, *Divine Horsemen*, 62.

51 Deren-Bateson correspondence, 1946–1947, reprinted in "Art and Anthropology," *October* 14 (1980).

52 Maya Deren, "Notebook," reprinted in "Art and Anthropology," *October* 14 (1980): 27.

53 Deren, "Notebook," 29–30.

54 Brakhage, *Film at Wit's End,* 112. Brakhage's claim has not been substantiated.

55 Deren, *Divine Horsemen*, 8.

56 Maya Deren, "Religious Possession in Dancing," originally published in 1942 in *Educational Dance,* reprinted in *The Legend of Maya Deren,* vol. 1, pt. 1, "Signatures, 1917–42," ed. Vèvè A. Clark, Millicent Hodson, and Catrina Neiman (New York: Anthology Film Archives, 1984), 491.

57 Ibid., 488.

58 Ibid., 496.

59 Deren, "Notebook," 24.

60 Ibid., 21.

61 Deren, "Religious Possession in Dancing," 482.

62 Neiman discusses the influence of Deren's father, who was a psychiatrist, on Deren's exploration of psychic phenomena. Catrina Neiman, *The Legend of Maya Deren,* vol. 1, pt. 2, "Chambers, 1942–47," ed. Millicent Hodson (New York: Anthology Film Archives, 1988), 108–9.

63 Deren, "Religious Possession in Dancing," 487.

64 Deren, *Divine Horsemen,* 259. The description continues for a page and a half, followed by a long footnote discussing the authenticity of the possession. Deren concludes that its authenticity was approved by those who witnessed it, although she points out that such discussions tend to "discuss the actions of a *loa* in great detail without thinking to make a single reference as to whose head that *loa* had entered." It is not customary to refer to "my possession by such and such a *loa*" in a proprietary manner (322 n).

65 This quotation from the film soundtrack is in *Divine Horsemen,* 112.

66 Deren, *Divine Horsemen,* 216.

67 Ibid., 102.

68 Deren, "Religious Possession in Dancing," 488.

69 Riefenstahl's Nuba footage has not been edited or released. A few scenes are reproduced in Ray Muller's *The Wonderful Horrible Life of Leni Riefenstahl*

(1993), including images of Riefenstahl herself surrounded by dancing Africans.

70 Walter Benjamin, "The Mimetic Faculty," in *Reflections: Essays, Aphorisms, Autobiographical Writings,* trans. Edmund Jephcott, ed. Peter Demetz (New York: Schocken Books, 1986), 334.

71 Antonin Artaud, "Witchcraft and the Cinema," in *Collected Works,* vol. 3, trans. Alastair Hamilton (1949; London: Calder and Boyars, 1972), 66.

72 Jean Rouch, "On the Vicissitudes of the Self: The Possessed Dancer, the Magician, the Sorcerer, the Filmmaker, and the Ethnographer," trans. Steve Feld and Shari Robertson, *Studies in the Anthropology of Visual Communication* 5, no. 1 (fall 1978): 3.

73 Rouch's books on the Songhay include *Le Niger en pirogue* (1954), *Les Songhay* (1954), *Rapport sur les migrations nigériennes vers la basse Côte d'Ivoire* (1957), and *La religion et la magie Songhay* (1960, 1989).

74 Rouch, "On the Vicissitudes of the Self," 7–8.

75 "Conversation between Jean Rouch and Professor Enrico Fulchignoni," trans. Anny Ewing and Steven Feld, *Visual Anthropology* 2, nos. 3–4 (December 1989): 272.

76 Rouch, "On the Vicissitudes of the Self," 8.

77 Michael Taussig, "Physiognomic Aspects of Visual Worlds," *Visualizing Theory: Selected Essays from V.A.R., 1990–1994,* ed. Lucien Taylor (New York: Routledge, 1994), 212.

78 Dan Yakir, "Ciné-transe: The Vision of Jean Rouch," interview, *Film Quarterly* 31 (spring 1978): 7–8; and Jeannette De Bouzek, "The 'Ethnographic Surrealism' of Jean Rouch," *Visual Anthropology* 2, no. 34 (1989): 304–5. De Bouzek's article is based on an interview with Rouch conducted in May 1988.

79 Rouch, "On the Vicissitudes of the Self," 7.

80 De Bouzek, "Ethnographic Surrealism," 307.

81 There is some disagreement about the title and date of this film. Mike Eaton's filmography dates the film as 1967 (in *Anthropology/Reality/Cinema: The Films of Jean Rouch,* ed. Mike Eaton (London: British Film Institute, 1979). Paul Stoller lists the film as *Les tambours d'avant: Turu et bitti* and dates it as 1971.

82 Eaton, "The Production of Cinematic Reality," in *Anthropology/Reality/Cinema,* 52.

83 Michel Marie, "Direct," in Eaton, *Anthropology/Reality/Cinema,* 35–39.

84 De Bouzek, "Ethnographic Surrealism," 307.

85 Paul Stoller, *The Cinematic Griot: The Ethnography of Jean Rouch* (Chicago: University of Chicago Press, 1992), 153.

86 Paul Stoller, "Artaud, Rouch, and the Cinema of Cruelty," in Taylor, *Visualizing Theory,* 90.

87 Teshome H. Gabriel, *Third Cinema in the Third World: The Aesthetics of Liberation* (Ann Arbor: UMI Research Press, 1982), 75–77.

88 Yakir, "Ciné-transe," 3.

89 Eaton, "The Production of Cinematic Reality," 6.

90 De Bouzek, "Ethnographic Surrealism," 310.

91 Stoller, *Cinematic Griot,* 154.

92 Fulchignoni, "Conversation," 279. Taussig claims that Rouch was afraid the participants would be provoked into an uncontrollable trance: "It's a kind of electroshock," he said, "to show a man a film of himself in trance." *Mimesis and Alterity: A Particular History of the Senses* (New York: Routledge, 1993), 243.

93 Rouch, quoted by Stoller, *Cinematic Griot,* 83.

94 De Bouzek, "Ethnographic Surrealism," 308.

95 Although Stoller describes this montage passage as Vertovian (*Cinematic Griot,* 152), it is much more Eisensteinian because it is dialectical, comparative, and of all the variations of dialectical montage, "intellectual" as Eisenstein describes it. Sergei Eisenstein, *Film Form: Essays in Film Theory,* trans. Jay Leyda (New York: Harcourt, Brace and World, 1949), 62. Taussig describes this passage as exemplary of cinematic magic, an instance of the flowering of primitivism within modernism, "the Western rebirth of the mimetic faculty" (*Mimesis and Alterity,* 242).

96 Peter Brooks, *Reading for the Plot: Design and Intention in Narrative* (New York: Vintage Books, 1984), 111.

97 Steven Feld, "Themes in the Cinema of Jean Rouch," *Visual Anthropology* 2, nos. 3–4 (December 1989): 225.

98 Stoller argues that not only *Les Maîtres fous* but many other of Rouch's films are instances of a cinema of cruelty in "Artaud, Rouch, and the Cinema of Cruelty."

99 Artaud, *The Theatre and Its Double,* 86.

100 Artaud, *Collected Works,* vol. 3, 60.

101 Artaud, *The Theatre and Its Double,* 49.

102 Rouch, "On the Vicissitudes of the Self," 6.

103 Homi Bhabha, *The Location of Culture* (New York: Routledge, 1994), 87.

104 "In photography, exhibition value begins to displace cult value all along the line" (Benjamin, "The Work of Art in the Age of Mechanical Reproduction," in *Illuminations,* 225).

105 The poster lists four movies, *The Set-Up* (Robert Wise, 1949), *Holiday in Havana* (Yarbrough, 1949, with Desi Arnaz), and *Cattle Stampede* and *Mark of Zorro* (probably Mamoulian, 1940, with Tyrone Power), but Rouch takes note only of the last, a remake of the Douglas Fairbanks swashbuckler of 1920.

106 Dennis Young has argued that *Les Maîtres fous* successfully achieves a schizophrenic scene of "group fantasy" as described by Deleuze and Guattari. Whereas this is possibly very true of the Hauka ritual itself, Young does not discuss Rouch's film as a text or a representation of the ritual. "Ethnographic Surreality, Possession, and the Unconscious," *Visual Anthropology* 7 (n.d.): 191–297.

107 The tape itself includes only a final credit for the Maha Devi temple in Suva, Fiji, and the name of the chief priest as explanation for the *puja*.

108 Artaud, *The Theatre and Its Double*, 102.

109 Ethnopoetics is the common ground of art and anthropology, but without the transgressive violence of Artaud, Girard, Buñuel, or Bataille, it can be only a passive universal humanism. *The Symposium of the Whole: A Range of Discourses Towards an Ethnopoetics* is an anthology edited by Jerome and Diane Rothenberg following a 1975 gathering at the Center for Twentieth Century Studies in Milwaukee. Although many of the collected texts are very interesting, as the title suggests, the humanistic thrust of the collection is toward the breaking down of cultural differences and a holistic conception of "man."

110 The money collected from tourists goes to the maintenance of the temple. Carolyn Henning Brown, "Tourism and Ethnic Competition in a Ritual Form," *Oceania* 54, no. 3 (March 1984): 224.

111 Adrian C. Mayer, *Peasants in the Pacific: A Study of Fiji Indian Ritual Society* (London: Routledge and Kegan Paul, 1961), 93.

112 A leaflet distributed to the spectators explains, in English, the purpose of the ritual: "The devotees feel that their body is the seat of the Supreme Mother. At the time of the walking on fire, they are not body-conscious. They are conscious only of the Divine Mother and identify their Spirit with Her. Is it a wonder then that the fire does not burn them, nor even leave a blister on their feet?" The pamphlet is authored by a Brahman from Madras, quoted in Brown, "Tourism," 228.

113 In the 1960s, it was said that Northern Indians who attempted to enter the procession failed because their bodies could not withstand the whipping (Mayer, *Peasants in the Pacific*, 93). Although the Fijians have their own aboriginal tradition of walking on hot coals, it is restricted to those of a certain lineage, whereas "any Indian who has faith in Devi can do it" (Brown, "Tourism," 242).

114 Brown, 223–25.

115 Ibid., 243.

116 Ibid., 240.

117 Raymond Bellour has developed the parallels between "the cinema-effect" and hypnosis, which he claims is a closer level of simulation than that of the dream. "Alternation, Segmentation, Hypnosis: Interview with Raymond Bellour," *Camera Obscura* 3–4 (1979): 101.

118 In Fredric Jameson's account of the schizophrenic character of postmodernism, he argues that schizophrenia is the "breakdown of the relation between signifiers." Words and images become material and literal, detached from their signified meanings. He interprets this as a form of loss, despite the "hallucinogenic intensification" that might be produced in the process. Fredric Jameson, "Postmodernism and Consumer Society," *The Anti-*

Aesthetic: Essays on Postmodern Culture, ed. Hal Foster (Port Townsend, Wash.: Bay Press, 1983), 120.

119 Deleuze and Guattari, *Anti-Oedipus,* 30.

120 See I. M. Lewis, *Ecstatic Religion: An Anthropological Study of Spirit Possession and Shamanism* (London: Penguin, 1971).

9 Archival Apocalypse

1 I'd like to thank Paul Arthur for this point.

2 Andreas Huyssen, *After the Great Divide: Modernism, Mass Culture, Postmodernism* (Bloomington: Indiana University Press, 1986), 15.

3 Andreas Huyssen, *Twilight Memories: Marking Time in a Culture of Amnesia* (New York: Routledge, 1995).

4 William C. Wees, *Recycled Images* (New York: Anthology Film Archives, 1993), 34.

5 Ibid., 45. The Michael Jackson video that Wees describes is *The Man in the Mirror* (1987).

6 Craig Owens, "The Allegorical Impulse: Toward a Theory of Postmodernism," in *Art after Modernism: Rethinking Representation*, ed. Brian Wallis (New York: New Museum of Contemporary Art, 1984), 208.

7 Ibid., 214.

8 The term "inauthentic art" is from James Clifford's Greimasian "semiotic square" in which he maps an art-culture system of authenticity, inauthenticity, masterpieces, and artifacts. Experimental ethnography clearly circulates within this conceptual machine that moves objects between the terms of art, culture, and their negations, not-art and not-culture. If experimental and ethnographic film occupy the top half of Clifford's grid, as "art" and "culture" respectively, video and TV documentary might occupy the lower half, as the "new and uncommon" not-culture and the "reproduced and commercial" not-art respectively. Scratch video would then be located between these two points as the epitome of the "inauthentic." *The Predicament of Culture: Twentieth Century Ethnography, Literature, and Art* (Cambridge: Harvard University Press, 1988), 224.

9 Patricia Zimmerman discusses a corpus of found-footage films that mobilize the historiography of archival practices. These films include Laura Kipnis's *Ecstasy Unlimited* (1985), Fernando Solanas's *Hour of the Furnaces* (1968), Eduardo Coutinho's *20 Years Later* (1984), Martha Haslanger's *Revolution* (1979–1983), and Pierre Gorin's *Routine Pleasures* (1986). Zimmerman compares these works to the "adventure" aesthetics promoted by a 1987 PBS documentary series, arguing that these texts offer an adventurous detour through the terrain of discursive history. "Revolutionary Pleasures: Wrecking the Text in Compilation Documentary," *Afterimage* 16, no. 8 (1969). See

also my essay, "David Rimmer's Found Footage: Reproduction and Repetition of History," *CineAction!* (spring 1989): 52–58.

10 Debord's films include *Hurlements en faveur de Sade* (1952), *Sur le passage de quelque personnes à travers une assez courte unité de temps* (1959), *Critique de la séparation* (1961), *La Société du Spectacle* (1973), *Réfutation de tous les jugements, tant élogieux qu'hostiles, qui ont été jusqu'ici portés sur le film 'La Société du Spectacle'* (1975), and *In Girium* (1978). Thomas Y. Levin, "Dismantling the Spectacle: The Cinema of Guy Debord," in *On the Passage of a Few People through a Rather Brief Period in Time: The Situationist International, 1957–1972,* ed. Elizabeth Sussman (Cambridge: MIT Press, 1991), 72–123.

11 Scott Bukatman, *Terminal Identity: The Virtual Subject in Postmodern Science Fiction* (Durham, N.C.: Duke University Press, 1993), 157.

12 Another film that engages with the archive as science fiction is Peter Greenaway's *The Falls* (1975), a film that uses some found footage along with false documentary footage of the fictional survivors of the VUE (violent unknown event). The postapocalyptic space of the film looks and sounds very much like 1970s England, as do his interviewees. As social actors, they are doubled as utterly banal "ordinary British people" and survivors who are gradually mutating into birds. The film thus enacts an allegory of transcendence in which ethnographic representation—the bodies in the film/the bodies of the film—becomes an excess of reality, a parallel universe to the fiction of the end of history.

13 Abigail Child, interview in Wees, *Recycled Images,* 77.

14 David James, *Allegories of Cinema: American Film in the Sixties* (Princeton, N.J.: Princeton University Press, 1989), 28.

15 Dana Polan, *Power and Paranoia: History, Narrative, and the American Cinema, 1940–1950* (New York: Columbia University Press, 1986).

16 Sharon Sandusky, "The Archeology of Redemption: Toward Archival Film," *Millennium Film Journal,* no. 26 (fall 1992): 6.

17 Leslie Thornton, "We Ground Things Now, on a Moving Earth," *Motion Picture* 3, nos. 1–2 (winter 1989–1990): 15.

18 Ibid.

19 See Thornton's interview in Wees, *Recycled Images,* 98.

20 Walter Benjamin, *Charles Baudelaire: A Lyric Poet in the Era of High Capitalism,* trans. Harry Zohn (London: Verso, 1983), 115–17.

21 Mary Ann Doane, "Temporality, Storage, Legibility: Freud, Marey, and the Cinema," *Critical Inquiry* 22 (winter 1996): 323.

22 Ibid., 343.

23 Wees, *Recycled Images,* 80.

24 Rosalind Krauss, "The Originality of the Avant-Garde: A Postmodern Repetition," in *Art after Modernism: Rethinking Representation,* ed. Brian Wallis (New York: New Museum of Contemporary Art, 1984), 13–30.

25 Bill Wees has suggested to me that this imagery is almost certainly from fa-

mous footage of Italian fascists who were executed by Italian partisans and hung upside down in the central square of Milan. Although it is always tempting to trace the sources of images in found-footage films, the effect of the images is precisely due to the unknown status of the sources, which is what provokes the images' radical ambiguity.

26 Mary Ann Doane, "Information, Crisis, Catastrophe," in *Logics of Television: Essays in Cultural Criticism,* ed. Patricia Mellencamp (Bloomington: Indiana University Press, 1990), 223.

27 Ibid., 232.

28 P. T. Saunders, *An Introduction to Catastrophe Theory* (Cambridge: Cambridge University Press, 1980), 1; quoted in Doane, "Information," 234.

29 This image of people who may be pygmies with the dead elephant is not unlike the Comerio footage in *From the Pole to the Equator* and, in its violence, also evokes Kubelka's imagery in *Unsere Africareise.*

30 Huyssen, *Twilight Memories,* 90.

31 Paul de Man, "The Rhetoric of Temporality," in *Critical Theory since 1965,* ed. Hazard Adams and Leroy Searle (Tallahassee: University Press of Florida, 1986), 202, 218.

32 Benjamin, *Charles Baudelaire,* 114.

33 Huyssen, *Twilight Memories,* 94.

34 Ibid., 90.

35 Wees, *Recycled Images,* 38.

36 Huyssen describes the MAD program as "the inherent absurdity and danger of technological progress and the politics of deterrence, or, in aesthetically coded terms, the dialectical closeness of chance and determination" (204).

37 Huyssen, *Twilight Memories,* 204.

38 This is, for Owens, "one of the fundamental strategies of allegory, and through it the symbolic is revealed for what it truly is—a rhetorical manipulation of metaphor which attempts to program response" ("Allegorical Impulse," 232).

39 Huyssen, *Twilight Memories,* 201.

40 Allan Sekula, "Reading an Archive," in *Blasted Allegories: An Anthology of Writings by Contemporary Artists,* ed. Brian Wallis (Cambridge: MIT Press, 1989), 122.

41 Ibid., 127.

42 Bill Nichols, *Blurred Boundaries: Questions of Meaning in Contemporary Culture* (Bloomington: Indiana University Press, 1994), 129.

43 The same disaster appears in the found-footage segment of *I Do Not Know What It Is I Am Like,* along with another selection of apocalyptic imagery. Viola also includes glimpses of various cultural rituals and a photo shoot of a zebra in this part of the tape, which eventually dissolves to a strobe light pulsating from the video monitor. One of the effects of relocating the collage form to video is the sense of it being the memory of the television itself.

44 Baldwin uses newsreel footage much more extensively in *RocketKitKongo-Kit* (1986) as a means of representing Africans caught up within a historical apparatus of power and paranoia centered around the leader of Zaire, Joseph Mobutu, and the omnipresent CIA.

45 Johannes Fabian writes: "Time is involved in any possible relationship between anthropological discourse and its referents." *Time and the Other: How Anthropology Makes Its Object* (New York: Columbia University Press, 1983), 28.

46 The term "Black," although out of fashion in North American critical discourse, tends to be used in British cultural studies to refer to people of both Asian and African descent. As Coco Fusco notes, the term expresses "a common social, political and economic experience of race that cuts across original cultures." Coco Fusco, "A Black Avant-Garde? Notes on Black Audio Film Collective and Sankofa," in *Young, British, and Black,* ed. Coco Fusco (Buffalo, N.Y.: Hallwalls, 1988), 9.

47 Ibid., 11.

48 Coco Fusco, "Interview with Black Audio Film Collective: John Akomfrah, Lina Gopaul, Avril Johnson, and Reece Auguste," in *Young, British, and Black,* 51.

49 The most notorious of these critiques was Salmon Rushdie's review of Handsworth Songs published in *The Guardian* and reprinted in Fusco's monograph (58–59).

50 Fusco, 19.

51 Huyssen, *Twilight Memories,* 33.

52 Michael Walsh, "Handsworth Songs: Rehabilitating the Real," unpublished paper, 6.

53 Stuart Hall, "Cultural Identity and Cinematic Representation," *Framework* 36 (1989): 70.

54 See Alan Sekula, "The Body and the Archive," *October* 39 (1986).

55 Joel Katz, "From Archive to Archiveology," *Cinematographe* 4 (1991): 99.

10 Autoethnography

1 Walter Benjamin, "A Berlin Chronicle," in *Reflections: Essays, Aphorisms, Autobiographical Writings,* trans. Edmund Jephcott, ed. Peter Demetz (New York: Schocken Books, 1986), 28.

2 Quoted from Benjamin's letter to Martin Buber (23 February 1927) by Gershom Sholem, preface to Benjamin's *Moscow Diary,* ed. Gary Smith (Cambridge: Harvard University Press, 1986), 6.

3 Susan Buck-Morss, *The Dialectics of Seeing: Walter Benjamin and the Arcades Project* (Cambridge: MIT Press, 1989), 31–32.

4 Michael M. J. Fischer, "Ethnicity and the Post-Modern Arts of Memory," in

Writing Culture: The Poetics and Politics of Ethnography, ed. James Clifford and George E. Marcus (Berkeley: University of California Press, 1986), 194–233.

5 Michael Renov has written about new modes of autobiography in "The Subject in History: The New Autobiography in Film and Video," *Afterimage* 17, no. 1 (summer 1989): 4–7, and "New Subjectivities: Documentary and Self-Representation in the Post-Verité Age," *Documentary Box* 7 (1995): 1–8. See also Jim Lane, "Notes on Theory and the Autobiographical Documentary Film in America, *Wide Angle* 15, no. 3 (July 1993): 21–36; Ruth Behar, "Expanding the Boundaries of Anthropology: The Cultural Criticism of Gloria Anzaldua and Marlon Riggs," *Visual Anthropology Review* 9, no. 2 (fall 1993): 83–91; José Muñoz, "The Autoethnographic Performance: Reading Richard Fung's Queer Hybridity," *Screen* 36, no. 2 (summer 1995): 83–99.

6 These terms are both used by Bill Nichols in *Blurred Boundaries: Questions of Meaning in Contemporary Culture* (Bloomington: Indiana University Press, 1994), 1–16.

7 Mary Louise Pratt, *Imperial Eyes: Travel Writing and Transculturation* (London: Routledge, 1992), 7.

8 James Clifford, *The Predicament of Culture: Twentieth Century Ethnography, Literature, and Art* (Cambridge: Harvard University Press, 1988), 94.

9 Renov, "The Subject in History," 4.

10 Muñoz, "Autoethnographic Performance," 87.

11 Francoise Lionnet has described autoethnography in literature as a form of *métissage* that "demystifies all essentialist glorifications of unitary origins, be they racial, sexual, geographical, or culture." *Autobiographical Voices: Race, Gender, Self-Portraiture* (Ithaca: Cornell University Press, 1989), 9.

12 P. Adams Sitney, "Autobiography in Avant-Garde Film," in *The Avant-Garde Film: A Reader of Theory and Criticism,* ed. P. Adams Sitney (New York: New York University Press, 1978), 246.

13 Janine Marchessault, "*Sans Soleil,*" *CineAction!* (spring 1986): 2–6.

14 Trinh Minh-ha, *When the Moon Waxes Red: Representation, Gender, and Cultural Politics* (New York: Routledge, 1991), 74.

15 Renov situates Mekas as a crucial contributor to the development of the new autobiography in "The Subject in History," 5–6. See also the anthology *To Free the Cinema: Jonas Mekas and the New York Underground,* ed. David E. James (Princeton, N.J.: Princeton University Press, 1992).

16 From David James's filmography in *To Free the Cinema* (321–22), the diary films include *Walden* (1964–1969, 3 hours); *Reminiscences of a Journey to Lithuania* (1971–1972, 82 minutes); *Lost Lost Lost* (1949–1975, 2 hours 58 minutes); *In Between* (1964–1978, 52 minutes); *Paradise Not Yet Lost* (1977–1979, 96 mins); *He Stands in a Desert Counting the Seconds of His Life* (1969–1985, 2½ hours).

17 David James, "Film Diary/Diary Film: Practice and Product in *Walden,*" in James, *To Free the Cinema,* 168.

18 Maureen Turim, "*Reminiscences, Subjectivities, and Truths,*" in James, *To Free the Cinema,* 210.

19 Renov, "The Subject in History," 6.

20 Filmmakers Co-op catalog 1989, p. 363; quoted in Turim, "Reminiscences," 207.

21 Turim, 208.

22 Turim, 206, James, "Film Diary/Diary Film," 160.

23 Jeffrey K. Ruoff, "Home Movies of the Avant-Garde: Jonas Mekas and the New York Art World," in James, *To Free the Cinema,* 294–311.

24 Filmmakers Co-op catalog 1975, p. 178; quoted in Turim, "Reminiscences," 202.

25 David James points out that Mekas's editing and "revising" of his footage entails a community practice, a language and a kind of writing that is quite removed from the immediacy of the filming stage ("Film Diary/Diary Film," 161).

26 See Marjorie Keller, "The Theme of Childhood in the Films of Jean Cocteau, Joseph Cornell, and Stan Brakhage" (Ph.D. diss., New York University, 1982).

27 Caren Kaplan, *Questions of Travel: Postmodern Discourses of Displacement* (Durham, N.C.: Duke University Press, 1996), 28.

28 Paul Arthur, "History and Crass Consciousness: George Kuchar's Fantasies of Un-Power," *Millennium Film Journal* 20–21 (fall–winter 1988–1989): 156.

29 Christine Tamblyn, "Qualifying the Quotidian," in *Resolutions: Contemporary Video Practices,* ed. Michael Renov and Erika Suderburg (Minneapolis: University of Minnesota Press, 1996), 19.

30 Kuchar described his editing technique at a post-screening discussion at Millennium, New York, 1986. Tamblyn reports the same thing (19). Kuchar started using the H-8 camera before it became a popular format, exploiting the feature of erasure/retaping as a medium-specific possibility. With the growing availability of editing suites, he has no doubt moved toward more conventional editing techniques.

31 See my "Culture as Fiction: The Ethnographic Impulse in the films of Peggy Ahwesh, Su Friedrich, and Leslie Thornton," in *The New American Cinema,* ed. Jon Lewis (Durham, N.C.: Duke University Press, 1998).

32 Sadie Benning is the daughter of James Benning, which may or may not account for her aesthetic sensibilities, but does suggest how she came to embrace the avant-garde at such an early age.

33 Chris Holmlund, "When Autobiography Meets Ethnography and Girl Meets Girl: The 'Dyke Docs' of Sadie Benning and Su Friedrich," in *Between the Sheets, in the Streets: Queer, Lesbian, Gay Documentary,* ed. Chris Holmlund and Cynthia Fuchs (Minneapolis: University of Minnesota Press, 1997), 130.

34 Muñoz, "Autoethnographic Performance," 84.

35 Laura Kipnis, "Female Transgression," in Renov and Suderburg, *Resolutions,* 340–41.

36 Tamblyn, "Qualifying the Quotidian," 13–28.

37 Homi K. Bhabha, *The Location of Culture* (New York: Routledge, 1994), 50.

38 Ibid., 52.

39 Ibid.

40 Fredric Jameson, *The Geopolitical Aesthetic: Cinema and Space in the World System* (Bloomington: Indiana University Press and British Film Institute, 1992), 192.

41 Jameson points out that the similar ideological lesson of *Perfumed Nightmare* (the title refers to the attraction to, and dangers of, modern technologies) is "of a type embarrassing if not inconceivable for First-World (realistic) film-makers" (204).

42 Benjamin, "The Author as Producer," in *Reflections,* 220–38.

43 Kidlat Tahimik, "*Why Is Yellow the Middle of the Rainbow?* An Interview with Kidlat Tahimik," interview by Arthur and Corinne Cantrill, *Cantrills Film-notes* 73–74 (May 1994): 55; cited hereafter as Tahimik, interview.

44 In the clips from the film-in-progress, it seems that Magellan's slave finally returns to the Philippines with his master, but the natives kill Magellan, thus freeing the slave. Tahimik describes the slave as someone who learned the dress codes and the language of the colonial Other, as well as the law of supply and demand.

45 Jameson, *Geopolitical Aesthetic,* 207.

46 In his critique of Jameson's theory of national allegory (which is the theory informing Jameson's discussion of *Perfumed Nightmare*), Aijaz Ahmad suggests that a global perspective of capitalist production is a more appropriate model for a theory that might encompass all Third World literatures. "Jameson's Rhetoric of Otherness," excerpted in *The Postcolonial Studies Reader,* ed. Bill Ashcroft, Gareth Griffiths, and Helen Tiffin (New York: Routledge, 1995), 80.

47 Tahimik's given name is Eric de Guia, and he told the Cantrills that he grew up as a bourgeois kid who wished he were an Igorot (Tahimik, interview, 47).

48 Ibid., 55.

49 Ibid., 59.

50 Some of the best articles on *Sans Soleil* are Yvette Biro, "In the Spiral of Time," *Millennium Film Journal* 14–15 (fall–winter 1984–1985): 173–77; Terrence Rafferty, "Marker Changes Trains," *Sight and Sound* 53, no. 4 (1984): 284–88; Janine Marchessault, "*Sans Soleil,*" *CineAction!* (spring 1986): 2–6; Michael Walsh, "Around the World, across All Frontiers: *Sans Soleil* as *Dépays,*" *Cine-Action!* (fall 1989): 29–36.

51 Marker includes "guerrilla" footage shot by Mario Marret and Eugenio Bentivoglio while the narrator comments on the incomparable reality of guerrilla fighting. The main theorization of guerrilla filmmaking is by Fernando Solanas and Octavio Gettino in "Towards a Third Cinema," in *Movies and Methods,* vol. 1, ed. Bill Nichols (1971; reprint, Berkeley: University of California Press, 1976), 44–64.

52 Bill Nichols uses this term in *Representing Reality: Issues and Concepts in Documentary* (Bloomington: Indiana University Press, 1991), 223.

53 *The Pillow Book of Sei Shonagon,* trans. and ed. Ivan Morris (London: Penguin Classics, 1971).

54 Ivan Morris, introduction to *The Pillow Book of Sei Shonagon.*

55 For Benjamin, the exchange of looks is also founded on sexual difference. The disintegration of aura, which for Benjamin is manifest in the cinema, is also found in Baudelaire's love poetry when he "describes eyes of which one is inclined to say that they have lost their ability to look" (Walter Benjamin, *Charles Baudelaire: A Lyric Poet in the Era of High Capitalism,* trans. Harry Zohn [London: Verso, 1983], 149). The look of the woman in the crowded metropolis is a "protective eye," one in which distance is collapsed; it promises sex without love and is assigned unambiguously to the prostitute. For Miriam Hansen, Benjamin's discourse on the gaze is thoroughly bound up in an Oedipal structure: "Benjamin undeniably participates in a patriarchal discourse on vision insofar as the auratic gaze depends upon a veil of forgetting, that is, a reflective yet unacknowledged form of fetishism which reinscribes the female body as source of both fascination and threat" ("Benjamin, Cinema, and Experience: 'The Blue Flower in the Land of Technology,'" *New German Critique* 40 [winter 1987]: 215).

56 Walsh traces the Orientalist background of Marker's film through Roland Barthes's *Empire of Signs* and the film studies literature on Japan.

57 Walsh, "Around the World," 35. Walsh supports his interpretation with the work of Andre Gunder Frank, Samir Amin, and Arghiri Emmanuel.

58 Walter Benjamin, "N [Theoretics of Knowledge; Theory of Progress]," trans. of *Passagen-Werk* by Leigh Hafrey and Richard Sieburth, in *Benjamin: Philosophy, Aesthetics, History,* ed. Gary Smith (Chicago: University of Chicago Press, 1983), 49.

59 The classical theorization of cinematic realism as a form of preservation is in André Bazin, *What Is Cinema?* vol. 1, trans. Hugh Gray (Berkeley: University of California Press, 1967).

Bibliography

Artaud, Antonin. *The Theatre and Its Double.* Trans. Mary Caroline Richards. New York: Grove Press, 1958.

Arthur, Paul. "Structural Film: Revisions, New Versions, and the Artifact." *Millennium Film Journal* 1–2 (spring 1978): 5–13; pt. 2, *Millennium Film Journal* 4–5 (summer–fall 1979): 122–34.

————. "The Last of the Last Machine? Avant-Garde Film since 1966." *Millennium Film Journal* 16/17/18 (fall–winter 1986–1987): 69–93.

Barkan, Elazar, and Ronald Bush, eds. *Prehistories of the Future: The Primitivist Project and the Culture of Modernism.* Stanford: Stanford University Press, 1995.

Barthes, Roland. *Camera Lucida: Reflections on Photography.* Trans. Richard Howard. New York: Hill and Wang, 1981.

Bataille, Georges. *Erotism: Death and Sensuality.* Trans. Mary Dalwood. San Francisco: City Lights Books, 1986.

Baudrillard, Jean. "The Precession of Simulacra." In *Art after Modernism: Rethinking Representation,* ed. Brian Wallis, 253–81. New York: New Museum of Contemporary Art, 1984.

Bazin, André. "Mort tous les aprés-midi." In *Qu'est-ce que le cinema?* Vol. 1, *Ontologie et langage,* 65–70. Paris: Editions du cerf, 1958.

Behar, Ruth. "Expanding the Boundaries of Anthropology: The Cultural Criticism of Gloria Anzaldua and Marlon Riggs." *Visual Anthropology Review* 9, no. 2 (fall 1993).

Behdad, Ali. *Belated Travelers: Orientalism in the Age of Colonial Dissolution.* Durham, N.C.: Duke University Press, 1994.

Belloï, Livio. "Lumière and His View: The Cameraman's Eye in Early Cinema." *Historical Journal of Film, Radio, and Television* 15, no. 4 (1995): 461–74.

Benjamin, Walter. *Illuminations.* Trans. Harry Zohn, ed. Hannah Arendt. New York: Schocken Books, 1969.

————. "A Short History of Photography." 1931. Trans. Stanley Mitchell. *Screen* 31, no. 1 (spring 1972): 5–26.

————. *The Origins of German Tragic Drama.* Trans. John Osborne. London: New Left Books, 1977.

———. *Charles Baudelaire: A Lyric Poet in the Era of High Capitalism.* Trans. Harry Zohn. London: Verso, 1983.

———. "N [Theoretics of Knowledge; Theory of Progress]." Translation of *Passagen-Werk* by Leigh Hafrey and Richard Sieburth. In *Benjamin: Philosophy, Aesthetics, History,* ed. Gary Smith, 43–83. Chicago: University of Chicago Press, 1983.

———. *Reflections: Essays, Aphorisms, Autobiographical Writings.* Trans. Edmund Jephcott, ed. Peter Demetz. New York: Schocken Books, 1986.

Berger, John. "Why Look at Animals." In *About Looking,* 1–26. New York: Pantheon Books, 1980.

Bhabha, Homi K. *The Location of Culture.* New York: Routledge, 1994.

Brakhage, Stan. *Film at Wit's End: Eight Avant-Garde Filmmakers.* New York: McPherson, 1989.

Brooks, Peter. *The Melodramatic Imagination: Balzac, Henry James, Melodrama, and the Mode of Excess.* New York: Columbia University Press, 1984.

Brownlow, Kevin. *The War, the West, and the Wilderness.* New York: Alfred A. Knopf, 1979.

Buck-Morss, Susan. *The Dialectics of Seeing: Walter Benjamin and the Arcades Project.* Cambridge: MIT Press, 1989.

Burch, Noël. *Life to Those Shadows.* Berkeley: University of California Press, 1990.

Cannizzo, Jeanne. "George Hunt and the Invention of Kwakiutl Culture." *Canadian Review of Sociology and Anthropology* 20, no. 1 (1983): 44–58.

Cantrill, Arthur, and Louise Cantrill. "*Why Is Yellow the Middle of the Rainbow?* An Interview with Kidlat Tahimik." *Cantrills Filmnotes* 73–74 (May 1994): 44–63.

Charney, Leo, and Vanessa R. Schwartz, eds. *Cinema and the Invention of Modern Life.* Berkeley: University of California Press, 1995.

Chow, Rey. *Primitive Passions: Visuality, Sexuality, Ethnography, and Contemporary Chinese Cinema.* New York: Columbia University Press, 1995.

Clark, A. Vèvè, Millicent Hodson, and Catrina Neiman, eds. *Chambers 1942–47: The Legend of Maya Deren.* Vol. 1, pt. 2. New York: Anthology Film Archives, 1984.

Clifford, James. "Of Other Peoples: Beyond the 'Salvage' Paradigm." In *Discussions in Contemporary Culture,* vol. 1, ed. Hal Foster, 121–30. Seattle: Bay Press, 1987.

———. *The Predicament of Culture: Twentieth Century Ethnography, Literature, and Art.* Cambridge: Harvard University Press, 1988.

———. "Traveling Cultures." In *Cultural Studies,* ed. Lawrence Grossberg, Cary Nelson, and Paula Treichler, 96–112. New York: Routledge, 1992.

Clifford, James, and George E. Marcus, eds. *Writing Culture: The Poetics and Politics of Ethnography.* Berkeley: University of California Press, 1986.

Cohen, Margaret. *Profane Illumination: Walter Benjamin and the Paris of Surrealist Revolution.* Berkeley: University of California Press, 1993.

Conley, Tom. "Documentary Surrealism: On *Land without Bread.*" In *Dada and*

Surrealist Film, ed. Rudolf E. Kuenzli, 176–98. New York: Willis Locker and Owens, 1987.

Corbey, Raymond. "Ethnographic Showcases, 1870–1930." *Cultural Anthropology* 8, no. 3 (1993): 338–69.

Crapanzano, Vincent, and Vivian Garrison, eds. *Case Studies in Spirit Possession.* New York: John Wiley and Sons, 1977.

Cubitt, Sean. *Videography: Video Media as Art and Culture.* New York: St. Martin's Press, 1993.

De Bouzek, Jeannette. "The 'Ethnographic Surrealism' of Jean Rouch." *Visual Anthropology* 2, no. 34 (1989): 301–32.

De Lauretis, Teresa. *Alice Doesn't: Feminism, Semiotics, Cinema.* Bloomington: Indiana University Press, 1984.

———. "Film and the Visible." In *How Do I Look? Queer Film and Video,* ed. Bad Object Choices, 223–64. Seattle: Bay Press, 1991.

Deleuze, Gilles, and Félix Guattari. *Nomadology: The War Machine.* Trans. Brian Massumi. New York: Semiotext(e), 1986.

———. *Anti-Oedipus: Capitalism and Schizophrenia.* Trans. Robert Hurley, Mark Seem, and Helen R. Lane. Minneapolis: University of Minnesota Press, 1992.

Deren, Maya. *Divine Horsemen: The Living Gods of Haiti.* 1953. Reprint, New York: Documentext, 1991.

Desmond, Jane. "Ethnography, Orientalism, and Avant-Garde Film." *Visual Anthropology* 4 (n.d.): 147–60.

Deveraux, Leslie, and Roger Hillman, eds. *Fields of Vision: Essays in Film Studies, Visual Anthropology, and Photography.* Berkeley: University of California Press, 1995.

Doane, Mary Ann. "Information, Crisis, Catastrophe." In *Logics of Television: Essays in Cultural Criticism,* ed. Patricia Mellencamp, 222–39. Bloomington: Indiana University Press, 1990.

———. *Femmes Fatales: Feminism, Film Theory, Psychoanalysis.* New York: Routledge, 1991.

———. "Temporality, Storage, Legibility: Freud, Marey, and the Cinema." *Critical Inquiry* 22 (winter 1996): 313–43.

Eaton, Mick, ed. *Anthropology/Reality/Cinema: The Films of Jean Rouch.* London: British Film Institute, 1979.

Elsaesser, Thomas, ed. *Early Cinema.* London: British Film Institute, 1990.

Fabian, Johannes. *Time and the Other: How Anthropology Makes Its Object.* New York: Columbia University Press, 1983.

Ferguson, Russell, William Geander, and Marcia Tucker, eds. *Discourses: Conversations in Postmodern Art and Culture.* New York: New Museum of Contemporary Art/MIT, 1990.

Fischer, Michael J. "Ethnicity and the Post-Modern Arts of Memory." In *Writing Culture: The Poetics and Politics of Ethnography,* ed. James Clifford and George E. Marcus, 194–233. Berkeley: University of California Press, 1986.

Foster, Hal. *Compulsive Beauty.* Cambridge: MIT Press, 1993.

——. *The Return of the Real: The Avant-Garde at the End of the Century.* Cambridge: MIT Press, 1996.

Foucault, Michel. *Madness and Civilization: A History of Insanity in the Age of Reason.* Trans. Richard Howard. New York: Random House, 1965.

——. *The History of Sexuality.* Vol. 1. Trans. Robert Hurley. New York: Pantheon Books, 1978.

——. *Discipline and Punish: The Birth of the Prison.* Trans. Alan Sheridan. New York: Vintage Books, 1979.

Frampton, Hollis. *Circles of Confusion: Film, Photography, Video Texts, 1968–1980.* Rochester, N.Y.: Visual Workshop Press, 1983.

Friedberg, Anne. *Window Shopping: Cinema and the Postmodern.* Berkeley: University of California Press, 1993.

Fulchignoni, Enrico. "Conversation between Jean Rouch and Professor Fulchignoni." Trans. Anny Ewing and Steven Feld. *Visual Anthropology* 2, nos. 3–4 (December 1989): 265–300.

Fusco, Coco, ed. *Young British and Black.* Buffalo: Hallwalls, 1988.

Gabriel, Teshome H. *Third Cinema in the Third World: The Aesthetics of Liberation.* Ann Arbor: UMI Research Press, 1982.

——. "Thoughts on Nomadic Aesthetics and Black Independent Cinema: Traces of a Journey." In *Out There: Marginalization and Contemporary Cultures,* ed. Russell Ferguson, Martha Gever, Trinh T. Minh-ha, and Cornel West, 395–410. New York: New Museum/MIT Press, 1990.

Gidal, Peter, ed. *Structural Film Anthology.* London: British Film Institute, 1976.

Gunning, Tom. "The Cinema of Attraction: Early Film, Its Spectator, and the Avant-Garde." *Wide Angle* 8 (1983): 63–70.

——. "An Unseen Energy Swallows Space: The Space in Early Film and Its Relation to American Avant-Garde Film." In *Film before Griffith,* ed. John L. Fell, 355–66. Berkeley: University of California Press, 1983.

——. "Before Documentary: Early Nonfiction Films and the 'View' Aesthetic." Unpublished paper, 1996.

Hall, Stuart. "Cultural Identity and Cinematic Representation." *Framework* 36 (1989): 68–81.

Hansen, Miriam. "Benjamin, Cinema, and Experience: 'The Blue Flower in the Land of Technology.'" *New German Critique* 40 (winter 1987): 179–224.

——. *From Babel to Babylon: Spectatorship in American Silent Film.* Cambridge: Harvard University Press, 1991.

Haraway, Donna. *Primate Visions: Gender, Race, and Nature in the World of Modern Science.* New York: Routledge, 1989.

——. "The Promises of Monsters: A Regenerative Politics for Inappropriate/d Others." In *Cultural Studies,* ed. Lawrence Grossberg, Cary Nelson, and Paula Treichler, 295–337. New York: Routledge, 1992.

Heath, Stephen. *Questions of Cinema.* Bloomington: Indiana University Press, 1981.

Henning Brown, Carolyn. "Tourism and Ethnic Competition in a Ritual Form." *Oceania* 54, no. 3 (March 1984): 223–44.

Hertogs, Daan, and Nico de Klerk, eds. *Nonfiction from the Teens: The 1994 Amsterdam Workshop.* Amsterdam and London: Nederlands Filmmuseum and the British Film Institute, 1994.

Hockings, Paul, ed. *Principles of Visual Anthropology.* 2d ed. New York: Mouton de Gruyter, 1995.

Hollier, Dennis. "The Use-Value of the Impossible." Trans. Liesl Ollman. *October* 60 (spring 1992): 3–24.

Holm, Bill, and George Irving Quimby. *Edward S. Curtis in the Land of the War Canoes: A Pioneer Cinematographer in the Pacific Northwest.* Vancouver: Douglas and McIntyre, 1990.

Holmlund, Chris. "Fractured Fairytales and Experimental Identities: Looking for Lesbians in and around the Films of Su Friedrich." *Discourse* 17, no. 1 (fall 1994): 16–46.

Holmlund, Chris, and Cynthia Fuchs, eds. *Between the Sheets, in the Streets: Queer, Lesbian, Gay Documentary.* Minneapolis: University of Minnesota Press, 1997.

Huyssen, Andreas. *Twilight Memories: Marking Time in a Culture of Amnesia.* New York: Routledge, 1995.

Imperato, Pascal James, and Eleanor M. Imperato. *They Married Adventure: The Wandering Lives of Martin and Osa Johnson.* New Brunswick, N.J.: Rutgers University Press, 1992.

Ivy, Marilyn. *Discourses of the Vanishing: Modernity, Phantasm, Japan.* Chicago: University of Chicago Press, 1995.

Jacknis, Ira. "Margaret Mead and Gregory Bateson in Bali: Their Use of Photography and Film." *Cultural Anthropology* 3, no. 2 (May 1988): 160–77.

James, David E. *Allegories of Cinema: American Film in the Sixties.* Princeton, N.J.: Princeton University Press, 1989.

———, ed. *To Free the Cinema: Jonas Mekas and the New York Underground.* Princeton, N.J.: Princeton University Press, 1992.

Jameson, Fredric. *The Political Unconscious: Narrative as a Socially Symbolic Act.* Ithaca: Cornell University Press, 1981.

———. "Postmodernism and Consumer Society." In *The Anti-Aesthetic: Essays on Postmodern Culture,* ed. Hal Foster, 111–25. Port Townsend, Wash.: Bay Press, 1983.

———. *The Geopolitical Aesthetic: Cinema and Space in the World System.* Bloomington: Indiana University Press and British Film Institute, 1992.

Jayamanne, Laleen. "Love Me Tender, Love Me True, Never Let Me Go . . . A Sri Lankan Reading of Tracey Moffatt's *Night Cries.*" *Framework* 38–39 (1992): 87–94.

Jenks, Chris, ed. *Visual Culture.* New York: Routledge, 1995.

Jensen, Gordon D., and Luh Ketut Suryani. *The Balinese People: A Reinvestigation of Character.* Singapore: Oxford University Press, 1992.

Kaplan, Caren. *Questions of Travel: Postmodern Discourses of Displacement*. Durham, N.C.: Duke University Press, 1996.

Krauss, Rosalind. "The Originality of the Avant-Garde: A Postmodern Repetition." In *Art after Modernism: Rethinking Representation,* ed. Brian Wallis, 13–30. New York: New Museum of Contemporary Art, 1984.

———. *The Optical Unconscious*. Cambridge: MIT Press, 1993.

Kubelka, Peter. Interview by Jonas Mekas. *Film Culture* 44 (spring 1967): 43–47.

Lakoff, Andrew. "Freezing Time: Margaret Mead's Diagnostic Photography." *Visual Anthropology Review* 12, no. 1 (spring 1996): 1–18.

Lastra, James. "Why Is This Absurd Picture Here? Ethnology/Heterology/Buñuel." Unpublished manuscript.

Le Grice, Malcolm. *Abstract Film and Beyond*. Cambridge: MIT Press, 1977.

———. *Materialist Film*. London: Routledge, 1989.

Lewis, I. M. *Ecstatic Religion: An Anthropological Study of Spirit Possession and Shamanism*. London: Penguin, 1971.

Lionnet, Francoise. *Autobiographical Voices: Race, Gender, Self-Portraiture*. Ithaca: Cornell University Press, 1989.

London, Barbara, ed. *Bill Viola*. New York: Museum of Modern Art, 1987.

Lyman, Christopher M. *The Vanishing Race and Other Illusions: Photographs of Indians by Edward S. Curtis*. Washington, D.C.: Smithsonian Institution Press, 1982.

MacDonald, Scott. *Avant-Garde Film: Motion Studies*. New York: Cambridge University Press, 1993.

Manganaro, Marc, ed. *Modernist Anthropology: From Fieldwork to Text*. Princeton, N.J.: Princeton University Press, 1990.

Marchessault, Janine. "Sans Soleil." *CineAction!* (spring 1986): 2–6.

Margulies, Ivone. *Nothing Happens: Chantal Akerman's Hyperrealist Everyday*. Durham, N.C.: Duke University Press, 1996.

Mayne, Judith. *The Woman at the Keyhole*. Bloomington: Indiana University Press, 1990.

Mead, Margaret, and Gregory Bateson. *Balinese Character: A Photographic Analysis*. New York: New York Academy of Sciences, 1942.

Mellencamp, Patricia. *Indiscretions: Avant-Garde Film, Video, and Feminism*. Bloomington: Indiana University Press, 1990.

Metz, Christian. *The Imaginary Signifier: Psychoanalysis and the Cinema*. Trans. Celia Britton, Annwyl Williams, Ben Brewster, and Alfred Guzzetti. Bloomington: Indiana University Press, 1982.

Moffatt, Tracey. Interview by Scott Murray. *Cinema Papers* 79 (May 1990): 19–22.

Morris, Rosalind C. *New Worlds from Fragments: Film, Ethnography, and the Representation of Northwest Coast Cultures*. Boulder: Westview Press, 1994.

Muñoz, José. "The Autoethnographic Performance: Reading Richard Fung's Queer Hybridity." *Screen* 36, no. 2 (summer 1995): 83–99.

Nichols, Bill. *Ideology and the Image: Social Representation in the Cinema and Other Media*. Bloomington: Indiana University Press, 1981.

———. *Representing Reality: Issues and Concepts in Documentary.* Bloomington: Indiana University Press, 1991.

———. *Blurred Boundaries: Questions of Meaning in Contemporary Culture.* Bloomington: Indiana University Press, 1994.

O'Pray, Michael, ed. *Andy Warhol: Film Factory.* London: British Film Institute, 1989.

Oshima, Nagisa. *Cinema, Censorship, and the State.* Trans. Dawn Lawson, ed. Annette Michelson. Cambridge: MIT Press, 1992.

Owens, Craig. "The Allegorical Impulse: Toward a Theory of Postmodernism." In *Art after Modernism,* ed. Brian Wallis, 203–35. New York: Museum, 1984.

Penley, Constance. "The Avant-Garde and Its Imaginary." *Camera Obscura* 2 (fall 1977): 3–33.

Penley, Constance, and Janet Bergstrom. "The Avant-Garde: History and Theories." *Screen* 19 (autumn 1978): 113–27.

Petro, Patrice, ed. *Fugitive Images: From Photography to Video.* Bloomington: Indiana University Press, 1995.

Pramaggiore, Maria. "Performance and Persona in the U.S. Avant-Garde: The Case of Maya Deren." *Cinema Journal* 36, no. 2 (winter 1997): 17–40.

Pratt, Mary Louise. *Imperial Eyes: Travel Writing and Transculturation.* London: Routledge, 1992.

Renov, Michael. "The Subject in History: The New Autobiography in Film and Video." *Afterimage* 17, no. 1 (summer 1989): 4–7.

———. "New Subjectivities: Documentary and Self-Representation in the Post-Verité Age." *Documentary Box* 7 (1995): 1–8.

Renov, Michael, and Erika Suderburg, eds. *Resolutions: Contemporary Video Practices.* Minneapolis: University of Minnesota Press, 1996.

Rony, Fatimah Tobing. "Those Who Squat and Those Who Sit: The Iconography of Race in the 1895 Films of Félix Regnault." *Camera Obscura* 28 (January 1992): 263–89.

———. *The Third Eye: Race, Cinema, and Ethnographic Spectacle.* Durham, N.C.: Duke University Press, 1996.

Rosen, Philip, ed. *Narrative, Apparatus, Ideology.* New York: Columbia University Press, 1986.

Rouch, Jean. "Vicissitudes of the Self: the Possessed Dancer, the Magician, the Sorcerer, the Filmmaker, and the Ethnographer." *Studies in the Anthropology of Visual Communication* 5, no. 1 (fall 1978): 2–8.

Rubinstein, E. "Visit to a Familiar Planet: Buñuel among the Hurdanos." *Cinema Journal* 22, no. 4 (summer 1983): 3–17.

Ruby, Jay. " 'The Aggie Will Come First': The Demystification of Robert Flaherty." In *Robert Flaherty, Photographer/Filmmaker: The Inuit, 1910–1922.* Exhibition catalog. Vancouver, B.C.: Vancouver Art Gallery, 1980.

Russell, Catherine. "David Rimmer's Found Footage: Reproduction and Repetition of History." *CineAction!* 16 (spring 1989): 52–58.

———. "David Rimmer: Twilight in the Image Bank." In *David Rimmer: Films and Tapes*, 17–54. Toronto: Art Gallery of Ontario, 1993.

———. "Culture as Fiction: The Ethnographic Impulse in the Films of Peggy Ahwesh, Su Friedrich, and Leslie Thornton." In *The New American Cinema*, ed. Jon Lewis, 353–78. Durham, N.C.: Duke University Press, 1998.

Sandusky, Sharon. "The Archaeology of Redemption: Toward Archival Film." *Millennium Film Journal* 26 (fall 1992): 3–25.

Sekula, Allan. "Reading an Archive." In *Blasted Allegories: An Anthology of Writings by Contemporary Artists*, ed. Brian Wallis, 114–28. Cambridge: MIT Press, 1989.

Sitney, Adams P. *Visionary Film: The American Avant-Garde, 1943–1978*. 2d ed. New York: Oxford University Press, 1979.

———, ed. *The Avant-Garde Film: A Reader of Theory and Criticism*. New York: New York University Press, 1978.

Sloniowsky, Jeannette. "The Cinema of Cruelty: Affective Rhetoric in the Cinema." Ph.D. diss., University of Toronto, 1992.

Sobchack, Vivian. "Synthetic Vision: The Dialectical Imperative of Buñuel's *Las Hurdes*." *Millennium Film Journal* 7–9 (1980–1981): 140–50.

———. "Inscribing Ethical Space: Ten Propositions on Death, Representation, and Documentary." *Quarterly Review of Film Studies* (fall 1984): 283–300.

Stoller, Paul. *The Cinematic Griot: The Ethnography of Jean Rouch*. Chicago: University of Chicago Press, 1992.

Taussig, Michael. *Mimesis and Alterity: A Particular History of the Senses*. New York: Routledge, 1993.

Taylor, Lucien, ed. *Visualizing Theory: Selected Essays from V.A.R., 1990–1994*. New York: Routledge, 1994.

Testa, Bart. *Back and Forth: Early Cinema and the Avant-Garde*. Toronto: Art Gallery of Ontario, 1992.

Thomas, Nicholas. "Colonial Surrealism: Louis Buñuel's Land without Bread." *Third Text* 26 (spring 1994): 25–32.

Trinh T. Minh-ha. *When the Moon Waxes Red: Representation, Gender, and Cultural Politics*. New York: Routledge, 1991.

Tyler, Stephen A. "Post-Modern Ethnography: From Document of the Occult to Occult Document." In *Writing Culture: The Poetics and Politics of Ethnography*, ed. James Clifford and George E. Marcus, 122–40. Berkeley: University of California Press, 1986.

Vaughan, Dai. "The Aesthetics of Ambiguity." In *Film as Ethnography*, ed. Peter Ian Crawford and David Turton, 99–115. Manchester: Manchester University Press, 1992.

Vertov, Dziga. *Kino-Eye: The Writings of Dziga Vertov*. Trans. Kevin O'Brien. 1922. Reprint, Berkeley: University of California Press, 1984.

Walsh, Michael. "Around the World, across All Frontiers: Sans Soleil as Dépays." *CineAction!* (fall 1989): 29–36.

Waugh, Thomas. "Cockteaser." In *Pop Out: Queer Warhol*, ed. Jennifer Doyle,

Jonathan Flatley, and José Esteban Muñoz. Durham, N.C.: Duke University Press, 1996.

Webster, Steven. "The Historical Materialist Critique of Surrealism and Postmodernist Ethnography." In *Modernist Anthropology: From Fieldwork to Text,* ed. Marc Manganaro, 266–99. Princeton, N.J.: Princeton University Press, 1990.

Wees, William C. *Recycled Images.* New York: Anthology Film Archives, 1993.

Williams, Linda. *Hard Core: Power Pleasure and the "Frenzy of the Visible."* Berkeley: University of California Press, 1989.

———. "Mirrors without Memories: Truth, History, and the New Documentary." *Film Quarterly* (spring 1993): 9–21.

———, ed. *Viewing Positions: Ways of Seeing Film.* New Brunswick, N.J.: Rutgers University Press, 1995.

Wollen, Peter. *Readings and Writings: Semiotic Counter-Strategies.* London: Verso, 1982.

Yakir, Dan. "*Ciné-transe:* The Vision of Jean Rouch." An interview with Jean Rouch in *Film Quarterly* 31 (spring 1978): 2–11.

Young, Dennis. "Ethnographic Surreality, Possession, and the Unconscious." *Visual Anthropology* 7 (1995): 191–297.

Zimmerman, Patricia. "Revolutionary Pleasures: Wrecking the Text in Compilation Documentary." *Afterimage* 16, no. 8 (1969): 6–9.

Filmography

Films

Atomic Café. Black-and-white and color film. The Archives Project (Kevin Rafferty, Jayne Loader, and Pierce Rafferty), United States, 1982. Facets Video.

Beauty #2. Black-and-white film, 66 min. Andy Warhol, United States, 1965. Museum of Modern Art.

D'Est. Color film, 107 min. Chantal Akerman, 1993. World Artists Releasing.

Divine Horsemen. Black-and-white film, 54 min. Maya Deren, United States,
1947–1985. Museum of Modern Art, Mystic Fire Video.

From the Pole to the Equator. Color film, 96 min. Yervant Giankian and Angela
Ricci Lucchi, West Germany and Italy, 1987. Museum of Modern Art.

Handsworth Songs. Color film, 58 min. Black Audio Film Collective, England,
1985. Third World Newsreel, Mongrel Media.

Hide and Seek. Black-and-white film, 62 min. Su Friedrich, United States, 1996.
Women Make Movies, Canadian Filmmakers Distribution Center.

The Human Figure in Motion. 4,789 black-and-white photographs. Eadweard
Muybridge, United States, 1887. Dover Publications.

I Do Not Know What It Is I Am Like. Video, 89 min. Bill Viola, United States,
1986. Museum of Modern Art.

In the Land of the Headhunters. Black-and-white silent film and sound video, 47
min. Edward Curtis, United States, 1914. Remade as *In the Land of the War
Canoes*, 1973. Milestone.

It Wasn't Love. Black-and-white video, 20 min. Sadie Benning, United States,
1991. Video Data Bank.

Kiss. Black-and-white film, 54 min. Andy Warhol, United States, 1963. Museum
of Modern Art.

Landscape Suicide. Color film, 95 min. James Benning, United States, 1986. Canadian Filmmakers Distribution Center.

Land without Bread (Las Hurdes). Black-and-white film, 27 min. Luis Buñuel,
Spain, 1932. Museum of Modern Art.

Les Maîtres fous. Color film, 24 min. Jean Rouch, France, 1954. Interama.

Living Canada. Black-and-white silent film. Joe Rosenthal/CPR, Canada and Britain, 1903.

Microcultural Incidents at Ten Zoos. Color film, 20 min. Ray Birdwhistell, United States, 1969. Pennsylvania State Audio-Visual Services.

A Movie. Black-and-white film, 12 min. Bruce Connor, United States, 1958. Canyon Cinema.

News from Home. 16 mm, color, 85 min. Chantal Akerman, United States, 1976. World Artists Releasing.

Night Cries: A Rural Tragedy. Color film, 16 min. Tracey Moffatt, Australia, 1990. Women Make Movies.

Peggy and Fred in Hell. Black-and-white and color film and video, 95 min. Leslie Thornton, United States, 1981–1994.

Pierre Vallières. Color film, 30 min. Joyce Wieland, Canada, 1972. Canadian Filmmakers Distribution Center.

A Place Called Lovely. Black-and-white video, 14 min. Sadie Benning, United States, 1991. Video Data Bank.

Real Italian Pizza. Color film, 13 min. David Rimmer, Canada, 1971. Canadian Filmmakers Distribution Center.

Reminiscences of a Journey to Lithuania. Color film, 89 min. Jonas Mekas, United States, 1972. Museum of Modern Art.

Sans Soleil. Color film, 100 min. Chris Marker, France, 1982. New Yorker Films.

Seashore. Black-and-white silent film, 11 min. David Rimmer, Canada, 1971. Canadian Filmmakers Distribution Center.

Simba: The King of Beasts. Black-and-white silent film and sound video, 83 min. Martin Johnson and Osa Johnson, United States, 1928. Milestone.

Trance and Dance in Bali. Black-and-white film, 22 min. Margaret Mead and Gregory Bateson, United States, 1952. Pennsylvania State Audio-Visual Services.

Tribulation 99: Alien Anomalies under America. Color film, 50 min. Craig Baldwin, United States, 1991. Canyon Cinema.

Uaka. Color film, 60 min. Paula Gaitan, Brazil, 1988.

Unsere Afrikareise. Color film, 13 min. Peter Kubelka, Austria, 1966. Filmmakers Cooperative, Canyon Cinema.

Voyage dans la lune. Black-and-white silent film, 12 min. Georges Méliès, France, 1903. Museum of Modern Art.

Weather Diary 1. Color video, 81 min. George Kuchar, United States, 1986. Video Data Bank.

Weather Diary 3. Color video, 24 min. George Kuchar, United States, 1988. Video Data Bank.

Why Is Yellow the Middle of the Rainbow? Color film, 175 min. Kidlat Tahimik, Philippines, 1981–1993. Yamagata.

Distributors

Canadian Filmmakers Distribution Center. 37 Hanna Ave., Suite 220, Toronto, Ontario, Canada M6K 1W8.http://www.cfmdc.org.

Canyon Cinema. 2325 Third St., Suite 338, San Francisco, CA 94107. 415-626-2255.

Filmmakers Cooperative. 175 Lexington Ave., New York, NY 10016.

Interama. 301 W. 53 St., New York, NY 10019-5766.

Milestone Film and Video Inc. 275 W. 96th St., Suite 28C, New York, NY 10025. 212-865-7449.

Mongrel Media. P.O. Box 68547, 581 Bloor St. W, Toronto, Ontario, Canada M6G 1K0.

Museum of Modern Art, Circulating Film Library. 11 W. 53 St., New York, NY 10019.

Mystic Fire Video. P.O. Box 422, New York, NY 10012-0008. 1-800-999-1319. http://www.mysticfire.com.

New Yorker Video. 16 W. 61st St., New York, NY 10023. 212-247-6110.

Pennsylvania State Audio-Visual Services. University Park, PA 16802.

Third World Newsreel. 335 W. 38th St., 5th Floor, New York, NY 10018. 212-947-9277.

Video Data Bank. The School of the Art Institute of Chicago, 37 S. Wabash Ave., Chicago, IL 60603. 312-899-5172.

Women Make Movies. 462 Broadway, Suite 500 D, New York, NY 10013.

Yamagata International Documentary Film Festival. Kitagawa Bldg., 4th floor, 6-42 Kagorazaka, Shinjuku-ju, Tokyo 162 Japan. 03-3266-9704.

Index

Boas, Franz, 104–5, 107
Boat Leaving the Harbour, A (Lumière brothers), 65–66
Body, the: in Archives Project's *Atomic Café* and Conner's *A Movie*, 258; in Benjamin's poetics, 9; in Birdwhistell's *Microcultural Incidents at Ten Zoos*, 137–38; colonial body, 57; in Deren, 207, 208; in early cinema, 51–75; embodied viewer in structural film, 160; as fetish in early cinema, 52, 56–57, 58, 75, 96; film as transforming, xiii–xiv; and found-footage filmmaking, 271, 272; in Kubelka's *Unsere Afrikareise*, 132; as mechanical apparatus, 67; in Moffatt's *Night Cries*, 43; Muybridge's motion studies, 66–74; in possession rituals, 193, 194, 197–98, 211, 227, 237; Regnault's study of native bodies, 55–56, 58; Rouch on writing with, 221; as sign system, 74; in Wieland's *Pierre Vallières*, 179
Bowser, Eileen, 330 n.39
Brakhage, Stan, 15, 149, 209, 317 n.34
Brault, Michel, 84–85
Bridge, The (Iven), 28
Brooks, Peter, 198
Brown, Carolyn Henning, 232
Buba, Tony, 278
Buck-Morss, Susan, 275
Buñuel, Luis: and surrealism, 29. See also *Hurdes, Las*
Burch, Noël, 18, 53, 73, 101
Bush, Stephen, 112
Byrne, David, 339 n.6

Cadenza #1 (Frampton), 323 n.32
Camera obscura model of spectatorship, 122, 160
Cannizzo, Jeanne, 104
Catastrophe theory, 248
Cauvel, Charles, 41
Cavalcanti, Alberto, 28
Chang (Schoedstack and Cooper), 333 n.42
Charney, Leo, 71

Child, Abigail, 241, 242
Children: in Archives Project's *Atomic Café*, 256, 257, 258; in Benning's *A Place Called Lovely*, 291–92; in Friedrich's *Hide and Seek*, 148, 152; in Marker's *Sans Soleil*, 305; in Muybridge's motion studies, 70, 71, 72; in Thornton's *Peggy and Fred in Hell*, 243–45; toys used by filmmakers, 299
Chow, Rey, 23, 318 n.46
Chronique d'une été (Rouch and Morin), 13, 220
Cinema. *See* Film
Cinéma direct, 84–85, 220
Cinemanalysis, 204
Cinéma vérité: the *flâneur* as first *vérité* observer, 7; in history of ethnographic film, 13; *Living Canada* series compared with, 84–85; and McBride's *David Holzman's Diary*, 293–94; Mead and Bateson's *Trance and Dance in Bali* anticipating, 203, 206; Mekas compared with, 285; and Rimmer's *Real Italian Pizza*, 177–78; and Rouch, 218, 219, 220–21; and surrealism, 221; and Vertov's *kinopravda*, 220; in Viola's *I Do Not Know What It Is I Am Like*, 229–30; Warhol's *Beauty #2* compared with, 174
Ciné-transe, 219, 220–21, 224, 228, 229, 235
Circle Dance (Indian film), 102
Citron, Michelle, 278, 279
City films, 27–28, 167
Clarke, Shirley, xvii
Clifford, James: on Boas, 105; on *Documents*, 27; on ethnographic surrealism, 26, 28, 40; on the exemplary cultural traveler, 104; on experimental ethnography, xi; and formal aspects of film and video, xvii; on inauthentic art, 346 n.8; on the salvage paradigm, 4–5; on self-fashioning, 277; on travel, 76
Cohen, Margaret, 72–73, 80
Cold War, 242

Experimental film (*continued*)
filmmaking, 266; canonization
debates, 14–19; critique of authenticity in, xii; Deren linking
surrealism with postwar, 207;
diversification of, 3; and early
cinema, 18, 53–54, 114; ethnographic aspect of, 17; ethnographic
film converging with, xi–xiii, 4;
feminist criticism of, 15, 16; in film
studies, 3–4; formalist orientation
of criticism of, 16; generational
split in, 15–16; idealist and materialist, 15; modernist origins of, 20;
the social in, 16; video in, xvi. *See
also* Structural film
Extremely Personal Eros (Kazuo), 278

Fabian, Johannes, 5, 238, 252, 264, 322
n.22, 349 n.45
Falls, The (Greenaway), 347 n.12
Feingold, Ken, 189
Feminism: in criticism of experimental film, 15, 16; ethnography
intersecting with, 22; postcolonial
theory grounded in critical strategies of, 21; "primitive" cinema as
inspiration for film of, 114; in Wieland's *Pierre Vallières,* 178. *See also*
Women
Fetish: the body as in early cinema,
52, 56–57, 58, 75, 96; means of representation as, 62; Muybridge's
female models as, 72
Fiji: firewalking ritual, 232–33, 345
nn. 112, 113; in Viola's *I Do Not
Know What It Is I Am Like,* 185,
229–34, 338 n.49
Film (cinema): as allegorical, 44;
as altering the status of art for
Benjamin, 7; as analogue of consciousness, 15, 159; in analysis of
behavior, 8; and anxiety of total
representation, 245–46; art and
science in, 8–9; Artaud on utopian
possibilities of, 217; and authenticity of the artwork, 10; the body
as transformed by, xiii–xiv; *cinéma*

direct, 84–85, 220; as fantasy of
nontechnologized reality, 8; gay
and lesbian film, 148, 149, 154, 170;
guerrilla cinema, 303, 352 n.51;
home movies, 242, 266, 285, 312;
identity as fragmented by, 313;
image and subjective experience as
separate in, 227; Indian film genre,
100, 102, 110, 328 nn. 5, 9, 330 n.39;
and intercultural social representation, xvii; as more than another
art form for Benjamin, xvi; New
Wave, 13, 218; pastoral allegory
exaggerated in, 5; personal filmmaking, 276, 278, 279, 312; possession rituals as trope of, 235; as
sharing its apparatus of vision,
183; social questions addressed
through, 3; travel by filmmakers,
76; as "vanishing culture," xviii,
311–14; video as extension of, xvi,
10; video as replacing, 7, 20, 311–14.
See also Cinéma vérité; Diary film;
Documentary film; Early film; Ex-
perimental film; Found footage;
Women's cinema
Firewalking ritual, 232–33, 345 nn.
112, 113
First contact, 37
Fischer, Michael, 276, 312
F Is for Fake (Welles), 279
Flaherty, Frances, 108–9
Flaherty, Robert: Curtis's *In the Land
of the Headhunters* compared with,
108–10; humanistic gaze of, 85;
Inuit footage of 1914, 109. *See also
Nanook of the North*
Flâneur, 7, 9, 60, 74, 85, 196, 245
Flicker films, 17, 158
Fluxus, 257
Ford, John, 298
Forest of Bliss (Gardner), 14, 189, 190
Foster, Hal, 22–23, 24, 45–46
Foucault, Michel, 119, 121–22, 124,
155, 199
Found footage, 238–72; as allegory
of history, 238, 240; apocalyptic
tenor of, 18, 241, 271; as arche-

age as historical inversion, 245; in Kubelka's *Unsere Afrikareise*, 130; postmodern view of, 253, 270. *See also* End of history

History (Gehr), 323 n.32

History and Memory (Tajiri), 278

Hitchcock, Alfred, 181, 292, 305, 309

Hoffman, Deborah, 278

Hollier, Dennis, 27, 36

Holm, Bill, 99–100, 111

Holmlund, Chris, 334 n.53

Holocaust, the, 259

Home movies, 242, 266, 285, 312

Hour of the Furnaces (Solana), 346 n.9

Human Figure in Motion, The (Muybridge), 66–74, 366

Humanism: benevolence of as condescension, 47, 321 n.50; Birdwhistell's *Microcultural Incidents at Ten Zoos* as circumventing, 139; Buñuel's *Las Hurdes* transgressing, 29; of the commodity, 61; cultural relativism produced by, 26; *Documents* challenging, 27; fascination hidden in scientific discourse by, 55; of Flaherty, 109, 110; in Mead and Bateson's *Trance and Dance in Bali*, 206; and New Age aesthetic, 230; otherness embraced by, 37; posthumanism, 36; of Rouch, 13; and Viola's *I Do Not Know What It Is I Am Like*, 233; zoos and ethnography as separate for, 123

Human Zoo, The (Morris), 140

Hunt, George, 104

Hurdes, Las (*Land without Bread*) (Buñuel), 28–40; as banned in Spain, 320 n.23; as colonialist, 29; disjunctive cutting of, 34; filmographical information, 365; Moffatt's *Night Cries* compared with, 46–47; narration in, 29, 30; as open modernist text, 34; primitivism in, 34–38; ritual sacrifice in, 38–39, 320 n.25; as shocking, 28, 36, 39–40; as sound film, 29–30; soundtrack of, 30–31; sources of,

319 n.7; subversive quality of, 34; as surrealist, xiii, 28; travelogues compared with, 30; visual evidence as unreliable in, 31–34

Huyssen, Andreas, 239, 251, 254, 257, 259, 266, 348 n.36

Hybridity, 293

Hyperrealism, 167–68, 181, 182

Identity: autoethnography as challenging imposed forms of, 276; Bhabha on postcolonial, 294–95; cinema as fragmenting, 313; *cinéma vérité* in Quebec's cultural, 84–85; as constantly transformed, 269; in diary film, 279; experimental ethnography distinguishing authenticity and, 21–22; in Friedrich's *Hide and Seek*, 149, 151, 152–53; as inscribed in technologies of representation, 291; in Marker's *Sans Soleil*, 306; in Moffatt's *Night Cries*, 41, 45; in Morris's *The Human Zoo*, 140; in new autobiography, 276; in possession rituals, 197, 237; self-fashioning of, 277; in Viola's *I Do Not Know What It Is I Am Like*, 187

Identity politics, 23, 24, 264

I Do Not Know What It Is I Am Like (Viola), 184–88; animals in, 119–20, 184–87; apocalyptic imagery in, 348 n.43; as canonical example of video art, 183; as demarcating limits of visual knowledge, xv; and the documentary gaze, 185; Fiji section of, 185, 229–34, 236, 338 n.49; filmographical information, 365; final stage of colonialism exemplified by, 185–86; five segments of, 184, 185, 338 n.49; mystical connotations of, 188; "Night of Sense" segment, 186; "Stunned by the Drum" segment, 188; and the unconscious, 234; visual economy of, 187

Igorots, 298–99

Ilê Aiyê (Byrne), 339 n.6

Inauthentic art, 240, 346 n.8

75; Clifford on, 4–6; Conner's *A Movie* as inverting, 251–52; in Curtis and Flaherty, 109–10, 113; and found-footage filmmaking, 18, 252, 264, 272; indigenous ethnography as inverting, 11; Rimmer's *Seashore*'s depiction of people as obverse of, 65; Rony on, 12–13; utopian form of memory preserved in, 113; zoos as instance of, 123

Sandusky, Sharon, 242–43

Sankofa, 11, 266

Sans Soleil (Marker), 301–11; Africa in, 301–2, 303, 304, 306, 308; and autoethnography, 277; as constantly turning back on itself, 305; as diary filmmaking, xv; disintegration of aura in, 311; epic scope of, 311; epistolary form of narration of, 311; as experimental ethnography, 301, 303; filmographical information, 366; Iceland scene, 304–5; incorrectness of, 303; Japan in, 301–2, 303, 304, 307–8; memory in, 305; *Pillow Book* as model for, 303–4; project of, 308; as radical attempt to disown images, 310; science fiction in, 309–10; soundtrack of, 304; textuality of, 301

Sao Paulo: Sinfonia de uma Cidade, 28

Schizoanalysis, 201

Schizophrenia, 200, 201, 205, 235–36, 243, 345 n.118

Schoedstack, Ernest, 333 n.42

Schwechater (Kubelka), 125

Science fiction: in Baldwin's *Tribulation 99,* 260, 263; and ethnography, 20–21, 76–79; Haraway's theory of cyborg culture, 318 n.37; in Marker's *Sans Soleil,* 309–10; Méliès's *Voyage dans la lune,* 88–92; as narrativization of distance, 24

Scientia sexualis, 124, 332 n.27

Scopophilia, 16, 120, 122, 124, 130

Scratch video, 240

Seashore (Rimmer), 63–66; early

cinema appropriated by, xiv, 54, 63; and ethnography as discourse of the body, 74; filmographical information, 366; formal devices of, 64; found footage in, 64, 66; repetition in, 65, 66; surface flaws, 64, 65

Sedgwick, Edie, 173, 174, 175

Sei Shonagon, 303–4, 310

Sekula, Alan, 259

Senghor, Blaise, 222

Sennett, Mack, 328 n.9

Sexuality: in Hauka ritual, 225–26; in Mead and Bateson's *Trance and Dance in Bali,* 205–6; in possession rituals, 198; *scientia sexualis,* 124, 332 n.27; in voodoo, 215–16; and voyeuristic gaze, 124; in Warhol, 172

Sharits, Paul, 17, 158

She (film), 141

Sherman's March (McElwee), 290

Shoot for the Contents (Trinh), 4

Siegfried (Lang), 108, 329 n.34

Simba: The King of the Beasts, A Saga of the African Veldt (Johnson and Johnson), 140–48; and American Museum of Natural History, 141, 145; black women in, 144–45; exploitation-entertainment context of, 141; filmographical information, 366; in Friedrich's *Hide and Seek,* 149, 153, 154; the gaze in, xiv, 120; native peoples in, 141–46; sound version of, 142; title cards for, 142, 146; women in, 144–45

Simulation aesthetic, 270

Sitney, P. Adams, 125, 158, 159, 207, 280, 322 n.20, 335 n.4

Situationism, 240–41

Sleep (Warhol), 160, 170, 174

Smith, Jack, 17

Snow, Michael: minimalism of, 17, 158; modernism of, 15; *La Region Centrale,* 175, 177; as structural filmmaker, 158; *Wavelength,* 175, 177

Sobchack, Vivian, 31, 130

on, 248; found footage as between photography and, 270–72

Testa, Bart, 63, 323 nn. 31, 32

Theater of cruelty, 215, 226

Thornton, Leslie: ethnography of, 244; in found-footage revival, 241. See also *Peggy and Fred in Hell*

Ties That Bind, The (Friedrich), 278

Time machine, 58, 92, 322 n.22

To Live with Herds (MacDougall and MacDougall), 14

Tom Tom the Piper's Son (Jacobs), 66, 323 n.32

Tossing the Photographer (*Living Canada* series), 82, 83

Tourists, The (Sennett), 328 n.9

Tour of the Dominions (British film), 86

Tourou et Bitti: Les Tambours d'Avant (Rouch), 220, 343 n.81

Toxic film artifact, 242–43

Trance and Dance in Bali (Mead and Bateson), 199–206; CBS broadcast of, 199; *cinéma vérité* anticipated by, 203, 206; as demarcating limits of visual knowledge, xv; Deren on, 206, 208–9, 210; disorientation of, 203; filmographical information, 366; as first systematic use of film in fieldwork, 195; mythic prehistoric setting of, 236; raw footage for, 341 n.32; sexuality in, 205–6; slow-motion footage of, 205; soundtrack of, 202; sponsorship of, 200; trance in, 204; two plays combined in, 202, 341 n.30

Trance films, xv, 207

Transcendental experience, 194–95

Transcendental gaze, 17

Travel: adventure-travel films of silent period, 140–41, 333 n.42; and diary film, 279, 280; ethnotopias of early cinema, 76–97; and experimental ethnography, 76; and Kubelka's *Unsere Afrikareise*, 127, 134; in *Living Canada* series, 80–87; Méliès's *Voyage dans la lune*, 88–92; travelogues compared with

Buñuel's *Las Hurdes*, 30. *See also* Safari films

Tribalism, 110

Tribulation 99 (Baldwin), 259–64; ambivalence of, 263; as articulating historiography of radical memory, xv; disaster images in, 262; and ethnographic potential of found footage, 239; filmographical information, 366; kitsch aesthetic of, 271; paranoid style of, 261; political activist discourse in, 262; premise of, 260–61

Trick films, 80, 326 n.18

Trinh T. Minh-ha: critique of ethnographic film, 4; as ethnographic revisionist, xvii; films of, 4; on humanism of the commodity, 61; on the Inappropriate Other, 104, 281; on meaning in early cinema, 87; *Naked Spaces*, 4, 93; on realism in ethnographic film, 12; *Reassemblage*, 4, 93, 119, 124–25; *Shoot for the Contents*, 4; on a third world in every first world, 36; on total meaning, 62

Turim, Maureen, 284

20 Years Later (Coutinho), 346 n.9

Tyler, Parker, 174, 337 n.31

Tyler, Stephen, xi, 19, 21, 44

Uaka (Gaitan), 92–96; as allegorical, 95; filmographical information, 366; fragmentation of the pastoral in, 93; Méliès's *Voyage dans la lune* in, 92, 93, 95–96; primitive cinema and primitive peoples in, 77; Trinh's films compared with, 93

Unsere Afrikareise (Kubelka), 125–35; aim of, 126; as anomalous, 126; death in, 125, 128, 129, 130; filmographical information, 366; the gaze in, xiv, 120, 128–30, 155; modernist anthropology in, 132; motion in, 133; the Other in, 134–35; realism of, 128–29, 130, 131; soundtrack of, 133; women in, 128, 133, 135

Utopias: American dreamworld, 247; Artaud on utopian possibilities of cinema, 217; Benjamin challenging modernist theories of, 254; early cinema's utopian imagination, 77; Jameson on literature of, 79; in Méliès's *Voyage dans la lune,* 91; in pornography and ethnography, 124; possession rituals as utopian, 197, 235; the primitive as utopian, 97; Rouch's utopianism, 193, 218, 221, 228; salvage paradigm preserving utopian form of memory, 113; in second-degree realism, 8; subjectivity as utopian space, 313

Vallières, Pierre, 178–80
"Vanishing Race, The" (Curtis lecture), 103
"Vanishing races" ideology, 102–8
Vaughan, Dai, 65–66, 112
Verne, Jules, 88–90
Vertigo (Hitchcock), 305, 309
Vertov, Dziga, 3, 21, 27, 219–20, 322 n.15
Very Nice Very Nice (Lipsett), 254
Video: diaries, 280–81, 286–95; early cinema on, 52; experimental filmmakers as drawn to, xvi; as extension of film, xvi, 10; film's replacement by, 7, 20, 313–14; intercultural social representation in, xvii; as media practice, xvi; and metaphor of consciousness, 184; scratch video, 240; social questions addressed through, 3; Viola's *I Do Not Know* as canonical example of, 183
"View" aesthetic, 81, 83–84, 85
Vigo, Jean, 28
Viola, Bill, 183–88; *Hatsu Yume (First Dream),* 183–84; as implicated in modernism and colonialism, 19; as last modernist, 186; minimalism of, xiv; mysticism of, 188; and New Age aesthetic, 230. See also *I Do Not Know What It Is I Am Like*

Virtual reality, 78, 88
Visual anthropology: and Benjamin's characterization of cinema as surgery, 57; expanding horizon of, 3; and Gaitan's *Uaka,* 95; indigenous ethnography's effect on, 11; of Mead, 204–5; as putting otherness on display, 55; Rouch in, 218
Visual culture: and early cinema, 53, 56, 60, 61, 79; evidentiary character of, 12; the gaze as ideologically constructed, 121; in *Las Hurdes,* 33; interdisciplinary interest in, 3; "just looking," 81–82; and Muybridge's motion studies, 67; otherness in, 153; and possession, 236; postmodern ethnography teasing apart layers of, 19; racial stereotype in, 56; and structural film, 17, 161
Visual Essays: Origins of Film (Razutis), 323 n.32
Voodoo, 208, 212, 215–16
Voyage dans la lune (Méliès), 88–92; colonial themes in, 88; Curtis's *In the Land of the Headhunters* compared with, 108; filmographical information, 366; in Gaitan's *Uaka,* 92, 93, 95–96; magic in, 90, 92; as ur-text of postmodern ethnography, 96–97; and utopia, xiv, 77; Verne's stories compared with, 88–90
Voyeuristic gaze, 124, 128, 160–61, 165–66

Walsh, Michael, 308
Warhol, Andy, 169–75; Akerman compared with, 171–72, 175; *Blow Job,* 172; *Eat,* 172, 174; *Empire,* 170; ethnographic undercurrent in, 17; found people used by, 174; *Haircut,* 174; letting the camera roll, 170; losing interest in film, 169; mark of death in, 174; and metaphysical film theory, 174–75; minimalism of, xiv, 170; realism of, 175, 337

n.30; as showman, 175; *Sleep,* 160, 170, 174; voyeuristic gaze in, 160. See also *Beauty #2; Kiss*

Waugh, Tom, 170

Wavelength (Snow), 175, 177

Way to My Father's Village, The (Fung), 278

Weather Diary 1 (Kuchar), 289, 366

Weather Diary 3 (Kuchar), 287, 289, 366

Weather Diary 4 (Kuchar), 287, 289

Webster, Gloria Cranmer, 113, 329 n.18

Webster, Stephen, 21, 336 n.17

Wees, William, 239–40, 255, 347 n.25

Wein, Chuck, 173

Welles, Orson, 279

Why Is Yellow the Middle of the Rainbow? (Tahimik): artistic process as represented in, 297; as autobiographical, 295; as diary film, xv; filmographical information, 366; as made for Western festival market, 295; Third World projector built in, 297

Wieland, Joyce: minimalism of, xiv, 17; *Pierre Vallières,* 178–80, 366; as structural filmmaker, 158

Williams, Linda, 69, 70, 72, 90, 124, 324 n.45, 332 n.27

Wollen, Peter, 15, 335 n.9, 336 n.18

Women: in Balinese drama, 205–6; bare-breasted women in pornography and ethnography, 124; in

Conner's *A Movie,* 251; in Hauka ritual, 225, 226; in the Johnsons' *Simba,* 144–45; in Kubelka's *Unsere Afrikareise,* 128, 133, 135; in Marker's *Sans Soleil,* 306; in Méliès's *Voyage dans la lune,* 90; in Muybridge's motion studies, 69–71, 72, 74; in voodoo dancing, 216. *See also* Feminism; Lesbians; Women's cinema

Women's cinema: Akerman's *News from Home,* 167; the empirical avant-garde, 45; the Hollywood woman's film, 42–43; lesbian filmmaking, 148, 149, 154; primitive cinema evoked by, 163

"Work of Art in the Age of Mechanical Reproduction, The" (Benjamin), xvi, 7–9, 189, 228

World's Columbian Exposition, 123

Young, Dennis, 344 n.106

Zebras, 131, 146, 147, 188, 334 n.51, 348 n.43

Zimmerman, Patricia, 346 n.9

Zoological gaze, 122–24, 183

Zoos: Birdwhistell's *Microcultural Incidents at Ten Zoos,* 135–40; as discipline, 124; in Friedrich's *Hide and Seek,* 153; as intermediate to pornography and ethnography, 122–23; and salvage paradigm, 123

Catherine Russell is Associate Professor in the School of Cinema at Concordia University. She is the author of *Narrative Mortality: Death, Closure, and New Wave Cinemas.*

Library of Congress Cataloging-in-Publication Data

Russell, Catherine.
Experimental ethnography : the work of film in the age of video /
Catherine Russell.
p.   cm.
Filmography: p.
Includes bibliographical references and index.
ISBN 0-8223-2287-0 (cloth : alk. paper). — ISBN 0-8223-2319-2
(pbk. : alk. paper)
1. Documentary films — History and criticism.   2. Experimental films —
History and criticism.   3. Motion pictures in ethnology.   4. Gaze —
Psychological aspects.   I. Title.
PN1995.9.D6R79   1999
070.1'8 — DC21   98-46549